John O'Brien

A History of the Mass and Its Ceremonies in the Eastern and Western Church

John O'Brien

A History of the Mass and Its Ceremonies in the Eastern and Western Church

ISBN/EAN: 9783743417267

Manufactured in Europe, USA, Canada, Australia, Japa

Cover: Foto ©ninafisch / pixelio.de

Manufactured and distributed by brebook publishing software (www.brebook.com)

John O'Brien

A History of the Mass and Its Ceremonies in the Eastern and Western Church

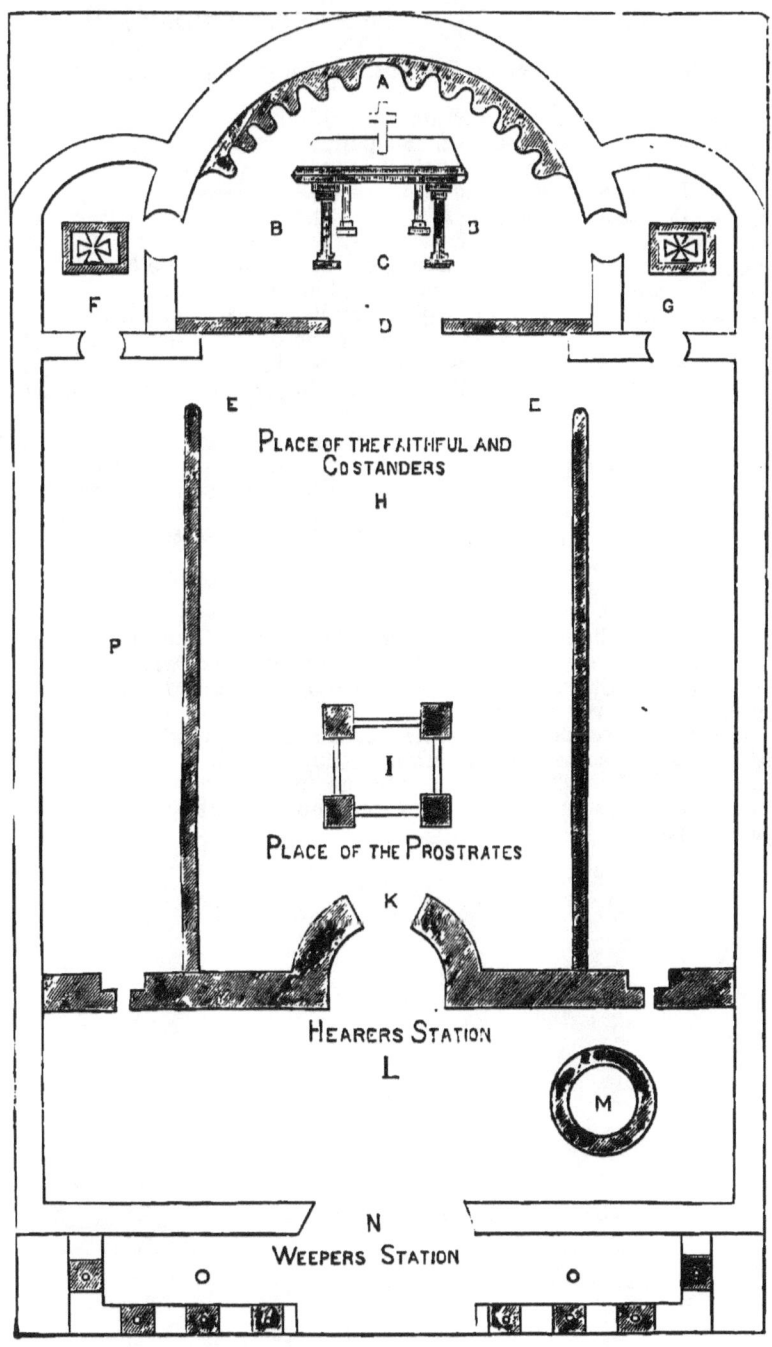

Plan of an Ancient Church showing the places of the Catechumens and Public Penitents.

EXPLANATION OF THE FRONTISPIECE.

A—The bishop's throne in the centre of the apse, with stalls on either side for the clergy.

B B—The sanctuary, or adytum.

C—The altar, supported on four pillars.

D—The sanctuary gates, or holy doors.

E E—The altar rails, called also *iconostasis* from the sacred *icons*, or images, that used to be placed there. The entire space within these rails was called the chancel, from a low, net-work partition which separated it from the rest of the church, called in Latin *cancelli*.

F—The prothesis, or cruet-table, veiled in by a screen.

G—The diaconicum, or sacristy, generally in charge of a deacon.

̈—The place of the male portion of the congregation, and of that : Public Penitents known as the Costanders.

he ambo, where the Epistle and Gospel were chanted and the ιs read.

/ ;he Beautiful Gates (portæ speciosæ), so called from the beauty
ι r workmanship. Here a subdeacon stood to see that the congre-
departed in order. Between I and K was the place of the Pros-
'enitents.

_ - 'he second porch, or narthex; also the Hearers' Station.

Я The Baptisterium.

'ɩ The Great Gates.

ɩ —The first porch and Weepers' Station.

'lace of the females, separated by a partition from the male por-
the congregation, and under the surveillance of what were called
ancient Church deaconesses. Men of note used to be sometimes buried in the porch or narthex.

The precise location of the catechumens is a disputed point; but inasmuch as the name was very often employed in that extended sense, meaning all who were forbidden to be present at Divine Service proper, it is generally supposed that they intermingled with the Penitents in the portico.

A

HISTORY OF THE MASS

AND ITS

CEREMONIES

IN THE

EASTERN AND WESTERN CHURCH.

BY

Rev. JOHN O'BRIEN, A.M.,

PROFESSOR OF SACRED LITURGY IN MOUNT ST. MARY'S COLLEGE,
EMMITTSBURG, MARYLAND.

FIFTH EDITION, REVISED.

"I would be willing to lay down my life for a single one of the Ceremonies of the Church."—St. Teresa.

New York:
THE CATHOLIC PUBLICATION SOCIETY CO.,
9 BARCLAY STREET.
—
1880.

Imprimatur:

John Card' McCloskey
Archbishop of New York

NEW YORK, MARCH 25, 1879.

A new work, entitled "A History of the Mass and its Ceremonies in the Eastern and Western Church," by the Rev. John O'Brien, of Mount St. Mary's College, Emmittsburg, having been carefully examined and commended by competent judges, is hereby approved by us.

✠ JAMES, *Archbishop of Baltimore.*

BALTIMORE, FEAST OF ST. BENEDICT, 1879.

Copyright, 1879, by JOHN O'BRIEN.

PREFACE.

As the question will doubtless be asked why we have presumed to write upon a subject which has already been treated so largely and so often by others, we make the same reply that one of the ancient Fathers did when a similar question was proposed to him. "This advantage," said he, "we owe to the multiplicity of books on the same subject: that one falls in the way of one man, and another best suits the level or comprehension of another. Everything that is written does not come into the hands of all, and hence, perhaps, some may meet with my book who have heard nothing of others which have treated better of the same subject."

Although it cannot be gainsaid that the subject which we have undertaken to touch has been largely treated already, and that by more eminent writers than we, still, when it is borne in mind that all those learned treatises have been written in one or other of the dead languages, and that, too, more for the sake of embellishing some public institution or library than for the enlightenment of the masses of the people, we think we owe no apology for writing a book of the present nature in English suited to the capacity of all. Another advantage, too, that our book has over any other which has hitherto appeared is this: that it does not confine itself to the ceremonies and liturgical customs of any church in particular, such as the Latin or the Greek, but gives the reader a general survey of all the churches of the East and West where a true Sacrifice of the Mass really exists. It therefore comprehends in its scope several churches which have long been separated from the centre of unity.

We wish our readers further to understand that the information embodied in these pages has been taken from the most approved sources, and but in a few cases, and these of minor note, taken second-hand. Where there was a doubt we have expressed it, and whenever we found ourselves obliged to copy the remarks of an author upon whom we could place but little reliance we have always noted the fact, in order not to give as certain what was at best but doubtful, and thus be made responsible for statements which could not stand the test of criticism.

We wish to remark, also, that our work has not been given to the public in undue haste. It has been compiled with a great deal of care and calm deliberation, and has been written over and over again, with new corrections and additions each time, in order that nothing might be asserted without proof and nothing stated at random; and although we have not followed to the letter the advice of the pagan poet to keep it in our drawer unto the ninth year, yet we can assure our readers of this much at least: that seven years of earnest and anxious labor have been expended on it. There is hardly a writer on sacred liturgy that we have not consulted; certainly we have passed over no one of any note; and in order that our readers, should they feel so inclined, may be enabled to collate our remarks with the sources from which we have drawn them, besides giving our authorities through the work, we have deemed it well also to attach an alphabetical list of them to the end of our treatise.

Regarding the order of the subject-matter, we have only to say that we have endeavored to treat each particular portion as fully as possible by itself, without running one part into another, and thus embarrassing the reader; and in order to aid the latter still more, we have appended so copious an index of words that it serves, in a measure, as a sort of compendium to the entire work.

As to the book's originality, we humbly confess that it is not new; and this confession we make, not through fear of running counter to what the Wise Man says, that "there is nothing new under the sun," but simply because we wish our readers to lay more stress upon the fact that it is a compilation of what the most learned writers have said upon the subject in hand rather than any effort of our own. Our book, then, can be called original only in so far as its name and the arrangement of parts are concerned. The labor of all this is ours, and ours only; as for the rest, we say in all sincerity with Montaigne: "I have here only made a nosegay of culled flowers, and have brought nothing of my own but the string that ties them."

THE TITLE OF THE BOOK.

We have called our book *A History of the Mass and its Ceremonies in the Eastern and Western Church*. At first sight it seems an easy matter to hit upon such a title as this, but we assure the reader that it did not seem so to us. Many an hour of serious meditation it cost us before we had satisfied ourselves that the designation was a happy one; and all this principally on account of the appellations of *Eastern* and *Western Church*. Almost every book that we take in hands— certainly every book of travels—has something to say about the Eastern Church and its liturgical customs; yet we candidly confess that we have never met with one which told us with any degree of satisfaction or clearness what this Eastern Church was, or which did not blunder from beginning to end in attempting to describe its ceremonies. Some are perpetually confounding the Eastern Church with the Greek Church, and the latter with the Russian, wholly forgetting that out of Greece itself no Greek Church exists, and that the

Russian Church is no more Greek than it is English or Irish. Others imagine that by the Eastern Church is meant that which is included within the Patriarchate of Constantinople; but this, after all, would be only a fraction of the East, for it would leave out both the Greek Church proper and the Russian Church, each of which is wholly independent of Constantinople and independent the one of the other. We have met some even who have gravely committed it to writing that by the Eastern Church is meant the Syrian and all its branches. Then add to this those neverending and high-sounding titles that are constantly dinning our ears and seen at the head of almost every review that we take in hand, such as "Holy Orthodox Church," "Orthodox Imperial Church," "Orthodox Church of the East," "Holy Eastern Church," and so on *ad indefinitum;* each, no doubt, meaning something, but quite unintelligible without much explanation. The fact is that since the fall of Constantinople, in 1453, there has existed no national church, if we except the Maronite alone, to which the appellation of *Eastern* could, with strictness, be given; and it is but too well known that the correlative appellation of *Western Church* went into desuetude centuries before that time. The two designations originally sprang up naturally and necessarily from the division of Constantine's empire in the fourth century, into that of the East, with Constantinople as its capital, and that of the West, with Rome. Strictly speaking, then, there are no such organizations now as the Eastern and Western Church, and here was our difficulty in choosing a title. "How, then," somebody will say, "can you justify the name of your book?" The question is answered in this way: If the book were a history, or a geography, or anything of that nature, it could not be justified at all, it would be a misnomer; but inasmuch as it is confined solely to ecclesiastical ceremonies and customs, all of which are the same to-day, with scarcely a perceptible difference, as they were when a real Eastern and Western Church existed, it cannot mislead as to its meaning, nor can it be said of it that it has been unaptly chosen. But it can be justified upon other grounds: Although the Catholic Church recognizes no Church to-day to which she gives the name of *Eastern* in its original acceptation, still it must not be forgotten that she has at this time several within her communion whose location is wholly in the East, and which yet retain all their ancient ceremonies and customs. The Maronite Church is one of these. It celebrates Mass and the Divine Office in Syriac; administers Holy Communion in both kinds to the laity; has a married clergy, and enjoys the privilege of electing its own patriarch. The Chaldean Church is another: it says Mass in the ancient Syro-Chaldaic; uses leavened bread in the Holy Eucharist; has a married clergy also; and, like all the other churches of the East, is under the immediate jurisdiction of a patriarch. Then there is the Church of the Uniat or Melchite Greeks; it still celebrates in the ancient Greek; like the Maronite and Chaldean, it has a married clergy; like them, also, it administers Holy Communion under both species, and enjoys the singular privilege of reciting the Creed, even in presence of the Pope himself, without being obliged to add the celebrated "Filioque." These are but a few of the many churches in the East which still retain their ancient ceremonies and customs; but as we shall have frequent occasion to refer to them again in course of the present work, this passing notice must suffice here.

THE ORIENTAL SCHISMATIC CHURCH.

Our duty would be but half discharged did we pass by unnoticed the Oriental Schismatic Church, which forms so large a part of Eastern Christendom and runs side by side with the Catholic Church in all the Eastern regions. This Church may be thus divided: First, into the Church of the Russian Empire; secondly, into that within the Turkish Empire, with Constantinople as capital; thirdly, into the Church of the kingdom of Greece. We ask the reader to bear this division carefully in mind, for numberless mistakes are made for want of due attention to it, and to remember at the same time that all these churches are wholly independent of one another, in temporals as well as in spirituals; and that they hold no intercommunion whatever, unless in so far as common charity or civility would dictate. The Church of the Russian Empire, at one time under the immediate control of the Archbishop of Moscow, and subsequently ruled by a patriarch, is now at the sole mercy of the "Holy Synod of St. Petersburg," and, though it would scorn to avow it, is to all intents and purposes a tool in the hands of the Czar, for without his sanction no change in the existing order of things can be made—not even can a council be convoked without first humbly asking his permission. This church uses the same liturgies and ceremonies as the Greek Church, and agrees with it in every point of discipline, save that it says Mass in the Sclavonic language.

The church within the Turkish Empire is made up of the four Patriarchates of Constantinople, Alexandria, Antioch, and Jerusalem. Constantinople, the headquarters of the Ottoman Empire, is also the chief patriarchal seat, and still rejoices in the proud title of New Rome. The Sultan is virtually the head of this church, and, though they would fain deny it, its bishops and patriarchs are forced to confess that he is the supreme and final arbiter in every important dispute. Of so vast an extent is this division of the Eastern Church that it includes within its limits people who celebrate Mass in nine different languages—viz., in Latin, Greek, Syriac, Armenian, Coptic, Ethiopic, Chaldean, Sclavonic, and **Wallachian.**

The Church of the kingdom of Greece, though nominally governed by the Synod of Athens, is as much a creature of the state as that of Constantinople or Russia, for it depends for its entire movement and being upon the will of the reigning monarch. It acknowledges no submission whatever to Constantinople, nor to any other branch of the Eastern Church.

Although these three great divisions of the Oriental Church include within their pale several churches which are both heretical and schismatical at the same time, still, as far as validity of orders is concerned, the Holy See has expressed her doubt of none save of the Abyssinian. The so-called Eastern Church has, therefore, a true priesthood, a true sacrifice of the Mass, and valid sacraments; hence its claim to our attention. But it has another claim which ought not to be passed by unnoticed here; its singular devotion to the ever-blessed Mother of God. This may be considered the great redeeming feature of the Eastern Church, and it is to be hoped that, in consideration of it, she whose glorious prerogative it is to destroy all heresies in the Church may, by her powerful intercession at the throne of her Divine Son, establish a lasting union between the East and West, so that Christ's Vicar may sing once more, as he sang at the Council of Florence, "Let the heavens rejoice and the earth burst forth in songs of gladness."

In concluding our Preface we beg leave to remark that no attempt whatever at what is called *style* has been made in the following pages. Our aim has been, from beginning to end, to give the reader plain facts, with little or no dressing, and to keep steadily in view that golden advice of St. Augustine, to wit, *that it is better to endure blame at the hands of the critics than say anything which the people might not understand*—" Melius est reprehendant nos grammatici, quam non intelligant populi " (*ad Ps.* cxxxviii.)

Whatever we have stated may be relied upon—if not relied upon as absolutely true, yet at least in the sense that it is a faithful rendering of the views of the author from whom it was taken. Further than this it would not be fair to hold us responsible. **J. O'B.**

MT. ST. MARY'S COLLEGE, EMMITTSBURG, MARYLAND,
Feast of the Immaculate Conception, December 8, 1878.

CONTENTS.

	PAGE
BRIEF DISSERTATION ON THE PRINCIPAL LITURGIES IN USE IN THE EAST AND THE WEST AT THE PRESENT DAY, . .	xix

CHAPTER I.

The Mass—Origin of the Word, ... 1

CHAPTER II.

Sacred Vestments, ... 35

CHAPTER III.

Sacred Vessels, ... 69

CHAPTER IV.

Chalice Linens, ... 83

CHAPTER V.

The Manner of Reserving the Blessed Sacrament, . . . 87

CHAPTER VI.

Incense, ... 92

CHAPTER VII.

Sacred Music and Musical Instruments, ... 95

CHAPTER VIII.
The Varying Rites within the Church, ... 103

CHAPTER IX.
The Altar, ... 113

CHAPTER X.
Relics, ... 121

CHAPTER XI.
Crucifixes and Crosses, ... 126

CHAPTER XII.
Lights, ... 132

CHAPTER XIII.
The Tabernacle, ... 137

CHAPTER XIV.
The Missal, ... 139

CHAPTER XV.
Bells, ... 146

CHAPTER XVI.
Bread used for Consecration, ... 153

CHAPTER XVII.
Wine, ... 165

CHAPTER XVIII.

Number of Masses that a Priest may say upon the Same Day, . 168

CHAPTER XIX.

Concelebration, ... 173

CHAPTER XX.

Customs relating to the Celebration of Mass, ... 176

CHAPTER XXI.

The Celebration of Mass—The Introit, ... 195

CHAPTER XXII.

The Sermon, ... 241

CHAPTER XXIII.

The Celebration of Mass—The Creed, ... 249

CHAPTER XXIV.

The Celebration of Mass—The Offertory, ... 266

CHAPTER XXV.

The Celebration of Mass—The Preface, ... 288

CHAPTER XXVI.

The Celebration of Mass—The Canon, ... 295

CHAPTER XXVII.

The Celebration of Mass—The Consecration, ... 324

CHAPTER XXVIII.
The Celebration of Mass—The Pater Noster, . . .

CHAPTER XXIX.
The Celebration of Mass—Communion of the People, . .

A BRIEF DISSERTATION

ON THE

Principal Liturgies in use in the East and West at the Present Day.

For the better understanding of the matter treated of in the following pages we deem it well to give the reader a brief account of the Liturgies in use in the Eastern and Western Church at the present day.

To give anything like a full history of the various Eastern Liturgies would, indeed, be a very laborious undertaking, and, we have serious reasons to fear, a very unsuccessful one also, for their name is legion—the Jacobites alone using as many as forty. We shall, therefore, wholly confine ourselves to such as are in general and daily use, and leave the rest to be treated of by those writers who make pure Liturgy the burden of their writing.

It would not be very bold to assert that the only living Liturgies in free circulation throughout the East at the present day are those of St. John Chrysostom and St. Basil the Great. Both of these are used now in their entirety, such as they were when they came from the hands of the great men whose names they bear; and this can be said of none of the other Eastern Liturgies. The Liturgy of St. Basil is very often called the Cæsarean Office, from the fact that its author was Bishop of Cæsarea, in Cappadocia. It is the parent of the Armeno-Gregorian Rite. The Liturgy of St. Chrysostom is usually inscribed "the Divine Liturgy of our Holy Father among the Saints, John of the Golden Mouth." From this many of the later forms in use among the Nestorians are derived. The Liturgy of St. James, first Bishop of Jerusalem, is very frequently spoken of in connection with the Maronites and Syrians, but it is a well-known fact that the living Liturgies of both these peoples have little more of St. James's in them than a few shreds. The Maronites are very fond of referring their Liturgy to that venerable norma because it has the impress of antiquity, it being the general opinion of liturgical writers that it is the oldest in existence; but in reality their Liturgy as it stands now is nothing else but a collection of *excerpta* taken from other Liturgies, and as often called by the name of St. John Maro as by that of St. James the Apostle. The fact is that, if we except the Church of Jerusalem and a few islands in the Archipelago which employ it on certain occasions, the Liturgy of St. James has no circulation to-day in its original form anywhere. The same may be said of the Liturgy of St. Mark, at one time in exclusive use throughout the Patriarchate of Alexandria, and, in fact, of every other primitive Liturgy known; so that we repeat what we stated at the outset, that the Liturgies of St. John Chrysostom and St. Basil the Great have almost undisturbed sway in the East to-day. They are used by Catholics and schismatics alike. Dr. Neale attributes all this to the influence of Balsamon, Catholic Patriarch of Antioch in the beginning of the thirteenth century, who, it appears, went heart and soul for shaping everything Eastern by the standard of the New Rome. Although Neale speaks somewhat disparagingly of this learned prelate, still, as he tells the story in full of how the Liturgies of Constantinople made their way into the East, we give his words without change of any kind. He speaks as follows: "Of the normal Liturgies, those of St. James and St. Mark were used by the churches of Antioch and Alexandria, respectively, till the time of Theodore Balsamon. This prelate was a complete Oriental Ultramontane; everything was to be judged by and squared to the rule of Constantinople. The Bellarmine or Orsi of the Eastern Church, he was for abolishing every formulary not adopted by the œcumenical patriarch, and endeavored successfully to intrude the forms of Constantinople on the whole East. Consulted by Mark of Alexandria as to the degree of authority which attached to the Liturgies of St. James and St. Mark, he wholly condemns them as not mentioned by Holy Scripture or the Canons, 'but chiefly because,' says he, 'the Catholic Church of the most holy œcumenical throne of Constantinople does in nowise acknowledge them.' The way in which Balsamon treats these offices, more venerable than his own, and that in which Rome has abrogated the Gallican and Mozarabic missals, are surely marvellously alike. From that time the Constantinopolitan Liturgies of St. Basil and St. Chrysostom have prevailed over the whole orthodox East, except that the Office of St. James is used in the Church of Jerusalem and in some of the islands of the Archipelago on the festival of that Apostle" (*History of the Holy Eastern Church*, General Introduction, vol. i. p. 318).

To enter, then, into more specific detail, the Liturgy of St. Chrysostom is used, first, by the Russian Church in the empire of Russia itself and throughout all the imperial dominions; not, indeed, in its Greek form, but in the Sclavonic, for that is the liturgical language in all those parts. It is also used in the kingdom of Greece and its dependencies, and has universal sway among the Mingrelians, Wallachians, Ruthenians, Rascians, Bulgarians, and Albanians, as well as with all the Uniat or Melchite Greeks of the four Patriarchates of Constantinople, Alexandria, Antioch, and Jerusalem. The United Greeks of Italy and those of the Austrian Empire use it also.

Together with this Liturgy, in all the places mentioned, runs that of St. Basil the Great, but it is not called as often into requisition. The Liturgy of St. Chrysostom is employed throughout the entire year, on week-days as well as on Sundays and festivals, with the following exceptions : viz., the vigils of Christmas and the Epiphany, the Feast of St. Basil (January 1), all the Sundays of Lent except Palm Sunday, Holy Thursday and Holy Saturday. On these excepted occasions the Liturgy of St. Basil is used, and on the ferial days of Lent the service of the Presanctified—called also the Presanctified Liturgy—is used instead of both.

THE LITURGIES OF THE WESTERN CHURCH.

The Liturgies of the Western, or Latin, Church need nothing more at our hands than a passing notice ; for, with the exception of one or two normas, which are better called rites than Liturgies—viz., the Ambrosian and Mozarabic—the Roman has undisturbed and universal sway. Of the two exceptions named—the former peculiar to the ancient Church of Milan, the latter confined to the city of Toledo, in Spain —a full account is given in another part of our work, so that more need not be said of them here. As for the so-called Gallican and Lyonese Liturgies, they are now things of the past. The few vestiges that yet remain to tell that they had at one time a place in the Church will be noticed in due course ; as will also the fragments that are left us of the celebrated Rite of Sarum, which at one time formed the chief glory of the English Church.

In concluding our dissertation we beg leave to direct the reader's attention to the following important fact : viz., that throughout the entire East the word *Liturgy* (from the Greek λεῖτον, public, and ἔργον, a work) means always the norma of the Mass, and no more; but in the West it is the complexus of all the rites and ceremonies that are used by the Church in the administration of the Sacraments and in all her sacred offices. It is well to keep this in mind, for some are perpetually confounding *Liturgy* and *Rubrics*, thinking that both mean one and the same thing. There is about the same difference between them as between mathematics and arithmetic. The one includes the other and a great deal more besides. The Rubrics, according to the primitive acceptation of the word, are nothing but the directions given in *red* letters for the due performance of any particular ceremony; when reduced to a regular system or science they are the elucidation of these directions, and nothing more. But the aim of Liturgy is of a far more comprehensive and elevated nature, for it takes in everything that is in any way connected with the sacred functions of the Church.

HISTORY OF THE MASS.

CHAPTER I.

THE MASS—ORIGIN OF THE WORD, ETC.

As to the origin of the word *Mass* liturgical writers are not entirely agreed. According to some, it comes from the Hebrew "מאסה," *Massah*, a debt or obligation; others derive its name from the Greek "μύησις," *Myesis*, initiation; whilst a third class maintain that it is nothing else but an improved form of the old obsolete *Mes* or *Messe*,[1] which, with the people of Northern Europe, meant a banquet or convivial gathering, and not unfrequently also a sacrifice.

The great body, however, of liturgical writers are in favor of deriving it from the Latin "Missa" or "Missio," a dismissal, referring to the custom in vogue during the first five or six centuries of the Christian Church—when the Disciplina Arcani, or Discipline of the Secret,[2] prevailed—of dis-

---

[1] From the same root are the affixes in such words as *Christmas, Childermas, Michaelmas, Lammas*, etc. (*Holy Days of the English Church*, p. 154).

[2] The Disciplina Arcani, or Discipline of the Secret, was a law enforced by the early Christian Church, in virtue of which the principal mysteries of our holy faith were concealed from pagans, infidels, and all who had not been regenerated by the saving waters of baptism; and this in accordance with the solemn admonition of our Divine Lord himself not *to cast pearls before swine* or *give what was holy to dogs* (Matt. vii. 6). This discipline prevailed in the Eastern Church until the end of the fifth century, and in the Western until about the middle of the sixth (Ferraris, art. *Discip. Arcani*, 735-12).

missing the Catechumens' and Public Penitents[4] from the house of God before the more solemn part of divine service began.

From the twofold dismissal—viz., that of the Catechumens at the beginning of Mass, and the other, of the faithful, at the end—the entire service used to be known by the plural appellations of *Missæ* or *Missiones* (that is, the *dismissals*); and hence the import of such phrases so often to be met with in the writings of the early Fathers, as "inter Missarum solemnia," "Missas facere," and "Missas tenere." Hence, also, the twofold division known as the "Mass of the Catechumens" and the "Mass of the Faithful," the former extending from the beginning to the Offertory, the latter from the Offertory to the end.

THE NAMES BY WHICH THE MASS WAS KNOWN IN THE GREEK CHURCH IN EARLY TIMES.

One of the strongest arguments against the Hebrew origin of the word Mass is that none of the Oriental Fathers ever made use of *Massah*, but always employed a different word. With them it was styled indifferently by the following names: *Mystagogia, Synaxis, Anaphora, Eulogia, Hierurgia, Mysterion, Deipnon, Teleion, Agathon, Prosphora,* and *Liturgia.*

It was called *Mystagogia* by St. Dionysius, from the fact

---

[3] Catechumen, from the Greek κατηχέω, I teach by word of mouth. Under the denomination of Catechumens came all those who were undergoing instructions at the hands of catechists previous to their reception of baptism. According to the most generally received opinion, there were two orders of Catechumens: the Hearers, or those who merely expressed a wish to become Christians; and the Elect or Competent, who had passed through the course of training that was necessary for the reception of baptism.

[4] Of the Public Penitents there were four distinct classes, viz.: the *Weepers*, whose place was in the porch, or first narthex; the *Hearers*, who stood in the second narthex; the *Prostrates*, whose place was near the ambo; and the *Costanders*, who stood with the faithful in the upper part of the nave. (See frontispiece.)

that it was a divine participation of, or initiation into, the sacred mysteries. It was termed *Synaxis*, or the *union*, because in virtue of it we are all united with Christ our Saviour. The name *Anaphora* was applied to it from the fact that it raises our minds and hearts to God. The term *Eulogia* was given it from its propitiatory nature; *Hierurgia*, because it was a sacred action; *Mysterion*, from the mysteries it contained; and *Deipnon*, or *banquet*, from the fact that it gave us the living Bread unto the eternal nourishment of our souls. Then, again, it was called *Teleion*, or *perfection*, because it was the sacrifice of that Holy Lamb, without spot or blemish, who came upon earth to be the perfection and completion of the ancient law. Its name *Agathon*, or *good*, was given it because it is the only lasting good upon which man can count; and from the fact that it finally conducts us to the happy end for which we were created, the appellation of *Prosphora* was given it also. Of all these names enumerated, that of *Liturgia* was most frequently used, and is exclusively used at the present day throughout the entire East.

DIFFERENT KINDS OF MASS.

From the various circumstances attending the celebration of Mass, from the ceremonies[b] employed, and the peculiar end for which it is offered, different names have been given to qualify it, such as Solemn High Mass, Simple High Mass, Low Mass, Conventual Mass, Bridal or Nuptial Mass, Golden Mass, Private Mass, Solitary Mass, Votive Mass, Dry Mass,

---

[b] The word *ceremony* owes its origin to a singular circumstance. When Rome was sacked by the Gauls, the Vestal Virgins, in order to escape with their lives and preserve their honor, fled the city, carrying with them all their sacred utensils, and repaired to the ancient city of Cære, in Tuscany. Here they received a most cordial reception, and here they remained until quietness reigned at Rome. To perpetuate the kind hospitality of the people of Cære towards the Vestals, the sacred rites, and all pertaining to them, were called ceremonies ever after (Gavantus, *Thesaur. Sacr. Rit.*, 2).

Evening and Midnight Mass, Mass of the Presanctified, Mass of Requiem, and Mass of Judgment.

Solemn High Mass.—When Mass is celebrated with deacon and subdeacon and a full corps of inferior ministers, it is denominated a Solemn High Mass. In many places of Europe the name *grand* is given it on account of its ritualistic display. It is called *high* from the fact that the greater part of it is chanted in a high tone of voice. When there is neither deacon nor subdeacon ministering, a Mass of this kind receives the name of Simple High Mass, or Missa Cantata.

Low Mass.—Low Mass is so called from its being said in a low tone of voice, in contradistinction to High Mass, which is chanted aloud. At a Mass of this kind the usual marks of solemnity are dispensed with. It is, in great part, read by the priest in an ordinary tone of voice, without any assistants save the server, who answers the responses in the name of the people and administers to the wants of the altar.

Conventual Mass.—Conventual Mass, strictly speaking, is that which the rectors and canons attached to a cathedral are required to celebrate daily after the hour of Tierce—that is, at about nine o'clock.

According to several authorities of note, this Mass is also of obligation in convents where the Blessed Sacrament is kept, and even in rural churches which enjoy the same privilege (De Herdt, i. 14). Conventual Mass is also known by the several names of *Canonical, Public, Common*, and *Major*. The last appellation is given it on account of the peculiar privileges it enjoys over ordinary Masses.

Bridal or Nuptial Mass.—It has always been the wish of the Church that at the solemnization of holy matrimony Mass should, if possible, be offered in behalf of the newly-married couple, in order that Almighty God may bless their union and favor them with a happy offspring. A special service is set apart in the Missal for this end, called in Latin " Missa pro Sponso et Sponsa "—*i.e.*, Mass for the Bridegroom and Bride—and the Mass itself is considered among the privileged, for it may be celebrated on days of greater rite (Bouvry, *Expositio Rubricarum*, ii. 601).

At a Mass of this kind a few ceremonies may be seen which are peculiar to it alone. As far as the " Pater Noster" it differs in nothing from an ordinary Mass; but when the priest has come to that part of the service immediately before the " Libera nos," he stands at the Epistle corner of the altar, and, having turned towards the bride and bridegroom, who are kneeling in front of him, reads over them from the Missal two prayers upon the nature and solemnity of their union. This being done, the bridal party retire to their places, and the Mass goes on as usual until the time of the last blessing. Here the priest turns round to the party again, and reads over them the following prayer: " The God of Abraham, the God of Isaac, and the God of Jacob be with you; may he shower his blessing upon you, that you may behold your children's children unto the third and fourth generation; and may you enjoy afterwards eternal, unending life through the help of our Lord Jesus Christ, who with the Father and the Holy Ghost liveth and reigneth God, world without end. Amen." After this the priest is directed to admonish the newly-married pair of the mutual faith and love they owe each other, and of the obligations they are under to remain continent on those occasions that the Church has set apart for special prayer and fasting. They are finally exhorted to live in the fear of God. The priest then sprinkles them with holy water, and Mass concludes as usual.

Bridal Mass according to the Sarum Rite.—According to the Sarum rite, of which we shall give a full account further on, Bridal Mass was celebrated with peculiar and interesting ceremonies. The marriage itself was performed at the church door, in order that all might witness it. From this the priest led up the married couple to the altar-steps, where he prayed over them and begged also the prayers of the people in their behalf. Mass was then begun, and the moment the "Sanctus" bell sounded the newly-married knelt near the foot of the altar, while some of the clerics of the sanctuary held over them a large pall commonly called the *care cloth*. This cloth was not removed until a little before the "Pax." The bride was required on this occasion to allow her hair to flow moderately upon her shoulders, and wear, if her circumstances allowed it, a wreath of jewels, or at least of flowers, upon her head.*

The dress of Margaret, eldest daughter of Henry VII., King of England, when going to be married to King James of Scotland, is thus described by Pauper: "She had a varey riche coller of gold, of pycrrery and perles round her neck, and the cronne apon hyr hed, her hayre hangyng." Just before the "Pax" the priest turned round to the new couple and imparted the marriage blessing, after which the *care cloth* was removed. The "Pax" was then given according to the ancient mode, and not with the *Pacifical*. The bridegroom received it first from the priest at the altar, and then bestowed it on his spouse. After Mass bread and wine, hallowed by the priest's blessing, used to be distributed among all the friends of the newly-married couple who happened to be in church during the ceremonies.

According to the rite followed at York, the nuptial blessing was generally given by the priest with the chalice, and this on account of the great dignity of the Sacrament of Matrimony. (The reader who wishes to see more upon this subject will do well to consult that excellent work of

* In mediæval art the Blessed Virgin is always represented in this way.

Dr. Rock known as the *Church of our Fathers*, vol. iii. part 2, 172.)

Golden Mass (Missa aurea).—Golden Mass was one that used to be celebrated formerly on the Wednesdays of the quarter tenses of Advent in honor of the Mother of God. It used to be a Solemn High Mass of the most gorgeous kind, and was often protracted three or four hours, in order to give full sway to the ceremonies and musical pieces employed on the occasion. The bishop and all his canons assisted at it, as well as the members of the different religious communities of the place where it was celebrated. It was customary, too, to distribute gifts, and those very often of the costliest kind, among the people who assisted at it; and, from the nature and excellence of the mystery in honor of which it was offered, it used to be written in letters of gold, hence its name (Gavantus, *Thesaur. Sacr. Rit.*, 27; Bouvry, ii. 105). Traces of this Mass may be witnessed yet here and there through Germany; but at the Church of St. Gudule, in Brussels, the regular Mass is celebrated every year on the 23d of December. Thousands assist at it on this occasion.

Private Mass.—Whenever the expression "Missa privata" is used by the rubrics, Low Mass, in contradistinction to High Mass, is always, or nearly always, meant. But by Private Mass we mean something entirely different. Strictly speaking, a Private Mass is one in which only the priest himself communicates (Gavantus, p. 29). It receives its name of *private* from the fact that no concourse of people assists at it, and that it is celebrated in some private oratory or chapel to which all have not access. According to the mind of the Council of Trent (session 22, chap. 6), no Mass is private in the Catholic acceptation of the word; for all, whether private or public, are offered by a public minister of the Church, not for himself alone, but for the entire household of faith (*ibidem*).

And that Masses of this kind have been practised from the very days of the Apostles themselves the most indubitable testimony proves; although the heretics of the sixteenth century would fain have it that such Masses were unheard of, nay, even forbidden, by the early Church. But Cardinal Bona shows to a demonstration that Private Masses have been in use always, and mentions, among others, the testimony of Tertullian, who lived away back in the second century, in proof of his assertion (Bona, *Rer. Liturg.*, p. 231).

The first daring attack made upon Masses of this kind was by the arch-heretic Luther himself, who declared that, in a conversation which he had had with the devil, it was revealed to him that such Masses were real idolatry (Bouvier, *Theol. Moral.*, iii. 224).

To put an end to all cavil on this subject, the Holy Council of Trent, in its 22d session, canon 8, thus decreed: "Si quis dixerit Missas in quibus solus sacerdos sacramentaliter communicat illicitas esse ideoque abrogandas, anathema sit." That is, *If any one shall say that those Masses in which only the priest communicates sacramentally are illicit, and that hence they should be abolished, let him be anathema.*

Solitary Mass.—When Mass is said by a priest alone, without the attendance of people, or even of a server, it is called a Solitary Mass. Masses of this kind were once very common in monasteries and religious communities (Bona, p. 230), and they are still practised to a great extent in missionary countries. They cannot, however, be said without grave necessity; for it is considered a serious offence by theologians to celebrate without a server, and this server must be always a male, never a female, no matter how pressing the necessity be.

Strangely enough, Solitary Masses were forbidden in days

gone by by several local councils, and this principally for the reason that it seemed ridiculous to say "Dominus vobiscum," *the Lord be with you;* "Oremus," *let us pray;* and "Orate fratres," *pray, brethren,* when there were no persons present. The Council of Mayence, held in the time of Pope Leo III. (A.D. 815), directly forbade a priest to sing Mass alone. The prohibition not merely to sing it, but to celebrate at all without witnesses, was repeated by the Council of Nantes, and for the reasons alleged. Gratian cites a canon in virtue of which two witnesses at least were required for the due celebration of every Mass; and this we find to be the rule among the early Cistercians.

Cardinal Bona (*Rer. Liturg.*, p. 230), from whom we copy these remarks, seems much in doubt as to whether Solitary Masses were wholly abrogated in his day. He instances, however, a well-known exception in case of a certain monastery which enjoyed the privilege from the Holy See of celebrating without having any person to respond.

According to the present discipline of the Church, whenever necessity compels a priest to celebrate alone he must recite the responses himself, and otherwise act as if he had a full congregation listening to him. He must not omit, abridge, add, or change anything to suit the peculiar circumstances of the occasion, but must do everything that the rubrics prescribe for ordinary Mass, and this under pain of sin.

Votive Mass.—As every day in the year has a Mass more or less peculiar to itself, whenever this order is broken in upon the Mass introduced is denominated *Votive*. Rubricists define it as a Mass not in accordance with the office of the day; and it receives its name *Votive* from the fact that it is celebrated to satisfy either the pious wishes of the priest himself or of some member of his congregation.

Masses of this kind are subject to various restrictions. They cannot be celebrated unless on days of minor rite, nor without a reasonable cause; for the rubrics of the Missal are very explicit in saying that, as far as can be done, the Mass ought to agree with the office of the day. St. Liguori says that a Votive Mass cannot be said merely on the plea that it is shorter than the Mass of the day, but that a more serious reason is required (Book vi., No. 419). A sufficient reason, however, would be if either the person asking such a Mass, or the person offering it, had a special devotion to some particular saint or mystery (De Herdt, i. 27).

Dry Mass.—When neither the consecration nor consumption of either element takes place the Mass is said to be a Dry Mass. In ancient times the word *Nautical* was applied to it, from the fact of its being confined principally to voyages on sea, where the difficulty of celebrating ordinary Mass would be very great on account of the rolling of the vessel and other causes. In celebrating a Mass of this kind all the sacred vestments were allowed; but, inasmuch as no consecration took place, the use of a chalice was forbidden. All those prayers which did not bear directly on the Offertory or Consecration could be recited, such as the opening psalm, the "Introit," "Kyrie eleison," "Gloria in excelsis," "Credo," Epistle and Gospel, as well as the "Preface." It was also allowed to impart the usual blessing at the end. It was customary, too, in some places to employ the services of deacon and subdeacon, in order to give it as solemn an air as possible. Genebrard, a Benedictine monk, who died towards the end of the sixteenth century, testifies that he himself was present at a Solemn Dry Mass celebrated at Turin one evening for the repose of the soul of a certain nobleman who had just departed life. These Masses were often said for the special gratification of the sick who could not attend church on account of their infirmities; also for prisoners, and, as has already been said, for seafaring people. But such Masses have long passed into desuetude. They are practised no more, and deservedly, for many well-meaning but simple-minded people were often led to put as much faith in their efficacy as in a real Mass (see Durandus, *Rationale Divinorum*, § par. 23; Bona, *Rer. Liturg.*, 235, 236; and Gavantus, *Thesaur. S. Rit.*, 33).

Evening Mass (Missa vespertina).—In the time of St. Augustine (fifth century) it was customary throughout Africa to celebrate Mass on Holy Thursday evening in memory of the institution of the Blessed Sacrament on that day. It used to be said by a priest who had already broken his fast (Martene, *De Antiquis Eccl. Ritibus;* Bona, *Rer. Liturg.*, 255). Touching this Mass the fourth Council of Carthage decreed as follows: "The Sacrament of the Altar must not be celebrated unless by a priest who is fasting, except on the anniversary of the institution of the Holy Eucharist."

Another custom, too, that prevailed in certain places was to say Mass for the dead at any time of the day that one of the faithful died, and this whether the priest had broken his fast or not (see article on the *Offertorium* of Masses for the Dead). But this practice was condemned almost as soon as its introduction by several councils, and among others by those of Carthage in Africa and Braga in Spain (Bona, 255).

Evening Mass in the Eastern Church.—As the majority of the Oriental churches do not reserve the Blessed Eucharist as we do, and this principally for the reason that leavened bread will soon corrupt in such climates as theirs, they are necessitated, in order to give the Holy Viaticum to the dying, to celebrate frequently in the evening, which, of course, they will do after having broken their fast.

The Copts never reserve the Blessed Sacrament from one

Mass to another, for reasons which we shall give when treating of Holy Communion, but will celebrate any hour of the day or night that they are called on to communicate the dying (Denzinger, *Ritus Orientalium*, p. 85).

Midnight Mass.—Midnight Masses, and Nocturnal Masses generally, were very frequent during the days of persecution, when the Christians were forbidden to assemble anywhere in daytime.

There were certain festivals, also, in later times for which Midnight Mass was prescribed, but all these privileges have long since been taken away, the only one remaining being that attached to Christmas. upon which night a Nocturnal Mass, as of old, is yet celebrated in many places.

In the Eastern Church Midnight Mass has never been much in vogue. One of the most gorgeous displays, however, of ritual ever known is to be witnessed in Russia at the Midnight Mass of Easter. As soon as twelve o'clock is announced all the bells of the Kremlin, whose number is legion, begin to toll, and they are immediately answered by all the other bells in Moscow. At the sound of these bells every inhabitant rises from sleep and repairs to church to hear the news of the risen Saviour. The whole city is in a blaze, for every window has a light, and a torch burns at the corner of every street. The great tower of the cathedral is illuminated from base to summit with myriads of lights, and lights burn in the hands of every man, woman, and child. The scene inside the different churches, but especially in the cathedral, defies description. The most costly vestments are used on this occasion, and neither labor nor expense is spared to make it worthy, in some way, of the great mystery it commemorates (Burder, *Religious Rites and Ceremonies*, p. 154).

Mass of the Presanctified.—This Mass receives its name, *Presanctified,* from the fact that it is celebrated with a Host consecrated on a previous occasion, and has no consecration of either element itself. In the Latin Church this Mass is celebrated but once a year—viz., on Good Friday—but in the Greek Church it is peculiar to every day in Lent except Saturdays, Sundays, and the Feast of the Annunciation, when the regular Mass is offered (Goar, *Euchologium Græcorum*, p. 205). This custom of not celebrating daily in the East during Lent is as old at least as the Council of Laodicea, held in A.D. 314. When the custom began in the Latin Church it is not easy to determine. Another difference in discipline between the Latin and Greek Church in regard to this Mass is this : that in the former no Communion is given during the service, but in the latter it is customary to communicate always on such occasions. The service in the Russian Church is thus spoken of by Romanoff :

"In the early days of the Christian Church the Fathers did not consider it seemly to celebrate the comforting feast on days of humiliation and mourning for sin, and permitted Mass to be sung on Saturdays and Sundays only during Lent, and on the Annunciation and Holy Thursday.[7] But as many pious Christians, accustomed to daily Communion, could not bring themselves to forego the strengthening and refreshing of their souls by the Body and Blood of Christ, the holy Church granted them the indulgence of the Liturgy of Preconsecrated Elements, when the bread and wine consecrated on the Sunday preceding are adminis-

---

[7] Whether there is a regular service in the Greek Church on Holy Thursday, as on the three other days mentioned, we have been unable to find. Goar says nothing about it. In the *Primitive Liturgies* (Introduction, xxxvii., note), by Neale and Littledale, a statement is made to the effect that the Liturgy of the Presanctified is not used on Holy Thursday at all, but only that of St. Basil, which is the one used also on Holy Saturday (Neale's *Holy Eastern Church*, vol. ii. p. 713). Whether we are to infer from this that the regular Mass is celebrated or not we are at a loss to determine ; but we strongly incline in favor of saying that it is not, for the Eastern canons only mention Saturdays, Sundays, and the Feast of the Annunciation.

tered on Wednesdays and Fridays to those who desire them" (Romanoff, *Rites and Customs of the Greco-Russian Church*, p. 123).

Mass of Requiem.—This is a Mass celebrated in behalf of the dead, and is subject almost to the same rules as a regular Votive Mass. If the body of the deceased be present during its celebration, it enjoys privileges that it otherwise would not, for it cannot be celebrated unless within certain restrictions. Masses of this kind are accustomed to be said in memory of the departed faithful, *first*, when the person dies—or, as the Latin phrase has it, "dies obitus seu depositionis," which means any day that intervenes from the day of one's demise to his burial; *secondly*, on the third day after death, in memory of our Divine Lord's resurrection after three days' interval; *thirdly*, on the seventh day, in memory of the mourning of the Israelites seven days for Joseph (*Genesis* 1. 10); *fourthly*, on the thirtieth day, in memory of Moses and Aaron, whom the Israelites lamented this length of time (*Numb.* xx.; *Deut.* xxxiv.); and, finally, at the end of a year, or on the anniversary day itself (Gavant., *Thesaur. Rit.*, 62). This custom also prevails with the Orientals.

Mass of Judgment.—The Book of Numbers, in its fifth chapter, has special directions for establishing the guilt or innocence of the wife who, whether justly or unjustly, had fallen under the suspicion of her husband. She was first to be taken before the priest with an offering of barley. The priest "took her before the Lord," as the expression goes, and put into her hand holy water mingled with some of the dust of the floor of the tabernacle. In this solemn condition the nature and enormity of the charges preferred were clearly explained to her, and she was assured that, if guilty of them, the water she held in her hand would, when she drank it, cause her "belly to swell and her thigh to rot," and she would be as a curse among the people; but if she were innocent she had nothing to fear. This was called the trial by the "waters of jealousy" (see Bannister's *Temples of the Hebrews*, p. 305), from which, no doubt, we are to trace what we are now going to treat of—the Mass of Judgment. That Masses of this kind were at one time very common we cannot deny, but we can deny, and that most emphatically, that they ever had the free sanction of the Church. They were altogether local abuses, and, when permitted to go on, it was wholly because, under the pressing circumstances of the times, better could not be done. Dr. Lingard, in his *History of the Antiquities of the Anglo-Saxon Church*, ii. 130, thus speaks upon this subject: "Before I conclude this chapter I must notice an extraordinary practice which united the most solemn rites of religion with the public administration of justice. To elicit, in judicial proceedings, a truth from a mass of unsatisfactory and often discordant evidence demands a power of discrimination and accuracy of judgment which it were vain to expect from the magistrates of a nation just emerging from ignorance and barbarity. The jurisprudence of an illiterate people is generally satisfied with a shorter and more simple process. While the Anglo-Saxons adored the gods of their fathers, the decision of criminal prosecution was frequently entrusted to the wisdom of Woden. When they became Christians they confidently expected from the true God that miraculous interposition which they had before sought from an imaginary deity." A little further on the author thus describes what used to take place on such occasions: "Three nights before the day appointed for the trial the accused was led to the priest; on the three following mornings he assisted and made his offering at Mass; and during the three days he fasted on bread, herbs, salt, and water. At the Mass on the third day the priest called him to the altar before the Communion.

and adjured him by the God whom he adored, by the religion which he professed, by the baptism with which he had been regenerated, and by the holy relics that reposed in the church, not to receive the Eucharist or go to the ordeal if his conscience reproached him with the crime of which he had been accused." The priest then administered Holy Communion with these words : " May this Body and Blood of our Lord Jesus Christ prove thee innocent or guilty this day." When Mass was finished the accused was again expected to deny the charge and take the following oath : " In the Lord I am guiltless, both in word and deed, of the crime of which I am accused." Dr. Lingard remarks in a footnote (p. 131) that the practice of ordeal prevailed among all the northern nations that embraced Christianity after the fifth century. But Masses of Judgment were by no means confined to the illiterate or to those newly emerging from barbarism. The most cultivated and civilized had recourse to them, and they were in vogue among some of the most refined nations of Europe. St. Cunegunda, wife of King Henry II. of Germany, proved herself innocent in this way of a charge of adultery. She went through the ordeal of walking over a number of red-hot ploughshares, from which she escaped unhurt (Butler's *Lives of the Saints;* Gavantus, *Thesaur. Sacr. Rit.*, p. 38). Queen Emma, mother of Edward the Confessor, subjected herself to a similar test, in order to establish her innocence of a foul calumny circulated of her. Lingard, however, seems to discredit this latter story ; but authorities of good standing make mention of it (see the *Month*, February, 1874, p. 214, for full particulars).

We have said that this practice of detecting crime by having immediate recourse to God through the holy sacrifice of the Mass was never directly sanctioned by the supreme authority of the Church, but only permitted because of the great difficulty and danger of eradicating it all at once.

Days upon which Mass is not Celebrated.

Our proofs of this are the following : Pope Gregory the Great condemned it as far back as A.D. 592 ; it was condemned expressly by the Council of Worms in 829, and Pope Nicholas I. repeated the condemnation upon his elevation to the chair of St. Peter in 858 ; Pope St. Stephen condemned it, too, and so did several other popes and councils (see Butler's *Lives of the Saints* and Alzog's *Universal Church History*; vol. ii. p. 155, by Pabish and Byrne). It is hardly necessary to add that Masses of this kind are now unknown in the Church.

DAYS UPON WHICH MASS IS NOT CELEBRATED.

From time immemorial it has been customary in the Latin Church to abstain from celebrating regular Mass on Good Friday, from the fact that it is the great mourning day of the year, and in a regular Mass there is more or less rejoicing ; and also because, as St. Thomas Aquinas says (p. 3, q. 83, art. 2), it is not becoming to represent the Passion of Christ mystically by the consecration of the Eucharist whilst the Church is celebrating it as if really happening.

Those who follow the Ambrosian rite (viz., the priests of Milan) have no service at all upon any Friday of Lent. This dates at least from the time of St. Charles Borromeo. They will not even on these days say Mass for the dead or to satisfy any demand, no matter how urgent it be (Bona, *Rer. Liturg.*, p. 219).

Mass is also forbidden, unless Solemn High Mass, on Holy Thursday, but an exception is made in case of minor churches where a sufficient number of priests cannot be had to go through the regular ceremonies. In such cases a Low Mass is permitted.

Holy Saturday is another day upon which Mass is not allowed—that is, Low Mass—unless in particular cases ; and although it is customary to celebrate Solemn High Mass on this day, yet, strictly speaking, this Mass belongs to Holy Saturday night or Easter eve, and not to the day itself, as may be clearly seen from its wording, where frequent mention is made of the time at which it used to be celebrated. Thus the first Collect reads : " O God ! who enlightenest this most sacred night by the glory of the Resurrection of our Lord, preserve in the new offspring of thy family the spirit of adoption thou hast given them ; that, being renewed in body and soul, they may serve thee with purity of heart." Allusion is also made to the *night* in the Preface, and in that prayer of the Canon called the "Communicantes."

THE FIRST MASS—BY WHOM CELEBRATED—WHEN, WHERE, AND IN WHAT LANGUAGE.

The opinion is sustained by the ablest liturgical writers that it was St. Peter, the Prince of the Apostles and head of Christ's Church, who said the first Mass, and this after the descent of the Holy Ghost, in the very same Cenacle[a] at Jerusalem where the Blessed Eucharist was instituted, and where our Lord uttered the words, "Do this in commemoration of me."

And as it will be asked why Mass was not celebrated before Pentecost, we give what the best authorities say upon

[a] The Cenacle, which stands upon Mt. Sion, is to-day one of the greatest objects of veneration in the Holy Land. It is remarkable as being the supposed place where the Last Supper was held ; where our Lord appeared to his disciples after his glorious resurrection on Easter morning ; where the Sacrament of Penance was first instituted, and where our Lord was seen to converse for the last time with his chosen band before he ascended into heaven. It was in this blessed spot also that St. James the Less, styled the brother of our Lord, was consecrated first bishop of Jerusalem ; and a pious tradition has it that it was here the "Beloved Disciple" said Mass in presence of the Blessed Virgin, who, it is said, departed this life there. Father Vetromile, *Travels in Europe and the Holy Land*, p. 200, describes the Cenacle as a large room divided by a kind of alcove, and says that a plenary indulgence is attached to a visit paid it, with, of course, the usual conditions.

the matter—viz., that, in the *first* place the Apostles would not presume to perform so august an action before they had received the plenitude of the Holy Ghost; and, in the *second* place, that inasmuch as the Ancient Law was not wholly abrogated in what pertained to the priesthood until after the descent on Pentecost, it was not deemed expedient to begin the sacred ministrations of the New Law until this abrogation had taken effect. The Holy Scriptures seem to corroborate this statement also, for we read in the Acts of the Apostles (i. 14) that *before* the descent of the Holy Ghost "they were all persevering with one mind in prayer," but *after* the descent the "breaking of bread"—*i.e.*, the celebration of Holy Communion—is mentioned (*Acts* ii. 42 and 46; see Gavantus and Merati, *Thesaur. Sacr. Rit.*, pp. 7, 12, 14; and Bona, *Rer. Liturg.*, book i. p. 206).

THE LANGUAGE IN WHICH THE FIRST MASS WAS CELEBRATED.

In the time of our Lord three particular languages were common throughout Judea. They were, in some sense of the word, the languages of the world in those days—viz., the Hebrew, Greek, and Latin. The *first*, better known as the Syro-Chaldaic, or more properly the Syriac, was the language of the greater part of Judea, especially of Jerusalem itself and its environs, and, without a doubt, was the vernacular of our Divine Lord and his Blessed Mother. This can be proved almost to a demonstration, both from the common consent of critics and from the numerous Syriac expressions that we find here and there in the New Testament yet in their original dress, such as "talitha cumi," "eloi, eloi, lamma sabacthani," and "ephphetha," all of which are Syriac, with a few euphonic changes made to suit Greek ears.

The *second*, or the Greek, obtained a large sway in Palestine also, as St. Jerome testifies (Proem, 1. 2, *Com. Epist. ad Gal.*) and various records show. "And this glory," says Brerewood in his *Languages and Religions*, p. 9—"this glory the Greek tongue held in the Apostles' time, and long after in the Eastern parts."

The *third*, or the Latin, had obtained a far wider sway in the Holy Land in the time of our Lord and his Apostles than either of the other two, for it was the language of imperial Rome ; and as Judea was a Roman province at that time, and for years previous, it was but natural to expect that the language of Rome would be forced on the conquered people. But as we shall have occasion to treat of these languages more fully a little further on, we dismiss them with these brief remarks, and take up the subject that heads our article, viz.: In what language was the first mass offered ?

Eckius, a learned German divine and antiquarian of the sixteenth century, was the first who broached the opinion that Mass was celebrated everywhere, in the beginning, in Hebrew. But this cannot be sustained, for the ablest liturgical writers and linguists hold that in the days of the Apostles Mass was celebrated in the language that prevailed in those places whither the Apostles went to spread the light of the Gospel ; hence, that at Jerusalem it was celebrated in *Syriac ;* at Antioch, Alexandria, and other Grecian cities, in *Greek ;* and at Rome, and throughout the entire West, in *Latin*. As the first Mass, then, was celebrated at Jerusalem, it is an opinion which it would be rash to differ from that the language in which it was offered was the Syriac (Bona, *Rer. Liturg.*, 207 ; Gavantus, *Thesaur. Sacr. Rit.*, 16, 17 ; Kozma, *Liturg. Sacr. Cathol.*, p. 111).

APPARATUS USED AT THE FIRST MASS.

Although neither Scripture nor history says anything definite about the apparatus or ceremonies employed by the Apostles in the celebration of the Holy Eucharist, still it is most probable that such an august sacrifice was not offered without what was suitable and becoming. The Apostles knew too well with what a gorgeous display of ritual the sacrifices of the Mosaic law used to be offered, and how Almighty God himself expressly regulated the kind of garments the priests should use and the special ceremonies that were to be employed on every occasion; and if this were done where the sacrifice consisted of nothing but bulls and goats, how much more ought to be expected when the victim offered was none else than the Son of God himself? It is very likely, then, that the apparatus used in the first Mass, and the ceremonies observed thereat, were communicated orally to the Apostles by our Lord himself, and that they did exactly as he prescribed.

Cardinal Bona, in treating this question, says that, without a doubt, lights were used after the manner of the ancient Hebrews; that vestments also were employed different from those of every-day life; and he mentions the fact that St. Peter's chasuble was conveyed from Antioch to the Church of St. Geneviève at Paris, and there carefully preserved (*Rer. Liturg.*, p. 206).

THE LANGUAGES IN WHICH MASS IS CELEBRATED TO-DAY THROUGHOUT CHRISTENDOM.

The Catholic Church of to-day celebrates the holy sacrifice of the Mass in nine different languages—viz., in Latin, Greek, Syriac, Chaldaic, Sclavonic, Wallachian, Armenian, Coptic, and Ethiopic.

Latin.—This is the language of the Mass in the entire

West and in a few places in the East, and has been so, without change, from the beginning of Christianity. It may, in fact, be called the vernacular language of the Western Church.

Greek.—At the present day Mass is said in Greek by the Uniat or Melchite[9] Catholics of the East. They are to be found in Syria, Jerusalem, Russia, in the kingdom of Greece, in Italy, and in several places of Europe; and they comprise the Mingrelians, Georgians, Bulgarians, Muscovites, and others. These Catholics are allowed by Rome to retain all their ancient rites, such as consecrating the Holy Eucharist in leavened bread, giving Communion in both kinds, saying the Creed without the "Filioque," and putting warm water into the chalice after Consecration. Nay, more, the Holy See even allows their clergy to marry.[10] They have three patriarchs, residing respectively at Antioch, Alexandria, and Jerusalem; and they use three different Liturgies for the celebration of the Mass—viz., the Liturgy of St. John Chrysostom, or that most generally used; the Liturgy of St. Basil the Great, used on all Sundays in Lent except

---

[9] The term *Melchite*, from the Syriac *Malko*, a king, was first applied at the Council of Chalcedon (451) to designate the orthodox party, at whose head was the Emperor Marcian. It has nearly the same meaning now in the East that the word *Papist* has through the West. The schismatics, however, often apply it to their body because of its expressing orthodoxy, for they rejoice in the title of the "Holy Orthodox Church of the East."

[10] When we say the Holy See allows the Eastern clergy in her Communion to marry, we must not be understood as implying that she allows those who are in Sacred Orders to do so. This would not be true. Her discipline in this matter is precisely as follows: Marriage is allowed all the inferior clergy from the subdeacon, *exclusive*, down. Should any member, then, of this inferior body be promoted to Sacred Orders, whether to the subdiaconate, diaconate, or priesthood, he is allowed to retain his wife and do for her as best he can from his living, but he can never marry again. Should he do so he would be degraded and forbidden ever to officiate. There is no such thing allowed or heard of as a clergyman getting married in Sacred Orders. If he is not married when a subdeacon he never can be afterwards. And as for bishops, patriarchs, metropolitans, and the other great dignitaries of the Oriental hierarchy, the rule is that they must all be single men. Hence it is that all, or nearly all, the Oriental bishops are taken from the monasteries; and this is the rule with the schismatics also.

Palm Sunday, on Holy Thursday, Holy Saturday, the Vigils of Christmas day and of the Epiphany, and, finally, on the Feast of St. Basil, January 1. The third Liturgy is denominated the *Presanctified*. It is only used during those days of Lent upon which there is no Consecration, but only a Mass similar to that which we have on Good Friday.

Syriac.—Mass is said in Syriac by the Maronites[11] of Mount Lebanon and the Syrian Melchites of the East. It is, in fact, the liturgical language of all those places where the Liturgy of St. James is used as the norma. It is the proud boast (and truly it is something to be proud of) of the people who say Mass in this language that they are using the very same language that was spoken by our Divine Lord himself and his Blessed Mother, as well as by the majority of the Apostles. The Maronites are allowed by the Holy See to retain all their ancient ecclesiastical rites and customs. They are governed by a patriarch, whose style is "Patriarch of Antioch of the Maronites." This dignitary is elected by the people themselves; but before he is installed in office his election has to await the confirmation of Rome. They use unleavened bread, as we do, in confecting the Holy Eucharist, and, like the rest of the Orientals, they communicate the people under both kinds; but when communicating the sick only the species of bread is used.

They use incense at Low Mass as well as at High Mass, and read the Gospel in Arabic after it has first been read in the Syriac, for Arabic is the language of the day in those parts.

[11] This people received the name of Maronite from a holy monk, St. Maro, who inhabited the Lebanon in the fifth century, and became celebrated all over the East for his eminent sanctity. Some say that they fell at one time into the Monothelite heresy, but they themselves deny the charge, maintaining that their faith has always been orthodox. By way of derision they are called the "Eastern Papists," so great is their loyalty to the Holy See.

Their secular clergy number about twelve thousand, and their regular about fourteen thousand. All the latter live in monasteries; and as they must be unmarried (for it is only the seculars who are allowed to have wives), it is from their body that the patriarchs and bishops are taken (Vetromile, *Travels in Europe and the Holy Land*, 77).

Chaldaic.—This language is peculiar to the Babylonian Catholics, who are chiefly converts from Nestorianism,[12] and who inhabit principally Mesopotamia, Armenia, and Kurdistan. They have a patriarch, who is titled "Patriarch of Babylonia." His residence is at Bagdad. All the liturgical books of this people are written in the Chaldaic, in that peculiar character known as the *Estrangelo*[13]—for the Chaldaic itself has as many different alphabets as eighteen (Antrim's *Science of Letters*, p. 88).

Sclavonic.—Mass is said in this language by the Catholics of Istria, Liburnia, and the maritime parts of ancient Dalmatia. It is, in fact, the liturgical language of all in union with Rome who belong to the Sclavonic nation. This privilege the Sclavonians first received from Pope Adrian

---

[12] The Nestorians, so called from Nestorius, a native of Germanicia, in Syria, and Patriarch of Constantinople in the fifth century, are found in great numbers to-day throughout the entire East. They have twenty-five metropolitans, and a patriarch who resides at Mosul, the ancient Nineveh. Strangely enough, they consider it an insult to be styled *Nestorians*, their proper name being, as they strenuously maintain themselves, *Soorâyé—i.e.*, Syrians. According to some they sometimes style themselves *Nusrani*—that is, " of Nazareth"—but this, if anything, must be a subterfuge to escape the name of the heretic Nestorius, which they disdain being called by (see *Nestorians and their Rituals*, vol. i. p. 178, by Rev. Geo. Percy Badger ; and Vetromile, *Travels in Europe and the Holy Land*, p. 90). The reader need hardly be told that the heresy for which Nestorius was condemned at the General Council of Ephesus in 431 was the ascribing of two distinct persons to our Lord instead of one, and refusing the title of "Mother of God " to the Blessed Virgin.

[13] According to Assemani (*Bibl. Orient.*, tom. iv. p. 378), this word comes from the Greek στρογγύλος, *round ;* but, as it is hard to see where the roundness comes into these characters, others derive the word from an Arabic compound meaning "gospel-writing" (see Phillips' *Syriac Gram.*, Introduction, p. 6).

II. in the ninth century, and it was confirmed by Pope John VIII., Adrian's immediate successor. This latter Pontiff, in renewing the grant, made it a condition that the holy Gospel, on account of its superiority over the other parts of the Mass, should be first read in Latin, and after that in Sclavonic. In A.D. 1248 Pope Innocent IV. acquiesced in all these concessions of his predecessors, as also did Pope Benedict XIV. in A.D. 1740; so that at the present day Mass is said in Sclavonic by quite a large body of Catholics. It is also the liturgical language of schismatical Russia and of thousands of Christians within the Turkish dominions (Bona, *Rer. Liturg.*, 216; Kozma, *Liturg. Sacr. Cathol.*, 112, note; Wouters, *Historia Ecclesiast.*, 258; Brerewood, *Languages and Religions*, p. 235; and Gavantus, *Thes. Rit.*, p. 25, xix.)

Wallachian.—Since the seventeenth century, when a great number of them came into the Church, the Wallachians, with the tacit consent of the Holy See, have been saying Mass in their own native language, which, however, is no longer that in daily use, but the old classic tongue. Concessions (if we may call that a concession which is allowed by tacit consent) of this kind are very rarely granted; and when granted at all, it is always in favor of some newly-converted people who cling with great tenacity to their national language and customs (Kozma, *Liturg. Sacr. Cathol.*, p. 112, note 9).

Armenian.—This is the liturgical language of all who are called by that name in the East to-day. They inhabit Armenia proper, or the modern Turkomania, and are found also throughout Asia Minor, Syria, Palestine, Turkey, Georgia, Greece, Africa, Italy, and Russia. In the last-named empire their sees were arranged by a ukase, March 11, 1836. They are at present governed by a patriarch, who is styled "Patriarch of Cilicia of the Armenians," and who resides at Bezourmar. In the island of San Lazaro, at Venice, they have a monastery which is famous all over the world for its printing-presses. Here most of the Armenian ecclesiastical books are turned out.

The Armenians, unlike all the other Christians of the East, save the Maronites, use unleavened bread in the Holy Eucharist as we do. The heretical Armenians, all of whom are *Monophysites*[14] (that is, believers in but one nature—viz., the divine—in our Lord, after the teaching of Eutyches), abstain from mingling water with the wine in the Mass, in order to give as great a prominence to their belief as possible; for water is symbolical of the human nature of our Saviour, which these people maintain was wholly absorbed by the divine, so that a vestige of it did not remain (Burder's *Religious Ceremonies*, p. 180; Smith and Dwight's *Travels in Armenia*, passim; Vetromile, *Travels in Europe and the Holy Land*, art. "Eastern Rites").

Coptic.—This language, which the natives maintain to be the same as the ancient language of the Pharaohs—that is, the *Egyptian*—is used by the Christians along the Nile in the celebration of their sacred rites. This people are called *Copts* from a paring down of the name they were given by the Greeks, viz., Αἰγύπτιοι—*i.e.*, *Egyptians*—which in many ancient manuscripts is written *Ægophthi*, *Copthi*, and *Chībthi*. This, at least, is the origin assigned by some of the ablest Oriental scholars, and Renaudot among others (see *Liturg. Orient. Col.*, dissert. *de Ling.*

---

[14] The term *Monophysite*, from the Greek μόνος, one, and φύσις, nature, first came in use after the General Council of Chalcedon in 451, at which the heretic Eutyches was condemned for asserting that there was but one nature in our Lord. In Syria and other parts of the East the followers of Eutyches are called Jacobites, from James Baradai, one of their chief reformers: but throughout Africa they are universally known by their more comprehensive name of *Monophysites*. As a peculiarity of their heretical tenets, they use only one finger in making the sign of the cross (Brerewood, *Languages and Religions*, p. 186).

Coptica, tom. i. p. cx.) But, according to Scaliger, Simon, and Kircher, the Copts are so called from an ancient city of Egypt known as Coptos, once the metropolis of the Thebaid. Renaudot, however, has clearly proved that this is at best nothing more than a guess; and the vast majority of modern linguists adhere to his opinion.[16]

The Copts use three different Liturgies in the celebration of Mass—viz., those of St. Basil, St. Cyril, and St. Gregory. The first, which is considered the most elegant and elaborate, and the one best suited to grand occasions, is dedicated specially to the Person of the Omnipotent Father. The second is dedicated to the Person of the Father also, but not in so special a manner. The third, or that of St. Gregory, is dedicated to the Person of our Divine Redeemer, for it dwells particularly on his Incarnation, Passion, Death, Resurrection, and Ascension. These are the three principal Liturgies; in fact, they may be said to be the only ones used by the Copts, for, although they have as many as twelve altogether, yet they never bring any others into requisition but the three specified (Renaudot, *Comment. ad Liturg. Copt. S. Basilii*, vol. i. p. 154).

The Copts at the present day—that is, the Catholic Copts—are governed by a vicar-apostolic residing at Cairo, but there is a movement on foot to give them a regular hierarchy of their own, with a patriarch at its head.

The schismatic Copts, all of whom are *Monophysites*, number about one hundred and fifty thousand—that is, about eighty thousand more than those in communion with the Holy See. They are governed by a patriarch, who is styled "Patriarch of Alexandria of the Copts"; but besides

---

[16] "Le terme Arabe, un Cophte, me semble une altération évidente du Grec Αἰγύπτος, un *Egyptien*, car on doit remarquer que y était prononcé *ou* chez les anciens Grecs, et que les Arabes, n'ayant ni g devant a, o, u, ni la lettre p, remplacent toujours ces lettres par g et b; les Cophtes sont donc proprement les représentans Egyptiens" (Volney, from the *Crescent and the Cross*, p. 93, by Warburton).

him they have another who resides at Cairo and takes his title from Jerusalem. He is, of course, subordinate to the Patriarch of Alexandria (see Vetromile, *Eastern Rites*, 87 ; Renaudot, *De Patriarcha Alexandrino*, passim, tom. i.) We shall have frequent occasion to refer to the Copts throughout our work.

Ethiopic.—This is the liturgical language of the modern Abyssinians, who differ but very little from the Copts either in discipline or ecclesiastical customs. Of the language there are two dialects—viz., the *Amharic* and the *Gheez*. The former, or court language, is considered much easier than the latter, in which nearly all the Abyssinian books are written. The Gheez is principally spoken in the kingdom of Tigre.

By some authors the Ethiopic is called the *Chaldaic*, from an opinion current among the natives that it originally came from ancient Chaldea ; and it is generally said that a fair knowledge of it is easily acquired by one skilled in Hebrew, for the principal difference, they say, that exists between both consists in the formation of the letters of the alphabet (Burder, *Rel. Rites and Customs*, p. 175 ; Brerewood, *Languages and Religions*, 300).

The Catholic Abyssinians now number about two millions. They are under a vicar-apostolic. The schismatics, who are Monophysites like the Copts, number about five times as many as the orthodox. They are governed by an official called the *Abouna* (from a Syriac word meaning "our Father), who ranks as a bishop and is sent them by the Patriarch of Alexandria. The great redeeming feature of this people is their extraordinary devotion to the Mother of God. So great is their reverence for her that when the common street-beggars fail to exact an alms for the love of God or for any of the saints, an appeal is at once made in honor of " Lady Mary," which is always sure to receive a favorable hearing (*Dublin Review*, July, 1863, p. 50). Furthermore, an oath taken in her name is considered the most solemn that can be administered, and, if taken rashly, is subject to the highest penalty the law can inflict (see Lobo's *Voyage to Abyssinia*, p. 26). Their Liturgy is called the "Liturgy of All the Apostles," but its official title is the "Ethiopic Canon." It is considered to be an amplification of that of St. Cyril.

It may be well to say that the Abyssinian ordinations are the only ones in the East which are held doubtful by the Holy See. For this reason priests coming into our Church from theirs are, in nearly every case, ordained *under condition*. I say in *nearly* every case, but not *always;* for where it is found that the Abyssinian ritual has been followed to the letter, no conditional ordination is needed. Their rituals have the valid form, but carelessness on the part of their bishops often causes it to be either badly vitiated or wholly disregarded (see Denzinger, *Ritus Oriental.*, p. 139).

Before we dismiss this subject we have some remarks to make that cannot but be of interest to the reader. We have said that the Catholic Church of to-day celebrates the holy sacrifice of the Mass in nine different languages, all of which we have given. We have said that the Greeks celebrate in *Greek*, the Armenians in *Armenian*, the Ethiopians in *Ethiopic*, etc. The reader must not understand by this, as some, such as Usher,[16] would fain do, that the language in any one case is the vernacular.

The Greeks, who celebrate in Greek, speak *Greek*, it is true, but so different is it from their liturgical language (for

---

[16] Usher was an Anglican bishop of the seventeenth century. He was a man of great erudition, and many works of merit, notwithstanding his own bigotry, issued from his pen. He published what he termed a *Catalogue of Irish Saints*, arranged in three divisions according to the age they lived in.

the latter is the ancient classic Greek) that hardly a man can be found who understands one word of it. The same may be said of the *Armenian*, the same of the *Ethiopic*, the same of any one of the nine specified. The Copts, for instance, are so little skilled in the *Coptic* used in the Mass that it has been found necessary to print the rubrics of their Missals in Arabic (the language of those regions) for the benefit of the clergy; for neither the clergy nor the people are much versed in the language used in the sacred offices. (The reader who wishes to see this subject fully discussed would do well to consult Renaudot, *Liturg. Oriental. Collectio*, tom. i., dissert. *de Liturg. Orient. Origine*, xxxviii.)

We do not consider it necessary to quote authorities for our assertion, for we challenge anybody to gainsay it. Protestants—we mean those who are not biassed and blinded by prejudice—and Catholics bear testimony to it. And since it is an indisputable fact that there is not to be found in Christendom a single instance of a people celebrating the Holy Mass in the language of the day, how is it that we of the Latin Church are called to task so often for " celebrating in an unknown tongue "? Why not call the Greek Church to task? Why not call the Armenian Church to task? Why not call the Russian to task? And yet, if there is reprehension deserved anywhere, these people deserve more than we, for the most illiterate of our congregations know far more about our liturgical language—there are translations of it in every prayer-book—than the most educated of the nations we have mentioned know about theirs. Ask a Nestorian or a Copt to roll you off only a few short sentences of the liturgical Syriac or Coptic; he could as easily tell you his thoughts in the language of the " Celestial Empire."

PRECEDENTS FOR USING AN UNKNOWN TONGUE, TAKEN FROM ANCIENT SOURCES.

Nor is the practice of celebrating divine service in a tongue unknown to the people without precedents in ancient and modern times. The Jews always celebrated the praises of Jehovah in "the language that the prophets spake"—*i.e.*, the ancient Hebrew. This was so far above the reach of the people that it was found necessary to supply them with translations in the shape of the so-called *Targums*,[17] in order that they might know something of what was done (see Renaudot in loc. cit.); and that this custom is yet kept up by the modern Jews in their synagogues innumerable witnesses prove (see Bannister's *Temples of the Hebrews;* Jahn's *Archæology;* Dr. Rock, *Hierurgia*, p. 216). We may be pardoned for taking another instance of praying in an unknown tongue from the Mahometans. It is well known in what deep veneration these people hold the Koran,[18] which is to them what the Bible is to Chris-

---

[17] *Targum*, from the Chaldaic *turgmo*, "interpretation," was originally a rendition of the Scriptures into the East-Aramæan dialect for the benefit of those Jews who, on account of their seventy years' absence in Babylon, could no more understand the pure Hebrew of the Bible. There are in existence yet ten of such Targums, the most ancient and valuable of which is the one ascribed to Onkelos, which is a very literal version of the original Hebrew Pentateuch. The Babylonian Talmud makes Onkelos a contemporary of Gamaliel, who flourished in the beginning of the Christian era.

[18] The Koran, from the Arabic *qurân*, "the reading," is looked upon with so much sacredness by the Mahometans that they deem no one worthy to behold it who is not a Moslem of the most orthodox kind. The book is held to be altogether a miraculous work; and so inimitable is its style that, according to the Mahometans, no one less than an angel from heaven could produce anything like it. Its miraculous nature is supposed to be proved from the following facts:

1st. Its elegance, diction, and melody are unsurpassed. 2d. Its structure cannot be equalled. 3d. Its consistency is marvellous, admitting of no contradiction. 4th. Its knowledge of divine things is admirable. 5th. Its knowledge of human and divine law. 6th. Its sayings have never been falsified. 7th. It removes all diseases of mind and body. 8th. It reveals mysteries known only to God.

It consists of one hundred and fourteen *Surâs*, or chapters, each bearing a title which serves as a sort of key or clue to what is to follow, as an antiphon does to its psalm. The first *Sura* is headed the "Cow," for in the body of the chapter the sacrifice of a

tians. It is written in the purest Arabic, and so much afraid are they of it becoming common that no one is allowed to attempt a translation of it in the Arabic spoken by the people. This pure Arabic is a dead language to the masses (see Guthrie's *Grammar of History*, p. 719). "Though it has long ceased to be spoken," says Murray (in his *Encyclopædia of Geog.*, vol. ii. 229), "it has continued to be the liturgic and learned language of all the numerous nations professing Islam," from the shores of the Indian Ocean to the westernmost corner of Morocco, and from the Wolga to Cape Delgado, in Africa."

Another example in point may be cited from the Hindoos, who allow none but the Brahmins to read the Veda on account of the great respect they have for the language in which it is written. The Hindoos carry this thing so far that they will not allow some of their minor ministers so much as even to listen to the reading of this book or to speak of it (Burder, *Religious Ceremonies and Customs*, pp. 528, 529); so also with the language known as the *Bali*, a half-sister of the Sanscrit, which has long since ceased to be spoken, yet it is the liturgical language of Ceylon, Bali, and Madura, of a great part of Java and Indo-China. It is also the religious language of all the Japanese who profess Lamaism (Murray, *Cyclop. of Geography*, vol. ii. p. 231). We have, therefore, clearly shown that if precedent be wanted for what is styled "a strange, unmeaning discipline," the

cow is spoken of. With but one exception every *Sura* begins thus : "Bismillah, ur-rahman-ur-raheem "—In the name of God, the compassionate, the merciful.

Mahomet was aided in composing the Koran by a Jew named Abdia Ben Salon, and by a monk who had apostatized, named Sergius, or Bahira. as the Orientals called him (see the Koran, translated by Sale, and the *Life and Religion of Mahomet*, translated from the Persian by Rev. James Merrick).

[19] Islam, Moslem, and Mussulman are all from the same root. *Aslam*, meaning to yield up, to dedicate, to devote to the service of religion ; something like our word *cleric*, which comes from the Greek κληρόω, I separate or choose for a religious purpose.

most critical mind can be satisfied by looking into the pages of antiquity and examining the religious customs of any ancient people. In nearly every case the liturgical language will be found different from that in use among the common people.

The principal reason why Protestants reprobate our use of a language not understood by the people is, as far as they themselves are concerned, very rational, but, as far as Catholics are concerned, highly absurd. A Protestant goes to church to utter a few prayers, or at least to hear the minister utter them, and nothing more. His service is essentially prayer, and nothing but prayer. Not so with the Catholic. His service is something higher and greater than mere prayer: it is a tremendous sacrifice; and as the sacrifice may be offered entirely independent of prayer, it matters but little whether the share prayer takes in it be little or great, provided everything else is duly ordered. For which reason some of the ablest spiritual writers have said again and again that one of the most efficacious ways of hearing Mass is to watch the actions of the priest at the altar with great attention from beginning to end, and look as little at the prayer-book as possible. A person who could do this without distraction would reap incalculable spiritual fruit from it, and would, without a doubt, be assisting at Mass in the strictest sense of the word.

WHY THE CHURCH RETAINS THE USE OF THE LATIN IN HER SERVICE.

The Catholic Church celebrates in Latin for a variety of reasons:

First. Because she did so in the beginning; and as she never changes her faith, she has never deemed it advisable to change her language. If her sacred language changed with those that are changing around her, there would be no end to the confusion that would result, and much disedification would unavoidably be given by using words and phrases in the hearing of the people to which the grossest meanings are sometimes attached.

Secondly. As order is heaven's first law, uniformity seems to be the first law of the Church, for which reason she makes it her endeavor to have her greatest charge, the due and respectful celebration of the Adorable Sacrifice of the Altar, conducted with the same ceremonies and said in the same language everywhere. This she could not do unless she had fixed on a common language.

Thirdly. Unity in respect to language goes a very great way in preserving unity of belief. A writer of high repute (Porubszky, *Jure suo Ecclesiast.*, p. 854) declares as his firm conviction that the various churches of the East which have severed their connection with the centre of unity, Rome, would hardly ever have done so had they been required from the beginning to make Latin their liturgical language. National languages always pave the way for national churches.

Fourthly. By preserving the Latin in her Liturgy, and requiring her ministers to cultivate it, the Catholic Church has secured for herself the accumulated literary treasures of eighteen centuries of Christianity. By this she has free access to the writings of some of the most illustrious doctors of the Church, to canon and civil law, to the decrees of ancient councils, and to many other documents of value which would have otherwise been totally out of reach. For which reason alone our Holy Church should receive the praise of Christendom. Hallam, in his *Middle Ages*, could not hide the fact that the sole hope of literature in these times depended principally on the Catholic Church, for wherever it existed the Latin language was preserved.

PRIEST OF THE LATIN CHURCH.
VESTED FOR MASS.

CHAPTER II.

SACRED VESTMENTS.

THE sacred vestments employed by a priest in celebrating the Holy Sacrifice are six in number—viz., Amice, Alb, Cincture, Maniple, Stole, and Chasuble.

THE AMICE.

The Amice, so called from the Latin *amicire*, to *clothe* or *cover*, is a rectangular piece of linen about three feet long and two feet wide. It has a string at each of its two upper corners by which to fasten it on the shoulders of the wearer, and a cross in the middle of the upper edge, which the priest kisses when vesting.

From the office which the Amice serves various names have been given it, such as *Humeral*, from the Latin *humerus*, a shoulder; *Anabolagium*, from the Greek $\dot{a}\nu a\beta o\lambda\acute{\eta}$ (anabole), a cloak; and *Ephod,* from its resemblance to the Aaronic garment of that name.

The Greek Church uses no article of this kind at the present time, although it did formerly. The priests of the Ambrosian or Milanese rite, also the canons of the Cathedral of Lyons, put on the Amice after the Alb, and not before it, as we do. This is also the discipline of the Maronites of Mt. Lebanon.

The Amice of the Armenians, called by them *Vakass*, has a breastplate attached, upon which are inscribed the names of the twelve Apostles, in imitation of the Jewish Ephod, whose breastplate displayed, in shining colors, the names of the twelve tribes of Israel (Neale's *Holy Eastern Church,* vol. i. p. 306).

Early History of the Amice.—Liturgical writers tell us that the Amice, in early days, served as a covering for the head and neck, and that it continued to be so used until about the tenth century, when its place was supplied by the ecclesiastical cap, or *berretta* then introduced (Bouvry, *Expositio Rubricarum,* vol. ii. 216).

This is corroborated by the practice yet prevailing with some of the religious orders, such as the Capuchins and Dominicans, of wearing the Amice over the head until the beginning of Mass, when they cast it back on their shoulders and adjust it around the neck. A vestige of its ancient use may also be seen in the ordination of a subdeacon, where the bishop draws the article first over the candidate's head, and then lets it fall loosely over his shoulders.

Mystical Meaning of the Amice.—The mystical meaning of the Amice may be gathered from the prayer recited in donning it : " Place upon my head, O Lord ! the helmet of salvation for repelling the attacks of the evil one." It is, then, part of the armor of a soldier of Christ, and serves to remind the priest of the obligation he is under of being ready at all times to fight the good fight of faith in accordance with that sacred admonition of the Apostle of the Gentiles, " Put ye on the armor of God, that you may be able to stand against the deceits of the devil. . . . And take unto you the helmet of salvation " (*Ephesians* vi. 11-17).

THE ALB.

The second vestment the priest clothes himself with is the Alb, so called from its white color—*albus* in Latin meaning *white.* It is an ample, loosely-fitting garment of pure linen, entirely enveloping the body, and fastened at the neck by means of strings.

The use of a vestment of this kind is of the highest antiquity, for we find it employed by all nations in their religious services. It is the same as the linen garment ordered to be worn by the priests of the Old Law (*Exod.* xxviii.; *Levit.* viii.) King David wore a linen Alb when translating the Ark of the Covenant from the house of Obededom to Jerusalem (1 *Paral.* xv. 27).

We have said that the Alb is made of linen; this, at least, is the present discipline in regard to it, but formerly it was often made of silk and ornamented with gold. King Ethelwolf, of Anglo-Saxon times, and father of Alfred the Great, presented the Church of St. Peter's at Rome, in A.D. 855, with a number of silken Albs richly ornamented in this way (*Church of Our Fathers*, by Dr. Rock, vol. i. p. 426). An ancient Roman ordo, published by Hittorp, prescribes *silken* Albs for Holy Thursday and Holy Saturday (*ibid.*)

The Alb, too, changed in color to suit particular occasions. The monks of Cluny used to wear one of pure cloth of gold in the High Masses of the greater festivals; and we find some of green, blue, and red in an old inventory of the celebrated monastery of Peterborough, in England (*ibid.*, pp. 430–433 et passim).

Pope Benedict XIV., *De Sacr. Missæ*, is our authority for saying that a garment of this kind, but of a black color, used to be formerly worn on Good Friday.

Figurative Signification of the Alb.—According to Pope Innocent III. (*De Sacr. Altaris Mysterio*, 57), the Alb, from the purity of its color, denotes newness of life, and reminds us of St. Paul's admonition to the Ephesians, chap. iv.: "Put off the old man with all his acts, and clothe yourselves with the new man, who, according to God, is created in justice and holiness of truth." This beautiful idea of a new life, as signified by the Alb, is very forcibly presented to us in Holy Baptism, where the newly-regenerated receives a white garment with these significant words: "Receive this white and spotless garment which you are to bear before the tribunal of our Lord Jesus Christ, that you may possess eternal life. Amen."

Oriental Usage.—The Greeks call the Alb *Poderis*, from its reaching to the feet (Bona, *Rer. Liturg.*, 281). This, however, is not the name that it is generally known by, for we find it mentioned in nearly all the Oriental Liturgies as the *Stoicharion* (Denzinger, *Ritus Orientalium*, pp. 129–405; Renaudot, *Liturg. Orient.*, i. 161). It is the first vestment of all the orders of the clergy, and, though anciently made of linen, is now, with many of the Oriental churches, of nothing else but white silk (Denzinger, 129).

In the Russian Church a *Stoicharion* of purple is prescribed for all days in Lent except the Feast of the Annunciation, Palm Sunday, and Holy Saturday (Neale's *Holy Eastern Church*, vol. i. p. 307).

With the Copto-Jacobites (or Monophysites of Egypt) it is known indifferently by the names *Jabat* and *Touniat*; and with those of Syria as the *Koutino*, evidently from the Greek χιτώνιον, an *under-garment* (Renaudot, i. 161, ii. 54). The Copts, too, sometimes call it *Kamis* (Denzinger, 129), from the Latin *camisia* and the French *chemise*,' an *under-gown*. They are very strict in their discipline regarding the wearing of it. No priest would dare enter the sanctuary without it. Should he present himself for Holy Communion, and neglect to have himself clothed with it, he is at once ordered to depart and communicate at the rails with the common people. One of their disciplinary

---

[1] It will interest the reader to know that the camisia, or under-gown, of Our Blessed Lady is yet preserved, with affectionate veneration, in a silver case at Chartres, in France. It is inscribed "La Chemise de la Sainte Vierge," and so well authenticated that it would be rash to entertain a doubt about it. For a full account of its miraculous history see Nicephorus Calixtus, *Hist. Eccl.*, lib. xv. chap. xxxiv.; or the *Truth of Supposed Legends*, by Cardinal Wiseman.

canons on this head runs thus : "It is unlawful for a priest to pray or receive Holy Communion [2] without his being vested with a Chitonion. The thing would be unbecoming and at variance with the canon of holy faith." And another: "Let not a priest approach Holy Communion on the steps of the altar unless vested with the Stoicharion. Should he not have this he must communicate outside the rails" (Renaudot, *Liturg. Orient.*, i. 160).

Priests of the Latin Church put on the Alb with the prayer : "Purify me, O Lord! and make me clean of heart, that, washed in the Blood of the Lamb, I may possess eternal joy." In the Russian Church the prayer is : "My soul doth magnify the Lord, who clothed me in the garment of salvation" (*Greco-Russian Church*, by Romanoff, p. 89).

THE CINCTURE.

The Cincture occupies the third place in the catalogue of sacred vestments. It is of as high antiquity as the Alb, which it always accompanies; its chief, in fact its only, office being to keep that garment in its proper place on the person of the wearer. Different writers give it different names, such as *zone, girdle, band, belt*, and the like. It is required to be of linen, and of such a length that, when doubled, it may encircle the body of the priest. Formerly it was wide like a sash, and was often made of the most precious materials—such as cloth of gold, silk, etc.—and

---

[2] We here beg to inform the reader that it is customary for all the priests of the East who assist at Mass, whether as concelebrants (that is, celebrating the self-same liturgy with the celebrant of the day) or as mere lookers-on, to receive Holy Communion from the hands of the priest at the altar. Should, however, the patriarch be present at such a Mass, but not celebrant, he approaches the altar and communicates himself (Denzinger, *Rit. Oriental.*, p. 405). The practice of thus receiving from the hands of the priest celebrating is observed in our Church on Holy Thursday, but on no other occasion.

used to be studded with gems (*Church of Our Fathers*, vol. i. p. 488, by Dr. Rock). A cincture found upon the body of a deceased bishop taken up in Durham Cathedral in 1829 is thus described by Raine : " Of the girdle, or *cingulum*, the portion which we were enabled to preserve measures twenty-five inches in length; its breadth is exactly seven-eighths of an inch. It has evidently proceeded from the loom ; and its two component parts are a flattish thread of pure gold and a thread of scarlet silk, which are not combined in any particular pattern, save that, at a very short distance from each selvage, there run two or three longitudinal lines, which serve to break the uniformity of the whole. The lining is of silk " (*ibid.* 489, note 22). It varied also in color formerly, to suit the different colors of the vestments ; but now it is rarely seen of any other color but *white*, although the rubrics do not forbid other colors to be used at the option of the priest. And as regards its material, according to the present discipline, it is required to be of pure linen, and of nothing else. Terminating both ends are two large tassels, which hang down equally on each side of the priest when vested.

Mentioned in Holy Scripture.—The Cincture is frequently alluded to in Holy Scripture, where many moral significations are attached to it. The prophet Isaias, in describing the Messias, says of him : " Justice shall be the girdle of his loins, and faith the girdle of his reins " (xi. 5). Our Divine Lord himself, when addressing his disciples, thus exhorted them : "Let your loins be girt, and lamps burning in your hands" (Luke xii. 35) ; and St. John, in the Apocalypse, says that he saw " in the midst of the seven golden candlesticks one like unto the Son of Man, clothed with a garment down to the feet, and girt about the paps with a golden girdle" (i. 13).

Cincture in the Old Law.—In the Old Law, as well as in

the New, the Cincture occupied a prominent place among the priestly vestments. According to the Jewish historian Josephus (p. 74), its width was four fingers, and it was woven in such a manner as to exhibit the appearance of serpents' scales. It used to be ornamented with floral embroidery in purple, dark-blue, scarlet, and white. The manner of weaving it was as now. The name given it by Moses was *Abaneth;* but the more recent Jews called it, in accordance with Babylonic usage, *Emia.*

Cincture of the Orientals.—The Cinctures of the Greeks and Syrians are much broader than ours, and, instead of being knotted on the person of the wearer, are buckled in front with a hook or clasp. These Cinctures are sometimes made of very precious silk, studded with precious stones. A gilt hook, shaped like an "S," is employed to fasten them around the waist (Dr. Rock, *Church of Our Fathers,* i. 490, 491). Renaudot (*Comment. ad Liturg. Copt. S. Basilii,* p. 161) tells us that, to draw as broad a line as possible between the followers of the Koran and the Christians of Egypt, some of the Caliphs[3] used to oblige the latter to wear a certain kind of Cincture always in common life. To exhort the faithful to bear this intended humiliation with true Christian fortitude, the Fathers of those days delivered many touching homilies to them. While this state of things lasted the Christians of those parts were commonly styled "Christiani de Cingulo"—that is, *Cincture-wearing Christians.*

The prayer recited in putting on the Cincture is worded as follows: "Gird me, O Lord! with the Cincture of purity, and extinguish in my loins the heat of concupis-

---

[3] Caliph—from the Arabic *kaleefah,* and the Chaldaic *chalaph,* to change, to succeed; hence, a ruler—is the official title of the highest Mahometan dignitary in spirituals and temporals. He is regarded as actually holding the place of Mahomet himself; therefore he must be considered in point of fact as his vicar on earth.

cence, that the virtue of continence and chastity may abide in me."

The Russian priests, who wear a Cincture exactly like ours, recite the following prayer in vesting themselves with it : " Blessed be the Lord, who girdeth me with strength, and maketh my path undefiled " (Romanoff, *Greco-Russian Church*, p. 89).

Venerable Relics.—Among the many sacred relics yet preserved, and exhibited every seven years for the veneration of the faithful, in the great church of Aix-la-Chapelle, in France, is the veritable Cincture worn by our Blessed Redeemer. It is entirely of leather, and bears at its extremities the imperial seal of Constantine the Great. Thousands flock thither from all quarters of the globe to behold this precious curiosity (*Catholic World*, Sept., 1872). The Cincture worn by Our Blessed Lady is said to be preserved also in the Church of Our Lady of Montserrat at Prato, in Tuscany (Burder, *Religious Ceremonies and Customs*, 235).

Moral Lesson taught by the Cincture.—The moral lesson intended to be conveyed by the wearing of the Cincture is easily gathered from the prayer recited in putting it on. It reminds the wearer of the great purity of mind and heart that he ought to be filled with in his ministrations before a God of infinite holiness and sanctity. The high-priests of the Old Law were reminded of this solemn obligation by being obliged to wear on their foreheads a golden plate with the words " קדש ליהוה "—Kadesh la Jehovah (Bannister, *Temples of the Hebrews*, p. 180)—inscribed upon it ; that is, *Holiness to Jehovah*. How much more holiness is required in priests of the New Law, where the Victim of sacrifice is none other than the Son of God himself, the Jehovah of the New Covenant ?

Other mystical meanings were also attached to the Cincture, such as *promptitude* in executing the commands of

God; *exactness* in religious observances; and *watchfulness* in regard to our eternal salvation, in accordance with that solemn admonition of our Divine Lord himself: "Let your loins be girt, and lamps burning in your hands" (Luke xii. 35). That is, be ready at all times to appear before the tribunal of divine justice.

THE MANIPLE.

The Maniple is the fourth article which the priest vests himself with. It is a small strip of precious cloth, of the same material as the Stole and Chasuble, having three crosses embroidered upon it—one in the middle, and one at each of its extremities. It is worn on the left wrist, to which it is fastened either by a pin or a string. Its whole length is generally about two feet, and its breadth about four inches. When fastened on, it hangs equally on both sides.

Ancient Names given the Maniple.—The Maniple was anciently known by as many as ten different names—viz., *Mappula, Sudarium, Brachial Cincture, Mantile, Linteum, Aer, Sacerdotale Cincticulum, Maniple, Mappa Parva,* and *Phanon* (Gavantus, *Thesaur. Sacr. Rit.*, p. 130).

Originally it was intended solely for wiping the perspiration from the face of the wearer, and drying the hands so that the sacred vestments may not be soiled by them. In fact, it served in every way as a handkerchief, as we see from what the ancients have written about it. Thus Alcuin, in the ninth century, speaks of it as follows: "The little kerchief which is worn on the left hand, wherewith we wipe off the moisture of the eyes and nose, designates the present life, in which we suffer from superfluous humors" (Bona, *Rer. Liturg.*, 281).

Amalarius also, who lived about the same period, writes

of it thus : "We carry a handkerchief (*Sudarium*) for the purpose of wiping the perspiration" (*ibid.*)

The Maniple, as we have said, was fastened to the left wrist. The ancient form of the Chasuble, of which we shall give a full account further on, required this disposition; for if it were kept anywhere else it would be almost wholly out of reach of the priest, who was enveloped on all sides, as our print will show (see figure). As long as the ancient ample Chasuble remained in use the Maniple was not allowed to rest on the wrist until the priest was about to ascend the altar-steps. Then the Chasuble was folded up by the deacon and subdeacon, and the left arm being thus entirely free, the Maniple was fastened to it, and thus did it remain until the end of Mass. A vestige of this ancient practice is yet preserved in a Bishop's Mass, where the Maniple is not fastened to the prelate's wrist until the "indulgentiam"—that is, a little before he ascends the steps.

According to the best authorities, the Maniple served the purpose of a handkerchief until about the twelfth century. After this it became a liturgical ornament (Kozma, *Liturg. Sacr. Cathol.*, 44), with no other office but a symbolic one. Our holy Church is always loath to part with any of her ancient apparel.

Material of the Maniple.—Whilst the Maniple served as a handkerchief it used to be made of fine white linen, and was frequently carried in the hand during divine service instead of being fastened to the wrist; but when it passed into a liturgical ornament, then the material of which it was made changed to suit that of the Stole and Chasuble. In some parts of England it was customary to attach little bells of gold and silver to its edging (Dr. Rock, *Church of Our Fathers*, i. 422).

The Maniple is put on with the following prayer : "May

I deserve, O Lord! to bear the Maniple of weeping and sorrow, in order that I may joyfully reap the reward of my labors." The reference in the words "weeping and sorrow" is to what frequently occurred in days gone by during the sacred ministrations at the altar, when many holy men wept, sometimes with joy at being allowed to assist at so tremendous a sacrifice, and sometimes with sorrow for their unworthiness. Durandus, in his *Rationale Divinorum*, p. 110, says that St. Arsenius used to be so affected.

Mystical Meaning.—The mystical meaning, then, of the Maniple is that it reminds the priest of the trials and troubles of this life, and the reward that awaits him if he bears them in a Christian-like manner.

Maniple of the Orientals.—The Orientals wear two Maniples, one on each arm, which are usually denominated *Epimanikia*, a barbarous word, from the Greek $\dot{\epsilon}\pi\iota$, upon, and the Latin *manus*, a hand—that is, something worn upon the hand. In form the Epimanikia differ from our Maniple considerably, although there is no doubt but that at one time both served the same purpose. They are shaped somewhat like the large, loose sleeves of a surplice, and are fastened to the wrist by a silken string. The rule requires that they be fastened tightly, for they are intended to remind the wearer of the cords that fastened our Lord's hands to the pillar of flagellation.

The Oriental bishops are accustomed to wear upon their Maniples an *icon*, or image of our Divine Saviour, which they present to the people to be kissed.

With the Syrians the Epimanikia are called *Zendo;* with the Armenians, *Pasban;* with the Russians, *Poruche* (hand-pieces); and with the Copts, *Manicæ*.

A Russian priest, in donning these articles, says, when putting on the right-hand one: "The right hand of the Lord hath pre-eminence; the right hand of the Lord bringeth mighty things to pass"; and when putting on the left-hand one: "Thy hands have made me and fashioned me; oh! give me understanding, that I may learn thy commandments." In the sentence, "the right hand of the Lord hath pre-eminence," there is a reference to the tradition that the Jews first nailed our Saviour's right hand to the cross, and then the left (see Goar, *Euchologium Græcorum*, p. 111; Neale, *Holy Eastern Church*, vol. i. p. 307; Renaudot, *Liturg. Orient. Collect.*, i. 162; Denzinger, *Ritus Orientalium*, p. 131; and Gavantus, *Thesaur. Sacr. Rit.*, 131).

THE STOLE.

The Stole ranks fifth in the catalogue. It is a long band of precious cloth, of the same width as the Maniple, but about three times its length. It is worn round the neck and crossed on the breast, in which position it is kept by the Cincture. It is universally admitted that originally the Stole was very similar to the modern Alb, and that, like the latter, it used to envelop the entire person (Durandus, *Rationale Divinorum*, lib. iii., v. 6, p. 108).

According to Cardinal Bona (*Rer. Liturg.*, 282), what we now call a Stole is nothing else but the ornamental band that used to form the selvage of what was really the Stole of the ancients; and that as soon as the practice of wearing that kind of Stole went into desuetude the band was retained as a sort of memorial of it, just as the Maniple is a memorial of the ancient *Sudarium*, or handkerchief.

Who may Wear the Stole.—The right to wear the Stole begins from the time of one's ordination as deacon. The deacon, however, cannot wear it as a priest does—that is, around both shoulders—but only as yet over the left shoulder, and fastened at the right side; and this to remind him of his inferiority in orders to a priest, and of his obligation to be as little encumbered as possible, especially about the right hand, when acting as his assistant minister. Upon this head the fourth Council of Toledo, held in A.D. 633, under Pope Honorius I., issued the following directions: "The levite (deacon) ought to wear one Orarion (Stole) on his left shoulder when he prays; but he must have the right shoulder free, to the end that he may be the more expeditious in administering to the wants of the priest" (Bona, *Rer. Liturg.*, 282).

The bishop wears the Stole pendent on both sides, without crossing it on the breast as a priest does, and this because he wears a cross already on his breast—viz., the Pectoral Cross [1]—whereby this necessity is obviated (Gavantus, 134).

The prayer recited by the priest while vesting himself with the Stole is worded thus: "Restore to me, O Lord! the Stole of immortality which I lost through the transgression of my first parents, and, though I approach unworthily to celebrate thy sacred Mystery, may I merit nevertheless eternal joy."

Many of the Anglo-Saxon Stoles and Maniples had little bells of silver and gold attached to them, which made a most agreeable, delicate sound whenever the sacred minister changed his position. Dr. Rock, in his *Church of Our Fathers*, vol. i. p. 415, note 60, tells us that there was once kept at Liege, in the Abbey Church of Wazor, the Stole of St. Foraunan, an Irish bishop who died in A.D. 982 while abbot of that monastery, which had hanging from its ex-

---

[1] The Pectoral Cross was originally a reliquary case, and received its shape from the fact that it used generally to contain a splinter of the true cross upon which our Lord was crucified. The reliquary, or neck-cross, as it used to be anciently called, worn by Pope Gregory the Great, was made of thin silver. Those now in use date no further back than the sixteenth century (Dr. Rock, *Church of Our Fathers*, vol. ii. 174). The Eastern bishops wear hanging from their necks what is called the *Panhagia*, a Greek word meaning "all-holy," in which there is inserted an enamelled medallion of our Lord and his Blessed Mother. This is often very richly ornamented with precious stones. It is suspended by a golden chain (Romanoff, *Greco-Russian Church*, 399).

tremities a number of little silver bells. These little bells were sometimes as many as twenty-seven (*ibid.*)

Stole of the Orientals.—The Stole of the Orientals, generally known as the *Epitrachelion*, from the Greek ἐπί, upon, and τράχηλον, the neck, is somewhat different from ours; for instead of being parted, so as to allow it to hang down equally on each side, it is made of one piece of stuff, with a seam worked along its middle, and having an opening at the top wide enough to allow the priest's head to pass through. It hangs down, when worn at Mass, in front of the priest, reaching nearly to the instep.

The Copts call the Stole *Bitarshil;* the Syrians, *Ouroro;* the Armenians, *Ourar* (Goar, *Euchol. Græc.*, p. 111; Neale's *Holy Eastern Church*, i. 308; Denzinger, *Ritus Orient.*, 133).

Touching the origin of this word *ourar*, or *orarium*, as applied to the Stole in ancient manuscripts and liturgical writings, there has always been much dispute. We incline, for our part, to the side of those who derive it from the Greek ὥρα, an hour, because it was by waving the *Orarium* that the deacon pointed out the different hours or stages during divine service at which the choir would sing or the congregation pray. And this is in keeping with the Oriental discipline yet. It must be remembered, too, that the name *Orarion* was peculiar only to the Stole of the deacon; that of the priest was always called *Epitrachelion*.

We had almost forgotten to mention that at one time, at least as far back as the ninth century, priests and bishops, even when they were not in church, always wore the Stole as part of their ecclesiastical dress and as a distinctive mark of their dignity. The Council of Mayence, held in A.D. 813 under Pope Leo III., thus decreed upon this subject : "Let priests use the Stole without intermission, on account of the difference of the priestly dignity." According to the

GREEK PRIEST IN CHASUBLE

present discipline, only the Pope wears the Stole in common daily life, and this in evidence of his jurisdiction over the universal Church (Kozma, *Liturg. Sacr. Cathol.*, p. 46). The papal Stole is ornamented with three crosses, the keys, and tiara (*ibid.*)

THE CHASUBLE.

The Chasuble, so called from the Latin *casula*, a little house (for, according to its ancient form, it enveloped the entire person of the priest, leaving nothing but the head visible), is the last in the catalogue of sacred vestments. In its present disposition it is open at both sides, and, as it rests on the priest, it reaches down in front to about the knees, and a few inches further behind. Its material is required to be of precious cloth, such as brocade, silk, or the like; and its color one of the five mentioned in the rubrics--viz., *white, red, violet, green,* or *black.* Without a dispensation from the Holy See no other kind of Chasuble may be used.

According to liturgical writers generally, the ancient ample-flowing Chasuble was in use up to the sixteenth century (Kozma, *Liturg. Sacr. Cathol.*, 49), but after that period a practice of clipping it set in, first at the shoulders and then down the sides, until it assumed its present shape, which, strange to say, was the work of private individual fancy rather than of any express wish or command on the part of the Church. "Id vero minime," says Mgr. Saussay, the learned Bishop of Toul, "contigisse ex ullo Pontificum judicio, ecclesiæque lege, sed ex privato genio quorundam" (Dr. Rock, *Church of Our Fathers,* vol. i. 329). Cardinal Bona makes the same assertion (*Rer. Liturg.*, lib. i. cap. xxiv. p. 237, ed. Sala), and so does Honorius of Autun.

The cause generally assigned for changing the ancient

form of the Chasuble was the difficulty that prevailed for a long time, especially about the sixteenth century, of procuring suitable pliant material for making it; for if made of hard, stiff, board-like cloth as it now is, while its ancient shape was preserved, it would greatly encumber the priest in his ministrations at the altar. Since, however, nothing else could be conveniently had but this stiff material, in order to save the Chasuble as much as possible from the wear and tear occasioned by lifting and folding it up so often during the Mass, it was deemed advisable to cut a slit in both sides of it, and in this way its present shape originated.

Another reason, too, and a very good one at that, contributed much towards effecting this change. As long as the ancient form was in use the difficulty of celebrating Mass without the aid of deacon and subdeacon was very great, for the Chasuble of the celebrant needed folding and lifting up at several parts of the service; and as it was not at all times easy to have assistant ministers, and as private Masses became more frequent, a form of Chasuble which the priest himself could manage seemed to be a desideratum; and this, as much as anything else, was the cause of introducing Chasubles of the present make (see *Hierurgia,* p. 440 ; *Les Cérémonies de l'Eglise,* par M. De Conny, p. 256).

The reader will see with what indignation this change in the style of the Chasuble was viewed at first from the following words thundered forth by De Vert.[s] Speaking of

---

[s] Claudius De Vert was a monk of Cluny and a native of Paris. His death is placed in 1701. He wrote a great work on the ceremonies, etc., of the Church, four volumes, in which he made himself singularly remarkable, and not unfrequently ridiculous, by looking for literal and natural meanings, wholly disregarding mystical ones, in everything that was done at Mass. Durandus is about as exact a match for him on the opposite side as could possibly be found. The *Rationale Divinorum* of this latter-named author is one of the most curious books ever written, and, to our mind, one of the most fanciful and mystical.

vestment-makers, he says : "They are allowed to have the liberty of nibbling, clipping, cutting, slashing, shortening, just as the whim may take, Chasubles, Dalmatics, Tunicles, and other priestly garments or ornaments which serve for the ministry of the altar; in a word, to give these robes what shape they like, without consulting the bishop on the matter" (*Church of Our Fathers*, vol. i. p. 330, note).

The prayer recited in putting on the Chasuble is as follows : "O Lord! who hast said, ' My yoke is sweet and my burden light,' grant that I may so carry it as to merit thy grace." In its figurative signification, the Chasuble is usually emblematic of charity, on account of its covering the entire person, as charity ought to cover the soul.

Chasuble of the Orientals.—The ancient form of Chasuble is yet in use with all the Oriental churches, whether Catholic or schismatic. The Maronites have obtained permission from the Holy See to use our form, but whether they do so or not we have been unable to learn.

The Coptic Chasuble, which the natives call *Albornos*, has an ornamental border at the top worked in gold, and denominated *Tkoklia;* the Arabs call it *Kaslet*. This, however, is not common to all the orders of their clergy, but is rather the Chasuble of a bishop (Denzinger, *Ritus Oriental.*, p. 130).

Many of the Greek Chasubles are covered over with a multiplicity of small crosses, to remind the priest that he is the minister of a crucified Master, whose Passion should be ever before his eyes. In the Russian Church the bishop's Chasuble has a number of little bells attached to the right and left sides, and also to the sleeves (Romanoff, *Greco-Russian Church*, pp. 89 and 399).

The Nestorian Chasuble is a square piece of cloth, of linen or calico, having a cross in the centre. They call it *Shoshippa* (Badger, *Nestorians and their Rituals*, i. p. 226).

The Chasuble of the Hungarian Greeks is so clipped in front that it hardly covers the breast (Kozma, *Liturg. Sacr. Cathol.*, p. 48, note 6).

The Chasuble of the Russian priests is now of the same style (Neale, *Holy Eastern Church*, i. 309).

The Syrians call the Chasuble *Philono*, a word evidently allied to the general denomination of the vestment with the Greeks—viz., *Phainolion*—and the ancient Latin name, *Penula*.

In concluding our article on the vestments, we have thought it appropriate to append what the best authorities have said concerning the reference of each to our Divine Lord. We take our remarks from Gavantus (*Thesaur. Sacr. Rit.*, p. 137):

1. The Amice is the veil which covered the face of our Lord.
2. The Alb, the vesture he was clothed in by Herod.
3. The Cincture, the scourge ordered by Pilate.
4. The Maniple, the rope by which he was led.
5. The Stole, the rope which fastened him to the pillar.
6. The Chasuble, the purple garment worn before Pilate.

The reader need hardly be told that all the vestments must be blessed by the bishop before being used at the altar. Faculties to do this are generally enjoyed by ordinary priests in missionary countries.

There are four other articles of clerical attire, which, though not denominated sacred vestments, yet, because of the important part they fill, we would consider it a great oversight to pass by in silence. These are the *Berretta, Zucchetto, Collar,* and *Cassock*.

THE BERRETTA.

The Berretta (Italian), a sort of diminutive of the Latin *birrus*, a cape or hood, is a square cap, with three corners or prominences rising from its crown, and having, for the most part, a tassel depending. When first introduced, which is generally supposed to have been soon after the ninth century, it had none of these corners, but was pliant and plain, something like an ordinary cap. The difficulty, however, of putting it on and adjusting it properly on the head while it continued in this way was sometimes very great, and hence it was deemed advisable to have it so fashioned that it could be put on and taken off without any trouble. This led to the introduction of the three corners, which are also symbolic of the Blessed Trinity (Ferraris, *Bibliotheca*, art. Bir).

Color of the Berretta.—The Berretta has but two varieties of color—viz., *red* and *black*. Red is peculiar and proper to cardinals, and to them alone. Black is the color for all other ecclesiastics, from cardinals down, whether patriarchs, archbishops, bishops, or priests. According to rule, a bishop's Berretta should be lined with green; in all other respects it differs in nothing from that worn by a priest (Martinucci, *Manuale Sacr. Cærem.*, v. p. 11; De Herdt, *Praxis Pontificalis*, i. pp. 44 and 45).

Cardinal's Berretta.—A cardinal's Berretta is generally made of red silk. It has no tassel to it, and never any more than three corners. A four-cornered Berretta is exclusively the cap of a doctor of divinity, and he can wear it by right only when teaching in the doctor's chair (Bouvry. *Explicatio Rubricarum*, etc., ii. 216, 217).

Ceremonies employed in Conferring the Doctor's Cap.[a]— By a recent decision of the Holy See the insignia of the doctorate—*i.e.*, the cap and ring—cannot be conferred upon

---

[a] The right of conferring the degree of doctor of divinity, with its insignia and the privileges attached, is enjoyed only by three institutions in the United States— viz., by the Jesuit colleges of Georgetown, D. C., and Spring Hill, Alabama, and by the Sulpician Seminary of St. Mary's, Baltimore.

any one who is not, together with being duly skilled in divinity, also of high standing in a moral point of view, and sound and solid in the faith. To this end, a profession of faith (that of Pope Pius IV.) is first exacted of the candidate on his knees, and he must swear that he will defend this faith even unto the shedding of his blood, if required.

Furthermore, he is to swear assent to the following articles, read to him by the person conferring the degree:

First. That he will never teach or write *intentionally* anything that is repugnant to Holy Scripture, tradition, the definitions of General Councils, or to the decrees of the Supreme Pontiffs.

Secondly. That he will be watchful in doing his share to preserve the unity of the Church, and not let the seamless garment of Christ be rent by divisions; also that he will be studious in seeing due honor paid to the Supreme Pontiff, and obedience and reverence to his own bishop.

Thirdly. He will swear to defend the Christian, Catholic, and Apostolic faith, to the effusion of blood.

After this the various prerogatives and privileges that are attached to the "D.D." are read, and the four-cornered cap and the ring are imposed. A book is then put into his hands—generally a theological work—as evidence of his right to the honors conferred upon him; and, if the whole ceremony be fully carried out, he is to be led to the doctor's chair, where, in pledge of brotherly feeling towards him, all the other doctors present impart to him a kiss.

It is customary on such occasions for the newly-created doctor to make an address in Latin to all the professors in the audience, and to express his thanks for the elevation to which he has been raised.

We have said that only cardinals wear a Berretta of a red color. This privilege was first granted them by Pope Paul II. in 1460; but the privilege of wearing the red hat goes back to the Council of Lyons, A.D. 1245, where it was granted by Pope Innocent IV. This, however, was only to cardinal legates; but the privilege was extended, in short, to all without exception, as was also the right to wear their other articles of dress of the same color. The precise symbolism attached to the *red* is that their Eminences must be ready to defend the rights of the Holy See even unto the shedding of blood (see Kozma, p. 72, note 2).

The Pope never wears a Berretta, but uses instead a tight-fitting cap, always white in color, called a *Solideo*, from the Latin *solus* and *Deus*, because it is only to God that he doffs it—that is, at the more solemn parts of the Mass. To no earthly ruler does the Pope ever take off this cap. Its material is usually white silk; and on its crown a large button is sewed to facilitate its being taken off and put on.

We have said that a four-cornered Berretta is peculiar to a doctor of divinity. From time immemorial, however, the clergy of France, Germany, and Spain have been accustomed to wear Berrettas of this kind (Bouvry, in loc. cit.)

In some of the French universities, in days gone by, the cap of a doctor of divinity used to be ornamented with a white silk tassel; that of a canonist with a green one; and a doctor's in civil law (D.C.L.) with a red one having a purple tuft in the middle.

In Germany the latter were allowed a scarlet cap. In the celebrated college of Salamanca, in Spain, in addition to the cap, which was black, but decorated with a large tassel of white silk, the "Beca" was also conferred, a curious kind of hood of red silk, which lay in graceful folds on the shoulders of the wearer (Rock, *Church of Our Fathers*, p. 70, vol. ii.)

When the Berretta may be worn.—Besides being worn in every-day life, the Berretta is also allowed to be worn in the sanctuary during the less solemn portions of the Mass. At the altar, however, when in actual celebration, no one may wear it, not even the greatest dignitary. The discipline in this respect is very strict, and admits of but one exception throughout the entire Church—viz., in case of the Catholic missionaries of the empire of China. It is well known how indecent it is held by the Chinese for a person to appear in public with head uncovered. A greater insult you could not offer one of these people than to violate this part of etiquette. Having these things in view, and remembering the salutary admonition of the great Apostle of the Gentiles, of becoming "all to all people in order to gain all to Christ," our Holy Father Pope Paul V., of blessed memory (1605-1621), granted to the missionaries of the Chinese Empire the privilege of wearing the Berretta all through Mass, even at the Consecration, with one proviso, however—that the said Berretta be not the one used in every-day life. In no other part of the world is this privilege enjoyed (De Montor, *Lives of the Popes*, vol. i. p. 943).

Berretta of the Orientals.—The Oriental Berretta differs considerably from ours in shape. That of the Greeks is round and close-fitting, and is generally of a violet color. Attached to it behind is an appendage shaped like a triangle, which the Greeks call περιστερά, *peristera*, or the dove, from its resemblance to the tail of that bird. It is intended to remind the priest that the grace of his holy ministry depends on the Holy Ghost, whom the dove symbolizes (Goar, *Euchol. Græc.*, 157). Throughout Russia all the "Black Clergy"[1] wear a high cap resembling a hat without a crown, having a veil covering it, which falls behind on the shoulders. This the Russians call *Klobouk*,

---

[1] The division of the Russian clergy into the "White" and "Black Clergy" is not from any peculiar distinction in dress, but only from their different modes of life. The term *Black* is applied to those who live in monasteries. All the rest are denominated *White*, no matter what the color of their dress may be (Gagarin, *Russian Clergy*, Introduction).

but its Greek name is *Kamelauchion* (Mouravieff, *History of the Russian Church*, notes, p. 399).

The Greek bishops, who never wear a mitre like ours, use a sort of low hat without a peak, over which a large veil is cast, something after the manner of the original Roman *birrus* (Neale, *Holy Eastern Church*, i. 314). They perform all the preliminary offices of the liturgy with this on their heads.

The cap of the schismatical Patriarch of Alexandria is crown-shaped, and is never removed at any part of divine service. This privilege is also assumed by the Patriarch of the Nestorians, who wears his cap even while distributing Holy Communion. All the rest of the Orientals celebrate with heads uncovered like ourselves (Goar, *Euchol.*, 157 and 220; Neale, in loc. cit.; Denzinger, *Ritus Oriental.*, 132).

The Coptic Berretta differs hardly in anything from the Greek, save that it has its crown ornamented with a variety of small crosses. The name they call it by is *Cidar*.

THE ZUCCHETTO.

The Zucchetto, from the Italian *zuccha*, a gourd, is a small, closely-fitting skull-cap, shaped like a saucer, and of a red, violet, or black color, according to the rank of the wearer. Originally it was introduced to protect that part of the head which had been made bare by the so-called clerical tonsure,[a] but now it is worn irrespective of the laws which regulated this ancient discipline.

[a] In ancient times there were three different forms of clerical tonsure. 1st. That of St. Peter, or the *Roman*, by which the top of the head was cleanly shaved, and the base left with an edging or crown of hair to symbolize the Crown of Thorns. 2d. That of St. Paul, in which the entire head was shaved, leaving no hair at all. 3d. That of St. John the Evangelist, in which the front of the head was shaved so as to resemble a crescent, and the hair allowed to fall down upon the back. This last was the form in use with the Irish and Britons up to the time of Colman, Bishop of Lindisfarne, A.D.

When the Zucchetto may be worn.—As the Zucchetto is not exactly considered a cap, it has privileges which the berretta never enjoys, for it can be worn upon occasions when the use of the latter would be wholly forbidden. Permission is often granted to wear it in the very act of celebrating, during the less solemn portions of the Mass—*i.e.*, from the beginning to the Preface, exclusive, and from the end of Communion to the completion of service. It must never be worn during the Canon, and permission to wear it at the times named must be had direct from the Pope. In case the celebrant should have permission to wear a wig he is never bound to remove it, for it ranks neither as a Berretta nor Zucchetto, but is rather esteemed as one's own hair. Permission to wear it, however, is very rarely granted by the Holy See.

Color of the Zucchetto.—We have said that the color of the Zucchetto varies with the rank of the wearer. That worn by cardinals is always red; patriarchs, archbishops, and bishops wear a violet-colored one ; for all the rest of the clergy the color is black. The privilege of wearing a violet Zucchetto was not enjoyed by bishops until June, 1867, when the concession was made by his Holiness Pope Pius IX. This concession, however, concerned but the Zucchetto, not the Berretta. The latter must be of the same color as that of a priest—viz., *black* (Martinucci, *Manuale Cærem.*, v. 14).

The Zucchetto is indifferently known by the several

661, when the Roman form was adopted in its stead (Alzog's *Church Hist*, vol. ii. p. 88, note 3, and p. 91, by Pabisch and Byrne).

According to the Roman Pontifical, the bishop, when conferring *tonsure*, cuts off with scissors five locks of hair from the head of the candidate for orders ; the *first*, over the forehead ; the *second*, at the back of the head ; the *third*, at the right ear ; the *fourth*, at the left ear ; and the *fifth*, on the crown of the head. In no case is the hair cut so deep that the head is exposed. This is what constitutes the clerical tonsure, the initiative step to Sacred Orders, and that which raises a layman to the rank and immunities of an ecclesiastic.

names *Calotte*, *Pileolus*, *Berrettino*, and *Submitrale*. It is called *Calotte* in French, from its resemblance to a shell; *Pileolus* is the Latin diminutive of *pileus*, a Roman cap; *Berrettino* is a diminutive of Berretta; and it received its name *Submitrale* from the fact that it used to be generally worn under the bishop's mitre. In common parlance it is always spoken of as the Calotte or Zucchetto.

THE COLLAR.

The clerical Collar, generally styled the Roman Collar, and in French *Rabat*, was unknown as an article of ecclesiastical attire, at least in its present form, prior to the sixteenth century. The religious orders have, as a rule, never adopted it generally; nor is it worn in the United States to any great extent, unless in a few dioceses where the statutes insist upon it as being the distinctive mark of a Catholic clergyman. Where it can be worn without exciting too much attention, or, as often happens in non-Catholic countries, exposing a priest to public insult, it ought to be; for it is wonderful, to pass over many other reasons, how much Catholics are comforted by seeing in their company, if travelling abroad, or even walking the street, if at home, a priest arrayed in this distinctive habiliment. There is no mistaking him then for a minister of one of the sects.

Before the introduction of the Roman Collar the article generally used was nothing else but a plain linen collar similar to those ordinarily used now by lay people, only a little wider. Some of the higher dignitaries wore *frills*, such as we see in paintings of the fourteenth and fifteenth centuries; but these were forbidden to the inferior clergy, who were required to wear their Collars as plain as possible, without even starch to stiffen them, or plaits to adorn them in any way. In France, Belgium, and

Italy laws were enacted prohibiting lace or fancy needlework to be used in making them up, for they were required to be of the plainest linen (*Church of Our Fathers*, vol. i. p. 474).

According to its present disposition, the Collar itself is a slip of thin linen about two inches wide, and long enough to encircle the neck of the wearer. This slip is folded down over a circular band or stock of some pliant but tolerably stiff material, such as fuller's board, to which is sewed a piece of cloth, generally large enough to cover the chest. The Collar is kept in its place by being buttoned behind or fastened to the neck by strings.

The Collar, like the other articles of clerical attire mentioned, varies in color with the dignity of the wearer. That of a cardinal is *red;* a bishop's, *violet;* a monsignore's, also *violet;* and a priest's, *black.* Canons, for the most part, wear one of *black*, with red buttons down the centre, and red trimmings.

Prothonotaries apostolic, of the class known as the *participantes*, who always rank as prelates, have the privilege of wearing a violet Collar like a bishop; but not so those who rank only as prothonotaries *titulares*, or honorary prothonotaries; theirs is *black* like a priest's (*Manuale Decretorum de Proton. Apostol.*, 753 and 759).

THE CASSOCK.

The Cassock, called in French *Casaque*, but more commonly *Soutane*, is that long outer black garment worn by priests in every-day life and at all the sacred functions. It is called in Latin *Vestis talaris*, from its reaching down to the feet. With many of the religious orders it is called the habit, and instead of being buttoned in front, as is the case generally with the secular clergy, it is fastened to the person by a large cincture.

In ancient times the Cassock used to be known as the *Pellicea*, or *Pelisse*, partly from the fact that it used to be made of the skins of animals, and partly also because in most cases it used to be lined with fur. Hence the origin of the word *surplice*—something worn over the *Pelisse* (Kozma, 49).

Color of the Cassock.—The color of the Cassock varies with the rank of the person and the religious order to which he belongs. Cardinals wear one of red generally, but during seasons of penance and mourning the color is *violet*. The color of a bishop's Cassock is violet, but on the occasions mentioned violet is changed for black. With priests who are not members of any particular order black is the color always.

The Camaldolese,[9] Cistercians,[10] Carthusians,[11] and Dominicans[12] wear white Cassocks. The Silvestrians[13] wear one of dark blue; the Third Order of Franciscans,[14] the Minor Conventuals,[15] and Minor Observants[16] wear an ash-colored one; the Jeromites[17] *gray*. When a member from any of these orders is promoted to the cardinalate he retains the color peculiar to his order, as far as the Cassock is concerned, but the berretta, zucchetto, and hat must be always *scarlet* (Martinucci, *Manuale Cærem.*, vi. 505).

The privilege of wearing a scarlet-colored Cassock was granted to the doctors in theology and canon law of the University of Paris by Pope Benedict XII. The same pontiff is supposed to have extended the like privilege to

---

[9] The Camaldolese, founded by St. Romuald in the early part of the eleventh century. So called from Maldoli, the name of the person who bestowed the ground upon them in the Apennines in the eleventh century. [10] So called from Cisterze, diocese of Chalons; founded by St. Robert, Abbot of Molesme, in 1098. [11] So called from Chartreuse, in France; founded by St. Bruno in 1084. [12] Founded by St. Dominic, a Spaniard, in 1215; called also Preaching Friars. [13] Called Silvestrians from their founder, Silvester Gozzolino, 1230. [14] The Third Order of Franciscans, or *Tertiaria*, was founded in 1221. [15] A branch of the Franciscans, established soon after 1302. [16] A branch of the Franciscans, established soon after 1302. [17] Founded in the fourteenth century by a number of solitaries.

Oxford (*Church of Our Fathers*, ii. 19, note 47). The Cassocks worn by the students of many of the European colleges have large pendants behind like wings. These commemorate a fashion once very prevalent in Rome, where tutors, in accompanying their pupils to school, held these pendants in their hands as evidence of their watchfulness over them.

Color of the Pope's Cassock.—In every-day life, and on all solemn occasions, the Pope wears a Cassock of white silk (Kozma, *Lit. Sacra Cathol.*, 72). This custom, it is said, dates from apostolic times, St. James the Less, first Bishop of Jerusalem, being its introducer. As his life states, this Apostle always appeared in fine white linen garments. St. Cyril assures us that the Patriarch of Jerusalem always appeared in white ; and it is also said that St. Peter used to wear garments of this color, in memory of the shining garments in which our Divine Lord appeared to him on the occasion of the Transfiguration on Thabor (see *Metropolitan*, "Letters from Abroad," January, 1855).

All the popes of primitive times, as we see from ancient mosaics, were vested in white ; so it may be very lawfully conjectured that the custom is as ancient as we have stated it to be.

COLORS OF THE VESTMENTS.

The Church employs at the present day five different colors in her sacred vestments—viz., *white*, *red*, *green*, *violet*, and *black*. Up to the sixth century she rarely used any color but white (Kozma, 73) ; and in the time of Pope Innocent III. (thirteenth century) there was no such color in use as *violet*, for that pontiff makes no mention of this color when he names the four employed in his day (*De Sacr. Altaris Myster.*, p. 86). That violet, however, was introduced soon after this pontiff's book appeared, is evident from

Durandus, who flourished about the year 1280 (Pope Innocent III. died in 1215), for in his great work, entitled *Rationale Divinorum*, violet is specially mentioned.

White, being symbolic of purity, innocence, and glory, is, as a general rule, employed on the special feasts of our Lord and the Blessed Virgin, and on those of the angels, virgins, and confessors.

Red, the symbol of fortitude, is the color proper to Pentecost, in memory of the "tongues of fire"; it is also used on the feasts of the apostles and martyrs, and on those of our Lord's Passion.

Green, symbolic of hope, is used as the color of the time from the octave of the Epiphany to Septuagesima, and from the octave of Pentecost to Advent.

Violet, the penitential color, is used on all occasions of public affliction and sorrow, in times of fasting and penance, and in all those processions which do not immediately concern the Blessed Sacrament. This color is also used on the Feast of the Holy Innocents, on account of the lamentations and weepings heard through Jerusalem when they were massacred by order of Herod. But should this feast fall on Sunday, the color of the occasion is red, as is also the color of the octave, from the fact that the lamentations taken up are supposed to have ceased by this time, and the eighth day is always significant of beatitude and glory (De Herdt, *Sacr. Liturg. Praxis*, i. p. 190 ; Bouvry, *Expos. Rubr.*, ii. 199).

Black, from its gloomy appearance, and because it is the negation of all color, is used in Masses and Offices of the Dead, and on Good Friday in memory of the profound darkness that covered the land when our Lord was crucified.

In ancient times it was customary with many churches to wear saffron-colored vestments on this latter day, to recall to mind the bitter vindictiveness of the Jews in putting our

Saviour to death, saffron being indicative of bile. Writing upon this, Bellotte thus remarks : " Croceo namque seu flavo colori bilis assimilatur, cujus sedes et imperium in præcordiis et visceribus Judæorum nedum iram sed et iræ furorem provocavit adversus Dominum et adversus Christum ejus " (*Church of Our Fathers*, ii. 263). For this same reason it was that the traitor Judas, in all mediæval paintings, is depicted with hair a shade of color between red and yellow. The Jews themselves were obliged, up to a recent date, to wear in many countries a yellow badge,so that all might know them from the rest of the people (*ibid.*)

Local Customs and Privileges.—In France red used to be used on feasts of the Blessed Sacrament instead of white. In-Spain the rare privilege of using sky-blue vestments on feasts of the Blessed Virgin has been enjoyed for some time past. Some, however, restrict this privilege to the Feast of the Immaculate Conception ; but we have not been able to learn whether it is so restricted or not. A set purchased for this occasion in 1843 cost the enormous sum of $14,000 (*Dublin Review*, 1845, article Spain, vol. xviii. ; *Church of Our Fathers*, ii. 259, note 32). That blue-colored vestments were once common in England, we have the most undeniable proofs. In Dugdale's history of St. Paul's,[18] London, we find enumerated among that cathedral's goods in 1295 several vestments of a blue color ; and in an inventory

---

[18] St. Paul's Church, London, was at one time one of the most venerable churches in existence. The cathedral known as "Old St. Paul's" dates from the time of Bishop Maurice, A.D. 1080. This wonderful edifice was nearly six hundred feet in length, and the summit of the spire rose to within a short distance of five hundred feet from the ground. It was made of wood covered with lead, and had relics placed in the ball beneath the cross. On Candlemas eve, 1444, the spire was struck by lightning and partly destroyed. One of the greatest treasures and curiosities that this church possessed for some time was a relic of the Holy Blood, sent from Jerusalem to King Henry III. by the Knights of St. John and those of the Order of Templars. This precious gift was afterwards conveyed to Westminster Abbey, where an indulgence of six years and one hundred days was granted all who visited it with the proper dispositions (*Ecclesiastical Antiquities of London*, by Alex. Wood, M.A.)

of the Church of Lincoln there is mentioned "a chesable of blew damask, a cope of the same color, a cope of cloth of gold, a bawdkin of blew color" (*Church of Our Fathers*, ii. 260, note 33). Bishop Wykeham bequeathed to his church at Windsor "his new vestment of blue cloth, striped and embroidered with lions of gold" (*ibid.*)

According to the Sarum Rite, there was no other color used through Lent but red. The great minster of Peterborough had twenty-seven "red albs" for Passion Week. The Ambrosian Rite also prescribed red for the same season, and so did many churches of France (*ibid.*)

On the third Sunday of Advent and the fourth Sunday of Lent, called respectively "Gaudete" and "Lætare" Sundays,[19] from the Introits on these days beginning with those words, cardinals wear, instead of their usual color, that of pale rose; and this is required to be the color also of their out-door dress on these occasions (Martinucci, vi. 504).

From an ancient Irish book called the *Leabhar Breac*, supposed to be written about the sixth century, the following curious extract is given by Dr. Moran, now Bishop of Ossory, in his *Discipline of the Early Irish Church*. It relates to the colors of the sacred vestments:

"The priest's mind should agree with the variety and meaning of each distinct color, and should be filled with

---

[19] The fourth Sunday of Lent is what is known as the "Sunday of the Golden Rose," from a custom observed at Rome of blessing a rose made of pure gold mixed with musk and balsam. The ceremony is performed by the Pope himself, and the rose thus blessed is carried in solemn procession in the hand of the pontiff to and from his chapel on this Sunday. The rose, symbolic of the eternal bloom and freshness of Paradise, is afterwards bestowed as a mark of special favor on some great potentate who has done service to the Holy See Pope Pius IX. sent a Golden Rose to Maria Theresa, Queen of Naples, for the kindness extended him by her and her husband when he was obliged to flee to Gaeta in 1848. He sent one also to the Empress Eugénie, wife of Napoleon III., and to Elizabeth, Empress of Austria (Kozma, 330; *Sacramentals*, by Rev. W. J. Barry, p. 110).

vigilance and awe, and be withdrawn from ambition and pride, when he reflects on what the various colors typify.

"The *white* typifies that he should be filled with confusion and shame if his heart be not chaste and shining, and his mind like the foam of the wave, or like the chalk on the gable of an oratory, or like the color of the swan in the sunshine—that is, without any particle of sin, great or small, resting in it.

"The *red* typifies that his heart should start and tremble in his breast through terror and fear of the Son of God, for the scars and wounds of the Son of God were red upon the cross when he was crucified by the unbelieving Jews.

"The *green* typifies that he should be filled with great faintness and distress of mind and heart ; for what is understood by it is his interment at the end of his life, under the mould of the earth, for green is the original color of all the earth.

"The *purple* typifies that he should call to mind Jesus, who is in heaven in the plenitude of his glory and majesty, and with the nine orders of angels who praise the Creator throughout all eternity.

"The *black* typifies that he should shed bitter tears for his sins, lest he be condemned to the society of the devil and dwell perpetually in endless pain."

From all this we clearly see that even so far back as the sixth century some churches had all the colors in use that we have now.

We conclude our remarks on sacred vestments by saying that those made of pure cloth of gold are tolerated at the present day, and may be used instead of *red, white,* or *green* (S. R. C., 28th April, 1866, 3644 [2]). Those of any other material of a yellow color are wholly interdicted, and cannot be used without permission of the Holy See.

Colors used by the Oriental Church.—The Greek Church

uses but two colors the whole year round—viz., white and red, in memory of what the Spouse says in the Canticle of Canticles : "My beloved is white and ruddy." White is their general color; red is used in all Masses for the dead and throughout the entire fast of Lent. According to the Greeks this latter color is better suited to Lent than any other, for during that season we are doing penance for the shedding of the innocent blood of our Divine Redeemer (Goar, *Euchol. Græcorum*, 113).

Renaudot tells us in his *Commentary on the Liturgy of St. Basil*, p. 160, that the Copts use no other color in their sacred vestments but white, and this for the reason that at his glorious transfiguration on Mt. Thabor it was in this brilliant color that our Lord appeared. One of the Coptic canons on this head reads as follows : "The vestments used for saying Mass ought to be of a white color, not of any other; for Christ when transfigured had vestments on brilliant as light" (*ibid.*) If we are to credit the reports of tourists to those regions, the Copts of to-day pay little regard to this canon, for vestments of every hue may be seen in use among them.

The Maronites use the same colors as we do.

The Syrians are partial to purple and green, and hence it happens not unfrequently that their chasubles unite these colors at one and the same time (Denzinger, 131).

The Armenians allow their lectors to wear a cope of *purple silk* similar to our pluvial. Their exorcists wear one of *hyacinth*; their acolytes of *red* (*ibid.* 133).

According to Badger (*The Nestorians and their Rituals*, i. p. 226), the vestments of the Nestorians are white ; still, the same author tells us that their girdle and stole consist of a narrow band or scarf, with alternate white and blue crosses worked on squares of the same colors.

Having now said all that to our mind it seemed necessary

to say about the sacred vestments and their colors, we pass on to another class of sacred appurtenances, called the vessels of the altar.

It may be well to remark here—we intended doing so earlier, but forgot it—that inasmuch as our book is not a Ceremonial, the reader must not expect to find in it all those little points and exceptions to rules which only a Ceremonial would comprehend. The main things are given; and, wherever we have thought it necessary for the reader's interest, we have descended to many minute particulars, for nothing is unimportant that directly concerns the Mass. We make this apology in order not to be misunderstood.

CHAPTER III.

SACRED VESSELS.

THE sacred vessels employed at the altar in the service of the Blessed Sacrament are five in number—viz., Chalice, Paten, Ciborium, Monstrance, and Lunette.

THE CHALICE.

The Chalice is the large Eucharistic cup in which the wine for consecration is placed. Regarding its shape, no precise rules are laid down, but custom would have it somewhat resemble the open calyx of a lily. In ancient times it was formed so as to resemble an apple, and this with a view to remind us that it is through the merits of Christ's Precious Blood, which the Chalice contains, that the sin of Adam, in eating the forbidden fruit, was atoned for.

Many liturgical writers tell us that the Chalice which our Divine Lord used at the Last Supper was made after the manner of the Roman cantharus, or mug—that is, with a handle on each side by which to lift it; and that its capacity was a sextary, or about a pint and a half (Bona, *Rer. Liturg.*, 290; see also the *Revelations* of Anne Catherine Emmerich). According to the testimony of Bede, quoted by Baronius (*Anno* 34, No. 63), this Chalice was made of silver, and was preserved for a long time at Jerusalem, where the people used to offer it much veneration. All this, however, or at least the main part of it, is contradicted by the gravest liturgical writers, and very justly; for it is now pretty well known that the Bede who fabricated the story was not the Anglican Bede called the *Venerable*, but a certain person of the name of Adamnamus Scotus, whose reputation for telling the truth did not stand very high (Kozma, *Liturg. Sacr. Cathol.*, p. 82, note).

The great majority are in favor of saying that the Chalice our Lord used was made of agate, and that by some means or other it came into the possession of the people of Valentia, who now preserve it with jealous care (Gavantus, *Thesaur. Sacr. Rit.*, p. 124).

Material of which the Chalice is made.—According to the present discipline of the Church, it is required that the Chalice be made of gold or silver, or at least that the cup be such. The privilege of using a Chalice of pewter is, however, sometimes granted to very poor churches, but always on condition that at least the inside of the cup be gilt. The stem or leg of the Chalice may be of any solid material whatever, provided it be decent and not easily broken. Chalices of brass, glass, or wood are wholly forbidden—of *brass*, on account of its liability to rust; of *glass*, on account of its brittleness; and of *wood*, on account of its great porosity. There is no doubt, however, but that in the very early days of Christianity, especially during the times of persecution, Chalices were often made of other materials besides gold and silver. In the Catacombs[1] many Chalices of glass have been found (*Roman Catacombs*, passim, by Northcote), and the most reliable testimony is given that such were often used in the celebration of Mass. Pope Gregory the Great, for instance, informs us that St. Donat, Bishop of Arezzo, used a Chalice of this material, and that when

---

[1] The term *catacomb*, from the Greek κατά, beneath, and κύμβος, a hollow or crypt, is applied to those subterranean vaults that are situated under the city of Rome, to which the Christians used to flee for shelter in the days of persecution, and where they buried their dead and celebrated Mass.

the same was broken by the pagans the holy man had it miraculously restored to its original form through means of earnest prayer (lib. i. *Dial.* cap. vii.)

St. Cæsar, Bishop of Arles, in France, used a glass Chalice frequently. And St. Gregory of Tours tells us of one that he himself used, and how when it was broken by accident he had it restored through the intercession of St. Lawrence (Bona, 290). It must be observed, however, that the use of glass Chalices was never general in the Church, and that whenever they were used at all it was from pressing necessity.

Chalices of Wood.—Sometimes, too, in difficult circumstances, Chalices of wood were used. An amusing saying upon this head is recorded of St. Boniface. Having been asked in the Council of Triers what he thought of the practice of saying Mass in wooden Chalices, he replied as follows: "In ancient times golden priests said Mass in wooden Chalices, but now wooden priests say Mass in golden Chalices" (Bona, *ibid.*) The canons of King Edgar of England (tenth century) wholly interdicted Chalices of wood (*ibid.*)

That Chalices of stone and marble were used at one time, at least on some pressing occasions, we see from the life of St. Theodore, Archimandrite,[2] commonly known as "Theodore of the Studium," from the great abbey of that name at Constantinople, where it is said that, when this holy man had enlarged his monastery, he changed his sacred vessels of marble for those of silver (Bona, *ibid.;* see also the saint's life).

---

[2] In the Oriental Church the term *Archimandrite* is applied to all those abbots who have jurisdiction over several monasteries. It is said to be derived from the Greek ἀρχός, a *chief*, and μάνδρα, a *monastery*. A head of a single monastery is styled *Hegumenos* but not exclusively, for the term is often applied to other ecclesiastics also. In the Latin Church the superior of the great monastery of Messina is styled Archimandrite.

It was customary, too, in some churches to use Chalices of precious stones—of onyx, sardonyx, chrysolite, etc.—also of horn and ivory. Among the ornaments donated by Pope Victor III. (eleventh century) to the famous monastery of Monte Casino, two Chalices of onyx are enumerated (*ibid.*) We find Chalices of horn prohibited as early as the eighth century in the Synod of Calcuith, in England (*ibid.*) In 813 the Council of Rheims decreed that both the Chalice and Paten should be of gold, or at least of silver. In case of great poverty it allowed a Chalice of pewter. It strictly forbade, however, no matter what the necessity, to consecrate in one made of wood or glass (Kozma, 83, note).

Ornamentation of Chalices.—From the great respect that the Christians of early times manifested for anything concerning our Divine Lord much care used to be bestowed and much artistic skill displayed in the ornamentation of Chalices. The devices were, as a rule, taken from some incident connected with our Saviour's life upon earth, such as the raising of Lazarus from the dead; changing the water into wine at Cana; multiplying the loaves; bringing back the "lost sheep"; healing the sick or consoling the afflicted.

The bottom of a glass Chalice found in the Catacombs, and mentioned by Father Northcote in his work on the *Roman Catacombs*, represents four different scenes taken from Scripture: first, Tobias and the fish; second, our Lord healing the paralytic; third, the children in the fiery furnace; fourth, the changing of water into wine at Cana. Another, taken from the same work, has enamelled figures of the Blessed Virgin and of the Apostles SS. Peter and Paul.

Ministerial Chalices.—Whilst the discipline of communicating the laity under both species prevailed,[3] Chalices called

---

[3] It prevailed up to the twelfth century, with few exceptions. It was wholly abrogated by the Council of Constance in 1414, and this, among other reasons, to confound the teaching of John Huss and his party.

Ministerial used to be employed for dispensing the Precious Blood to the communicants. The deacon, as a rule, had charge of these, and it was upon him that the duty devolved of communicating the people from them. The Chalice used by the priest was then known as the *Offertorial Chalice*, and was reserved for himself and the sacred ministers who assisted him. As all the other Chalices obtained their supply from this, it used to be, in days gone by, of considerable proportions. It was customary, however, when the number of communicants was very great, to use large ministerial Chalices, and mingle with the Precious Blood they contained ordinary wine in small proportions, in order that the supply might not run short (Benedict XIV., *De Sacrosanct. Missæ Sacrif.*, p. 27; Bona, 291, 292; Kozma, 83; Bellarmine, *De Sacrif. Missæ*, lib. iv. cap. xxiv.)

Baptismal Chalices.—These were used solely for communicating children after they had been baptized—a custom which once prevailed in the Church of the West, and is yet in vogue in the Eastern Church.

Silver Tubes attached to Ancient Chalices.—The first Roman Ordo, in laying down the rules that regard the distribution of the Precious Blood, says that, after the Pope and his ministers had taken their portion from the Chalice employed at the altar, the remainder was to be poured into a large cup (*scyphus*) and dispensed to the people through a reed or tube (*Church of Our Fathers*, vol. i. 164). In Masses celebrated by an ordinary priest the deacon used to pour unconsecrated wine first into the Chalice intended for the people before he poured the Precious Blood, and then "confirm" all, as the saying went—that is, allow each to taste of the Blood thus mingled through a reed made of gold, silver, ivory, or glass, as the case might be (*ibid.* note 35).

These reeds were in many cases, but not in all, fastened

on a pivot to the inside of the Chalice, and were so adjusted that there was no difficulty whatever experienced in allowing the proper quantity of the Precious Blood to pass through. The material of which they were made was often of the most precious kind, and much labor used to be expended in their workmanship. St. Paul's, London, had in 1295 two reeds of silver gilt; and among the presents bestowed on the Cathedral of Exeter by its bishop, Leofric, was one "silfren pipe" (*ibid.* 168, note 39). As late as A.D. 1200 the Cathedral of Pavia had reeds of glass (*ibid.*)

Up to a very recent date the silver tube was employed in the Monastery of Cluny, and at that of St. Denis in Paris, on Sundays and Holydays (*ibid.*) Kozma (p. 84) would lead us to infer—in fact, he asserts it—that this ancient custom is yet kept up in the Monastery of St. Dionysius, of the Congregation of St. Maur, near Paris, where, by a special indult of the Holy See, the deacon and subdeacon, at Solemn High Mass, yet communicate under both kinds. With this exception the ancient practice is now seen nowhere else unless in Solemn Mass celebrated by the Pope, where his Holiness always receives the Chalice through one of the forementioned reeds. The deacon assisting him on such occasions receives the Precious Blood through the reed also, but the subdeacon receives it from the Chalice itself (Kozma, 84, note 13).

For purifying these reeds a long golden needle used to be employed after they had first been rinsed with wine and water. Dr. Rock, in his very valuable work, *The Church of Our Fathers*, vol. i. p. 167, exhibits one of these needles having a head of sapphire. The papal needle depicted in the same place has two chain ornaments at its head, in which the pontiff is expected to put his fingers when receiving the Precious Blood.

Before we dismiss our subject we must not forget to

mention that, no matter how numerous the communicants were when the discipline of receiving under both species prevailed, there was but one Chalice used at the altar in the act of consecrating. Pope Gregory II., A.D. 726, having been asked by St. Boniface if it were lawful to employ any more than one, thus replied : "In the celebration of Mass that must be observed which Our Lord Jesus Christ observed with his disciples; for he took the Chalice, saying, 'This is the Chalice of the New Testament in my Blood; this do as often as you shall receive.' Whence it is not fitting to place two or three Chalices on the altar at the celebration of Mass" (*Church of Our Fathers*, i. 165, note).

Chalices of the Orientals. — The extraordinary respect shown by all the Orientals, schismatic as well as orthodox, for the sacred vessels concerned immediately with the Blessed Sacrament is worthy of all commendation. The Copts will allow nothing to enter into the composition of the Chalice but the most precious material; and notwithstanding their almost universal poverty as a people, yet care is always taken to see that their Chalices are of the purest silver or gold (Renaudot, *Liturg. Orient. Collect.*, comment. ad *Liturg. Copt. S. Basilii*, vol. i. p. 175).

Regarding the consecration of the Chalice the majority of the Orientals are not particular. But this is not through any carelessness whatever or disrespect on their part; if anything, it is a mark of the lively faith they have in the real presence of our Divine Lord in the Blessed Sacrament, and of their belief in the virtue that accompanies this Sacred Presence everywhere. Their reasons for not paying more attention to the consecration of their Chalices is that to their minds the simple contact of the Precious Blood is sufficient of itself to consecrate them without any additional ceremony. In proof of this belief many examples of a miraculous nature are cited. The Copts, for instance, have it on record in the patriarchal history of Alexandria that when one of their Chalices was stolen by the Mahometans and sold to an artisan, the latter observed blood flowing from it the moment he broke it. Another story is related in a history of the Nestorians, to the effect that a man who had been almost crushed to death by the falling of a wall was instantly restored to health and strength by drinking the water which was poured out of a Chalice. Many other miracles are cited, but those given we deem enough at present. Nor was the belief that the Chalice is consecrated by contact with the Precious Blood solely confined to the Orientals; some very able theologians of the Latin Church, and Diana among others, held the same belief also (Renaudot, *ibid.*; Merati, *Thesaur. Sacr. Rit.*, 126). But the practice of our Church has always been to consecrate in every case, irrespective of what theologians or others say upon the subject.

It must be observed, however, that although many of the Orientals do not consecrate their Chalices, yet there is a form for so doing in all their rituals. According to the Coptic Ritual, the form runs as follows: " O Lord Jesus Christ, God and man together, whose divinity and humanity are inseparable, who didst by thine own free-will pour out thy blood for the sake of thy creatures, stretch thy divine hand over this Chalice, sanctify and purify it, to the end that the same Precious Blood may be borne in it as a remedy and pardon for all who truly partake of it." The Chalice is then anointed within and without with holy chrism, whilst the following words are said : " Sanctity, purity, benediction, and protection to all who drink of thy true and precious blood. Amen." According to the Greek Ritual, given by Goar (*Euchology*, p. 853), the ceremony of consecration is almost the same.

THE PATEN.

The Paten is that small silver or gold dish, something like a saucer, which covers the mouth of the Chalice, and upon which the large bread for consecration is placed up to the Offertory. It is required to be of the same material as the Chalice, and to be perfectly plain on its concave surface (Bouvry, ii. 239).

In ancient times the Paten was much larger than now, for it was made to hold all the bread that was to be consecrated at Mass. Hence we must not be surprised when we hear or read of Patens which weighed twenty-five and thirty pounds (Bona, *Rer. Liturg.*, 292; Kozma, 84).

Patens of the Orientals.—The Greeks call the Paten ἅγιος δίσκος, or *holy tray*. Theirs is much larger than ours, as must needs be to keep their large Particles from falling off, for their Hosts are not thin and flat like ours, but thick and square.

THE CIBORIUM.

When the number of communicants is great it is customary to administer the consecrated Particles to them from a sacred vessel shaped somewhat like the Chalice, but much more shallow and wide in the cup, called a Ciborium, from the Latin *cibus*, food. In ancient times the Ciborium meant the canopy of the altar, from which a contrivance shaped like a dove, and generally fashioned of gold or silver, used to hang for the purpose of reserving the Blessed Sacrament (Kozma, p. 87). Whilst the Ciborium contains the Holy Eucharist it is always kept under lock and key in the tabernacle, unless when it is necessary to give Holy Communion or to purify it.

THE MONSTRANCE.

The Monstrance, called also the Ostensorium and Portable Tabernacle, and sometimes, but less properly, the Remonstrance, is that large appurtenance in which the Blessed Sacrament is exposed at Benediction, and borne in solemn procession outside the church on certain occasions. It has a large stem something like that of the Chalice, and its upper part is so formed as to resemble the rays issuing from the radiant sun. In its centre there is a circular aperture in which the Lunette, with the Blessed Sacrament enclosed, is placed during exposition.

Monstrances date their origin from the institution of the Feast of Corpus Christi,[4] which was first set on foot by Robert, Bishop of Liege, in the year 1246, at the instigation of a holy nun named Juliana, who frequently saw in a vision a luminous moon with one dark line on its surface. The moon, she was given to understand by special revelation, was the Church; and the dark line denoted the absence of a certain feast from those annually celebrated, and which she was afterwards given to understand meant one specially directed towards the Blessed Sacrament. This led to the institution of Corpus Christi, which Pope Urban IV., in 1264, extended to the universal Church. Other rea-

---

[4] In order to invest this glorious Feast with as much solemnity and grandeur as possible, Pope Urban caused a Mass and Office to be specially composed for it, which he entrusted to two of the most illustrious and eminent scholars of the day—St. Bonaventure and St. Thomas Aquinas. Both set to work with the most ardent zeal, but when the great Franciscan saint went to compare his work with what the " Angelic Doctor" had done, he was so dissatisfied with his own efforts that he threw his manuscript into the fire and abandoned the task ; and hence the whole work devolved upon, and was finished by, St. Thomas (*Life of St. Thomas*, by Most Rev. Dr. Vaughan, p. 880). This Saint wrote out and arranged the Mass as it stands to-day for this feast. He composed as a *Sequence* for it the inimitable " Lauda Sion " ; and for Divine Office, among other hymns, the " Pange, lingua," of which the " Tantum ergo " forms a part.

Besides the office framed by St. Thomas, there was another in use for some time, said to be composed by an ecclesiastic named John, of Mount Cornelio. It is the opinion of several writers that when this Office was suppressed on account of some things in it that did not wholly square with the disposition of the Roman Breviary—for it was framed according to the Gallic Rite—St Thomas utilized much of it in the Office he himself composed (Romsee, iii. p. 183 ; Gavantus, *Thesaur. Sacr. Rit.*, 458).

sons, too, are given for the institution of this feast, such as an apparition that a certain priest of little faith had after the Consecration, when our Divine Lord appeared to him on the Corporal in form of a beautiful infant. Another legend says that the priest through some accident upset part of the Precious Blood on the Corporal, and that an image of a Host was seen wherever it fell (see Gavantus, *Thesaur. Rit.*, p. 458 ; Kozma, 88 and 388 ; and Romsee, iii. p. 183).

For some time after the institution of Corpus Christi the Monstrance took the shape of those little towers in which the Blessed Sacrament used to be kept in ancient times.

In some of the churches of the Cistercian Order in France, instead of a regular Monstrance such as we use, there is employed a small statue of the Blessed Virgin, so constructed that the Sacred Host may be placed in its hand during the time of exposition (Kozma, 89, note 6).

The present shape of the Monstrance, imitating the radiant sun, forcibly recalls to mind the divine splendor of our Lord's countenance on the occasion of his Transfiguration on Thabor, and that saying of the royal Psalmist: "He has placed his tabernacle in the sun" (*Ps.* xviii. 6 ; *ibid.*)

The material of the Monstrance is generally the same as that of the other sacred vessels mentioned. When borne in solemn procession, a large canopy, called a Baldachinum, is carried over it.

WHO MAY TOUCH THE SACRED VESSELS.

So very particular is the Church regarding the respect that should be paid to the sacred vessels immediately concerned with the Holy Eucharist, that she forbids them, under pain of sin, to be touched by any one but a cleric.

Nay, even clerics, unless they have reached the rank of sub-deacon, are not allowed to touch them without special permission. Should any one wilfully touch the Chalice whilst it contains the Precious Blood, and not be at least in deacon's orders, all theologians hold that he would by so doing commit a mortal sin. When permission is granted a lay person to touch the sacred vessels, he should always wear a glove or have his hand covered with a cloth or clean napkin (De Herdt, vol. i. No. 175).

APPALLING PUNISHMENTS WITH WHICH ALMIGHTY GOD SOMETIMES VISITS THE PROFANERS OF THE SACRED VESSELS AND VESTMENTS OF THE ALTAR.

The Old Testament is full of examples that show how indignantly Almighty God takes the slightest disrespect shown to any of the sacred vessels used in his service. Look at the history of the Ark of the Covenant, and see what miracles were wrought in testimony of its sanctity. First, it is captured by the Philistines, and insult is offered it by being brought into the temple of Dagon; but it has scarcely entered when Dagon falls to the ground (1 *Kings* v.), and for the indignity offered it, the whole city of Azotus is severely punished. The Gethites carry the Ark about from one place to another, and wherever it entered the mortality was so fearful that, as the Scripture says, "The fear of death was in every city" (*ibid.*) Then, again, look at the sorrowful example made of the Bethsamites. For looking with curiosity into the Ark as many as fifty thousand of them were slain (*ibid.* cap. vi.) But the most appalling example of all is that recorded of Heliodorus in the second book of Machabees, chap. iii. This infamous man, to gratify the wishes of Seleucus, son of Antiochus the Great, set out for Jerusalem in order to plunder the Temple of its valuable treasures. Onias, a very saintly man, was High-Priest at the time. All that could possibly be done by prayer and earnest entreaty was done on that occasion to hinder Heliodorus from persisting in his wicked design, but to no purpose. He entered the Temple, and was about to lay hands upon the sacred treasures, when lo! the judgment of God fell upon him. "There appeared," says the sacred text, "a horse with a terrible rider upon him, adorned with a very rich covering: and he ran fiercely and struck Heliodorus with his fore-feet, and he that sat upon him seemed to have armor of gold. Moreover, there appeared two other young men beautiful and strong, bright and glorious, and in comely apparel: who stood by him, on either side, and scourged him without ceasing with many stripes. And Heliodorus suddenly fell to the ground." These are but a few of the many others that are found here and there in the Old Testament, where we see the malediction of God visiting the profaners of His sacred temple. Those furnished by historians and annalists of the Christian Church are in nowise less astounding.

It is well known, for instance, how, when the Donatists broke down the altars of the early Christian churches and cast the Blessed Eucharist to the dogs, the latter turned upon the wicked wretches themselves and tore them to pieces. St. Gregory of Tours tells us of an English nobleman who entirely lost the use of his feet on account of having dared to wash them in a Paten which he had brought from a neighboring church (Kozma, 85, note 17). But what Theodoret relates in his third book, chap. xii., of the soldiers of Julian the Apostate is the most appalling that could be recorded. There was at that time a very beautiful church at Antioch, called the "Golden" from its wonderful magnificence. Its valuable treasures were immense, and all the donation of Constantine the Great. Julian sent two of his men to plunder this church and bring the spoils to himself. They obeyed his commands; but mark the result. Not content with desecrating the sacred house itself, one of them ascended the main altar and defiled it in a most shameful manner, while the other kept crying out in blasphemous derision : " Behold what fine vessels they use in the worship of the Son of Mary !" Divine vengeance in an instant overtook both of them. The first was seized with an ulcer which turned his inside to putrefaction, so that he died vomiting his bowels through his blasphemous mouth. The other was taken with a violent hemorrhage, which continued without interruption until all the blood in his body had been drained off; then he expired amidst the most excruciating pains. This dire occurrence is also related by Protestant historians. Another singular visitation of God is related by Victor Uticensis in his work on the Vandal persecutions (lib. i. p. 593). This historian tells us that a man named Proclus, agent of one of the Vandal kings, once entered a Christian church, and, having stripped the altar of its sacred coverings, converted them to his own private uses. He made himself shirts of some of the coverings and drawers of others; but the very instant he put them on he was seized with so frightful an attack of mental delirium that he died biting his tongue off.

These examples are sufficient to show how inviolable and sacred the smallest article of the sanctuary is held in the eyes of Almighty God.

CHAPTER IV.

CHALICE LINENS.

CORPORAL.

The Corporal in its present form is a square piece of linen about the size of a handkerchief, folded in four parts, and having a small black cross worked near the middle of its anterior edge. It is spread out on the altar, at full length, at the beginning of Mass, and the Chalice is placed upon it. The name *Corporal* is given to it from the fact that our Divine Lord's Body under the Sacred Species rests upon it. It is of strict obligation that it be of linen, and this principally to commemorate the "linen garments" in which our Lord's Body was shrouded in the sepulchre. So particular is the Church about this sacred cloth that she will allow none to touch it but those who have the privilege of touching the Chalice; and when it needs washing the duty devolves upon a subdeacon or one in major orders. It must be washed with great care in three separate waters, and should, if possible, be made up without starch. This latter precaution is necessary on account of the danger of mistaking a particle of the starch, which may often adhere to it, for a Consecrated Particle. When the Corporal is not in use it is kept folded up in the Burse.

We have said that the Corporal must be made of linen. Pope Silvester I., A.D. 314, strictly forbade it to be made of silk or of any tinctured cloth ; and a council held at Rheims repeated this prohibition, adding that it must be of the purest and neatest linen, and be mixed with nothing else, no matter how precious (Kozma, 85). According to Durandus (*Rationale Divinorum*, p. 217), the original injunction requiring the Corporal to be of linen was promulgated by Pope Sixtus I., A.D. 132. The same author gives a very beautiful but rather far-fetched reason, as nearly all his reasons are, for having it of this material. "As linen," says he, "attains to whiteness only after much labor and dressing, so the flesh of Christ by much suffering attained to the glory of the Resurrection" (*ibid.*)

In ancient times the Corporal was large enough to cover the entire table of the altar, and the duty of spreading it out, which was not done until coming on the Offertory, was the peculiar office of the deacon, who also folded it up after the Communion (Kozma, 86). To-day it is only at Low Mass that the Corporal is spread out on the altar, from the beginning; at Solemn High Mass the ancient discipline of spreading it out at the approach of the Offertory is still in vogue.

Corporal of the Orientals.—The Greeks call the Corporal εἰλητόν, *eileton*—that is, *something rolled up*, referring to the wrapping up of our Lord's Body in the linen shroud procured by Joseph of Arimathea (Goar, *Euchol. Græc.*, p. 130). The Corporals used by the Orientals scarcely differ in anything from those used in the Greek Church.

PURIFICATOR.

The Purificator, called also the Mundatory, is a piece of linen about twenty inches long, and in width, when folded in three, about four inches. It has a small cross in the centre, and when not in use it is kept wrapped up by the priest in the Amice.

That the Purificator is of modern introduction, we are justified in asserting from the fact that it is mentioned by none of the ancient liturgists. All that we learn concerning it is that formerly the custom prevailed with the monks of certain monasteries of appending a piece of linen to the Epistle side of the altar by which the Chalice used to be wiped after Communion (Bona, *Rer. Liturg.*, p. 297 ; Kosma, p. 86). When the Purificator became one of the Chalice linens, is not easy to determine ; certain it is that no mention is made of it by any writer prior to the thirteenth century. Pope Innocent III., who died in 1216, makes no allusion to it, although he wrote a very exhaustive work on the Mass and its ceremonies ; neither does Durandus speak of it, although he describes the other linens minutely.

Instead of a Purificator like ours, the Greeks use a sponge, and this with reference to the sponge employed at our Lord's Crucifixion (Goar, *Euchol.*, p. 151). The Greeks rarely use anything in their service which has not a reference of some kind to our Saviour's life upon earth.

PALL.

The Pall is a stiff piece of linen about five inches square, having a cross worked in its centre. It is employed for covering the mouth of the Chalice to prevent dust or flies from falling in, and when not in actual use it is kept with the Corporal shut up in the Burse.

For the first eleven or twelve centuries, the Corporal was so large that it served to cover the Chalice instead of the Pall now in use. To this end its hinder part was so arranged that immediately after the Offertory it could be drawn over the Host and chalice together. The Carthusians observe this discipline yet (Bona, 207).

VEIL.

The Veil which covers the Chalice is generally of the same material as the Chasuble ; but if that of the latter be very stiff it is recommended to have the Veil made of silk, on account of its pliancy, but in color it must always agree with the regular vestments.

THE BURSE.

The Burse, in which the Corporal and Pall are placed out of Mass, ought to be of the same material and color as the rest of the vestments, and a cross should be worked in its centre.

CHAPTER V.

THE MANNER OF RESERVING THE BLESSED SACRAMENT.

WE have said that in ancient times the Blessed Sacrament used to be kept in a golden dove suspended from the canopy of the altar. This was the way in which it was generally kept, and it was on this account that many of the ancient fathers used to designate the church by the appellation of "Domus Columbæ"—that is, the House of the Dove (Selvaggio, b. i. p. 1). Reference, of course, to the Holy Ghost, who is so often represented by a dove, is the ultimate intent of the expression.

The Church of Verona used to keep the Blessed Sacrament in an ivory vessel of costly workmanship (Martène, *De Antiquis Ecclesiæ Ritibus*), and this was the custom also with many British churches. Sometimes it was kept in a small tower, and sometimes in a neat little basket of delicate wicker-work, in allusion to the baskets that were used at the miraculous multiplication of the loaves by our Divine Lord. This latter way of keeping it was in vogue at Rome in the time of Pope Gregory XI., A.D. 1370 (*ibid.*)

In many of the Anglo-Saxon churches, whilst the custom prevailed of keeping the Blessed Sacrament in the golden dove, a sort of aureola, formed of very brilliant lights, used to surround it. In all cases a light burned before it day and night (Dr. Rock, *Church of Our Fathers*, vol. i. 200).

HOW THE BLESSED SACRAMENT IS RESERVED NOW.

The Catholic reader need hardly be told that the Blessed Sacrament is now reserved in a ciborium placed in the Tabernacle and covered with a silken veil. Here it is to be had whenever it is needed, whether to communicate the people during Mass or go on its errand as the Holy Viaticum to the dying. A little lamp filled with pure olive-oil burns before it constantly, and a bell is rung whenever it is to be taken away outside of Mass. In order that there may be no danger of the Sacred Particles becoming stale or unpleasant to the taste, it is customary to renew them every eight or ten days. Then the old Particles are either distributed at the rails to the communicants or consumed by the priest at the altar whilst he yet remains fasting.

RESERVATION OF THE HOLY EUCHARIST BY THE ORIENTALS.

The Greek Church reserves the Holy Eucharist in a little satchel placed near the main altar, in what is termed the *Artophorion*, and keeps a light constantly burning before it (Goar, *Euchol. Græc.*, 15). When conveying it to the sick as the Holy Viaticum, the priest must always be preceded by two deacons with torches in their hands, who keep up a continual recital of psalms the whole way. In some places the law of the land requires all to kneel down on such occasions until the Blessed Sacrament has passed, and this whether the parties who come in the way be Turks, Jews, or heathens (Martène, *De Antiq. Eccl. Rit.*, q. 2).

The Abyssinians reserve the Blessed Sacrament in what they call the *Tabout*, or ark, for a tradition of long standing among them says that the real "Ark of the Covenant" is yet preserved in their land; and hence their desire to perpetuate the fact by applying the name to the tabernacle in which the Blessed Sacrament is kept. The prayer for the consecration of this ark is thus given in the Ethiopic Canon : "O Lord our God, who didst command Moses thy servant and prophet, saying, 'Make me precious vessels, and put them in the tabernacle on Mount Sinai,' now, O Lord God Almighty, stretch forth thy hand upon this ark, and fill it with the virtue, power, and grace of thy Holy Ghost, that in it may be consecrated the Body and Blood of thine only-begotten Son, our Lord" (Neale, *Holy Eastern Church*, i. 186 ; Renaudot, *Liturg. Orient.*, i. p. 474).

The Copts never reserve the Blessed Eucharist outside of Mass ; and they defend their strange discipline by saying that it was forbidden the chosen people of old to reserve any portion of the paschal lamb from one day to another, but that all of it had to be consumed at one meal. So that if a Coptic priest should be summoned any time of the day or night to the bed of a dying person, in order to procure the Holy Viaticum, he will say Mass, whether fasting or not, without the slightest scruple (Denzinger, *Ritus Orientalium*, p. 86). There are two other reasons, however, besides the one mentioned, for this strange discipline. The first is that, inasmuch as the Copts are wholly under dominion of the Mahometans, they are apprehensive that the latter might break into their churches at any time and offer insult to the Blessed Sacrament. The second reason why they do not reserve it, is owing to a strange fear they have that it might be devoured by some of those treacherous serpents for which their land is remarkable. An accident of this kind happened once, and ever since the Coptic patriarchs have forbidden all reservation of the Blessed Sacrament outside of Mass (*ibid.*)

THE PYX.

The Pyx is a small box, generally of gold or silver, in which the Blessed Sacrament is carried to the sick. In shape it exactly resembles the case of a watch, and seldom or never exceeds the latter in size. When carried on the person of the priest it is enclosed in a silken purse, to which a string is attached for fastening it around the neck. In Catholic countries, instead of the Pyx, the ciborium is carried in procession, and a ringing of bells is kept up all the time as a warning to the people that our Lord is passing by on his mission to the sick.

Out of respect for the Blessed Sacrament the priest is required to walk with a slow, dignified pace on these occasions, and this must characterize his movements whether he go on foot or horseback. Some of the very best authorities maintain that a priest should not run or make any undue haste on such occasions, even though he were quite certain that by not doing so the sick person would be dead before he had reached him (De Herdt, *Sacr. Liturg.*, iii. 234).

A solemn silence is also enjoined ; and no salutes or reverences must be paid to any one on the way.

When the distance is short, walking is considered the most respectful way of travelling ; when long, a carriage or horse may be employed ; but care must be taken to move slowly in every case.

Propriety also requires—in fact, the rubric directly prescribes it—that the Pyx be fastened round the neck and secured somewhere on the breast, but never enclosed in the pocket ; and all the time that the priest holds it on his person, while a Particle is in it, he must not sit down unless in case of real necessity.

Oriental Usage.—Unless the person be very dangerously ill the Oriental priests will not carry the Blessed Sacrament outside of church, but will require the sick person to be conveyed thither and communicated there. When communicated out of church it is always, at least with the majority of the Orientals, the rule to administer only under one kind—viz., that of bread (Denzinger, 93 et passim).

The demonstrations made in the East before the Blessed Sacrament, when going to the sick, are very great. A solemn recitation of psalms and pious hymns is kept up all the time, and deacons and acolytes head the procession with torches and incense. No one of the party must ever dare to sit down; and the most solemn decorum must be observed by all until the journey has been completed.

With the Syrian Jacobites it is strictly forbidden to put the Blessed Sacrament in one's pocket when conveying it to the sick. It must be carried in a purse fastened around the neck; and should the journey be made on horseback, on no account must this purse be fastened to the saddle, or conveyed in any other way but on the person of the priest (*ibid.* 92). That this is also the rule observed by the Copts we see from Renaudot (*Commentarius ad Liturg. Copt.*, 270.)

CHAPTER VI.

INCENSE.

OF the use of Incense in divine service so much is said in the Old Testament that it is not necessary to say much about it here. Suffice it to say that its use in the Latin Church is principally confined to Solemn High Mass and Vespers, to expositions of the Blessed Sacrament, and to the obsequies of the dead. In the Eastern Church, especially with the Maronites, it is used on almost every occasion, whether the Mass be High or Low, as we shall see further on.

Its spiritual meaning is as follows: *First,* by its burning we are reminded how our hearts should burn with the fire of divine charity. *Secondly,* it represents the good odor of Christ our Lord, in accordance with that saying in the Canticle of Canticles, "We run in the odor of thy ointments." Therefore, as Incense spreads its odor through the entire church and refreshes our bodies by its agreeable scent, so also does our Lord spread his graces to refresh and nourish our souls. *Thirdly,* Incense has, both in the Old and New Law, been ever looked upon as symbolic of the virtue of prayer, agreeably to that saying of the royal Psalmist, "Let my prayer, O Lord, be directed as incense in thy sight" (*Ps.* cxl.); and that of St. John in the Apocalypse, chap. viii.: "Another angel came, and stood before the altar, having a golden censer; and there was given him much incense, that he should offer of the prayers of all the saints"

(Bouvry, ii. 21; Bona, *Rer. Liturg.*, 295; Durandus, *Rationale Divinorum*, 165).

When Incense is offered to a person it is always indicative of the highest respect. Thus, the Magi offered it to our Lord at his birth on Christmas morning. Our bodies, too, when placed in the grave, are incensed, for the principal reason that on account of the participation of the sacraments during life they became the temples of the Holy Ghost (Bouvry, ii. 594).

THE THURIBLE.

The vessel in which the Incense is burned is called the *Thurible*, a word of Greek origin, meaning the same as our word *censer*, by which it is more generally designated. Accompanying the Thurible is a little vessel, shaped like a boat, in which the Incense is kept, and from which it is taken by a small spoon.

In ancient times the material of the Thurible was sometimes very precious. Constantine the Great, as we read in Anastasius (*Vita S. Silvestri*, i. 31), presented, among other things, to the basilica of St. John Lateran at Rome a number of Thuribles of the purest gold, set with a profusion of gems and precious stones.

In the ancient Anglo-Saxon Church particular attention was paid to the material as well as to the form of the Thurible. Nor was the use of Incense wholly confined to the sanctuary, for we have it recorded that in many churches large Thuribles used to hang down from the roof; or, as was often the case, from a specially-constructed framework supported by columns. On the greater festivals Incense was placed in these and allowed to burn throughout the entire service (Dr. Rock, *Church of Our Fathers*, i. 206). That these hanging Thuribles were also in vogue at Rome we read in the life of Pope Sergius, A.D. 690. Around the altar, too, it was customary in many places to have curiously-wrought vessels for the same purpose. Some of them used to be made so as to resemble various kinds of birds. In these an aperture with a lid to it was formed in the back, so that when fire was put in and Incense cast upon it the fumes would issue through the bird's beak. Conrade, a writer of the twelfth century, describes the hollow-formed silver cranes that he saw in the church of Mentz, and how the Incense issued from them when fire was applied (*ibid.* p. 208, note).

ORIENTAL USAGE.

In the Oriental churches a free use of Incense is kept up all through divine service; and this is not confined to Mass alone—it forms part of nearly every exercise of devotion (Renaudot, *Liturg. Orient.*, i. p. 183).

The Copts use it before pictures[1] of the Blessed Virgin (*ibid.*); so also do the Greeks and Russians, both of whom are particularly careful to keep a lamp burning besides, upon which they throw grains now and then through the day (Dr. Rock, *Church of Our Fathers*, i. p. 209, note; Burder, *Religious Ceremonies and Customs*, pp. 150, 151; *Rites and Customs of the Greco-Russian Church*, passim, by Romanoff).

---

[1] Throughout the East generally, instead of statues of saints, *pictures* are used, for the Orientals maintain that the clause of Deuteronomy in which "graven things" are forbidden should be literally observed even now.

CHAPTER VII.

SACRED MUSIC AND MUSICAL INSTRUMENTS.

SACRED MUSIC.

As it would not be exactly in the line of this book to enter into a full history of Ecclesiastical Music, we think we shall have done our part when we have given the reader a brief account of the place that it holds to-day in the service of the Church.

And first let us remark that it is only in High Mass that music forms part of divine service. For Low Mass it is not prescribed.

For the preservation and cultivation of ecclesiastical music, or Chant, as it is generally called, in the Latin or Western Church, we are principally indebted to the zealous labors of St. Ambrose, Archbishop of Milan (fourth century), and to the illustrious pontiffs, Gelasius and Gregory the Great. Most of the hymns of the Divine Office, or Breviary, are the work of the first named; and these, at least in great part, he was led to compose, as he says himself, in order to counteract the evil tendencies produced in the minds of the faithful by the circulation and recital of the Arian hymns which, during his day, had been gaining such vantage-ground all through Christendom. Of the Ambrosian Chant, strictly so-called, the only specimen we have in the Mass of to-day is that found in the celebrated composition sung at the blessing of the Paschal Candle on Holy Saturday, and called, from the word with which it begins, the "Exultet." It is almost universally admitted that the composition of this is the work of St. Augustine, but that the chant itself is Ambrosian.

As St. Ambrose lived a considerable time in the East, where Church music had already been zealously cultivated, it is generally believed that it was in that region that he received his first impressions of its singular beauty, and that thence he introduced it into his own church at Milan, after much study had been expended in reducing it to a system suitable to Western ears. Whether the chant thus introduced was built upon the "eight modes"[1] of Greek music or not, we are unable to say with certainty; very likely it was. Certain it is, however, that his system was rather intricate, and in many instances far above the compass of ordinary voices; for which reason it was deemed advisable to give it a new touching, and so suit it to the capacity of all, that all might comply with the wishes of the Church in singing the praises of God together. The task of doing this good work was undertaken by Pope Gregory the Great, who also established a regular school at Rome to see that his modified system was duly observed and practised everywhere. And this is the origin of the so-called *Gregorian Chant*. It is called *plain* from its great simplicity, and "canto firmo" by the Italians, from the singular majesty that pervades it throughout.

As to the precise merits of the Ambrosian Chant we know but little now; whether that in use at Milan to-day be the same as that used in the fourth century we leave others to determine. Certain it is, however, that the ancient chant was full of majesty and divine sweetness; this we have

---

[1] The eight modes or tones of the Greek music were: the *Dorian, Hypodorian, Phrygian, Soft-Hypophrygian, Lydian, Hypolydian, Mixed-Lydian, Hyperlastian*. Each of these was distinguished by peculiar characteristics, such as *soft, sweet, martial, furious*, etc.

from the illustrious St. Augustine, whose big heart melted into tears of compunction whenever he listened to its solemn strains. "When I remember," says he in his *Confessions*, "the tears which I shed at the chants of thy Church in the first days of my recovered faith, and how I am still moved by them—not, indeed, by the song, but by the things which are sung, . . . I acknowledge the great usefulness of this institution."

The merits of the Gregorian Chant are known to all; and who that has ever heard it rendered as it should be will not say that it has a divine influence over the soul? If St. Augustine wept upon hearing the Ambrosian Chant, many more recent than he have wept, too, upon hearing the simple but soul-stirring strains of the pure Gregorian. The Venerable Bede, for example, tells us how deeply affected St. Cuthbert used to be when chanting the Preface, so much so that his sobbing could be heard through the entire congregation; and, as he raised his hands on high at the "Sursum corda," his singing was rather a sort of solemn moaning than anything else (*Vita S. Cuthbert*, cap. xvi.) The renowned Haydn was often moved to tears at listening to the children of the London charity schools sing the psalms together in unison according to the Gregorian style; and the great master of musicians and composers, Mozart, went so far as to say that he would rather be the author of the Preface and Pater Noster, according to the same style, than of anything he had ever written. These are but a few of the numerous encomiums passed upon this sacred chant by men who were so eminently qualified to constitute themselves judges.

The great distinguishing feature of the Gregorian Chant is the wonderful simplicity, combined with a sort of divine majesty, which pervades it throughout, and which no words can exactly describe. It must be heard to be appreciated. Then, again, another great feature that it possesses is the power of hiding itself behind the words, so as to render the latter perfectly audible to the congregation. In this way it is made a most solemn kind of prayer, so very different from the great bulk of modern compositions, whose entire drift seems to be to drown the words completely, or so mutilate them as to render them perfectly indistinct and unintelligible.

For many years Rome preserved this sacred chant in its original purity, and watched with jealous care to exclude from it everything that smacked of the world's music. But, careful as Rome was, innovations and corruptions set in; so much so that, after a few years, hardly a trace of Gregorian music could be distinguished in what was once the pride of the Church. As might naturally be expected, the corruption began in France. For the space of seventy years (from Pope Clement V., in 1309, to Pope Gregory XI.) the Roman pontiffs resided at Avignon, and, as was reasonable to expect, the papal choir was composed entirely of French performers. They treated the Gregorian Chant just as they pleased; but little would that have mattered had it not been for the fact that Pope Gregory XI., upon his return to Rome, brought his French choir with him with all their fantastic vagaries. The impression made at Rome by the efforts of this musical body was of the most disedifying kind, for not a word could be heard or understood of all that they sang. So ridiculous was their singing that when Pope Nicholas V. asked Cardinal Capranica what he thought of it, his Eminence humorously replied: "Well, Holy Father, I compare it to a sackful of swine squeaking away; they make a tremendous noise, but not a word is articulated distinctly."

Church music went on in this way until about the time

of the Council of Trent, when it was determined to ameliorate it or banish it entirely from the Church. A committee of cardinals was formed by Pope Pius IV. for the purpose of seeing whether it was possible to compose a Mass the music of which would be harmonious and the words distinct and intelligible. St. Charles Borromeo and Cardinal Vitelozzi were among the number selected for the important task. There was at this time attached to the choral staff of St. Mary Major a man of great musical renown and of singular originality. To him the committee applied. He accepted their proposal and set earnestly to work at writing a Mass to suit their taste. He composed two off-hand which were greatly admired, but the third was the climax of perfection. It was simple, harmonious, and very devotional. Every word of it was articulated distinctly. It was produced before the Pope and the College of Cardinals, and with one consentient voice all pronounced in favor of it. Thus the music of the Church was saved. The person who figured in this momentous juncture was the celebrated Palestrina,[2] ever since known as the great reformer of ecclesiastical chant. He is looked up to as the father of Church harmony; and his great Mass, denominated "Missa Papæ Marcelli" (from Pope Marcellus II., A.D. 1554, before whom it was sung), will ever be venerated as one of his greatest and happiest efforts. The Mass is performed on every Holy Saturday in the Papal Chapel. It was originally in eight parts, but was reduced by Palestrina himself to six. The other great reformers, or rather embellishers, of Church music were Allegri, author of the famous "Miserere" of the Sistine Chapel; Pergolesi,

---

[2] His real name was Pierluigi (Giovanni Pierluigi), but he generally went by the name of his native city, Palestrina, the ancient Præneste, in Italy, where he was born in 1524. His death took place in 1594, and he was buried in St. Peter's. St. Philip Neri attended him in his last moments.

author of the inimitable music of the "Stabat Mater"; and Mozart, whose renown will ever be known the world over.

MUSICAL INSTRUMENTS.

That the Gregorian Chant was at its introduction performed without the aid of instruments everybody is willing to admit. Instruments are not in use to-day with the Cistercians or Carthusians, nor at the ancient church of Lyons, in France; and we see also that they have no place in the service of the Oriental Church, if we except the few sorry ones employed by the Abyssinians and Copts, of which Pococke speaks in his *Travels in Egypt*. From the papal choir, too, all instruments are excluded save a trumpet or two, which sound a delicate harmony at the Elevation. This choir, which is justly esteemed the most select in existence, always accompanies the Holy Father whenever he sings Solemn High Mass in any of the churches of Rome. Its members are strictly forbidden to sing anywhere else, and none but male voices are admitted among them.

The Organ.—It is generally believed that the introduction of the organ into the service of the Church was the work of Pope Vitalian, or at least that it happened during his pontificate, from A.D. 657 to 672. The first which appeared in France was that which the Emperor Constantine Copronymus sent in the year 757 to King Pepin, father of Charlemagne. This was placed in the Church of St. Corneille, in Compiègne. At first organs were of very small compass, but not many years after their introduction they assumed larger proportions. This may fairly be gathered from an expression of St. Aldhelm, who in his poem, "De Laudibus Virginitatis," tells the admirer of music that if he despises the more humble sound of the harp he must listen to the thousand voices of the organ. The ancient cathedral of Winchester, in England, had a monster organ, which could be heard at an incredible distance. Its sound, we are told, resembled the roaring of thunder; and so huge was it that it required seventy stalwart men to feed it with air. It had four hundred pipes, twenty-six feeders, and a double row of keys. So famous was it that it formed the theme of many of the poetic effusions of the day. Wolston, the monk, wrote much about it.

Other Musical Instruments. — Besides the organ, the Anglo-Saxon Church employed a variety of other wind instruments, foremost among which was a sort of hoop sheathed in silver plates, having a number of bells hung around it. These were generally prescribed for processions out of church, but they were used also in the regular choir within.

In closing our chapter on Church music we cannot resist calling the attention of the reader to the great care our forefathers took to see that nothing should ever be sung in divine service that was not of the purest and gravest nature. To carry this out the better, some of the greatest nobles of the land would now and then volunteer their services and take an humble part with the rest of the choir in leading the sacred chant on Sundays and festivals. What a glorious and edifying thing it was, for instance, to see Richard I., Cœur de Lion—the Lion-hearted King, as he was familiarly called—take part in the choir of his own chapel and sing from the beginning to the end of service! Yes, that mighty warrior, who spread terror throughout the East by the formidable army he led to Palestine in defence of the Holy Land on the occasion of the Third Crusade, put himself on a level with his humblest subjects in singing the praises of God. "He would go up and down the choir," says Radulf, Abbot of Coggeshall, " and arouse all the members to sing out and sing together ;

and he would raise his hands aloft, and take the greatest delight in directing the music on the principal solemnities."

(For the principal matter of this chapter on Church Music and Musical Instruments we are indebted to the following works: *Divina Psalmodia*, by Cardinal Bona; *Antiquities of the Anglo-Saxon Church*, vol. ii., by Lingard; *Church of Our Fathers*, vol. iii. part 2, and *Hierurgia*, by Dr. Rock; *Holy Week in the Vatican*, by Canon Pope; and an article in the *Dublin Review* for 1836, denominated "Ecclesiastical Music." The rest we have found in places which we cannot now recall to mind. We have been careful, however, to say nothing at random.)

CHAPTER VIII.

THE VARYING RITES WITHIN THE CHURCH.

As we shall have occasion to refer frequently in the course of this work to several rites that do not accord in everything with that which is strictly termed *Roman,* we have thought it well to give the reader a general survey of them here, in order to make our remarks hereafter more intelligible and to save unnecessary repetition.

The learned Cardinal Bona, in speaking of the different rites within the Church, compares them to the dress of the spouse in the Canticle of Canticles, which abounded with such a variety of colors. At one time there was hardly a locality which had not some peculiarity of its own in celebrating the Holy Sacrifice. This, of course, was nothing touching the substance of the Sacrifice itself, nor, indeed, could it be considered a change in the general norma of the Mass. It was rather "præter Missam," as theologians would say, than "contra Missam." It was some embellishment or other in the ceremonies which was not prescribed in the ordinary rules laid down for the celebration of divine service. But as these peculiarities often gave rise to much dissension, and tended in some cases to the formation of national churches, the Holy See thought well to direct immediate attention to them and stay their rapid progress. The matter was taken in hand by the Sacrosanct Council of Trent, under the auspices of Pope Pius V. His Holiness issued a decree to the effect that all those rites which had

not been approved of by Rome from time immemorial, or
which could not prove an antiquity of two hundred years,
should be abolished then and for ever. The result was that
only three orders could prove an antiquity of two hundred
years—viz., the Carthusians, Carmelites, and Dominicans—
and only two of the other class could show that they had
been approved of from time immemorial—viz., the Mozarabics and Ambrosians or Milanese. All these were allowed
to stand and retain their own peculiar ceremonies and liturgical customs, but the rest were abolished at once. Some
of the French primatial churches, such as that of Lyons, and
one or two others throughout Germany and Naples, were
permitted to retain some laudable customs of a minor nature; but as these did not constitute what would be technically called a rite, we shall give them but a passing notice.

CARTHUSIANS.

This religious body, so called from La Chartreuse, near
Grenoble, in France, the wild valley in which their first monastery was built, was founded in the year 1084 by St. Bruno, a
priest of Cologne. It is regarded as the strictest order in the
Church, and is the only one which a member from one of
the mendicant orders can join as being of a higher order of
perfection than his own. It has as its device a cross sur-
mounting a globe, with the inscription, "Stat crux dum
volvitur orbis"—that is, "The cross stands as long as the
earth moves." In England they are called the "Charter-
House" Monks, a corruption of Chartreuse. Their habit is
entirely white, but abroad they wear over it a black cowl.
One strange and rare privilege enjoyed by the nuns of their
order is that, at the solemn moment of making their vows,
they put on a maniple and stole, and are allowed to sing the
Epistle in Solemn High Mass (Romsee, iv. 356, note). They

use no musical instruments whatever in their service, but sing everything according to the pure Gregorian style.

The peculiarities of their Mass are as follows : They put the wine and water in the chalice at the beginning, and say the introductory psalm and Confiteor, not at the centre, as we do, but at the Gospel side, with face towards the altar. Their form of confession is much shorter than ours, and instead of saying the "Oramus te, Domine," when they ascend the altar-steps, they say a Pater and Ave, and then sign themselves with the cross. They say the "Gloria in excelsis" at the Epistle corner, where the book is, and turn round in the same place to say the "Dominus vobiscum." They kiss the margin of the missal after the Gospel instead of the text itself, and only make a profound bow instead of a genuflection at the "Et homo factus est" of the Creed. In fact, at no part of the entire Mass do they touch the ground with the knee when they make a reverence, as we do. They bless both water and wine by one single cross at the Offertory, and make the oblation of Host and chalice one joint act by placing the paten and the large bread on the mouth of the latter. From the beginning of the Canon to the "Hanc igitur" they stretch out their arms in such a manner as to exhibit the form of a cross, and at the Consecration they elevate the chalice only a few inches from the altar, never high enough to be seen by the people, just as we do at the "Omnis honor et gloria" before the "Pater noster." After consecration they extend their hands again in form of a cross until the "Supplices te rogamus," when they bow and cross one upon the other.

At the end of Mass they do not bless the people, as we do, nor say the Gospel of St. John, but come down and return to the sacristy the moment they have recited the "Placeat." A few of their other peculiarities will be noticed throughout this work.

CARMELITES.

This order, so called from Carmel, in Palestine, where Elias, the holy prophet, dwelt in a cave, owes its origin principally to Berthold, a monk and priest of Calabria, who with a few companions erected in 1156 some huts on the heights of Mt. Carmel. The Carmelites themselves claim Elias as their founder.

The peculiarities of their manner of saying Mass are these: They recite the psalm "Judica me, Deus," on their way to the altar, and not standing in front of it, as we do; and, like the Carthusians, pour water and wine into the chalice before the beginning of Mass. On the greater festivals of the year they repeat the "Introit" three separate times; on other occasions only twice, as with ourselves. The moment they uncover the chalice at the Offertory they make the sign of the cross over the bread and wine, in the name of the Father, and of the Son, and of the Holy Ghost; then they make the oblation of both Host and chalice under one form of prayer—viz., "Suscipe Sancta Trinitas"—which we are accustomed to say after the oblation has been finished; but their prayer has an addition to it that ours has not. They say before the "Secreta": "Domine, exaudi orationem meam, et clamor meus ad te veniat." At the "Hanc igitur" they incline to the altar and remain in that posture until the "Quam oblationem." They extend their arms in the form of a cross from the time they begin the "Unde et memores" until they reach the part at which the crosses are to be made. After the last of the three prayers preceding Communion they say (in Latin, of course) : "Hail, Salvation of the world, Word of the Father, Sacred Host, Living Flesh, Deity Complete, True Man." In saying the "Domine, non sum dignus," they bow the knee a little and strike the breast as we do. After having blessed the people they recite the "Salve Regina," with its responses and prayer, for which, in Paschal time, they substitute the "Regina Cœli." After the Gospel of St. John they say, "Per evangelica dicta," etc., as we do at the first Gospel, and then, covering their heads with their cowl, return to the sacristy reciting the "Te Deum."

DOMINICANS.

The Dominicans are so called from St. Dominic, a Spaniard by birth, who founded them in the year 1215. They are very generally known by the name of Friars Preachers from their peculiar mission. In England their general appellation is the Black Friars, on account of their wearing an overdress of a black color; when at home their habit is entirely white. Throughout France their familiar designation is Jacobites, from the fact that the principal house of their order in Paris was first known by the name of St. James, which in Latin is *Jacobus*.

Like the Carmelites and Carthusians, the Dominicans put the water and wine into the chalice before they begin Mass. They do not say the "Judica me, Deus," but recite instead of it certain verses beginning with "Confitemini Domino quoniam bonus." They say the opening words of the "Gloria in excelsis" at the middle of the altar, but return to the book at the Epistle side to finish the rest of it. Here also they say the "Dominus vobiscum." They observe somewhat similar ceremonies in reciting the Credo. First they say "Credo in unum Deum" at the middle ; then they return to the missal at the Gospel side, and continue reciting it there until the "Incarnatus est," when they go to the middle again, and there, spreading out the anterior part of the chasuble on the altar, kneel so as to touch the ground at the "Homo factus est." They extend the chasuble in like manner whenever the "Flectamus genua" is to be said.

After the "Homo factus est" they return and finish the Credo at the book. They read the Offertorium at the Gospel side, after the manner of a collect, and make the oblation of the Host and chalice as the two fore-mentioned orders do. After the Gospel of St. John they make the sign of the cross upon themselves, and then go to the middle, where they fold up the corporal and put it in the burse, and afterwards return to the sacristy with the amice covering their head as at the beginning of Mass. They recite the "Benedicite" after Mass, as we do.

MOZARABIC LITURGY.

The ancient Spanish Liturgy introduced by St. Torquatus and his companions resembled the Roman in all essential points. When Spain was invaded by the Suevi, Alani, Vandals, and Visigoths (fifth century), all of whom were Arian, its Liturgy and the Arian Liturgy commingled, and ran hand-in-hand for many years; and from the fact that a constant intercourse was kept up between the Spanish Church and that of Constantinople, the headquarters of the East in the beginning of the fifth century, several Greek customs, as well as those that were rank with Arianism, entered the Spanish Liturgy, so that it stood much in need of renovation. In the year 537 Profuturus, Archbishop of Galicia, wrote for advice in the matter to Pope Vigilius, then the Sovereign Pontiff. His Holiness sent him the Canon of the Mass according to the Roman norma, together with a copy of the entire Mass of Easter, in order that he might shape his new Liturgy by them. Towards the end of the sixth century the Visigoths were converted to the faith, and then the Liturgy of Spain assumed its most important appearance. In the fourth Council of Toledo, A.D. 633, the Spanish bishops, at whose head was St. Isidore of Seville, resolved to banish from the country every foreign rite, and have but one Liturgy throughout the land. From the fact that St. Isidore headed this work, he is generally looked upon as the author of the Liturgy of Spain. The Liturgy so formed, and called by the name of *Gothic*, was used in Spain without being in any way influenced by the reform of Pope Gregory the Great. A new state of things set in towards the beginning of the eighth century, when the land fell into the hands of the Moors.[1] Those who yielded to the Moorish yoke were called "Mostarabuna," an Arabic participle meaning "mixed with Arabs,"[2] and this Liturgy was denominated accordingly *Muzarabic* or *Mozarabic*. During the dominion of the Moors, which lasted nearly eight hundred years, the Liturgy kept constantly changing and receiving new corruptions, so that at the Synod of San Juan de la Peña, held under the auspices of Pope Alexander II. (1601), Sancho Ramirez, King of Aragon, caused the Gregorian or Roman Rite to supersede the Gothic. The Council of Burgos in 1085 issued a solemn proclamation to this effect. It was no easy matter, however, to effect the introduction of the Gregorian Rite entirely, for people cling with wonderful tenacity to ancient customs. Some were for it, others against it. To settle the matter, strangely enough, an appeal was made to the "judgment of God." A powerful fire was accordingly made, and a copy of each Liturgy cast into it; whichever came out unhurt was to be the Liturgy of the land. The Gregorian was thrown in first, but scarcely had it

---

[1] The Moors, or Mauri, were the people of Mauritania, or Morocco, in the north of Africa. They embraced Mahometanism in the seventh century at the instigation of their Arabian conquerors, and became so identified with the latter in everything that *Arab* and *Moor* were synonymous terms. They were finally driven from Spain by Ferdinand and Isabella in 1492.

[2] The Arabs divide their people into three classes: first, those called "el Arab el Arabeh"—*i.e.*, pure Arabs; second, "el Arab el Mota' arribeh," or those who speak and know the language; and, third, "el Arab el Mosta' ribeh"—that is, *mixed* or *naturalized* Arabs.

touched the flames when it rebounded and fell uninjured by the side of the fire. The Mozarabic was then cast in, and, singular to behold, it remained intact in the midst of the flames! As both liturgies were miraculously preserved, it was decided that both were equally good, and that consequently each should hold a place in Spain. Predominance, however, was soon given to the Gregorian, so that it became the Liturgy of the whole land, with the sole exception of the city of Toledo, where the Mozarabic was employed in six churches—viz., St. Justa, St. Luke, St. Eulalia, St. Mark, St. Sebastian, and St. Torquatus; but as time wore on the Mozarabic was even superseded in these, and solely confined to the cathedral chapel. Cardinal Ximenes, however, by very earnest entreaties, whilst Archbishop of Toledo, caused it to be readopted in five of the churches mentioned, and instituted as its custodians what he termed "Sodales Mozarabes," a company of thirteen priests, to whom he assigned the Chapel of Corpus Christi. The rite is yet kept up in these places, but nowhere else (see *Life of Cardinal Ximenes*, by Hefele; Bona, *Rer. Liturg.*, p. 219; Kozma, 157; and Gavantus, *Thesaur. Rit.*, 23). We shall have occasion to refer to the peculiarities of the Mozarabic Rite throughout our work.

AMBROSIAN LITURGY.

The Ambrosian Rite,[3] so called from St. Ambrose, Bishop of Milan, A.D. 374, claims a very high antiquity. According to the Milanese themselves, its main structure is the work of St. Barnabas, Apostle; but as it received a fresh

---

[3] Strictly speaking, neither the Mozarabic nor Ambrosian Rite can be called a *liturgy*. The latter name, taking it in its general acceptation, only applies when the language used and the ceremonies employed are different from those of Rome; but as there is no difference in either case here mentioned in language, and but very little in ceremonies, the term *rite* is more proper than *liturgy*.

touching-up at the hands of St. Ambrose, it is generally ascribed to him and called by his name. Many attempts have been made to abolish this rite altogether and substitute the Roman in its stead, but all to no purpose. The Milanese cling to it with a dying man's grasp, and the Holy See, to choose the less of two evils, and make itself all to all where nothing trenches upon faith, permits them "to abound in their own sense." In the year 1497 Pope Alexander VI. solemnly confirmed its use, and ever since then it has been strictly adhered to at Milan ; not, however, in all the churches, for some even now follow the Roman Rite, but in a few belonging to the diocese (Kozma, 156). St. Charles Borromeo did much to uphold this rite during his time (1590). Some of the peculiarities of the rite are as follows : It allows the "Agnus Dei" only in Masses for the dead. The text of Scripture used is not that followed by the Roman Rite, but one of those versions in use before St. Jerome's Vulgate was published. On Easter Sunday two Masses are prescribed, one for the newly baptized, the other of the day itself. Throughout the whole of Lent there is no Mass on Friday of any kind (this was an ordinance of St. Charles Borromeo). On Sundays and feasts of great solemnity a lesson from the Old Testament is read before the Epistle, together with some versicles, after the manner of our Gradual. Immediately before consecration the priest saying Mass goes, according to this rite, to the Epistle corner of the altar and washes his hands in silence. The other peculiarities will be noticed as we go on (see *Institutiones Liturgicæ*, vol. ii. p. 300, by Maringola ; Cardinal Bona, 218 ; Gavantus, 22 ; Kozma, 156).

We mention, in passing, that according to this rite the Sacrament of Baptism is administered by *immersion*, and not by *infusion*, as with all who follow the Roman Rite.

GALLIC RITE.

We devote here but a passing notice to this rite, for the reason that it never made any headway, if we except a few ceremonial embellishments, after the time of Charlemagne —that is, after the ninth century. In one of the cities of France—viz., the ancient Lugdunum of the Romans, now Lyons—a few peculiar liturgic customs are yet kept up, such as reading the Gospel from the ambo, and singing without the aid of the organ or any musical instrument whatever. The Lyonese ascribe the introduction of their rite into Gaul to St. Irenæus, Bishop of their city in the early part of the third century (see *Recherches sur l'Abolition de la Liturgie Antique dans l'Eglise de Lyon*, by M. De Conny; Kozma, 157; Cardinal Bona, *Divina Psalmodia*, p. 559).

CHAPTER IX.

THE ALTAR.

ACCORDING to the best authorities the word altar is formed from the Latin *altus*, high, and *ara*, a mound or elevation. It is the sacred table upon which the Holy Sacrifice of the Mass is offered.

According to rule it ought to be about three and a half feet high, three feet wide, and six and a half feet long; and to denote the perfection of our Lord, whom it is made to represent in sacred symbolism, it should be solid throughout (Bouvry, ii. 223). Before Mass may be celebrated on it, it must first be consecrated by the bishop.

MATERIAL.

According to the present discipline of the Church the Altar must be made of stone, or at least that part of it upon which the chalice and its appurtenances are placed. When not entirely of stone the rubrics require that an appendage called an *antipendium* should hang always in front of it to cover its anterior surface.

In ancient times, especially during the days of persecution, altars were for the most part made of wood; in fact, it would have been loss of time and useless to make them of any more durable material, for the reason that the pagans might have desecrated and destroyed them at any moment; but after peace was restored to the Church the costliest materials sometimes entered into their composition.

THE ALTAR USED AT THE LAST SUPPER.

It is the general opinion of liturgical writers that our

Divine Lord instituted the Blessed Eucharist on an ordinary wooden table, such as the Jews in his day were wont to eat from.

According to Martène (*De Antiquis Eccl. Ritibus*) there are yet preserved at Rome two wooden altars, one in the Church of St. John Lateran, the other in that of St. Pudentiana, upon which St. Peter used to say Mass during his Roman pontificate. The one in the latter-named church is now almost eaten up with age, but is preserved from utter destruction by being covered over with a stone casing. The following inscription appears upon it: "In hoc altari Sanctus Petrus pro vivis et defunctis ad augendam fidelium multitudinem, Corpus et Sanguinem Domini offerebat"—that is, "Upon this altar St. Peter used to offer the Body and Blood of our Lord, in behalf of the living and the dead, for increasing the number of the faithful."

Pope Silvester (314) is said to have been the first who made stone altars obligatory; but some count this as doubtful, both because the decree so ordaining cannot be found among those attributed to this Pope, and because it is a well-known fact that altars of wood existed and were used after his time (Merati, 118). This much, however, is certain: that the Council of Epaon, held in the year 517, forbade any altars except those of stone to be consecrated. The same prohibition may be seen in several of the capitularies of Charlemagne (*ibid.*)

ALTARS OF GOLD, SILVER, AND PRECIOUS STONES.

During the reign of Constantine the Great (from A.D. 312 to 336), who published many edicts in favor of the Christians, stately altars of gold and silver, and sometimes even of precious stones, were to be seen in several cities of the East and West. The emperor himself had caused to be erected at Rome, in the basilica called after his name—now the Church of St. John Lateran—seven different altars of the purest silver (Kozma, 29, note 4). The Empress Pulcheria bestowed upon the great basilica of Constantinople an altar formed of gold and gems (*ibid.*) There is still to be seen at Chartres, in France, a very ancient altar made of jasper (*ibid.*)

But the greatest of all altars was that of the famous Church of Holy Wisdom[1] at Constantinople, justly regarded as one of the wonders of the age. Everything that was precious on sea or land was purchased and brought together to form this singular altar. Gold, silver, and the richest metals, with every variety of precious stones, were collected by the Emperor Justinian and used in its erection. The most experienced artisans of the day were employed in superintending its construction, and neither labor nor expense was spared to make it perfect of its kind. When finished, the following inscription appeared upon it : " We, thy servants, Justinian and Theodora, offer unto thee, O Christ! thine own gifts out of thine own, which we beseech thee favorably to accept, O Son and Word of God ! who wast made flesh

---

[1] This church, from the fact that it is generally called Sancta Sophia, is often falsely rendered *Saint Sophy*, by those who think that it was dedicated under the name of some such saint; whereas it was really dedicated to Holy Wisdom, in Greek "Ἁγία σοφία," but "Sancta Sophia" in Latin. This world-renowned church was first built by Constantine the Great in the year 325. The second of the same name, and on the same foundation, was built by Constantius in 359. Theodosius the Great built a third one on the same site in 415. The fourth and last was the temple of Justinian. It was commenced at eight o'clock A.M., February 23, A. D. 532. The architects were Anthemius of Tralles and Isidore of Miletus, both eminent mechanicians. Artists from the four quarters of the globe were invited to take part in its construction, and foremost among the workmen, we are told, was the emperor himself, girt in a tunic and equipped with hammer and trowel. From the date of its commencement to its completion was five years, ten months, and three days. When Justinian saw it finished, and beheld what a magnificent edifice it was, he cried out in a transport of admiration, "I have conquered thee, O Solomon ! Glory be to God, who hath accounted me worthy of such a work !" In 1453, when Constantinople fell into the hands of the Turks, this famous church was converted into a Mahometan *Jami*, or greater mosque, and most of its embellishments, but not all, were destroyed (Neale, *Holy Eastern Church*, i. 235, 236 ; *Catholic World*, August, 1865 ; Gibbon, *Decline and Fall of the Rom. Emp.*, vii. 117).

and crucified for our sakes ; keep us in the true orthodox faith ; and this empire which thou hast committed to our trust augment and preserve to thine own glory, through the intercession of the Holy Mother of God and Virgin Mary" (Martène, *De Antiquis Ecclesiæ Ritibus*, art. "Altare").

SACRED SYMBOLISM OF ALTARS.

The precise symbolism of the altar is that it denotes Christ our Lord, in accordance with what St. Paul says in his first Epistle to the Corinthians : "They drank of the spiritual rock which followed them, and the rock was Christ" (Bouvry, ii. 222). According to Venerable Bede, the altar is the body of Christ, or all the saints in whom a divine fire ever burns, consuming all that is flesh.

RIGHT AND LEFT OF THE ALTAR.

Up to the fifteenth century the *right* and *left* of the altar were settled by the position of the priest standing before it. The part which was opposite his right hand was the altar's *right*, and that opposite his left the altar's *left*. This ordinance is now exactly the reverse, for the designations of *right* and *left* are taken from the Crucifix, and not from the position of the priest ; so that the right of the altar now is the part to the right of the Crucifix—that is, the Gospel side ; and the left, the left of the Crucifix, or Epistle side. According to Father Le Brun (*Explication de la Messe*, i. 171, note), this change was first introduced by Patricius, Bishop of Pienza, in Italy, about the year 1488, and Pope Pius V. adopted it afterwards in his recension of the missal. It is well to bear this in mind when reading such works as those of Durandus and Pope Innocent III., who wrote prior to this time, for what they invariably call *right* is the *left* according to the present discipline. This rule also holds good in every other case, at Mass and out of Mass, where it becomes necessary to make a distinction of this kind—such, for instance, as in sprinkling with holy water, in putting incense in the thurible, and in incensing anything.

COVERING AND FURNITURE OF THE ALTAR.

It is of strict obligation that every altar upon which the Holy Sacrifice is offered should be covered with three linen cloths. The first two must be large enough to cover the entire table or upper surface; the third, or outer one, must cover the latter two and hang down on both sides so as to touch the ground. In case three cannot be had, it is permitted to fold the under cloth in two, and thus make up the complement. Before these cloths are used they must be blessed by the bishop, or by one to whom he delegates his power in this matter. Three are used in honor of the Blessed Trinity (Gavantus, p. 115), as well as to commemorate the linen cloths in which our Lord's Body was wrapped when laid in the sepulchre (Kozma, 32). They are mentioned as far back as the fourth century, at which period they were not spread on the altar until after the exclusion of the catechumens—*i.e.*, before the Offertory (*ibid.*)

ALTARS OF THE ORIENTALS.

The discipline of the Oriental Church on the subject of altars differs but little from our own. With them the altars must be of stone also. However, in the absence of a regular altar they will say Mass on certain cloths called *Antimens;* nay, even on a leaf of the Gospel, if necessity presses.

Antimens.—This word is sometimes written *Antimins*, and nearly always so by the Greeks; but as it is evidently derived from *anti*, instead of, and *mensa*, a table or altar, we prefer writing it as here, because it is more suggestive of its origin. These antimens are held in great veneration by the Orientals. Their material is generally silk, but in some cases linen also is used, after the manner of our corporals. They are consecrated with much ceremony, relics being pounded up with fragrant gum, and holy oil being poured out together with them by the bishop and cast upon them. Then the Office of the Holy Eucharist is celebrated on them for seven successive days before they are fully consecrated. The date of their consecration is generally worked upon them, also the name of the consecrating prelate (Neale, *Holy Eastern Church*, vol. i. p. 186; *Hierurgia*, 504; Goar, *Euchol. Græc.*, 653). They measure about sixteen inches square, and have generally a figure stamped upon them representing the burial of our Lord by Joseph of Arimathea and the holy women (Romanoff, *Rites and Customs of the Greco-Russian Church*, pp. 84, 85). The discipline of the Russian Church is so strict regarding these sacred cloths that no church can be consecrated without them. When not in actual use, they are carefully folded up in a silken cloth called the *Iliton* (*ibid.*) Instead of these antimens, the Syrians use, when pressed by necessity, slabs of wood called *Mensæ*, which they also employ, when the notion takes them, even though regularly consecrated altars can be had (Neale, 187).

HOW THE ALTARS OF THE ORIENTALS ARE DRESSED.

The Orientals also, like ourselves, use three coverings. The manner in which they vest the altar is thus described by Neale: "At the angles of the mensa are placed four small pieces of cloth, symbolizing the four Evangelists, and adorned with their respective emblems. Over these the *catasarka* of silk or stuff is spread, having four strings or tassels at its extremities, and over this the ἐπενδύ- σις, *ependusis*, or exterior covering, generally worked with crosses" (i. p. 187). Although Neale agrees with Goar regarding the number of altar coverings used by the Orientals, still the latter mentions one—viz., the *eileton*—not named by the former (*Euchol. Græc.*, p. 849).

According to the Ritual of Russia, the altar's first covering is a white linen cloth made in the form of a cross, the four ends of which hang down to the floor. It is called the *stratchitza*, and by it is meant the linen cloth left by our Lord in the sepulchre after his glorious resurrection (Romanoff, 85). The second covering resembles this in everything, only that its material is of a richer kind. This is denominated the *inditia*, and signifies the "glory of God." The third article is called the *iliton* (same as the Greek *eileton*); it is intended to call to mind the napkin which bound the head of our Lord, and which the Apostles Peter and John saw "wrapped in a place by itself" (*Greco-Russian Church*, p. 85).

The first cloth put on by the Copts is of a black color (*mappa nigra*). With them, and in fact with the majority of the Orientals, the altar is always bare and unfurnished except at Mass; nor must it ever be dressed unless when the priest is standing before it making his acts of preparation for the Liturgy (Renaudot, *Liturg. Orient. Collectio*, tom. i. 166).

On Holy Thursday the Latin Church strips the altar of all its coverings and ornaments, leaving nothing but the *candelabra* and crucifix. This is intended to recall to mind the denudation of our Divine Lord during his bitter Passion (Bouvry, ii. 515).

ALTAR CARDS.

For the greater convenience of the priest there are always placed on the altar three large cards, standing upright, containing certain portions of the Mass which may be read at sight. The priest, it is true, is expected to have these already committed to memory; but as the memory often fails when we least expect it, it has been deemed advisable to have certain prayers always in sight, and not trust to uncertainty of any kind.

The card at the Gospel side contains the Gospel of St. John. That in the centre the "Gloria in excelsis" and "Credo," as well as all the prayers said at the Offertory; also the "Qui pridie," or beginning of the Canon, the form of consecration, the prayers before Communion, and the last prayer, or "Placeat." The card at the Epistle side contains the prayer recited in putting the water into the chalice, and that said at the washing of the fingers. Strictly speaking, only the centre card is necessary, and it is the only one the rubric calls for; the other two have been introduced by custom.

CHAPTER X.

RELICS.

ANCIENT CUSTOMS.

DURING the persecutions[1] the faithful were accustomed to turn the tombs in which the martyrs were interred into altars, and offer the Holy Sacrifice upon them. This can be proved by innumerable testimonies, and even by ocular demonstration at this great distance, if trouble be taken to visit the Roman Catacombs and read their sacred inscriptions. "In the midst of these venerable symbols," says D'Agincourt (tom. ii. p. 86), "upon a large slab of marble which completely covered the sarcophagus of the martyr, the first ministers of the Christian worship celebrated the mysteries of our faith in the time of persecution." Hence the origin of such appellations as "Memoria," "Confessio," "Martyrium," and "Apostolia" given by the ancient Fathers to such places, and subsequently applied to the churches erected over or near them (Kozma, 21, note; *Hierurgia*, 496). The name "Martyrium," however, was not always confined to the altar nor to the church built over a martyr's tomb; it was sometimes given even to an ordinary church when the latter was erected through the zeal of any

---

[1] It is generally admitted that there were ten persecutions of the Christians in the early days of Christianity. The first began under Nero; the second, under Domitian; the third, under Trajan; fourth, under Marcus Aurelius; fifth, under Severus; sixth, under Maximin; seventh, under Decius and Gallus; eighth, under Valerian; ninth, under Claudius and Aurelian; and the tenth, under Diocletian and Maximian. The date of the last was A.D. 303.

private individual. Thus, Constantine the Great called the church he built at Jerusalem a "Martyrium," as being a monument or witness of his good feelings towards the Christian people (Riddle, *Christian Antiquities*, p. 704).

PRESENT CUSTOMS.

When peace was restored to the Church the custom of saying Mass on the tombs of the martyrs gradually died away and gave place to the present discipline of depositing some portions of the martyrs' bodies in the newly-consecrated altars. Hence the import of that prayer now said by the priest as he lays his hands on the sacred table at the beginning of Mass: "We pray thee, O Lord! through the merits of thy saints whose relics are here placed, and of all the saints, that thou wouldst vouchsafe to forgive me all my sins."

The relics of the martyrs are placed in the altar by the bishop who consecrates it; and, in order to verify the words of the above prayer, it is required that a plurality be inserted. It is customary to enclose with the martyrs' relics some also of the saint to whose name the church is dedicated. Hereupon it is well to remark that a portion of the saint's or martyr's dress is not enough; the relic must be a part of the body (S. R. C., April 13, 1867, N. 5379; De Herdt, i. No. 178). Liturgical writers tell us that it was Pope Felix (third century) who first enjoined this practice (Merati, *Thesaur. Rit.*, 115). The holy relics, before being deposited in the altar, are first enclosed in a little case made of silver or other metal, and have generally accompanying them the names of the saints whose relics they are, and the name of the bishop who deposited them (Martinucci, vii. 306; Catalanus, *Pontif. Roman.*, iii. 403). They are deposited with these words: "Under the altar of God ye saints of God have received a place; intercede for us with our Lord Jesus Christ."

HOLY EUCHARIST DEPOSITED IN PLACE OF RELICS.

A very singular custom prevailed at one time in many places of depositing the Sacred Host in the altar when no relics could be obtained. Durandus, Bishop of Mende, who died and was buried at Rome in 1296, says in his *Rationale Divinorum*, p. 54, that when genuine relics cannot be had the altar must not be consecrated without the Holy Eucharist. The same custom was once very prevalent in England while that country was Catholic. This we learn, among other sources, from the Council of Calcuith, held in A.D. 816, where the following enactment was made: "When a church is built let it be hallowed by the bishop of the diocese; afterwards let the Eucharist which the bishop consecrates at that Mass be laid up, together with the relics contained in the little box, and kept in the same basilica; but if he cannot find any other relics, then will the Eucharist, most of all, serve the purpose, for it is the Body and Blood of our Lord Jesus Christ" (*Church of Our Fathers*, vol. i. p. 41, note). This custom lasted in England up to the fifteenth century (*ibid.*) Three particles of incense, as is also the rule now, used to be enclosed in the little box where the relics were deposited (*ibid.* 42).

Another custom that prevailed in certain places was to enclose with the regular relics portions of the instruments employed in torturing the martyrs, as well as documents of high veneration. From a record of St. Paul's Church, London, in 1295, we find that its jasper altar had deposited in it, besides the relics of SS. Philip and Andrew and those of SS. Denis and Blasius, a relic also of the veritable cross upon which St. Andrew was crucified (*ibid.* 254).

LETTER OF THE BLESSED VIRGIN ENCLOSED.

At Messina, in Sicily, there is said to be an altar in which is enclosed, as a most precious relic, a letter written by the Mother of God herself. The history of this curious letter is as follows: Tradition has it that the Messinese received the faith direct from the Prince of the Apostles himself during his Roman Pontificate. Their cathedral is one of the most august in Europe, and the most venerable by reason of its great antiquity, for it was founded in A.D. 1197. In the year A.D. 42, as the legend goes, St. Paul visited Messina, and having found the people there well disposed, and eager to hear the word of God from his lips, he preached them two sermons, one on our Lord's Passion, the other on the perpetual virginity of our Blessed Lady. This latter had such a telling effect upon the inhabitants that they cried out with one acclaim, "Our city must be placed under the protection of the Virgin Mother." The story goes on to say that an embassy, at the head of which was St. Paul himself, was sent to Jerusalem, where the Mother of God was then living, and that as soon as the Blessed Virgin received the embassy she sent a reply to the Messinese in Hebrew, stating that she was willing to accede to their pious wishes. This letter was afterwards done into Greek by St. Paul, and deposited in the ancient church of Messina, whence in course of time it was removed to its present place in the altar of the cathedral church. The following is a copy of this singular document:

"Mary, Virgin, daughter of Joachim, most lowly handmaid of God, Mother of the Crucified Jesus Christ, of the tribe of Juda, from the race of David, to all the people of Messina salutation and blessing from God the Father Almighty. It is certified by public documents that all of you have, in great faith, sent emissaries and ambassadors to us. Led to know the way of the truth through the preaching of Paul the Apostle, ye confess that our Son, the Only-Begotten of God, is both God and man, and that he ascended into heaven after his resurrection. For this reason we, therefore, bless ye and your city, whose perpetual Protectress we desire to become.—Year of our Son 42; Indiction I.; iii. nones of June; xxvii. of the moon; feria v. from Jerusalem. MARY, Virgin, who hath approved the handwriting above" (*Catholic Italy*, by Hemans, vol. ii. p. 511).

To establish the genuineness of this letter the learned Jesuit, Father Melchior Inchofer, wrote a very learned Latin work, entitled *Epistolæ B. Virginis Mariæ ad Messinenses Veritas vindicata*—"The truth of the Epistle of the Blessed Virgin Mary to the people of Messina vindicated."[3]

RELICS OF THE ORIENTALS.

The Orientals agree with us also in the discipline regarding sacred relics. These, with the Eastern churches, are often placed under the altar in a little box, and are held in the greatest veneration by the people. According to the Ritual of Russia,[2] this little box is only placed there when the archbishop consecrates the church in person and not by deputy (Romanoff, 84). Without these relics the Nestorian Rituals forbid any altar whatever to be consecrated (Smith and Dwight, *Travels in Armenia*, ii. 236).

---

[2] The Russian Church uses the same liturgies and ceremonies as the Greek Church, but the language of the Mass is Slavonic. There are, of course, a few other differences of minor note.

[3] By order of the Sacred Congregation of the Index the word *truth*, as herein applied, was afterwards changed into *conjecture*.

CHAPTER XI.

CRUCIFIXES AND CROSSES.

CRUCIFIXES.

ACCORDING to the best liturgical writers, the custom of placing the Crucifix—that is, a cross with the image of our Lord crucified upon it—has been derived from the Apostles themselves. Mention is made of it by all the early Fathers, and, as we shall see a little further on, it has always been used by the Orientals (Bouvry, ii. 225 ; Kozma, 33). It is intended to remind all that in the Holy Sacrifice of the Mass the same Victim is offered which was offered on Calvary, but in an unbloody manner. "The Church omits nothing," says Pope Benedict XIV., "to impress upon the minds of the priest and people that the Sacrifice of the altar and that of the Cross are the same" (Bouvry, ii. 22, note).

Whenever there is an exposition of the Blessed Sacrament it is recommended to take away the Crucifix as long as the reality is present ; but, if this cannot be conveniently done, it is not insisted upon. In fact, every church is allowed to follow its own custom in this respect (De Herdt, i. 181).

DIFFERENT KINDS OF CROSSES.

While on the subject of Crosses we deem it well to mention the different kinds, as erroneous notions are prevalent about some of them. There are usually enumerated six different kinds of Crosses—viz.: 1st. The Latin Cross, where the transverse beam cuts the upright shaft near the top. 2d. The Greek Cross, where two equal beams cut each other in the middle. 3d. The Cross commonly known as St. Andrew's, because the saint was crucified on it; it resembles the letter X. 4th. The Egyptian, or St. Anthony's Cross, shaped like the letter T. 5th. The Maltese Cross, so called because worn by the Knights of Malta, formed of four equilateral triangles, whose apices meet in one common point. 6th. The Russian Cross, having two transverse beams at the head, and one near the foot of the upright shaft, slightly inclined, to favor a tradition of long standing with the Russians—viz., that when our Lord hung on the Cross one of his feet was lifted a little higher than the other (Coxe, *Travels in Russia*, p. 593).

Triple Cross.—A Cross with three transverse bars or transoms is generally denominated the Papal Cross; but this is nothing more than pure imagination, for no such Cross ever existed among papal insignia, and it exists nowhere to-day. When the Holy Father moves in procession nothing but the simplest kind of Cross—viz., that with one transverse beam—is carried before him, and it is well known that he never uses a bishop's crook, or crosier, as it is called. A triple Cross, therefore, is a misconception, invented by painters, but never authorized by the Church.

Double Cross.—The double Cross, or that with two transverse beams at the head, one a little longer than the other, owes its origin evidently to the fact that upon the true Cross whereon our Lord suffered a board was placed above the head with the inscription in Hebrew, in Greek, and in Latin, "Jesus of Nazareth, King of the Jews." This board is represented by one transom; and that on which our Lord's head rested, and to which his hands were nailed, forms the second, and hence the so-called double Cross.

Archiepiscopal Cross.—We are entirely at a loss to know how this double Cross came to be an archiepiscopal ensign. Neither the *Cæremoniale Episcoporum* nor the *Pontificale Romanum* gives a word to distinguish it from any other; nor is it spoken of by any liturgical writer of our acquaintance, and there are few whose works we have not perused. It cannot be denied, however, that such Crosses are in use, and that they were formerly in vogue in certain places, particularly with the English prelates. It is generally supposed that they found their way into England from the East in the time of the Crusades. It is supposed, too, that his lordship Anthony Beck, Bishop of Durham, whom Pope Clement V., in 1305, created patriarch of Jerusalem, had something to do with their introduction, for they were very common with the Greeks (Dr. Rock, *Church of Our Fathers*, vol. ii. pp. 218–223). It may interest the reader to know that the only two prelates in the Church who are mentioned by name as having a peculiar right to the double Cross are the Patriarch of Venice[1] and the Archbishop of Agria, in Hungary (Kozma, 73, note 3).

Jansenistic Crosses.—Crosses in which the arms of our Lord are but partly extended are called *Jansenistic*, from Cornelius Jansens, Bishop of Ipres, or Ypres, in Belgium, A.D. 1635, who maintained the heretical doctrine that Christ died not for all mankind but only for the *good*. To conform with the true doctrine that Christ died for all, a regular Catholic Crucifix would represent our Lord's arms fully extended.

---

[1] Although the term patriarch is now nothing more than a mere honorary title, still it is well for the reader know that there are twelve such dignitaries in the Catholic Church to-day—viz., the patriarchs of Constantinople, of Alexandria, of Antioch of the Maronites, of Antioch of the Melchites, of Antioch of the Syrians, of Antioch of the Latins, of Jerusalem, of Babylon, of the Indies, of Lisbon, of Cilicia, and of Venice (*Gerarchia Cattolica*, 1873).

NUMBER OF NAILS BY WHICH OUR LORD WAS FASTENED TO THE CROSS.

It is commonly supposed that our Lord's feet were separately nailed to the Cross, and not placed one over the other and fastened by a single nail, as is the tradition in the Greek Church. Pope Benedict XIV., commenting on this point, pertinently remarks that it would be almost impossible to avoid breaking some of the bones of the feet if one rested on the other and a nail were driven through both. There would be danger in that case of making void the Scriptural saying to the effect that not a bone of our Saviour was to be broken.

Before the twelfth century the paintings representing the Crucifixion always exhibited our Lord's feet nailed separately; and, therefore, four nails instead of three were the entire number that fastened him to the cross. St. Gregory of Tours and Durandus speak of four nails, but the latter writer also alludes to three without saying which number he himself inclines to (*Rationale Divinorum*, p. 537). From time immemorial the Latin Church has kept to the tradition that four nails were employed, and not three, and she represents our Lord as thus crucified (see *Notes, Ecclesiological and Historical, on the Holydays of the English Church*, p. 172).

It is commonly believed that one of the nails of the Crucifixion is kept yet in the Church of the Holy Cross at Rome, and that the cathedrals of Paris, Treves, and Toul have the others. When St. Helena first discovered them it is said that she attached one to the helmet of her son, Constantine the Great, and another to the bridle of his horse. Tradition has it that she threw a third into the Adriatic Sea to appease a storm. The crown of Italy contains a portion of one of these nails, and filings from them are kept as precious relics in many churches of Europe (*The Sacramentals*, by Rev. W. J. Barry).

THE PRACTICE OF THE ORIENTAL CHURCH REGARDING THE CRUCIFIX.

The Oriental disciplinary canons regarding the sacred symbol of salvation are very strict. No service must take place without having the Cross prominent. There is one placed on the altar for the people to kiss the moment they enter the church. It may be seen in all the principal streets of Eastern cities, especially within the Russian dominions, and there is hardly a private house in which the Crucifix and an image of our Blessed Lady, with a lamp burning before them, are not prominently in view (see Porter's *Travels*, p. 54; Romanoff, *Greco-Russian Church*, pp. 84 and 93).

The Armenians have an extraordinary reverence for the Cross. Before they apply it to use it is first consecrated with much ceremony. To this end it is washed in wine and water, in imitation of the blood and water which flowed from our Saviour's side, and is then anointed with the sacred oil, or *meiron*, in token of the Holy Spirit who descended upon him. Following this, several passages from the Psalms, the Prophets, and from the Epistles and Gospels are recited; after which the priest sends up a prayer of invocation that God may give to this Cross the power of casting out devils, of healing diseases, and of appeasing the wrath that visits us on account of our sins. A Cross when thus consecrated is called by the Armenians the "Throne of Christ," his "Chariot," his "Weapon for the conquest of Satan" (Smith and Dwight, *Researches in Armenia*, vol. i. pp. 157, 158).

The Nestorians, also, have a singular reverence for it. In order that they may enter the house of God filled with holy recollections, it stands at the very threshold of all their churches (Badger, *Nestorians and their Rituals*, ii. 135), and not unfrequently is it worn with the prints of their kisses. The two authors just quoted inform us that the first act a Nestorian Christian performs upon entering the church, and before he takes his seat, is to doff his shoes and pay his obeisance to the Cross, which stands on a side altar, by humbly approaching and kissing it (ii. p. 210). One of the greatest festivals in the Nestorian calendar is "Holy-Cross Day," which is celebrated with great pomp on the 13th of November. As the Rev. Mr. Badger admits, volumes might be written about the veneration paid the Cross by the Nestorians, heretics though they be.

Nor are the Copts[2] behindhand in this sacred duty. Their reverence for it is so great that, in order to have it always before their eyes, they inscribe it on their arms by a process of tattooing; and when any one asks them whether they are Christians or not, the arm thus tattooed is at once displayed in testimony of their belief (Pococke, *Travels in Egypt*, p. 370).

Protestant missionaries to the East would do well to resume their reverence for the sacred symbol of salvation. As long as they reject it from their service, and ridicule the pious veneration paid to it East and West, their proselytes will be very few. In many parts of the Orient they are looked upon as heathens on this account alone. The authors above cited are forced to make open confession of this fact.

[2] In speaking of the Eastern Christians throughout this work we have not deemed it necessary, unless in a few particular cases, to specify their doctrinal tenets. As far as ceremonies and liturgical customs are concerned, there exists hardly any difference between the orthodox and the heterodox. It is well that the reader should bear this carefully in mind, as it will serve as a key to many a difficulty.

CHAPTER XII.

LIGHTS.

ALONGSIDE the crucifix there are placed on every altar for the celebration of Mass two candlesticks with candles of pure wax burning in them during the entire time of divine service. At Solemn High Mass the rule requires at least six. At a Low Mass celebrated by a bishop it is customary to light four. An ordinary priest can never employ more than two. When the Holy Father celebrates High Mass the candles used are always ornamented (Martinucci, ii. p. 31, note).

The rule requiring the candles to be of pure wax is very stringent, and dispensations from its observance are rarely granted unless in difficult circumstances. The Catholic missionaries in some parts of the empire of China and throughout Hindostan have, when pressed by necessity, been allowed by the Holy See to use oil instead of candles. Sperm candles and those known as *paraffine* are wholly interdicted, unless in case of churches whose poverty is so great that none others can be purchased. Besides the natural reason for prohibiting the use of any lights but those of pure wax—viz., because those of any other material usually emit an offensive odor—there are many spiritual or mystical reasons also, the principal of which is that the pure wax symbolizes our Lord's humanity, which was stainless and sinless; and the light his *divinity*, which always shone forth and illuminated his every action.

ANTIQUITY OF LIGHTS UPON THE ALTAR.

It is an opinion which it would be rash to differ from that the use of lights at the celebration of Mass is of apostolic origin. Cardinal Bona and all liturgists of note strongly maintain this, and many passages of the New Testament seem to warrant it (Bona, *Rer. Liturg.*, pp. 206-294).

MYSTIC SIGNIFICATION OF LIGHTS.

There are many mystic significations, besides the one we have mentioned, to be found in the use of lights at Mass. In the first place, they represent our Divine Lord's mission upon earth in a very striking and happy manner. He is called by the Prophet Isaias "a great Light," who also says that "to them who dwelt in the region of the shadow of death a Light is risen" (chap. ix. 2). The same prophet calls him the "Light of Jehovah," and calls upon Jerusalem to arise and be enlightened by him. When the aged Simeon first saw him and held him in his arms in the Temple, he designated him as "a Light to the revelation of the Gentiles" (*Luke* ii. 32). He calls himself *the Light of the world:* "I am the Light of the world" (*John* viii.); and St. John describes him as "the true Light which enlighteneth every man coming into this world." The Rabbis also had this idea of our Divine Lord, or the "great Expected of nations," as he was called, for they looked to him as the Light of God who was to guide them in the way of peace (*Essays on the Names and Titles of Jesus Christ*, p. 216, by Ambrose Serle; London, 1837). Then, again, his teaching is aptly compared to a light; for as the latter dispels physical darkness, which hides all the beauties of nature from our gaze, so the former dispels all the darkness of the soul and enables it to see what is beautiful and true and good in the spiritual order. "Thy word is a lamp to my feet," says the royal Psalmist, "and a light to my paths" (*Ps.* cxviii.) But more especially is the word of the holy Gospel this lamp and light, for which reason, when it is chanted in the Mass, the Church wisely ordains that lights should accompany it in solemn procession. "Whenever the Gospel is read," says St. Jerome, writing to Vigilantius, "lights are produced; not, indeed, to banish darkness, but to demonstrate a sign of joy, that under the type of a corporal light that light may be manifested of which we read in the Psalmist: 'Thy word, O Lord, is a lamp to my feet and a light to my paths'" (*Hierurgia*, p. 401).

Lights in the Old Law.—The use of lights in the Jewish ceremonial is so well authenticated that we need not stay to prove it. The Holy Scriptures themselves attest it. Nor need we dwell particularly on the seven-branched candlestick which God himself ordered to be made and to be kept filled with oil, in order that it may burn always (see *Exod*. xxv. and xxvii. 20), for it is not certain whether this candlestick gave light also during the day. If it did not it would not help our purpose much to cite it as an example. Josephus, however, who is a very reliable authority in this matter, distinctly says that three of its lamps burned also in the daytime (*Antiquities of the Jews*, book iii. chap. viii. 3); and in his account of the building of the Temple by Hiram of Tyre he says that ten thousand candlesticks were made, one of which was specially dedicated for the sacred edifice itself, "that it might burn in the day-time, according to law" (book viii. chap. iii. 7).

LIGHTS GIVEN THE NEWLY-BAPTIZED.

One of the most impressive ceremonies of the entire rite of holy baptism is witnessed at that place where the priest puts into the hand of the newly-baptized a lighted candle, with the following solemn admonition: "Receive this burning light, and preserve your baptism blamelessly: keep the commandments of God, in order that when the Lord shall come to the marriage-feast you may run to meet him with all the saints in his celestial palace, and may have life everlasting and live for ever and ever. Amen."

LIGHTS AS MARKS OF RESPECT.

Lights are significant of great respect, and hence they were used on occasions of great moment. The Athenians employed them on the feasts of Minerva, Vulcan, and Prometheus, and the Romans used them on all their solemn days (*Notes and Illustrations on the Reasons of the Law of Moses*, by Rabbi Maimonides, p. 411). Out of the great respect that the Jews had for the garments of their highpriest, a light was kept constantly burning before them as long as they remained deposited in the tower called "Antonia" at Jerusalem (Josephus, *Antiq. of the Jews*, book xviii. chap. iv. 3). The grand lama, or sovereign pontiff, of Tartary is never seen in his palace without having a profusion of lamps and torches burning around him (Burder, *Relig. Customs and Ceremonies*), and it is a well-known fact that a certain European dignitary—a son of one of the crowned heads—upon occasion of his visit to this country some years ago, refused to sit down in the apartments assigned him in one of our fashionable hotels until two wax candles had been brought and lighted before him. This etiquette is very common in the East (see *Religious Ceremonies and Customs*, by Burder, p. 502 and passim).

Lights at Funerals and Graves.—Eusebius gives a glowing account of the profusion of lights used at the funeral obsequies of Constantine the Great, who died A.D. 337, and St. Jerome speaks of the quantity used at the burial of the pious St. Paula. When the body of St. John Chrysostom was conveyed from Comana to Constantinople vast crowds of people came to meet the *cortége* in ships on the Bo.-

phorus, and so numerous were the lights that burned on the occasion that the whole sea appeared as if ablaze (*Hierurgia*, p. 403). Lights were kept constantly burning in Westminster Abbey, London, before England's great heroes, and the old story of lamps being found burning in sepulchres after the lapse of ages clearly shows how important it was considered by the ancients to show this mark of respect to the dead.

LIGHTS AT SOLEMN HIGH MASS.

Besides the regular lights placed upon the altar at the beginning of Mass, others are brought out by acolytes at the approach of consecration, and are kept burning as long as our Divine Lord is present on the altar—that is, until after the Communion.

Oriental Practice in this Respect.—The discipline of the Oriental Church and ours is in perfect agreement on this point, as every one can testify who has ever travelled in the East or looked into any of the Oriental Liturgies. The Copts on no account will say Mass without two candles at least. "Liturgia non celebretur," says one of their canons, "absque cereis duobus majoribus aut minoribus qui altare luceant"—that is, "Let not the Liturgy be celebrated without two large wax candles or two small ones to burn on the altar" (Renaudot, *Liturg. Orient. Col.*, i. p. 179). The rest of the Oriental churches are equally strict in their observance of this practice.

We have designedly dwelt on this subject in order to show that Protestants have no grounds whatever for saying that our practice of burning lights in the open day is *ridiculous, and without any meaning or precedent to justify it.*

CHAPTER XIII.

THE TABERNACLE.

The small structure in the centre of the altar, resembling a church in appearance, is called the Tabernacle of the Blessed Sacrament. It is here that the Holy Eucharist is always reserved under lock and key; and so particular is the Church about the respect that should be paid it that the most minute directions are given regarding its exterior and interior ornamentation. In shape it may be square, hexagonal, heptagonal, or any other becoming form; but it must not be crowned with any profane devices, or be made so as to suggest anything else than the sacred purpose for which it is intended; hence, as far as can be, a cross should surmount its top, and its outside, if means admit, should be finished in gold. As wood is less liable to contract dampness than any other material, it is advisable to have the Tabernacle made of it; but if made of marble, metal, or any kind of stone, its inside at least should be lined with wood out of reverence for the Blessed Sacrament. No matter what its material be, the interior must always be covered over with silk, and a clean corporal must lie under the vessel in which the Blessed Sacrament is enclosed.

It is strictly forbidden to make the Tabernacle a base for anything to rest on, even though the thing were a reliquary containing a portion of the true cross or a relic of the greatest saint in heaven; and it is forbidden, too, to have any drawers over or under it for the purpose of keeping the holy oils or any utensils belonging to the altar or sanctuary. Upon no consideration can any empty vessels be kept within it, such as the chalice, ciborium, lunette, monstrance, or the like. Nothing, in fact, is allowed there but the sacred vessel containing the Blessed Sacrament; and if for any reason this should not be there, the door should be always open, in order that the people may not be deceived.

The Tabernacle should have two keys, made of gold or silver, or at least gilt, one of which should be kept by the pastor himself, the other by one of his priests.

A lamp fed with pure olive-oil must burn before it perpetually—a discipline which, as we have seen, prevails also in the Oriental Church, and by which we are reminded of the "perpetual fire" of Solomon's Temple, and of that sacred mystic fire of divine charity with which our Lord's heart ever burns in the adorable Sacrament of the Altar.

CHAPTER XIV.

THE MISSAL.

THE Missal is the next thing that claims our consideration. It is a large book in folio, printed in Latin in red and black letters, and containing all the Masses that are to be said throughout the year. It begins with the first Sunday of Advent.[1] The portions printed throughout in red letters are termed the *rubrics*.[2] They give the directions by which a priest is to be guided in performing the various actions of the Mass. Attached to the Missal are five large ribbons, or book-marks, corresponding in color to the five colors used in the sacred vestments. It is customary to mark the Mass of the day with the ribbon that suits it in color. That part of the Missal called the "Canon" has slips of leather attached to its leaves for the greater convenience of the priest.

---

[1] The First Sunday of Advent has no fixed date. According to the present discipline, it is always the nearest Sunday to St Andrew's Feast (November 30), whether before or after it. In case this feast should fall on a Sunday it is transferred to some other day, and that Sunday is the first of Advent. The old rule for finding Advent Sunday was thus expressed :

"Saint Andrew the king
Three weeks and three days before Christmas comes in ;
Three days after, or three days before,
Advent Sunday knocks at the door."

[2] The word *rubric*, which comes from the Latin *ruber*, red, was first applied by the ancient Romans to a species of red chalk with which they marked the titles of their books and statutes ; in process of time the red writing itself received the name, and in this way has it descended to us. What the Romans called *rubrica* the Greeks called *miltos*. The latter used it in painting their ships (Homer, *Iliad*, ix. 125).

MISSAL STAND.

Although the rubric calls for a cushion to support the Missal, general custom justifies the use of a regular book-stand for this purpose. The precise symbolism of the cushion is this : it denotes the tender hearts of the true hearers of the word of God, and not the hard hearts such as were manifested for it by the Jews (Gavantus, 116).

ANCIENT MISSALS.

Who the author of the first Missal was it is not easy to determine. Some are of opinion that it was St. James the Apostle,[a] first Bishop of Jerusalem, and that he composed it in the Cenacle of Sion (Kozma, 97; Renaudot, *Dissert. de Liturg. Orient. Origine et Auctoritate*, vol. i.) Be this so or not, all are agreed that the Liturgy which bears the name of this Apostle is the most ancient in existence. It was committed to writing about A.D. 200.

Following closely upon the apostolic age we find no less than four special books employed in the service of the altar —viz., an Antiphonary, an Evangeliary, a Lectionary, and a Sacramentary. The Antiphonary contained all that was to be sung by the choir and sacred ministers. It was some-

---

[a] There were two apostles who bore the name of James. One, called James the Greater from his seniority in age, was the son of Zebedee and Mary (surnamed Salome). The other, called James the Less, also the *Just* from his great sanctity, and "Brother of the Lord" because allied to him as cousin-german, was the son of Alphæus and Mary (sister of the Blessed Virgin). He was appointed Bishop of Jerusalem soon after our Lord's ascension, where he met death at the hands of the Jews by being cast from the battlements of the Temple and then despatched with a blow from a fuller's club. According to Josephus, he was esteemed so holy a man that it was generally believed the final overthrow and destruction of Jerusalem was a divine visitation in punishment for his cruel death. He is the author of the Catholic Epistle which goes by his name.

thing like our modern gradual. The Evangeliary contained the series of Gospels for the Sundays and festivals of the year. In the Lectionary were to be found all the lessons that were read in the Mass from the Old and New Testaments; and whatever the priest himself had to recite, such as the Collects, Secrets, Preface, Canon, etc., was found in the Sacramentary.

The authorship of these four volumes is yet an unsettled question. John the Deacon (l. 2, c. 6), who wrote the life of Pope St. Gregory the Great, tells us that he saw with his own eyes the Antiphonary which was composed by that pontiff; but whether we are to consider this as the first written, or only as a new edition of the first, the writer does not state. Many, however, are of opinion that this really was the first written, so that Pope Gregory may be considered its true author (Kozma, 99, note; Gavantus, 5).

Of the Lectionary we find mention made as far back as the middle of the third century, for St. Hippolytus, Bishop of Porto, in Italy, alludes to it in his so-called *Paschal Canon* (Kozma, *ibid.*) Its precise author is unknown. Towards the end of the fourth century it underwent a thorough revision at the hands of St. Jerome, who was specially appointed for the task by His Holiness Pope St. Damasus. The Epistles and Gospels to be read throughout the year were inserted in it, after much care had been expended in assigning to the different Sundays and festivals the particular lessons that were best suited to them. This codex is sometimes called the Hieronymian Lectionary, from St. Jerome (*Hieronymus* in Greek), its compiler; and it is from it that the series of Epistles and Gospels in our present Missal has been taken (Kozma, 177, note; Gavantus, *Thesaur. Sacr. Rit.*, 5).

The authorship of the Evangeliary is still unsettled. Mention is often made of it by ancient writers, yet little attempt has been made at discovering its precise author, and this principally on account of its great antiquity.

Regarding the Sacramentary, called also the Book of the Mysteries, much dispute has been raised. Although generally ascribed to Pope Leo the Great (fifth century), and called *Leonine* from him, yet some of the ablest liturgical writers deny it to be his composition. Besides this so-called Leonine Sacramentary, two others appeared in course of time : one edited by Pope Gelasius, the other by Pope Gregory the Great. The Gelasian was, to all intents and purposes, a recast of the Leonine, and the Gregorian was formed from them both. Whenever allusion is now made to a Sacramentary, that issued under the appellation of the *Gregorian* is always understood, for it was more complete than any other (Kozma, p. 99, note 9).

As it was oftentimes very embarrassing for a priest, especially if celebrating Low Mass, to have to turn from one to another of these four volumes whenever he wanted to read a particular prayer or lesson, the necessity of having one book in which the matter of all the four would be combined was soon felt, and this led to the subsequent introduction of what were termed Plenary Missals. Although Missals of this kind were in use long before the Council of Trent (1545 to 1563), still, inasmuch as they received greater perfection in being remodelled by a special decree of the Fathers of this august assembly, their origin is generally ascribed to it. The Sacramentary of Pope Gregory the Great was the norma employed in preparing the new Plenary Missal. The task, first taken in hand by Pope Pius IV., was brought to a termination by his successor, Pius V., who in 1570 produced a new Missal and issued a bull enjoining its observance on all. This is the Mass-Book that we use to-day (Kozma, p. 101, note 3).

Of course the reader must not suppose that any change

of a substantial nature was made in the Ordinary of the Mass when preparing this new edition of the Missal. All that Pope Pius V. did was to reduce it to a better form and expunge those errors and interpolations from it which were introduced about the period of the Reformation. He did, it is true, make some things obligatory which it had been customary to say or omit at pleasure before his time, such as the Psalm "Judica me, Deus," at the beginning of Mass, and the Gospel of St. John at the end; but this was all. The rest of his emendations principally concerned certain rubrical observances which affected in no way the norma of the Mass.

MISSALS OF THE ORIENTALS.

The Orientals use many more books in the service of the altar than we. The Greeks alone employ as many as eighteen, the principal of which are the following: 1, the *Euchology*, which contains the three Liturgies used by all who follow the Greek Rite—viz., the Liturgy of St. Chrysostom, that of St. Basil, and the Liturgy of the Presanctified; 2, the *Praxapostolos*, so called from its containing the Acts of the Apostles and their Epistles; 3, the *Anagnoseis*, or book containing the lessons read from the Old Testament; 4, the *Panegyricon*, or collection of sermons for the various festivals of the year (this book is generally in manuscript).

As Dr. Neale very justly remarks in his *History of the Holy Eastern Church*, vol. ii. p. 819, it is next to impossible to get any clear idea of the books used by the Oriental Church in the service of the altar. Their number is interminable, and there is nothing but confusion in their service, on account of the constant turning backward and forward from one book to another in order to find the particular portion to be read. Add to all this that there is no such thing known with them as a *translation* of a feast; and hence when an occurrence[4] of feasts happens all are celebrated together, with a jumble of rubrics which it is impossible to describe. The *Typicon*, or Ordo, for the feast of St. George, for example, fills about ten pages of a quarto volume, and this on account of all the other feasts that occur with it or fall on the same day.

NESTORIAN MISSALS.

The Nestorians also employ a vast number of service-books, but they do not trouble themselves much about rubrics. In the first place, they have what is termed the *Euanghelion*, or book of the Gospels. This they read at every Mass. Second, the *Sliho* (in Syriac, ܫܠܝܚܐ), or book of Epistles, containing nothing but extracts from the Epistles of St. Paul. Third, the *Karyane* (Syriac, ܩܪܝܢܐ =*koruzo*, a preacher, hence the word *Koran*), which contains extracts from the Old Testament and from the Acts of the Apostles. Fourth, the *Turgama* (Syriac, ܬܘܪܓܡܐ =*turgmo*, interpretation, whence Targum), consisting of a variety of hymns chanted responsively around the altar by the deacons before the Epistle and Gospel, calling upon the people to give ear to the words of the New Testament.

The Karyane is read by the Karoya, or lector, at the altar door, on the south side; the Sliho, on the north side, by the subdeacon; the celebrant himself reads the Euanghelion at the middle of the altar. During the reading of all these the sacred ministers are facing the congregation. In case a Shammasha, or full deacon, is present the onus of reading the Gospel devolves on him. The pulpit in which

---

[4] In liturgical language, when two or more feasts fall on the same day there is said to be an *occurrence* of feasts; when one feast meets another only at Vespers it is said to constitute a *concurrence*. It is well to bear in mind that the ecclesiastical day always begins in the evening and ends the evening following.

the Nestorians formerly read the Sliho was denominated Gagolta (same as Golgotha, the name of Mount Calvary), from the steps by which it was ascended.

The Chaldeans⁶ use the same books in divine service, with little difference, as the Nestorians (Badger, *Nestorians and their Rituals*, vol. ii. p. 19). This difference touches, of course, the Nestorian heresy of holding that there are two Persons in our Divine Saviour instead of one.

COPTIC MISSAL.

All that we know of the Coptic Missal is that it is printed throughout in the ancient Coptic language, and that its rubrics are in the native Arabic, the language spoken by the people; for, as Dr. Neale very justly remarks, hardly three persons can be found in all Cairo (the headquarters of the Copts) who can speak the Coptic of the Missal, not excepting even the clergy, and hence the necessity of having the rubrics printed in the vernacular.

---

[b] The name *Chaldean* is generally used in the East as the distinctive appellation of all who join our communion from Nestorianism. The Chaldean Catholics, as we have said in another place, are governed by a patriarch with the title of "Patriarch of Babylon of the Chaldean Rite." This prelate generally resides at Bagdad.

CHAPTER XV.

BELLS.

THE use of bells in divine service is very ancient. We find mention made of them in the books of Exodus and Ecclesiasticus, where they are enumerated among the ornaments of the high-priest's ephod, in order that "their sound might be heard whenever he goeth in and cometh out of the sanctuary." (We have stated in another place that this ancient custom of attaching little bells to the fringes of the priestly garments is yet very common in the Eastern Church.) Besides these little bells the ancient Hebrews employed others of a larger kind, called *Megeruphita*, which used to be sounded by the Levites on certain occasions. Of these the Mishna [1] says that when they were struck their noise was so deafening that you could not hear a person speak in all Jerusalem. They were sounded principally for three purposes : First, to summon the priests to service ; secondly, to summon the choir of Levites to sing ; thirdly, to invite the stationary-men to bring the unclean to the gate called Nicanor (Bannister, *Temples of the Hebrews,* p. 101). The Mishna further states that when these megeruphita were sounded to their full capacity they could be heard at Jericho, eighteen miles from Jerusalem.

For the first three or four centuries of the Christian

---

[1] The Mishna, or oral law of the Jews, consists of various traditions respecting the law of Moses. The Mishna and Gemara (or commentary on the Mishna) form what is called the Talmud, of which there are two kinds—viz., that of Jerusalem and that of Babylon. The latter is held to be the greater of the two.

Church's existence the faithful were compelled to assemble at divine service with as little noise as possible, for fear of attracting the attention of their pagan enemies, and thus bringing about fresh persecution ; hence we must not expect to find bells in use during those days.

According to Polydore Virgil it was Pope Sabinian (seventh century), the immediate successor of Pope Gregory the Great, who first introduced the practice of ringing bells at Mass (Bona, *Rer. Liturg.*, 259). The same thing is corroborated by Onuphrius Panvinius, who, when writing of this pontiff, says : " Hic Papa campanarum usum invenit, jussitque ut ad horas canonicas, et Missarum sacrificia pulsarentur in ecclesia "—that is, " This pontiff introduced the use of bells, and ordained that they be rung in the church at the canonical hours and during the Sacrifice of the Mass." The usual ascription of the introduction of bells to St. Paulinus of Nola stands upon little or no foundation.

The name *campanæ*, sometimes given to bells, from Campana, in Italy, where large quantities of them were made, generally denotes the larger kind, and *nolæ* (also from an Italian town) the smaller kind. Small bells went generally by the name of *tintinnabula*, from their peculiar tinkling sound.

ANCIENT SUBSTITUTE FOR BELLS.

Before the use of bells had become general in the Church it was customary to employ in their stead signal or sounding boards, called *semantrons*, which used to be struck with a mallet of hard wood. These are yet in use in most of the Oriental churches, especially in those within the Turkish dominions ; for it is the belief of the followers of the Koran that the ringing of regular bells disquiets the souls of the departed dead. Hence it is considered a great privilege in the East, wherever Mahometanism prevails, to be allowed the use of bells in divine service, and but few churches enjoy it. Ali Pasha, in order to conciliate his Christian subjects and win their esteem, granted the privilege to the churches of Joannina, capital of Albania (Neale, *Holy Eastern Church*, i. p. 216). They were also allowed at Argentiera, or Khimoli, in the Archipelago (*ibid.*) ; and of late their use was extended to the Church of the Holy Sepulchre at Jerusalem, where the sound of a bell had not been heard since the time of the Crusades.

Of the semantrons there were two kinds, one made of wood, the other of iron. The former consisted for the most part of a long piece of hard, well-planed timber, usually of the heart of maple, of from ten to twelve feet in length, a foot and a half in breadth, and about nine inches thick. In the centre of this piece of wood was a catch in which to insert the hand while striking with the mallet. Persons who have heard these semantrons assure us that the noise they make when struck by this mallet is perfectly deafening. The sound emitted by the semantrons called *hagiosidera* (because made of iron) is generally very musical, and consequently less grating on the ear than that produced by those made of wood. These hagiosidera are generally shaped like a crescent, and their sound differs little from that of a Chinese gong. They are much in use in the East.

With the Syrians the semantron is held in the greatest veneration, for the reason that a tradition of long standing among them ascribes its invention to Noe, who, according to them, was thus addressed by Almighty God on the eve of the building of the ark : " Make for yourself a bell of boxwood, which is not liable to corruption, three cubits long and one and a half wide, and also a mallet from the same wood. Strike this instrument three separate times every day : once in the morning to summon the hands to the ark, once at midday to call them to dinner, and once in the evening to invite them to rest." The Syrians strike their semantrons when the Divine Office is going to begin and when it is time to summon the people to public prayer (Lamy, *De Fide Syrorum et Discip. in re Eucharistiæ*). The peculiar symbolism attached to this "Holy Wood," as the semantron is often denominated, is, to say the least, very significant and touching. The sound of the wood, for instance, recalls to mind the fact that it was the wood of the Garden of Eden which caused Adam to fall when he plucked its fruit contrary to the command of God; now the same sound recalls another great event to mind—viz., the noise made in nailing to the wood of the cross the Saviour of the world who came to atone for Adam's transgression. This idea is beautifully expressed in the "Preface of the Cross."

That the Nestorians use bells in their service we are informed by Smith and Dwight (*Researches in Armenia*, ii. p. 261), who, though rather dangerous to follow on account of their narrow-minded bigotry, yet may be relied on when treating of subjects which do not excite their prejudices. They tell us that when the small bell is sounded the people cross themselves and bow their heads a minute or two in silent adoration. This is, very likely, at the Elevation.

With the Armenians there is an almost incessant ringing of bells during Mass. These bells are for the most part entrusted to the custody of deacons, who carry them attached to the circumference of circular plates held in the hand by long handles. Large bells suspended from the domes of their churches are also employed (*ibid.* ii. p. 101).

The Abyssinians, or Ethiopians, ring large bells during the elevation of the Sacred Species.

According to Goar (*Euchol.*, p. 560), bells were not used by the Oriental Church before the end of the ninth century, when Urso, Doge of Venice, sent twelve as a present to the Emperor Michael, who afterwards placed them in the campanile of the Church of Holy Wisdom at Constantinople (Bona, p. 259).

At Mount Athos—called in the East the "Holy Mountain," from the vast number of its monasteries—bells are very much in vogue. The Monastery of St. Elias, on the island of Crete, has some of rare excellence ; and that they are held in general esteem by the Cretans themselves may be inferred from one of their ancient ballads, a stanza of which runs thus (Neale, 216) :

> " It was a Sunday morning,
> And the bells were chiming free
> To welcome in the Easter
> At Hagio Kostandi."[2]

The attachment of the Russians to bells is known the world over. Every church in the Kremlin[3] is loaded with them ; and they are of such enormous size that several men are required to ring one of them. The great tower of Ivan Veliki has as many as thirty-three, among which is the famous bell of Novgorod, whose sound used to call people together from very distant parts. This immense bell is, however, but a hand-bell in comparison to the great monster bell of the world, known as "Ivan Veliki," or Big John, of Moscow, for which no belfry could be built strong enough. It weighs 216 tons—that is, 432,000 pounds. It is yet on exhibition in the Kremlin, where for years past it has been

[2] The words "Hagio Kostandi" refer to Constantinople—*i.e.*, the Holy City of Constantine.

[3] As there is nothing more contemptible than pedantry, we follow general custom in spelling this word as it is spelled here, although we know it is properly spelled *Kreml*, which in Arabic means a fortified place. The Kremlin at Moscow is two miles in circumference, and contains a vast number of magnificent churches ; that of the Assumption is where the czars are always crowned.

serving as a chapel, the people entering through the large crack made in its side when in process of casting (Romanoff, *Rites and Customs of the Greco-Russian Church*, p. 259; Porter's *Travels*, p. 163; *Encyclopædia Britannica*, art. "Bell").[4]

HOW THE FAITHFUL WERE SUMMONED TO CHURCH DURING THE DAYS OF PERSECUTION.

Some writers have asserted, but altogether gratuitously, that during the days of persecution the faithful were summoned to divine service by the sound of those boards called semantrons, of which we have been speaking; but a moment's reflection will convince us that this cannot be true, for it is well known that in those times of trouble the utmost care had to be taken in order that the gatherings of the faithful might be entirely private, lest the pagans, hearing of them, might make them a pretext for new persecution. It is false, then, to assert that any public signal was given for gathering together the Christians, but rather that they were assembled by some secret signs known among themselves, or carried from one quarter to another by specially-deputed persons. This is the view taken by Cardinal Bona (see *Rer. Liturg.*, p. 259), by Baronius, and many other eminent writers. We have stated already that semantrons were used instead of bells in the early days, but by early days we meant not the days of persecution, but only those which followed closely upon the age of Constantine the Great.

BELLS SILENT IN HOLY WEEK.

As there is a mixture more or less of joy and solemnity in the ringing of bells, it has been customary from time imme-

---

[4] The largest bells in the world in actual use are: the second Moscow bell, which weighs 128 tons; the Kaiserglocke of Cologne Cathedral, 25 tons; the great bell of Pekin, 53 tons; the bell of Notre Dame, 17 tons; Big Ben of Westminster, 14 tons; Tom of Lincoln, 5 tons.

morial to suspend their use during the last days of Holy Week, when the entire Church is in mourning for the Passion and death of our Divine Saviour. Hence it is that in many ancient documents this week is called the "Still Week"; in others, the "Week of Suffering." The bells are silent from the "Gloria in excelsis" in the Mass of Holy Thursday until the "Gloria" on Holy Saturday, when a joyful and solemn peal is rung in memory of the glorious resurrection of our Saviour. During the silence of the bells little wooden clappers are used after the manner of the ancient semantrons, and are rung at all those parts of the Mass, such as at the "Sanctus," Elevation, Communion, etc., at which the usual bell would be sounded.

According to Pope Benedict XIV. (*De Festis*, No. 174), bells are silent this week for the mystic reason that they typify the preachers of the word of God, and all preaching was suspended from our Lord's apprehension until after he had risen from the dead. The apostles, too, when they saw his bitter torments, and the indignities he was subjected to by the Jews, stole away from him silently and left him alone. Durandus gives many more mystic reasons for the silence observed these three days (*Rationale*, p. 512).

The reader will do well to bear in mind that inasmuch as the divine offices of Holy Week have a greater antiquity than any others within the annual cycle, they bear the impress yet of many early liturgical customs, all of which, as we have taken care to note elsewhere, the Church clings to with fond tenacity.

CHAPTER XVI.

BREAD USED FOR CONSECRATION.

FOR the valid consecration of the Holy Eucharist bread made of wheat (*panis triticeus*), and no other, must be employed. According to the discipline of the Latin Church, this bread must be *unleavened*, must have nothing tempering or mixing it but water, and must be baked after the manner of ordinary bread, and not stewed, fried, or boiled.

LEAVENED AND UNLEAVENED BREAD.

No question has given rise to more warm dispute than that which touches the use of leavened or unleavened bread in the preparation of the Holy Eucharist. Cardinal Bona tells us in his wonted modest way what a storm of indignation he brought down upon himself when he stated in his great work on the Mass and its ceremonies that the use of leavened and unleavened bread was common in the Latin Church until the beginning of the tenth century, when unleavened bread became obligatory on all. We shall not now go over the ground which the learned cardinal did to prove this assertion, but we shall simply say for the instruction of the reader that his opinion is embraced by almost all writers on sacred liturgy. That the use of unleavened bread, or azymes, was never intermitted in the Latin Church from the very institution of the Blessed Eucharist itself all are willing to admit; but it is very commonly held that when the Ebionite heretics taught that the precepts of the ancient law were binding upon Christian people, and that, in consequence, the Eucharist could not be celebrated at all unless the bread our Lord used —viz., *unleavened*—were employed, the Church also sanctioned the use of leavened bread to confound this teaching, and that this remained in force until all traces of the Ebionites had died away. This statement has for its supporters several eminent theologians, among whom are Alexander of Hales, Duns Scotus, St. Bonaventure, and St. Thomas Aquinas (see Cardinal Bona, *Rer. Liturg.*, lib. i. cap. xxiii.; Kozma, 238; Neale, *Holy Eastern Church,* "On the Controversy concerning the Azymes," vol. ii.)

In so far as the validity of the sacrament is concerned, both the Latin and Greek churches have always held that consecration takes place in either kind, and that the use of leavened or unleavened bread is altogether a matter of discipline and not of dogma. The latter Church, too, acknowledges (at least the ancient Greek Church did), equally with the former, that our Lord used unleavened bread at the Last Supper, but that for very wise reasons the early Church thought well to introduce leavened bread, and that when itself (*i.e.*, the Greek Church) adopted this custom it held on to it without change (Neale, ii. 1059, and 1073-34). It must not be concealed that the turbulent Michael Cerularius, Patriarch of Constantinople in 1043, in order to make the rupture between the two churches as great as possible, went so far as to assert that consecration in any other bread but leavened was invalid, and that hence the whole Latin Church was heretical because it used unleavened. But the Eastern theologians never adopted this teaching; nor is it held to-day, although, with the exception of the Armenians and Maronites, all the Oriental churches follow the Greek discipline in the use of leavened bread.

We have said that, according to the consent of both

churches, consecration is valid in either kind; the discipline, however, of the Latin Church is so strict in the matter of unleavened bread that, were a priest of her communion to consecrate in any other kind without a special dispensation, he would sin mortally. He could not even do so were it to fulfil the precept of hearing Mass on Sunday or give the Holy Viaticum to the dying. The only case in which it is allowed is when, through some accident or other, the Sacred Host disappears immediately after consecration, and no other bread is at hand but leavened. The latter may then be used in order to the completion of the Sacrifice (De Herdt, ii. p. 167, No. 3).

HOW THE BREADS ARE BAKED.

The breads for the use of the altar are baked between heated irons upon which is stamped some pious device, such as the Crucifixion, the Lamb of God, or a simple cross. The instrument used for this purpose somewhat resembles a large forceps in appearance. It has two long handles, and at its extremities is a pair of circular heads, one overlapping the other. After this instrument has been sufficiently heated in the fire a little lard or butter is rubbed over its surface to keep the paste from adhering. A thin coating of this paste is then spread over the surface of the under disc, and the upper one being allowed to rest on it a moment or two, it is taken out perfectly baked. The irons are then separated, and the bread is taken out and trimmed for use.

DEVICES USED IN STAMPING THE BREAD.

At the present day there is no particular device prescribed to be impressed upon the altar-breads. Every church is allowed to abound in its own choice in this respect. In some places a representation of our Lord crucified is the impression; in others the "Agnus Dei." We have also seen breads upon which the first and last letters of the Greek alphabet were stamped, in allusion to our Lord's saying in the Apocalypse, "I am Alpha and Omega, the first and the last, the beginning and the end." The most general device, however, is, as we believe, the ancient and sacred monogram "IHS," or, as it was formerly written, "IHC." As to the precise interpretation of this "IHS" there has been much dispute; some contending that it means (at least that its letters are the initials of) "Jesus Hominum Salvator"—*Jesus, the Saviour of Men*—others that they are the initials of "I Have Suffered." Other interpretations are given of them which we do not deem necessary to state. The truth, however, is that they are the three first letters of our Lord's sacred name in Greek, viz., *IHΣOYΣ*, and that as such they were very commonly employed as a sacred device on the Christian tombs during the days of persecution. They are yet to be seen inscribed in many places in the Roman catacombs (see *Justorum Semita; or, The Holydays of the English Church*, p. 335; *Holy Name of Jesus*; also, *Dublin Review*, vol. xliv., 1858, art. "Primacy of St. Peter").

The interpretation "Jesus, the Saviour of Men" first originated with St. Bernardine of Sienna, in 1443, and was brought about in this way: The saint, it seems, had occasion to reprove a certain man for selling cards with dangerous devices impressed upon them. The man tried to defend his cause by saying that he could not earn a living in any other manner, but that if Saint Bernardine offered a device instead of those he himself used, and assured him that he would not be a loser in adopting it, he would at once abandon those he had; whereupon the saint recommended the letters "IHS," telling the man that they stood for "Jesus Hominum Salvator." They were at once adopted, and their success was complete (see *Gleanings for the Curious*, by C. C. Bombaugh, A.M., pp. 98, 99).

BY WHOM THE BREADS ARE MADE.

Although it would be more proper that the breads for altar purposes should be made by the sacred ministers themselves, yet, as the modern way of making and preparing them for use is open to no abuse, the duty is often entrusted to pious members of the congregation—for the most part to the Sisters who may be attached to any particular church.

In ancient times it was considered a great honor to be allowed to make these breads, and we find some of the nobles of the land offering their services for this pious work. It is related of St. Wenceslaus, Duke of Bohemia (tenth century), that he used to sow the wheat in the field with his own hands, cut it down afterwards when ripe, winnow it himself, grind it into flour, and finally make it into bread for the use of the Holy Sacrifice (Martène, *De Antiquis Eccl. Ritibus*, f. 13 ; *Lives of the Saints*, September 28). A similar story is related of St. Radegunde, Queen of France, in the sixth century.

In the good old days of Catholic England the synodical decrees relating to the making of the altar-bread were very strict, as the following will show : "We also command that the ofletes[1] which in the Holy Mystery ye offer to God ye either bake yourselves or your servants before you, that ye may know that it is neatly and cleanly done" (Dr. Rock, *Church of Our Fathers*, vol. i. p. 156, note). The Bishop of Lincoln (thirteenth century) thus addressed the clergy

---

[1] This was the Anglo-Saxon name for the altar-bread. It was also called *obley* (evidently from the Latin *oblata*) and "singing-bread." Dr. Rock conjectures that the latter name must have been given it from the fact that it was used at High Mass ; but we venture to say that it was so named because during its preparation a constant singing of psalms and hymns was kept up, which, as we shall see, is yet the practice in the East.

of his diocese: "More care than ordinary must be taken to see that the ofletes be made of pure wheat. While the work of preparing them is going on the ministers of the church who make them ought to sit in a decent place and be dressed in surplices. The instrument for baking these ofletes ought to be anointed with wax only, not with oil or any greasy material" (*ibid.*)

SIZE OF THE ALTAR-BREAD.

Up to the eleventh century the custom was almost general of communicating the people from particles of the large Host which the priest used; hence this must have been of far greater proportions than it is now (Kozma, 239). When the custom of thus communicating the people ceased, small Hosts were introduced, which still bore the name of particles, and the priest's Host became smaller in size.

FORM OF THE HOST.

From time immemorial it has been customary to have the Host, or altar-bread, of a circular form. This can be traced as far back at least as the third century, for Pope Zephyrinus, who died A.D. 217, calls the bread a "crown of a spherical figure"—*Corona sive oblata sphericæ figuræ* (Benedict XIV., c. 5). Severus of Alexandria, styled the "Christian Sallust," who flourished in the fourth century, calls it simply the "circle" (Martène, *De Antiquis Ecclesiæ Ritibus*, 14). According to Durandus, who is never at a loss for a mystical meaning, the bread is circular, in the shape of a coin, to remind us that the true Bread of Life, our Divine Redeemer, was sold by Judas for thirty pieces of silver (*Rationale Divinorum*, p. 256).

BREADS OF THE EASTERN CHURCH.

It is very generally known that the entire Eastern Church,

with the sole exception of the Armenians and Maronites, uses leavened bread in the preparation of the Holy Eucharist. Whether it has kept up this practice from the beginning or not we leave others to settle. Some are of opinion that it has, and others, for very weighty reasons, say that it has not; but the point is one of small consequence so long as all agree in admitting that consecration takes place, no matter which of the two kinds is used.

According to Pococke (*Travels in Egypt*), the Copts also use unleavened bread; but this is certainly a mistake, for no author that we have seen makes such an assertion. If this were the case, Renaudot, who describes the Coptic ceremonies and customs most minutely, would certainly have made mention of it, or it would be referred to by Denzinger in his *Ritus Orientalium*.

Brerewood, in that hodge-podge entitled *Enquiries touching the Diversity of Languages and Religions*, London, 1674, asserts that the Abyssinians do the same—*i.e.*, consecrate in unleavened bread. But as this author paid little or no attention to what he said, and took his information, in most cases, second hand, little reliance is to be placed on any statement that he makes which does not square with what has been said by approved authorities. He says also that Thecla Haimonout, an Abyssinian priest, stated that they celebrate ordinarily in leavened bread, but that they use unleavened on Holy Thursday (p. 203). This may have been done at one time, but it is not now.

CEREMONIES ATTENDING THE MAKING OF THE ALTAR-BREAD IN THE EAST.

The respect manifested by the Orientals even for the unconsecrated bread, to say nothing of the Holy Eucharist itself, is worthy of all admiration. And to begin with the Copts, of whom we have been speaking: So very particular are they about the sacrificial bread that they deem it profane to purchase the grain used in making it with any other money than that which has been set aside for church purposes. The wheat, too, when made into flour, must always be kept in the church, where is also the oven in which the breads are baked. During the process of making these breads a constant chanting of psalms is kept up by the clerics to whom the work is entrusted, and the whole thing is looked upon as a sacred duty (Pococke, *Travels in Egypt*). Their discipline requires that the bread be *new, fresh,* and *pure;* in fact, according to their canons, that of yesterday's making could not be used in saying Mass to-day, but newly-made bread must be offered—*i.e.*, bread made the same morning that Mass is said. On no account must this be made by a female. A violation of this rule would subject the offender to excommunication. "It is meet," says one of their constitutionary laws, "that the Eucharistic bread should be baked nowhere else but in the oven of the church. Let not a female knead it or bake it. He who acts contrary to this, let him be anathema" (Renaudot, *Liturg. Oriental. Coll.*, i. p. 172).

The Syrian bread, called *Xatha*, is made of the finest and purest flour, and is tempered with water, oil of olives, salt, and leaven. They defend the use of oil in making it by saying that it is merely employed in order that the paste may not adhere to the hands. The entire operation is carried on within the church by a priest or deacon; it is wholly forbidden to entrust its preparation to any one not in sacred orders (*ibid.;* and Lamy, *De Fide Syrorum et Discip. in re Eucharistiæ*). One of the Syrian canons on this head runs as follows: "Let the priest or deacon who prepares the bread of oblation take care to have the mould clean, and to have a vessel for the purpose of straining the water and oil; he must be careful not to let it be handled by a lay person. Besides this, he must have his loins girt, shoes on his feet, be turned towards the east, and have his face veiled with an amice. Psalms must accompany this ministry" (Lamy, *ibid.*)

The discipline of the Armenians also requires that the bread be made by the sacred ministers. Their bread is unleavened, like ours.

BREAD USED BY THE GREEK CHURCH.

The bread used by the Greeks is round, like a large griddle-cake, and rising from its surface is a square projection denominated the Holy Lamb, which, when cut off

HOLY LANCE.

afterwards by the Holy Lance, becomes, properly speaking, the sacrificial Host. What remains of the loaf when the square projection has been taken away is divided into several small particles, which are arranged in groups and dedicated to the Blessed Virgin, the apostles, saints, and martyrs, as well as the living and the dead (Goar, *Euchol. Græc.*, p. 116; *Primitive Liturgies*, pp. 120 and 183, by Neale and Littledale). The square projection itself is divided into four equal portions after consecration. When cutting off the Holy Lamb from the large loaf the Greek

HOST OF THE GREEKS.

priest says, as he inserts the lance in the right side of the seal (that is, the impression stamped upon the bread), "He was led as a sheep to the slaughter"; when inserting it into the left, "And as a blameless lamb dumb before his shearers, he opened not his mouth." Inserting it into the upper part, he says, "In his humiliation his judgment was taken away"; into the lower, "And who shall declare his generation?" The deacon says at each incision, "Let us make our supplications to the Lord." By the quadrangular form of the holy bread the Greeks intend to signify that Christ our Lord suffered for the four quarters of the globe (Martène, *De Antiquis Eccl. Ritibus*, f. 15).

INSCRIPTIONS IMPRESSED ON THE HOLY BREAD.

Considerable diversity exists in the East in relation to the devices employed in stamping the altar-bread. The Syrians use only a number of small crosses; the Nestorians the same. The Coptic Host has upon one side, "$Ἅγιος$, $Ἅγιος$, $Ἅγιος$, $Κύριος$ $Σαβέωθ$"—that is, *Holy, Holy, Holy, Lord of Hosts;* and upon the other, "$Ἅγιος$ $Ἰσχυρός$"—*Holy Strong One*. The latter is part of the famous *Trisagion* which the Eastern Church employs in every day's service, but which the Latin Church only repeats once a year, in the Mass of Good Friday. This sacred hymn has a peculiar and interesting history attached to it. In the time of Theodosius the Younger, A.D. 446, Constantinople was threatened by so dreadful an earthquake that all believed the end of the world at hand. The wildest confusion reigned throughout the city as the first signs of this untoward calamity manifested themselves. Men, women, and children ran frantic through the streets, and the utmost consternation was depicted on every countenance. In this dreadful juncture Theodosius addressed a petition to St. Proclus, archbishop of the imperial city, earnestly beseeching him to ask of Almighty God to avert the impending calamity. The saintly man acceded at once to the emperor's wishes. He accordingly formed a procession of all his clergy and people, and, with the attendance of all the members of the royal court, marched a little outside the city, and then knelt down with the entire multitude in solemn and earnest prayer. They had not been kneeling long when, to the great astonishment of all, a child was seen in the clouds above them, moving from one place to another, and singing loud enough to be heard by the spectators. After the lapse of about an hour the child descended, singing, "Ἅγιος Ἰσχυρός, Ἅγιος ὁ Θεός, Ἅγιος Ἀθάνατος, ἐλέησον ἡμᾶς"—that is, Holy Strong One, Holy God, Holy Immortal One, have mercy on us! Upon being questioned as to the object of this singing, the child replied that he had heard the angelic choir sing this sacred anthem at the throne of God, and that if the people wished to avert the terrors of the earthquake they should sing it also. It was taken up at once, and tranquillity was restored (Goar, Euchol. Græcorum, p. 126 ; Neale, Holy Eastern Church, i. p. 367). The emperor afterwards issued a decree causing it to be universally adopted, and it is said that St. Proclus had it inserted in the liturgies of Constantinople (Ferraris,

HOST OF THE COPTS.

Bibliotheca; Butler's *Lives of the Saints,* Oct. 24, St. Proclus).

The small crosses that appear on the face of the Coptic bread are in memory, it is said, of a celebrated discourse of St. John Chrysostom on the divinity of our Lord, in which the word *cross* appears several times. Martène tells us that the seals used by the Oriental patriarchs for stamping the altar-bread differ much from those used by the priests. The inscription on the Greek Host—viz., "IX. NIKA"—is translated "Jesus Christ conquers."

CHAPTER XVII.

WINE.

IF we except the Aquarians alone, who said that water may be employed instead of wine in the consecration of the chalice, no dispute has ever arisen upon this subject; all are at one in holding that for the valid consecration of this species the juice of the grape (*vinum de vite*) is necessary. Nor does it matter as to the color of the wine; some prefer red, others white wine, but this is altogether a matter of taste. One great advantage that red wine has is this: that there is no danger of mistaking it for water, owing to its resemblance in color to blood.

WINE OF THE ORIENTAL CHURCH.

The discipline of the Oriental and the Western Church are in perfect agreement regarding the sacrificial wine. An abuse, however, exists among the Copts which, though not resorted to save in extreme cases, is still deserving of condemnation. We refer to the employment of what is called *zebib* instead of pure juice of the grape. Pococke, in his *Travels in Egypt,* art. "The Religion of the Copts," describes the process of making this very doubtful wine as follows: "In the Catholic churches they must use wine, but in the others they use what they call zebib. . . . Zebib is a sort of raisin wine. They put five rotolas of new grapes to five of water, or more grapes are used if they are older. It is left to steep seven days in winter and four in summer. The deacons strain it through two bags, one after another, to make it fine. This keeps seven years, and tastes like a sweet wine that is turned a little sour. They keep the zebib in a jar, and cover it closely so that no wind can come to it." Be all this as it may, the canons of the Coptic Church are very clear and strong upon the point that no other wine but the unadulterated juice of the grape must be used for Mass purposes; and so particular are they that this shall be of the finest quality that they will allow no one to have anything to do with its preparation but the ministers of the altar. To this end the grapes are picked with great care, and are bruised between the hands in extracting the juice from them, instead of being trodden out by the feet, as is the custom when the wine is destined for ordinary use. While the wine remains in the casks it is considered a mortal offence for any one to meddle with it before the quantity necessary for altar uses has first been set aside (Renaudot, vol. i. pp. 176 and 177). The Copts will not say Mass with wine which has been purchased in a store, for the reason that it may not be pure (*ibid.*)

CRUETS.

The wine and water necessary for the Holy Sacrifice are kept in two glass vessels termed Cruets. Although it is not specially required that they be made of glass, still, for the greater convenience of those who have to keep them clean, but above all for the advantage Cruets of this material have over those which are not transparent, it is better that they should; for accidents of a very serious nature are liable to happen unless it can be seen at a glance in which vessel the wine is and in which the water.

In early times these Cruets were often made of the most precious materials. Gold, silver, and precious stones frequently entered into their composition, and the most elaborate workmanship was displayed in making them. John of Hothum, Bishop of Ely,[1] gave to his church, as a private donation, in A.D. 1336, a set of golden Cruets studded with rubies and pearls (*Church of Our Fathers*, by Dr. Rock, i. p. 159, note). Beauchamp, Earl of Warwick, bequeathed in A.D. 1400, to his lord the king, an image of the Blessed Virgin, with two cruets, silver and gilt, made in the shape of two angels (*ibid.*) In those good old days the highest nobles of the land strove with holy zeal to see how much each could do towards beautifying the house of God and having the sacred vessels of the altar and sanctuary of the most ornate kind.

[1] Ely, an ancient city of Cambridgeshire, England, was once a resort of much note. It is about seventy miles from London. It had a venerable Catholic cathedral in 1107, which was 517 feet long, with a tower 270 feet high.

CHAPTER XVIII.

NUMBER OF MASSES THAT A PRIEST MAY SAY UPON THE SAME DAY.

DURING the very early days it was entirely at the discretion of every priest whether he said daily a plurality of Masses or not (Gavantus, *Thesaur. Sacr. Rit.*, p. 19). It was quite usual to say two Masses, one of the occurring feast, the other for the benefit of the faithful departed. A plurality of Masses, however, was soon restricted to occasions upon which a greater concourse of people than ordinary was gathered by reason of some solemnity. Then, in order to afford all an opportunity of assisting at the Holy Sacrifice, as many Masses as were deemed necessary could be said, and these even by the same priest. Pope Leo III. (ninth century), we are told, said as many as nine Masses on a single day to meet an exigency of this kind (*ibid.* p. 19). This practice, however, kept gradually falling into desuetude until the time of Pope Alexander II. (from A.D. 1061 to 1073), when that pontiff decreed that no priest should say more than one Mass on the same day. The decree was thus worded: "It is sufficient for a priest to say one Mass the same day, because Christ suffered once and redeemed the whole world. The celebration of one Mass is no small matter, and very happy is the man who can celebrate one Mass worthily" (*ibid.*) This is the present discipline of the Church in this matter. Faculties, however, are granted to priests in charge of two churches to say Mass in each church on Sunday, in order to give the people an opportunity of complying with the precept requiring them to assist on that day at the Holy Sacrifice. But under no circumstances can more than two be said by the same priest on these occasions.¹ Permission to *duplicate* may be also had for one church where two Masses are required.

CHRISTMAS DAY AN EXCEPTION.

Christmas day is now the only day of the year upon which a plurality of Masses may be said. On this great feast the Church extends to every priest the privilege of celebrating the Holy Sacrifice three times the same morning, without, however, binding him to celebrate any more than one, if he does not wish to do so. According to Durandus (*Rationale Divin.*, p. 419, No. 17), this privilege was granted by Pope Telesphorus, A.D. 142. Liturgical writers assign to these three Masses the following mystic meaning: first, the eternal birth of the Son of God in the bosom of his Father; secondly, his birth in time in the womb of his Immaculate Mother; thirdly, his spiritual birth in the hearts of the faithful by a worthy reception of his sacraments, but, above all, by the reception of himself in the adorable sacrament of the altar (Benedict XIV., *De Festis Dom. Nostr. J. Christi*, No. 668; Bouvry, *Expositio Rubr.*, i. 437).

Throughout the kingdom of Aragon, in Spain (including Aragon, Valentia, and Catalonia), also in the kingdom of Majorca (a dependency of Aragon), it is allowed each secular priest to say two Masses on the 2d of November, the Commemoration of all the Faithful Departed, and each regular² priest three Masses. This privilege is also enjoyed by the Dominicans of the Monastery of St. James

---

[1] Father Vetromile (*Travels in Europe and the Holy Land*, p. 171) is our authority for saying that the priests attached to the Chapel of Calvary at Jerusalem can say Mass there at any hour of the day, and as often as they please.

[2] The term *regular* is applied to all priests who live together in community. Those who live outside of community life are termed *seculars*.

at Pampeluna (Benedict XIV., *De Sacrif. Missæ*, Romæ, ex. Congr. de Prop. Fide, an. 1859 editio, p. 139). This grant, it is said, was first made either by Pope Julius or Pope Paul III., and, though often asked for afterwards by persons of note, was never granted to any other country or to any place in Spain except those mentioned. For want of any very recent information on the subject I am unable to say how far the privilege extends at the present day. A movement is on foot, however, to petition the Holy Father for an extension of this privilege to the universal Church, in order that as much aid as possible may be given to the suffering souls in Purgatory.

THE PRACTICE OF THE ORIENTAL CHURCH REGARDING THE CELEBRATION OF MASS.

The practice of the Oriental Church regarding the celebration of Mass is somewhat lax; but in so far as relates to the number a single priest may say the same day, if we except the Copts, that Church and ours agree. Daily Mass is very rare in the East, except among the Papal Catholics (as those of our communion are termed), and even in many places there is no celebration on Sunday, unless it be one of great note.

According to the Nestorian Ritual, Mass is prescribed for every Sunday and Friday and every Church festival throughout the year. It is also prescribed every day of the *first*, *middle*, and *last* week of Lent, except Good Friday; daily also the week following Easter. At present, however, Mass is restricted to Sundays and principal holydays; and in some places whole weeks pass without a celebration. The Rev. Geo. Percy Badger, whom we are quoting, says that on some occasions it is the practice for the priest to read the Liturgy, omitting the prayer of consecration and other parts of the office, after the manner of a Dry Mass. This the Nestorians call by the name of *d'Sh-heeme,* or *Simple* (*Nestorians and their Rituals,* vol. ii. p. 243).

Smith and Dwight, in their travels through the East, were informed by some Nestorian priests that a whole year sometimes passes without there being any more than three Masses celebrated (*Researches in Armenia,* vol. ii. p. 230). They state, however, that the more devout celebrate very regularly, especially during the season of Lent.[3]

According to the discipline of the Armenians, daily Mass is enjoined, and is rarely omitted where there is a sufficiency of priests (*ibid.* 103). Neale, however, flatly contradicts this in his *Holy Eastern Church* (vol. i. p. 380, note *a*), where he distinctly states that it is a regulation of the Armenian Church that the Liturgy is not to be celebrated excepting on Saturday and Sunday, and when any great festival of our Lord or his Mother occurs. On ordinary days, instead of Mass, they recite Tierce, Sext, and None of the Divine Office. Neale adds, however, that during Lent celebration is more frequent.

[3] The season of Lent is very strictly observed throughout the entire East. In fact, it is not merely one Lent they have, but several, and these are kept with all the ancient rigor even at the present day. Besides fasting on every Wednesday and Friday of the year, the Nestorians fast also for twenty-five days previous to Christmas; fifteen days before the Feast of St. Mary—that is, before the Assumption of the Blessed Virgin; three days before the Feast of the Holy Cross; three before the Feast of St. John; fifty days before Easter; and fifty before Pentecost. The fast of Wednesday and Friday is so strict that no meat is eaten from the evening before until the evening following (Smith and Dwight, *Researches in Armenia,* ii. 208, 209). The total number of fasting days with the Armenians in one year amounts to one hundred and fifty-six (*ibid.* i. p. 156).

According to Dr. Neale, the fasts in the Greek Church amount to two hundred and twenty-six per annum. He further states that during the "Great Fast," as Lent is called, nothing can equal the rigor observed everywhere and by all. The only relaxations given are the allowance of more than one meal on Saturday and Sunday, and the use of fish on the Feast of the Annunciation. At all other times meat, fish, cheese, eggs, butter, oil, and milk are strictly forbidden. So strictly is this "Great Fast" kept by old and young that poor men will throw away their only loaf if a drop of oil or other forbidden substance should accidentally touch it (*Holy Eastern Church,* ii. 744).

In case of a death occurring Mass is never omitted. The Armenians say one on the day of burial and one on the seventh, fifteenth, and fortieth after death; also one on the anniversary day. This holy practice of praying for the dead and saying Mass in their behalf is very common throughout the entire East, with schismatics as well as Catholics.

According to Pococke, the liturgical days of the Copts are Sundays and holydays, and the Wednesdays and Fridays of the fasting seasons. The same author remarks that, under pretext of not being able to obtain grapes from Cairo for wine purposes, their priests say they cannot celebrate Mass oftener than once a month. These remarks, of course, wholly refer to the schismatic Copts and not to the Catholic. The latter celebrate regularly.

CHAPTER XIX.

CONCELEBRATION.

UNTIL about the beginning of the thirteenth century the custom of having several priests unite in offering the same Mass was very prevalent on the more solemn festivals of the year. The priests who lent their aid on such occasions were said to *concelebrate*—that is, to perform one joint action with the regular celebrant of the Mass; and no matter how great their number was, no one ever supposed that more than a single Sacrifice was offered (Bona, *Rer. Liturg.*, p. 246). Touching this peculiar custom Pope Innocent III., in his fourth book on the Mass, chap. xxv., writes as follows: " The cardinal priests have been accustomed to stand around the Roman Pontiff and celebrate together with him; and when the Sacrifice is ended they receive Communion at his hands, signifying thereby that the Apostles who sat at table with our Lord received the Eucharist from him; and in their celebrating together it is shown that the Apostles on that occasion learned the rite by which this Sacrifice should be offered."

This custom of concelebrating must have gone into desuetude in the early part of the thirteenth century, for Durandus, who flourished in A.D. 1260, speaks of it as a thing already passed away. The only vestige of it that now remains in the Latin Church is to be found in the Mass of the ordination of a priest and the consecration of a bishop. In the former case the candidate, or *ordinandus*, as he is called, takes up the Mass with the bishop ordaining at the

Offertory, and goes on with him to the end, reciting everything aloud, even the form of consecration of the Host and Chalice; in the latter case the bishop-elect takes up the Mass at the very beginning with the bishop consecrating, and follows him in everything to the end, except that he does not turn with him at any time to the people when saying "Pax vobis," "Dominus vobiscum," or "Orate fratres." At the Communion he receives part of the Host used by the consecrating bishop; and with him, also, part of the Precious Blood, from the same chalice.

Regarding this Mass of concelebration many curious questions are asked; but as it would be entirely beyond our purpose to delay in discussing them, we shall give only the most important to our readers. This is, Whether the consecration of the bread or wine is to be ascribed to the bishop ordaining or to the *ordinandus,* in case the latter should have pronounced the entire form first? Some theologians formerly held that, in order to avoid all scruple on this head, the newly-ordained priest ought to recite the words of consecration *historically* (*historico modo*), and have no personal intention of effecting transubstantiation at all. According to others, it mattered nothing whether the *ordinandus* pronounced the form before the bishop or not; consecration was in every case to be ascribed to the latter. The third opinion is the one accepted to day—viz., that although the newly-ordained priest may through haste have pronounced the sacred words of institution before the bishop ordaining, still the whole thing must be considered as one joint moral action, in virtue of which consecration is effected only when all parties have pronounced the entire form. This is supported by Pope Innocent III. among others, and by the great doctor, St. Thomas Aquinas (see *Pontificale Romanum,* by Catalanus, newly edited by Mühlbauer, fascic. i. p. 167).

All are at one in saying that the newly-ordained priest really offers a true sacrifice on this occasion, and that hence he must have the intention of consecrating the same bread and wine with the bishop (Benedict XIV., sect. 2, No. 142; Bouvry, ii. 493, q. 4).

ORIENTAL USAGE IN THIS MATTER.

The ancient custom of concelebrating is yet in use with nearly all the Oriental churches. Wherever the Greek rite prevails it is strictly observed; and Badger tells us that it is common with the Nestorians (*Nestorians and their Rituals*, i. p. 286). That the custom is also in vogue with the Maronites we see from their liturgy and liturgical customs. Goar tells us (*Euchol.*, p. 299) that whenever the patriarch celebrates a Mass of this kind he is attended by several bishops and priests, who celebrate and communicate with him. When the bishop is the celebrant all the priests who are present assist him, and the same is done when the celebrant is a protopope.[1] All this, however, applies only to the greater festivals of the year; on ordinary occasions this display is dispensed with.

[1] A protopope in the Eastern Church is nearly the same as our archdeacon. His precise jurisdiction is the same as that of the ancient chorepiscopus, or rural bishop.

CHAPTER XX.

CUSTOMS RELATING TO THE CELEBRATION OF MASS.

MASS MUST BE SAID WITH SHOES ON.

WHETHER in imitation of the high-priest of the old law, who always celebrated barefooted, or through profound respect for the Holy Eucharist, there were some in times past who used to say Mass in their naked feet. This was the practice of certain monks of Egypt until forbidden by the Holy See (Cassianus, *Institut.*, lib. i. cap. vi.) It is never allowed by the existing order of things to celebrate barefooted; the rubric distinctly says that the priest must have shoes on (*pedibus calceatus*).

With the Nestorians, however, the case is very different; for, according to them, it is considered a great offence to say Mass with the feet covered. They require them to be entirely bare from beginning to end, as an evidence of deep respect towards the Blessed Sacrament (see, among others, Smith and Dwight, ii. 229). According to Burder (*Religious Ceremonies and Customs*, p. 180), the Armenian clergy, when assisting in choir, never wear anything on the feet, but the celebrant of the Mass always wears a light black slipper.

Ancient Rules regarding the Color of the Shoes worn at Mass.—Although bishops in the early days could wear any color they pleased in what was termed their sandals, yet for priests and those of the lower order of clergy black was always prescribed. The Council of Exeter, held in A.D.

1287, ordained that the clergy should wear no other than black boots; and in a council held in London in 1342 it was enacted that they should not wear green or scarlet leggings. Bishop Waneflete, in the statutes he drew up for his college at Oxford, strictly forbade the use of a low kind of shoe called high-lows; also red peaked boots, and everything of that kind which was not suitable to the priestly state and the holy canons (Dr. Rock, *Church of Our Fathers*, ii. 244).

At the adoration of the cross on Good Friday the sacred ministers doff their shoes out of respect. The Romans, we are told, walked barefooted at the funeral of Augustus, in testimony of the great respect that should be paid such a man.

MASS MUST BE CELEBRATED FASTING.

According to Cardinal Bona (*Rer. Liturg.*, p. 255), the practice of celebrating fasting is of apostolic origin, and was always strictly observed in the early Church. St. Augustine says that, out of respect for the Holy Eucharist, we should partake of no food whatever before communicating. To this rule there was, however, one signal and special exception in ancient times—viz., in case of the Mass celebrated on Holy Thursday. On this day, in memory of the Last Supper, it was customary for some years, at least in Africa, to celebrate after having taken food. The decree regulating this discipline, and issued by the Council of Carthage in A.D. 397, was thus worded: "The sacrament of the altar must not be celebrated unless by those who are fasting; an exception, however, is made on the anniversary upon which the Lord's Supper was instituted" (*ibid.*) Some claimed an exception, also, in case of Masses for the dead, but the practice gained but little favor. To-day the rule enjoining fast is of universal obligation, and admits of no relaxation, except in one or two special cases—viz., where an accident should befall a priest after consecration, rendering him unable to go on any further, and there is no other priest at hand to complete the Sacrifice but one who has already broken his fast. Some theologians make another exception in the case where people had been deprived of Mass for a long time, and could not, on account of their great distance from church, be early enough for the regular Mass. But as such things rarely happen, they are hardly exceptions to the universal rule.

Practice of the Eastern Church in this respect.—We have said in another place that the Copts will say Mass any time of the day or night, whether fasting or not, in order to give Holy Viaticum to the dying, as they do not reserve the Blessed Sacrament. This, however, must be considered a solitary case, for the discipline of all the Oriental churches in this matter is precisely the same as our own.

According to many of the Coptic and Ethiopic disciplinary canons, the priest who is to say Mass must be fasting from the previous evening, and must not even take a glass of wine before he has celebrated (Denzinger, *Ritus Orientalium*, p. 66; Renaudot, *Liturg. Oriental.*, i. 268). So fearful are they of violating this sacred law that it is quite common to find a priest taking up quarters in the sacristy the previous day, and remaining there, secluded from all danger of breaking the fast, until Mass has been celebrated.

WASHING OF THE HANDS.

On account of the profound respect that is due to our Lord in the Holy Sacrament of the altar, as well as to signify that interior purity of heart which we should always possess when celebrating the tremendous Sacrifice of the new law, it is of strict obligation that the priest should wash his hands immediately before donning the sacred vestments. All are unanimous in saying that this practice is as old as the Christian Church itself. While performing this ablution the priest recites the following prayer: " Grant, O Lord! such virtue to my hands that they may be cleansed from every stain, to the end that I may serve thee without defilement of mind or body."

In early times not only was the priest who was to say Mass required to wash his hands, but also every member of the congregation as he entered the sacred edifice. For which reason there used to be placed at the entrance of all the ancient churches fonts filled with water (Riddle, *Christian Antiquities*, p. 739). These fonts were sometimes elaborately finished, and inscriptions of a pious nature were engraved upon them. The celebrated Church of Holy Wisdom (Sancta Sophia) at Constantinople had an inscription on its font which read the same way backwards and forwards. It was printed in Greek characters, thus: "ΝΙΨΟΝ ΑΝΟΜΗΜΑΤΑ ΜΗ ΜΟΝΑΝ ΟΨΙΝ"—that is, " Wash away your sins, and not your countenance only" (Neale, i. 215). In the Oriental Church the ablution of the hands is performed after having vested, and not before, as with us. On such occasions the Oriental priests recite the psalm "Lavabo inter innocentes."

Whenever a bishop celebrates he washes, according to our rite, four different times: the first before vesting; the second, after he has read the Offertorium; the third, after the Offertory; and the fourth time, after Communion.

After the priest has washed his hands he goes to prepare the chalice by first placing upon it a clean purificator, over which he also places the paten with a large Host resting upon it, and over this the pall. He then covers all with the chalice veil, and rests the burse with the corporal in it on the top. The chalice is then said to be dressed.

The priest proceeds now to vest himself, putting on each article in the order which we have described already, and with the same ceremonies. This is done in the sacristy; but should the celebrant be a bishop, he always vests at the altar.[1]

Having put on all the sacred vestments, he takes the chalice in his hands and proceeds to the altar with a solemn, dignified gait; and, to show the great importance of the work he is about to engage in, he must salute no one as he passes along, unless the person be some great dignitary, and then only by a moderate bow of the head. We have a remarkable precedent for this in the solemn discourse made by our Lord to his disciples when sending them to preach the Gospel; he commanded them to "salute no man by the way" (*Luke* x. 4).

When the priest has arrived in front of the altar he takes off his cap, or berretta, and having made a low bow to the crucifix, or a genuflection if the Blessed Sacrament be in the tabernacle, he ascends the steps, and, having spread out the corporal in the middle of the altar, places the chalice with its appurtenances on it. (At Solemn High Mass the chalice is not brought to the altar until the Offertory.) After this he proceeds to the Epistle side, and, having opened the missal at the Mass of the day, returns to the front of the altar, at the lowest step, and there begins the service. (A server, or altar-boy, kneeling at his left, answers the responses in

---

[1] The reason of this distinction is founded on the fact that in all the ancient churches there used to be built, generally in the nave, a small altar, at which the bishop would seat himself before Mass to receive the obeisance of the people as they passed in, and impart them his blessing; for which reason this altar used to be generally known as the *Salutatorium*. When the entire congregation had gathered, his lordship would vest at this small altar, and then proceed in solemn procession to the sanctuary, where he would begin Mass. When the practice of building these appurtenances ceased, the main altar of the church served in their stead; and hence the origin of the present practice. This may be gleaned from the *Cæremoniale Episcoporum* and the other works that mention the *Secretarium*, as the Salutatorium was sometimes called.

the name of the people.) He first makes a low bow, or a genuflection if the Blessed Sacrament be present, and then

THE SIGN OF THE CROSS,

by touching his forehead, breast, left and right shoulder, as he says, "In nomine Patris, et Filii, et Spiritus Sancti, amen"—that is, "In the name of the Father, and of the Son, and of the Holy Ghost, amen." When he touches his forehead he says, "In the name of the Father"; when he touches his breast, "and of the Son"; and as he passes his hand from the left to the right shoulder he concludes by saying, "and of the Holy Ghost, amen." We call the reader's special attention to this distribution of the words, for they are very frequently misplaced, it being quite common to hear nothing but "Amen" said as the right shoulder is touched. This is wholly incorrect, as may be seen at once from the rubrics describing the manner of making the sign of the cross. It is hardly necessary to add that it is always the right hand which is used in going through this ceremony.

Ancient Customs regarding the Manner of Making the Sign of the Cross.—In the Christian Church in early times the custom of making the sign of the cross on the forehead only was very common. Tertullian (A.D. 200) alludes to it in his *De Corona Militis*, cap. iii., as does also the Roman Ordo in its directions for saying Mass. Sometimes, too, only the mouth was signed, and sometimes nothing but the breast. Customs varied in different places. Anxious, however, to retain vestiges of all these ancient and pious practices, the Church still preserves them in some part of her sacred offices. The three may be seen united in one ceremony at the reading of the Gospel, where the priest signs himself on the forehead, mouth, and breast as he pronounces the initial words. The signing of the mouth only is seen in the Divine Office of the Breviary at the words "Domine, abia mea aperies"— "Lord, thou wilt open my lips."

When all the ancient practices died away, and the present discipline was introduced, for quite a long time it was the rule to trace the right. hand from the right to the left shoulder after having touched the breast, instead of, as now, from the left to the right. The latter came into general use in the time of Pope Pius V. (sixteenth century).

The Spanish peasantry, in making the sign of the cross, use the formula, "By the sign of the Holy Cross deliver us from our enemies, O God our Lord! In the name of the Father, and of the Son, and of the Holy Ghost. Amen, Jesus."

Regarding the disposition of the fingers in making this sacred sign, different practices existed, too, at one time. The most general way, however, in the Latin Church was to close the small and annular fingers of the right hand and extend the other three; then to make with the hand thus disposed the required sign. Bishops and the members of the Carthusian and Dominican orders have retained this custom. The two fingers united in this way symbolize the duality of natures in our Divine Lord, against the Eutychians, who maintained that there was but one; and the three other fingers typify the Blessed Trinity (Romsee, iv. 56; Bona, *De Divina Psalmodia*, p. 507). It will interest the reader to know that our Holy Father the Pope always observes this ancient disposition of the fingers whenever he imparts his blessing, as may be seen from any correct picture representing him in this attitude.

Customs of the Oriental Church.—The ancient practice of touching the right shoulder before the left is yet in vogue with all who follow the Greek Rite, but the disposition of the fingers is entirely different. In making the sign of the

GREEK BISHOP IN CHASUBLE.
HOLDING THE DIKERION AND TRIKERION.

cross the Greek priest first crosses his thumb on the annular or fourth finger of the right hand, and bends his little finger so as to have it resemble the curve of a crescent; he allows the index finger to stand perfectly erect, and, having bent the middle one so as to form the same figure as that formed by the little finger, raises his hand aloft, and then traces the sign. The interpretation of all this is very interesting. The outstretched finger stands for the Greek letter *I;* the bending of the middle finger represents the letter *C*, one of the ancient ways of writing *Sigma*, or the English *S;* the letter *I*, and this *C* or *S*, form the well-known contraction for "Jesus," being its first and last letters. The thumb, crossed upon the fourth finger, is the Greek letter *X*, equivalent to our *ch;* and this, with the small finger shaped as the middle finger, and representing *C* or *S*, forms the contraction for "Christus," or Christ. Hence, "Jesus Christ" is the interpretation of the whole action. The Greeks are so careful to keep the fingers thus adjusted when making the sign of the cross that we find them so disposed when blessing the people with the *Dikerion* and *Trikerion*[2] (see figure).

In the great church of Holy Wisdom at Constantinople, of which we have said so much already, there was a very celebrated painting of our Lord in the inner porch over the central door, with St. John the Baptist on one side and the Blessed Virgin on the other, in the act of blessing the Emperor Justinian, who lay prostrate before him. The manner in which our Lord's fingers are adjusted in this painting is in accordance with the practice we have just described. Although the great temple itself is no longer a house of Christian worship, it being converted into a Mahometan

---

[2] The Dikerion is a sort of candlestick with two lights, signifying the duality of natures in our Lord; and the Trikerion, with its three lights, symbolizes the ever Blessed Trinity. With these the Greek bishop blesses the people before Mass.

jami,[3] traces of the ancient painting may yet be seen there, though in a very dingy condition.

The Maronites,[4] in making the sign of the cross, use the formula, "In the name of the Father, and of the Son, and of the Holy Ghost, one True God" (*Syriac Maronite Breviary*, Ferial Office).

The Monophysites,[5] in order to give as much prominence as possible to their heresy of holding that there was but one nature in our Lord, make the sign with one finger only. The orthodox of the East, as a set-off against this, make it with two (Smith and Dwight, *Researches in Armenia*, i. 159, note; Bona, *De Divina Psalmodia*, pp. 507, 508). According to the first-mentioned authority, the Armenians make the sign of the cross exactly as we do.

We will now return to where we left off. Having made the sign of the cross upon his person, the priest, alternately with the server, recites the "Judica me, Deus," or Forty-second Psalm. The peculiar adaptation of this Psalm for this part of the Mass is very happy when we consider that, according to the most general acceptation, it was originally written by King David when exiled from his house and home by the treachery of his son Absalom and his kinsman Saul. The only consolation that was left him in his misery was the hope he fondly cherished of returning again to the

---

[3] The *jami* is to a Mahometan what a cathedral is to a Christian. Ordinary churches the Mahometans call *mosques;* the greater ones, or those in which the office of Friday (the Turkish Sunday) is performed, are called *jamies*. The service peculiar to them is denominated *Jumanamazi*.

[4] We have said in another place that the name *Maronite* comes from Maro, a holy recluse of Mt. Lebanon. We deem it well to mention here that the Maronites themselves derive it from *Moran*, our Lord, and say that this better applies to them than any other name, inasmuch as they never lost the faith which they received from our Saviour (Bona, *Divina Psalmodia*, p. 567).

[5] All through Africa the followers of the heretic Eutyches are called *Monophysites*—*i.e.*, believers in one nature; but in the East they are universally styled *Jacobites*, from James Bardai, one of their leaders.

tabernacle where, better than anywhere else, he could pour out his soul to God in humble prayer.

Before the time of Pope Pius V. the recital of this Psalm was entirely at the option of the priest, somewhat in the same way as the "Benedicite" after Mass is at present; but in the new edition of the missal, published by order of the Council of Trent and supervised by the pontiff named, its recital was made a *red letter*, and since that time it has become obligatory. Those who were allowed to retain their ancient rites by the above-mentioned pontiff, such as the Carthusians, Carmelites, Dominicans, Ambrosians, etc., do not recite it now, at least not before the altar as we do. The Carmelites say it on the way out as they are going to celebrate, and that in an undertone of voice, without the antiphon "Introibo." Inasmuch as it is more or less a psalm of jubilation, it is omitted in Masses for the dead and in those of Passion-time. Such expressions as "Why art thou sad, O my soul?" and "Why dost thou disquiet me?" are but ill-suited to Masses which are said on mournful occasions. According to Pouget, another reason may be given for its omission in these cases—viz., that a vestige of the ancient custom of not reciting it at all may be preserved (Romsee, iv. 60).

The Psalm is concluded with the minor doxology, "Glory be to the Father, and to the Son, and to the Holy Ghost. As it was in the beginning, is now, and ever shall be, world without end. Amen."

Regarding the antiquity of the "Gloria Patri," there seems to be unanimous consent that, with the exception of a few words, it originated with the Apostles themselves, who in conferring Holy Baptism had frequent occasion to pronounce the greater part of it at least in the sacred formula (Kozma, 164). Up to the Council of Nicæa, A.D. 325, its form was this: "Glory be to the Father, and to the Son, and to the Holy Ghost, world without end. Amen." The part, "as it was in the beginning, is now, and ever shall be," was added by the fathers of that council against the heretic Arius, who denied that our Lord was coequal in eternity and in glory with God the Father (Selvaggio, l. ii. p. i. c. 10). According to Durandus (*Rationale Divin.*, p. 330), Pope Damasus (366-384), at the suggestion of St. Jerome, ordered the "Gloria" to be said after every psalm. The Greeks say it only after the last, and then not precisely as we do, but as follows : " Glory be to the Father, and to the Son, and to the Holy Ghost, now and ever, and to all ages." They, in common with ourselves, call it the *minor doxology*, in contradistinction to the " Gloria in excelsis," which is denominated the *major*, or *greater*. It is never said in the Masses or offices of the dead, on account of their lugubrious nature. With the Nestorians it is recited thus: " Glory be to thee, O God the Father ! Glory be to thee, O God the Son ! Glory be to thee, O thou all-sanctifying Spirit. **Amen**" (Burder, ii. 236).

CONFITEOR.

Following closely upon the "Gloria Patri" is the Confiteor, or Confession, which the priest recites bowed down in profound humility. It is worded as follows : " I confess to Almighty God, to blessed Mary ever Virgin, to blessed Michael the Archangel, to blessed John the Baptist, to the holy Apostles Peter and Paul, and to all the Saints, and to you, brethren, that I have sinned exceedingly in thought, word, and deed, through my fault, through my fault, through my most grievous fault. Therefore I beseech the blessed Mary ever Virgin, the blessed Michael the Archangel, the blessed John the Baptist, the holy Apostles Peter and Paul, and all the Saints, and you, brethren, to pray to the Lord our God for me."

Although the form of confession precisely as it now stands

is not of very high antiquity, yet all are agreed that its main structure is of apostolic origin. It must not, however, be supposed that ever since the days of the Apostles it has formed part of the Mass; the best authorities say that it was not introduced into it until about the eighth century (Romsee, 'iv. 69). Cardinal Bona conjectures that some form of confession must have been in use all the time, but what it was and where it came in he ventures not to say (*Rer. Liturg.*, p. 310). According to Merati (*Thesaur. Sacr. Rit.*, p. 158), the Confession was reduced to its present form of wording, out of the many then in use, by the third Council of Ravenna, held in the year 1314, and all the others were suppressed.

Of the many that formerly appeared and were used in the Mass we select the following from the celebrated Missal of Sarum,* as being the shortest : " I confess to God, to blessed Mary, to all the Saints, and to you, that I have sinned grievously in thought and in deed, through my fault. I beseech blessed Mary, all the Saints, and you to pray for me."

With the Dominicans the form of confession is as follows : " I confess to Almighty God, to blessed Mary ever Virgin, to our blessed father Dominic, and to all the Saints, that I have sinned exceedingly in thought, in speech, in work, and in omission, through my fault. I beseech the blessed Mary

---

* Sarum was an ancient borough in Wiltshire, England, a little north of Salisbury. It was rendered famous and of venerable reminiscence from the great St. Osmund, who was bishop of the place in 1078, and who, after much labor and careful study, instituted the so-called Sarum Rite, or "Use of Sarum," so well known throughout the land for the magnificence of its ceremonies. This rite prevailed throughout Great Britain generally until the reign of Queen Mary, in 1560, when, through the mediation of Cardinal Pole, Archbishop of Canterbury, the regular Roman Rite was introduced in its stead. (For a full account see Butler's *Lives of the Saints*, under the history of St. Osmund, December 4, and Dr. Rock's *Church of Our Fathers*, vol iii. part ii) The Sarum Rite never obtained at either Lincoln, Hereford, or York ; but it did at the famous cathedrals of Peterborough, Ely, and Durham. In a great many of its ceremonies it resembled the Carthusian and Dominican rites, as will be seen further on in the present work.

ever Virgin, and our blessed father Dominic, and all the Saints to pray for me." As the priest says, "'Through my fault, through my fault, through my most grievous fault," he strikes his breast three separate times in token of the sorrow that he feels for having offended God in the manner specified. This is a very ancient practice, for we find it done by the poor publican when he entered the Temple to pray, and by the people who witnessed our Lord's crucifixion on Calvary; for, as the Holy Scripture says, "They returned striking their breasts" (*Luke* xxiii. 48). The custom, too, was very prevalent in the early Church. "We enter the temple," says St. Gregory Nazianzen, "in sackcloth and ashes, and day and night between the steps and the altar we strike our breasts" (Bona, p. 311). According to Durandus (*Rationale*, p. 163), striking the breast three times at the Confiteor is intended to remind us of the three essential parts of the Sacrament of Penance—viz., *contrition, confession*, and *satisfaction*.

Confession in the Old Law.—That confession also preceded the offering of sacrifice according to the Aaronic ritual the Rabbi Moses Maimonides and other Jewish doctors assure us (Bona, p. 309). The manner in which this confession was to be made was fully explained in the *Mishna*, and the *Cabala*[7] unravelled its spiritual signification. The form of

---

[7] The *Cabala*—called by the Jews the "Soul of the Soul of the Law," in contradistinction to the *Mishna*, which they called simply the "Soul of the Law"—comprehended all the decisions of the rabbins on civil and religious points. Strictly speaking, it was the unwritten word handed down from sire to son in sacred tradition, and containing all that was necessary to know in order to understand the law and the prophets. According to the Jewish doctors, it was first delivered to Moses by Almighty God himself on Sinai, but was never committed to writing. It was intended to explain all the difficult passages of the law and to give their mystical interpretation. Those versed in this species of exegesis are called Cabalists. Their principal commentaries are contained in the book named *Zohar*, said to have been written by Rabbi Ben Jochai, who died about the year A.D. 120. Others ascribe to it a later date (see *The Reasons of the Law of Moses*, from the *More Nevochim* of Maimonides, done into English by James Townley, D.D., London, 1827; and Bannister's *Temples of the Hebrews*, p. 359).

its wording was as follows: "Truly, O Lord! I have sinned; I have acted iniquitously; I have prevaricated before thee, and am ashamed of my deeds; nor shall I ever return to them more." This the Jews called "Viddin Haddenarin" (Merati, *Thesaur. Sac. Rit.*, p. 158).

Without the express permission of the Holy See nothing can be added to the Confiteor. The privilege of adding the names of their founders to it is enjoyed by several religious orders, such as the Benedictines, Carmelites, Dominicans, Franciscans, and Augustinians.

Confession in the Oriental Church.—All the Eastern churches, as we see from their liturgies, observe the practice of making some sort of confession before the beginning of Mass. Save that of the Armenians alone, the form in no case agrees, as far as words are concerned, with ours, but the sentiments are the same. The confession used by the Maronites is as follows: "I ask thee, O God! to make me worthy of approaching thy pure altar without spot or blemish; for I thy servant am a sinner, and have committed sins and done foolish things in thy sight. Nor am I worthy to approach thy pure altar nor thy holy sacraments, but I ask thee, O pious, O merciful, O lover of men, to look upon me with thine eyes of mercy." After the Confiteor, which the server also recites, the priest says: "May Almighty God be merciful unto you, forgive you your sins, and bring you to life everlasting!" The server having answered "Amen," the priest subjoins, "May the Almighty and merciful God grant us pardon, absolution, and remission of our sins," to which "Amen" is also responded. In beginning the last prayer, or "Indulgentiam," the priest makes the sign of the cross upon his person to show that it is only through Him who died upon the cross for love of man that he expects indulgence and pardon. He then recites a few verses taken from Holy Scripture, principally from the Psalms, and ascends the altar-steps repeating that beautiful prayer, "'Take away from us, we beseech thee, O Lord! our iniquities, that we may be worthy to enter with pure minds the Holy of Holies, through Christ our Lord."

The expression "Holy of Holies," or, as it is in Hebrew, קֹדֶשׁ קֳדָשִׁים, *Kodesh Kodeshim*, refers away back to that portion of the Temple of Solomon which was inaccessible to all save the high-priest alone, and even to him unless on the great Day of Atonement, which was celebrated yearly in the month of Tisri. At all other times it was considered sacrilegious even to look into this hallowed place, whence the very light of day itself was excluded, and where nothing was allowed to remain save the Ark of the Covenant, over the lid of which, or Propitiatory, as it was called, shone the divine *Shechinah*,[a] or visible manifestation of Jehovah's presence, in the form of a luminous cloud.

The adaptation of this prayer to this part of the Mass is admirable. In Solomon's Temple the Holy of Holies was entirely shut in from the rest of the building, and from the gaze of everybody, by a thick veil, which no one was ever permitted to draw aside but the high-priest on the Day of Atonement, and not then until after much time had been spent in prayer and in per-

---

[a] The presence of the Shechinah (from the Hebrew *Shak*, to dwell) was one of the rare privileges of Solomon's Temple, neither of the subsequent ones possessing it. By it the Jews understood the presence of the Holy Ghost; and hence it is that in the Targums we find the distinctive appellations of *Jehovah*, or God; *Memra*, or the Word; and *Shechinah*, or the Holy Spirit. According to the rabbins, the presence of the Shechinah drove the princes of the air from the Temple, terrified the demons, and communicated a peculiar sanctity to all around the sacred edifice (Bannister, *Temples of the Hebrews*, p. 142). A tradition of long standing among the Jews says that when the Temple was destroyed by the Chaldeans the Shechinah was seen to fly away from it in the shape of a beautiful dove, never more to return.

forming the purifications required by the law. In asking Almighty God, therefore, to take away from us our iniquities, we, as it were, ask him to take away the veil alluded to, for our sins as a veil keep us from seeing Him as He is, and keep us from the true Holy of Holies, where not a mere Shechinah resides, but the great Jehovah of the New Testament, the Son of God himself, Body and Blood, Soul and Divinity. By as much, then, as a substance exceeds its shadow, by so much does our Holy of Holies exceed that of Solomon's Temple; and the Tabernacle in which the Holy One is kept is infinitely more holy and more precious than ever the Ark of the Covenant was. The prayer alluded to is very ancient, as it may be seen in all the early Roman Ordos, and mention is made of it by Micrologus,* who wrote in the eleventh century (Romsee, iv. 75).

When the priest has reached the altar he places his hands upon it, and, having made a slight inclination, recites the prayer "Oramus te, Domine," which may thus be rendered in English: "We pray thee, O Lord! through the merits of thy saints whose relics are here present, and of all the saints, that thou wouldst vouchsafe to forgive me all my sins." As he pronounces the words "whose relics are here present," he kisses the altar out of respect for the sacred relics themselves, as well as to testify his love for our Divine Lord, whom the altar mystically represents. As we have already devoted several pages to the custom of enclosing relics in the altar, we shall only say here that, even though for some reason or other there should be no relics at all enclosed, as is often the case in this country, still the prayer "Oramus

---

* It is not certain whether "Micrologus" was the name of an author or the name of a book. The production, at any rate, dates from the time following closely upon the death of Pope Gregory VII., which happened A.D. 1085.

te, Domine," must not be omitted. At Solemn High Mass the altar is incensed at this place, but at Low Mass the priest, after having recited the "Oramus te," goes immediately to the missal, placed on its stand at the Epistle corner.

Ancient Customs.—Although the prayer we have been speaking of may be found in missals which date as far back as the ninth century, still with many churches it was never customary to recite it at all; and we see that it is not recited now by either the Carthusians or the Dominicans. The former say in its stead a "Pater" and "Ave"; the latter kiss the altar simply, and say nothing but the "Aufer a nobis."

In ancient times the custom prevailed of kissing at this place, instead of the altar itself, a cross which used to be painted on the missal (Romsee, iv. 77). A vestige of this is yet to be seen in Pontifical Mass, where the bishop, after he has said the "Oramus te, Domine," kisses the altar first, and then the Gospel of the day, presented to him by a subdeacon. Some used to kiss a sign of the cross traced upon the altar with the finger. The Dominicans observe this practice yet.

Oriental Customs in this Respect.—The Nestorian priests kiss the altar, as we do, upon first reaching it, and repeat this act of reverence frequently through the Mass (Smith and Dwight, *Researches in Armenia*, ii. 261 et passim). The Armenians kiss a beautifully-wrought cross on the back of the missal (*ibid.* 112). The practice with the rest of the Orientals is precisely like our own, as we see from their various liturgies.

Here we beg to call the reader's particular attention to a fact well worthy of remembrance—viz., that there was hardly a ceremony or liturgical custom ever used which may not yet be found, either whole or in part, in the ceremonies employed by the Church to-day. What is not seen in Low Mass may be seen in High Mass; and what is not seen in the Mass of an ordinary priest may be seen in that celebrated by a bishop; then, again, what a bishop's Mass has not a pope's has. We shall illustrate what we mean by examples. In ancient times the "pax," or kiss of peace, was common to every Mass, and every member of the congregation received it in due order; now it is only given at Solemn High Mass, and then only to the members of the sanctuary. The custom once prevailed, too, of pinning a handkerchief or maniple to the priest's left wrist a little before he ascended the altar-steps, for purposes that we have already explained; this custom is now reserved for a bishop's Mass, where the maniple is fastened to his lordship's arm at the "Indulgentiam." Again, when the people communicated under both species, other chalices besides that used by the priest were employed, which received the name of *ministerial*, from the fact that the Precious Blood was administered from them by means of tubes or long reeds; these tubes are yet employed whenever the pope celebrates Grand High Mass. Many things, too, may be seen in Masses for the dead which date away back to the early days, such as not saying the opening psalm, or "Judica me, Deus"; omitting the blessing of the water at the Offertory, and of the people at the end of Mass. Many other vestiges of ancient practices might be enumerated, but we rest content with the citation of one more, taken from the Divine Office of the Breviary. It is a well-known fact that while the *Disciplina Arcani*, or "Discipline of the Secret," prevailed, the Lord's Prayer was one of those things that the catechumens were not allowed to learn, or even hear recited. Now, as all these were allowed to be present at the recital of the Divine Office, this prayer was never said aloud, lest it might be heard by the *uninitiated :* but at Mass the case was otherwise. No catechumen could remain in church after the Gospel, and hence, as no fear was to be apprehended from the presence of any but the faithful, when the priest came to the "Pater Noster" he said it loud enough to be heard by all. The same is observable in the Office and Mass of to-day.

CHAPTER XXI.

THE CELEBRATION OF MASS.

THE INTROIT.

THE priest, having reached the Epistle corner of the altar, after the "Oramus te, Domine," stands before the missal and reads from it the Introit, or beginning of the Mass of the day. In pronouncing its initial words he makes the sign of the cross upon himself, thereby calling to mind a memorable ancient custom so often alluded to by the early Fathers—viz., of making the sacred sign at the beginning of every important work. "At every step and movement," says Tertullian (second century), "whenever we come in or go out, at the bath, at table, whatever we are doing, we make the sign of the cross upon our foreheads" (*De Corona Militis*, c. ii.) Strictly speaking, the Introit is the beginning of Mass, for all that precedes it may be considered as a preparation for celebration; and we have seen that the greater part of it has not been long of obligation. With the Ambrosians, or Milanese, the Introit is called the *Ingress*. The Mozaràbic Missal calls it the *Office*, as does also that of the Carthusians, Dominicans, and Carmelites; and by this name was it designated, too, in the ancient Missal of Sarum (*Church of Our Fathers*, vol. iii. p. 147).

According to Merati (*Thesaur. Sacr. Rit.*, p. 70), the introduction of Introits into the Mass is to be ascribed to Pope Celestine (A.D. 423–432). Previous to this pontiff's time

Mass began with the lessons, and in some cases with the litanies, vestiges of which custom we have yet in some Masses of Lent. All liturgical writers are agreed in ascribing the arrangement of the Introits as they stand now, at least of all those that are taken from the Psalms, to Pope Gregory the Great. He placed these, together with the Graduals, Offertories, Communions, etc., in a separate book by themselves, called the *Antiphonary*, and afterwards drew upon them as occasion demanded. It is well to note here that in compiling this *Antiphonary* the pontiff made use, not of the Hieronymian translation of the Vulgate that was then in circulation, but of that which was in general use before St. Jerome's time, and called indifferently the *Versio Communis*, *Vetus Itala*, and *Editio Vulgata*. This accounts for the difference in wording between those passages of the Psalms used in the Mass and those that are said at Vespers and at other parts of the Divine Office. For example, the psalm "Beatus vir," or the Cxith, has, in the version that is used in the Mass, "metuit" and "cupit" where, according to St. Jerome's version, we read "timet" and "volet." And in the Cxlviith Psalm, or the "Lauda Jerusalem," instead of St. Jerome's rendition, "Mittit crystallum suam sicut buccellas," that read in the Mass has "Emittit christallum suam sicut frusta panis," and so on with many others. Those of the Mozarabic and Ambrosian rites, though not following closely the ancient *Versio Communis*, yet approach nearer to it by far than to St. Jerome's version in the portions that are used in the Mass. The versions used by them (they are not the same) are evidently some of those of which St. Augustine speaks as being innumerable about his time.

Whence the Introits are taken.—We have said that Pope Gregory is the author of all—at least so far as regards their arrangement—the Introits that are taken from the Psalter. There are several which are not taken from the Psalms at all, and a few which are taken from no part of Scripture, being the composition of some pious individuals. Nay, more, there is one which is taken from an apocryphal book—viz., the fourth book of Esdras—of which we shall presently speak. Those Introits which are not from the Psalms but from other parts of Scripture are by Durandus termed *irregular*, probably because they are not found in the Gregorian *Antiphonary*. Of such is the Introit for the third Mass of Christmas morning, the "Puer natus est nobis," taken from Isaias, chapter ix., and that for the Epiphany, "Ecce advenit Dominator Dominus," from Malachias, chapter iii. Those that are not Scriptural at all are the "Salve sancta parens," common to nearly all the Masses of our Blessed Lady, the Mother of God, and the accredited composition of the Christian poet Sedulius, or Shiels,[1] who flourished in the fifth century; the "Gaudeamus omnes in Domino" of the Feast of the Assumption; and the "Benedicta sit Sancta Trinitas" for the Feast of Holy Trinity. This latter is generally marked in our missals as being from the book of Tobias, chapter xii., but this is a mistake; in no part of Scripture do we find the Adorable Trinity mentioned expressly by one name. That the greater part, indeed, of this Introit is framed on the sixth verse of the said chapter is undoubtedly true, but it is incorrect to say that all of it is taken thence. We have said that there is an Introit which is taken from an apocryphal book; this is the one used in the Mass for the third feria after Pentecost Sunday, be-

---

[1] According to the general opinion, Sedulius, or Shiels, was an Irishman by birth. At an early age he is said to have settled in Italy, where, having prosecuted his studies with much success, he was ordained priest, and, according to some, advanced to the episcopacy. All pronounce him an eminent scholar and profound divine. The Church uses many of his hymns in her service, the principal of which are, "A solis ortus cardine," proper to Lauds of Christmas day; and "Herodes hostis impie," or, as the Roman Breviary has it, "Crudelis Herodes." The reader must be careful not to confound this Sedulius with another of the same name, but styled the *Younger*, who was bishop in Spain in the eighth century, and who wrote a history of the ancient Irish.

ginning thus: "Accipite jucunditatem." It is from the fourth book of Esdras,[2] chapter ii.

Scope of the Introit.—As a general rule the scope of the Introit is a key to the entire Mass of the day. If the occasion be one of great solemnity, and the Introit be taken from the Psalter, it is generally from those psalms that are most expressive of joy and exultation. Thus, on Easter Sunday, when the whole earth bursts forth in songs of praise over the glorious Resurrection of our Divine Lord, the Introit is taken from one of the most beautiful psalms among the entire one hundred and fifty—viz., the Cxxxviiith.

On occasions of great sorrow the Introit is generally from those psalms known as the *elegiac*, such as that for Septuagesima Sunday, when the Church puts on her penitential garments, and earnestly exhorts her children to prepare themselves by fasting and penance for the sorrowful tragedy that is to be enacted the last week of Lent.

On the feasts of particular saints it is generally formed so as to favor some special feature in the saint's career. Thus, for instance, in the case of St. Jerome Æmilianus, who was known the world over for his singular compassion in behalf of forlorn children, the Introit is taken from the Lamentations of Jeremias: "My liver is poured out upon the earth, for the destruction of the daughter of my people, when the children and the sucklings fainted away in the streets of the city" (chap. ii. 11).

Structure of the Introits.—The Introits, as a general rule, are made up of a few verses from some of the Psalms or other portions of Holy Scripture, followed by the minor doxology. Formerly the entire psalm used to be repeated at

---

[2] There was a very spirited discussion in the Council of Trent about the propriety of putting this book on the list of canonical Scripture. Some of the Fathers, considering its rare worth in general and the lofty tone of its sentiments, argued strongly in favor of it, while others opposed it. The latter, however, ruled ; and so it yet remains.

this place (Bona, p. 312), either by the priest himself or more generally by the choir. Pope Benedict XIV. is our authority for saying that this custom prevailed in the majority of churches up to the sixteenth century (*De Sacro. Missæ Sacrif.*, c. xvii.)

When the priest has read the entire Introit he reiterates it as far as the psalm appended to it. Taken in a mystic point of view, this initiatory prayer recalls to mind the clamors and anxious expectations of the patriarchs and prophets of old for the coming of the Messias, and its double repetition signifies the renewed earnestness with which this great event was looked for (Durandus, *Rationale Divin.*, p. 153). In many of King David's Psalms we find examples of this holy importunity, where we see the most important verses recited sometimes twice and thrice over; see, among others, Psalm xli. The Canticle of Canticles affords many more instances, and striking ones at that. Thus, in the fourth chapter the spouse is invited from Lebanon three different times: "Come from Lebanon, my spouse, come from Lebanon, come."

The priests of the Carmelite Rite repeat the Introit as we do, on ordinary occasions; but on the more solemn feasts of the year they repeat it three times. According to Le Brun, the literal or natural reason of thus lengthening out this part of the Mass was to give time for the incensing of the altar, etc., at Solemn High Mass, where the duty of singing the Introit always devolved upon the choir (see *Explication des Prières et des Cérémonies de la Messe*, i. 176).

Almaricus, Bishop of Treves, as related by Fortunatus (*De Ord. Antiph.*, cap. xxi.), says that Almighty God, in order to testify His approval of this portion of the Mass, caused His angels to sing for the Introit of the Mass in the Church of Holy Wisdom, at Constantinople, on the Feast of the Epiphany, the ninety-fourth Psalm, or the "Venite exultemus."

In Masses for the dead the priest does not make the sign of the cross on himself when beginning the Introit, but rather over the book, towards the ground, as if to bless the earth where the dead lie sleeping (Kozma, p. 226).

Introits in the Eastern Church.—In the Mass of the Eastern Church there are two Introits, although neither is precisely the same thing as ours, but rather a minor and greater procession. The former takes place a little before the expulsion of the catechumens,[3] and consists only of the translation of the book of the Holy Gospels to the altar by the deacon. The latter, or greater Introit, called by the Greeks ἡ μεγάλη εἴσοδος, *megale eisodos*, follows the expulsion of the catechumens, and is attended with such a gorgeous display of ritual that many have taken umbrage at it. To understand the ground of offence it must be borne in mind that on the occasion of this major Introit the unconsecrated elements are carried in solemn procession from the *prothesis*, or cruet-table, to the main altar amid fumes of incense and a multitude of blazing torches. An army of deacons and acolytes accompanies the procession, and the people of the congregation as it passes along prostrate themselves in silent adoration. It was this latter feature that formed the chief cause of complaint, and that led the censors sent out by the Holy See to the Eastern regions to abolish this rite in the liturgies of the orthodox. The Orientals attempt a defence of their seemingly strange custom by saying that no adoration whatever is here intended, but only what may be termed a sort of anticipatory reverence in view of what the elements will be changed into in course of the Holy Sacrifice—viz., the Body and Blood of Christ. This is the explanation given by Gabriel, Exarch of

---

[3] Although the ceremony of expelling the catechumens has long since ceased in the East as well as in the West still these expressions are yet retained by the Orientals.

Philadelphia, in Lydia, Asia Minor (Neale, *Holy Eastern Church*, i. 375).

KYRIE ELEISON.

When the priest has finished the Introit he proceeds to the middle of the altar, and there recites alternately with the server the "Kyrie eleison," or Minor Litany, as it used to be called in the early days. When it is a Solemn High Mass this is recited at the book. "Kyrie eleison," and its accompanying "Christe eleison," are two Greek expressions meaning "Lord have mercy on us," "Christ have mercy on us." Including what is said by the priest of this solemn petition for mercy, and what is said by the clerk or server, we have in all nine separate petitions, which liturgical writers interpret as follows : "Kyrie eleison" is said three times to God the Father for his manifold mercies ; "Christe eleison" is said three times to God the Son, the author of our redemption ; and "Kyrie eleison" is thrice repeated again to God the Holy Ghost, the sanctifier and consoler (Kozma, 168).

There is a very ancient tradition, and, to say the least of it, a very beautiful one, to the effect that our Divine Lord, on the occasion of his glorious ascension into heaven, tarried one day with each of the nine choirs of angels before he reached the celestial throne, and that in memory of this the "Kyrie" is repeated nine times (Neale, *Song of Songs*, p. 86). This tradition, according to some of the early Fathers, furnishes a key to the interpretation of that passage in the Canticle of Canticles where the spouse is represented as "leaping upon the mountains" and "skipping over the hills" (chap. ii. 8). The *mountains* and *hills*, say they, are the grades of the angelic choir through which our Lord passed (*ibid.*)

Some attribute the introduction of the "Kyrie" into the Mass to Pope Gregory the Great ; but this cannot be correct, for that holy pontiff himself said that he only caused it to be recited by both priest and people, because in the Greek Church it was solely confined to the latter, and even then there was no mention whatever of the "Christe eleison." Another very strong proof of the earlier introduction of it is that the Fathers of the second Council of Vaison, held in A.D. 529, speak of it as if well known throughout the whole Church; and this was at least sixty years before Pope Gregory's pontificate. We deem it well to quote the words of this council : "Let that beautiful custom of all the provinces of the East and of Italy be kept up—viz., that of singing with grand effect and compunction the 'Kyrie eleison' at Mass, Matins, and Vespers—because so sweet and pleasing a chant, even though continued day and night without interruption, could never produce disgust or weariness" (*Summa Conciliorum*, p. 89).

In many churches the custom prevailed for some time of intermingling with the "Kyrie," certain intercalary expressions touching the nature of the feast of the occasion. Thus, on feasts of the Blessed Virgin it would read after this manner : " O Lord, thou lover of virginity, illustrious Father and Mary's Creator, have mercy on us"; and so on with the rest of it (Romsee, p. 84).

The Ambrosians, or those who follow the Milanese Rite, recite the "Kyrie" at three different periods of the Mass— viz., after the "Gloria in excelsis," after the Gospel, and at the conclusion of divine service.

Why said in Greek.—There are certain words and expressions so peculiarly adapted to the language in which they were first conceived that they lose all their force and beauty when translated into another. Of such a nature are the words "alleluia," "hosanna," and "Kyrie eleison." But there is a deeper reason than this for retaining them in the Mass. Originally the Church was principally formed out of three different nations—viz., the Latin, the Greek, and the Hebrew—and in order to testify that the belief of these three nations was one and the same, the Western or Latin Church thought it proper to preserve the memory of the fact by adopting phrases from each of them. From the Greek we have "Kyrie eleison, Christe eleison," and in the *Improperia* of Good Friday, "Agios Theos, Agios Ischuros, Agios Athanatos"; and from the Hebrew, "amen," "alleluia," "hosanna," "Sabaoth," "cherubim" and "seraphim," and several others which occur now and then in the Epistles and Gospels. But liturgical writers give several other reasons for the retention of these languages in the Mass, foremost of which is that they have ever been looked upon as venerable and sacred, from the fact that the title of the cross was written in them; and as the sacrifice of the Mass and that offered on the cross are one and the same, except that the former is offered in an unbloody manner, what could be more appropriate than to give these hallowed languages a place in it? The Greek has innumerable other claims to the place it holds. It was the vernacular of some, in fact we might say of the vast majority, of the early heroes and defenders of the faith—of St. John Chrysostom, St. Gregory Nazianzen, St. Basil the Great, St. John Damascene, and hosts of others. It was in it that the very valuable and venerable translation of the Scriptures called the Septuagint was made, from which our Lord and his blessed Apostles drew so largely in their addresses to the people (Dixon, *Introduction to the Sacred Scrip.*, p. 98).

One thing alone, to pass over all others, should entitle the Hebrew to a place in the Mass—viz., it was the language of Melchisedec, the prototype in the old law of our Divine Lord himself in relation to his sacred and eternal priesthood. It was also the vernacular of our Lord and his ever-blessed Mother, not to say of the majority of his disciples in the new law. We do not think it necessary to enter here into a full history of the ancient Hebrew and what it is so often known by—viz., the Syro-Chaldaic, or Syriac. Let it suffice to say that since the Babylonic captivity there has been no true Hebrew spoken by the Jews; and that what goes by that name in the New Testament was an Aramean branch of the Semitic family of languages known as the Syriac. It can be proved, almost to a demonstration, that this was the language our Lord spoke.

Oriental Usage regarding the "Kyrie eleison."—The Liturgy of St. James[4] is the only Eastern Liturgy which enjoins the recital of the "Kyrie" on the priest. In all the others it is solely confined to the choir and people, who, however, on no occasion say "Christe eleison." The Liturgy of St. Chrysostom[5] prescribes the recital of the "Kyrie" after all the principal supplications.

GLORIA IN EXCELSIS.

After the recital of the "Kyrie" follows that of the "Gloria in excelsis," or major doxology, during which the priest makes several reverences by bowing the head slightly at some of its principal clauses, and terminates it by making the sign of the cross upon his person.

[4] The Liturgy of St. James lays claim to the first place among all the liturgies of the East. It is said to be the oldest in existence, having been committed to writing somewhere about the beginning of the third century. Though now rarely used in its entirety, still it is the basis of all those liturgies used by the Maronites, Syrians, and Nestorians, and is the one accredited to the churches within the patriarchate of Jerusalem. It is used in some of the islands of the Archipelago on St. James' day. [5] The Liturgy of St. Chrysostom, derived and abbreviated from that of St. Basil, as the latter is from that of St James, has the largest circulation at present of any known Liturgy in the East. It is in general use wherever the Greek Rite, no matter what the language be, prevails. It is therefore the Liturgy of Russia and of the four patriarchates, Constantinople, Alexandria, Antioch, and Jerusalem, as well as of the kingdom of Greece. On those occasions upon which it is not employed—viz., on the Sundays of Lent, except Palm Sunday, and Holy Thursday, Holy Saturday, and the vigils of Christmas and the Epiphany—the Liturgy of St. Basil supplies its place.

Regarding the authorship of the opening words of this sublime anthem no doubts can be entertained, for the Evangelists record them as having been sung by the Heavenly Host over Bethlehem on Christmas morning. Much dispute, however, has arisen regarding the remainder; some attributing them to one author, others to another. A very widely circulated opinion accredits it to St. Hilary, Bishop of Poictiers, in France, A.D. 353. Whoever be its author, this much is certain: that it existed word for word as it stands now before the Council of Nicæa, held in A.D. 325 (Kozma, p. 170; Bona). Rather, then, than ascribe it to any one in particular, in the absence of substantial proof, it is better to say, with the Fathers of the fourth Council of Toledo, in Spain, held A.D. 633, that *the remainder was composed by doctors of the Church, whoever these were* (Merati, *Thesaur. Sacr. Rit.*, p. 72).

So careful was the ancient Church of securing for this sacred anthem all the veneration that was due to it that she restricted its recital to very grand occasions, and even then confined it solely to bishops. But it was not at its introduction confined exclusively to the Mass, for we find it prescribed for the Morning Service, or Matins, of the Divine Office (Romsee, iv. 90). The precise date of its introduction into the Mass, or who introduced it, is not easy to settle. Those who ascribe its introduction to Pope Telesphorus are evidently incorrect in so doing, for it is now very well ascertained that he only caused to be said the initial sentence, or the part chanted by the angels, and had nothing to do with the rest of it (Bona, p. 317). Until the entire hymn was composed, the first part of it, or the angelic words, used to be sung—not, however, in every Mass, but only in the Midnight Mass of Christmas, as the above-named pontiff decreed (*ibid.*) According to Pope

Innocent III. (*De Sacr. Altaris Mysterio*, cap. xx. p. 113), it was Pope Symmachus (498–514) who extended it in its present form to every Sunday in the year and to the feasts of all the holy martyrs. Some maintain that the decree regulating this discipline was to be viewed as a general one, and that hence it included priests as well as bishops; others hold that it affected the latter only. Whether it did or did not, this much is certain : that when Pope Gregory the Great attained to the pontificate (590–604) no priest was accustomed to say it in any Mass, unless in that of Easter Sunday ; and bishops were not allowed to recite it except on Sundays and festivals. From a very ancient Roman directory yet preserved in the Vatican Library we derive the following information in point: "Dicitur 'Gloria in excelsis Deo,' si episcopus fuerit, tantummodo die Dominico, sive diebus festis. A presbyteris autem minime dicitur nisi in solo Pascha" (Bona, p. 317)—that is, "If the bishop celebrates, the 'Gloria in excelsis' is said only on Sundays and festivals. On no account must it be said by priests, unless on Easter Sunday alone." This same restriction was approved of and enjoined by Pope Gregory, who also caused it to be inserted in a conspicuous place in the missal made out under his supervision ; and in this way did it continue, according to Cardinal Bona, until about the middle of the eleventh century, when the restriction was taken away and the privilege of reciting it extended to priests and bishops alike in every Mass that admitted of it.

According to Martène and others, this hymn used to be chanted in early times at Rome on Christmas morning, in Greek first and then in Latin. The same custom prevailed also among the clergy of Tours, where it was said in Greek at the first Mass, and at the second in Latin (*Enchiridion de Sacr. Missæ ex opere Ben. XIV.*, p. 31).

When the "Gloria in excelsis" may be said.—As the Angelic Hymn is one of joy and festivity, its recital is forbidden to all during seasons of penance and mourning. Hence it is not heard during Lent or in Masses for the dead. Durandus tells us, with no small amount of holy indignation, that in times gone by the bishop of Bethlehem arrogated to himself the right of reciting it on every occasion, no matter whether it was a joyful or a sorrowful one, and this for the reason that an exception should be made in case of the city where the sacred anthem had first been heard (*Rationale Divinorum*, p. 172). The present rule regarding its recital is that which was laid down by Pope Pius V.—viz., that whenever the "Te Deum" is recited in the Divine Office this hymn is said in the Mass. This, however, admits of a few exceptions; but as we are not writing a ceremonial, we do not think it our duty to name what they are, and we wish our readers to bear this in mind in similar cases.

How the Dominicans, Carthusians, and Others recite it. —The Carthusians and Dominicans, as their ceremonials direct, go to the middle of the altar, as we do, to recite this hymn, but after they have said its initial words they return and finish the remainder at the missal. This custom prevailed also in the Mass according to the Sarum Rite (*Church of Our Fathers*, iii. 148).

Practice of the Oriental Church.—Singularly enough, the Nestorians are the only Christians of the East who recite this hymn in the Mass (Neale, *Holy Eastern Church*, i. 471). The Greek Church recites it frequently in the Divine Office, but never in the Liturgy or Mass. It appears, to be sure, in the Liturgy of St. James, but not the entire hymn, only the angelic part, or that which used to be said at first in the Latin Church. And this cannot but be a strong argument against those who would have the authorship of it accredited to Pope Telesphorus, who died in A.D. 154: for undoubtedly, if it existed in its entirety then as now, it would be so inserted in that Liturgy, which, in the opinion of the ablest critics, was not edited earlier than the year 200.

DOMINUS VOBISCUM.

At the conclusion of the "Gloria in excelsis" the priest stoops down and kisses the altar; then, having turned to the people, salutes them with "Dominus vobiscum"—"The Lord be with you"—words evidently taken from the Old Testament, where we see them employed on various occasions (see *Ruth* ii. 4 ; 2 *Paral.* xvi. et passim). The Jews were very particular in having the name of God in all their salutations, or at least an allusion to some one of God's good gifts. Their other salutations used to be : 1, The blessing of Jehovah upon thee ; 2, May God be with thee ; 3, Be thou blessed of Jehovah ; 4, Peace be to thee. It was this last form that the Angel Gabriel used when he announced to our Blessed Lady that she was to be the favored Mother of the "Long-expected of nations," our Saviour and Redeemer. What in English is rendered by "Hail to thee" is in Syriac—the vernacular of the Blessed Virgin at that time, and evidently the language in which the angel addressed her—ܫܠܳܡ ܠܶܟܝ *Slom lek*—"Peace to thee."

PAX VOBIS.

We have seen that the recital of the "Gloria in excelsis" was at its introduction into the Mass solely confined to bishops, and continued to be peculiar to them for many centuries afterwards. Now, inasmuch as *peace*—*i.e.*, the peace of God, which, as the apostle saith," surpasseth all understanding"—is the most prominent feature set forth in this sacred anthem ; and as our Divine Lord always made use of the word in his salutations to his disciples after his resurrection, it was deemed appropriate to deviate from the usual "Dominus vobiscum" after the recital of this hymn, and say in its stead, "Pax vobis"—"Peace be to you" To keep up an old custom, and to establish a slight difference between a bishop's manner of saying Mass and that of a priest, the former was allowed to retain the use of "Pax vobis" after the privilege of reciting the "Gloria" had been extended to the latter (Bona, p. 318; Le Brun, i. 205). But it is only at the end of this anthem that the bishop salutes with "Pax vobis"; upon every other occasion he says "Dominus vobiscum" like an ordinary priest. Some Spanish bishops, it is true, arrogated to themselves the right of saying it upon every occasion, but we see how severely they were reprehended for so doing by the first Council of Braga, in A.D. 561 (Bona, *ibid.*)

Oriental Customs.—The Greeks never use the salutation "Dominus vobiscum," but always say in its stead "Εἰρήνη πᾶσιν," *eirene pasin*—that is, "Peace to all"; to which is responded, "Καὶ τῷ πνεύματι σοῦ," *Kai to pneumati sou* —"And to thy spirit." The same forms are observed in all the other churches of the East, with very little difference. At several parts of the Mass it is customary with the Nestorian priests to make the sign of the cross upon themselves when using this salutation, which is generally, "Peace be with you all." Their deacons, for the most part, say, "Peace be with us" (Badger, *Nestorians and their Rituals*, ii. 237 et passim).

After having said the "Dominus vobiscum," the priest returns to the Epistle corner of the altar, and there, extending his hands in the manner of a suppliant, reads from the missal before him the prayers proper to the occasion. As he is about to read the first he invites all to unite with him in the sacred act by reciting aloud "Oremus"—"Let us pray." In former times it was customary to turn entirely around to the congregation after this invitation had been pronounced, and explain to them the precise nature of the prayer that followed, a vestige of which is still retained in the long series of prayers recited in the Mass of Good Friday, where we see a particular object prefixed to each. Another custom, too, that obtained in ancient times was for the people to enter into a sort of silent prayer after they had heard "Oremus," and remain in this quiet meditation until the general prayer was announced. This general prayer was denominated "ἐπίκλησις," *epiklesis*, by the Greeks, from ἐπί, upon, and καλέω, I call—that is, an invocation—but in Latin it received the name of *collecta*, or collect, from the verb *colligere*, to gather together; because the common wants of the whole people were, as it were, brought together in it and laid before Almighty God. These prayers go by the name of collects even to-day (Bona, p. 319; Selvaggio, *Inst. Christian Antiq.*, i. p. 1).

MANNER OF RECITING THE PRAYERS.

The priest recites all the prayers with outstretched and extended hands. This practice is not new, for we find that it was observed also in the old law. Moses thus prayed in the wilderness, and the Holy Scripture tells us that as long as he kept his hands thus uplifted on high while his kinsmen fought against the Amalekites in the valley of Raphidim, the former were always victorious, but that when he let them down a little, victory fell to the latter (*Exod.* xvii.) Many touching allusions are made to this extending of hands in prayer throughout the Old Testament; and we see it also strongly recommended in the New, for St. Paul says, "I will that men pray lifting up pure hands" (1 *Tim.* ii. 8). And that this holy and venerable attitude was observed by the ancient Christians in their devotions, innumerable testimonies prove. The Catacombs bear witness of the fact in the pictures they furnish us of men and women praying in this way. But it is only the priest at Mass who observes this practice now. The people pray that way no longer, but rather with hands united. Dr. Rock tells us in his *Hierurgia* (p. 61) that while travelling in Europe he noticed the people in many of the churches of Munich praying after the ancient manner. In the mystic interpretation of this posture there is reference, first, to Adam's uplifting of his hand in reaching for the forbidden fruit; and, secondly, to the lifting up and outstretching of our Divine Lord's hands on the cross, by which Adam's transgression was atoned for (Bona, p. 322). Praying with the hands fully extended in the form of a cross is yet observed at certain parts of the Mass by the Carthusians, Carmelites, and Dominicans, as we see from their ceremonials.

The reader, no doubt, will be curious to know something more about the manner in which the ancient Christians assisted at Mass than what we have given. As a general rule the ancient churches had no seats for the people to sit on, as that position was deemed ill in keeping with the gravity becoming the house of God. As the services, however, in the very early days were much longer than at present, those who, through feebleness of health or other causes, could not stand, were allowed the use of staves to lean upon, and in some rare cases even of cushions to sit upon, a practice which is yet quite common in the churches of Spain, and in many of those of the rest of Europe. It was the rule to stand always on Sunday, in memory of our Lord's glorious resurrection, and to kneel the rest of the week (Selvaggio, b. 10). As kneeling is a sign of humiliation, it was the rule to observe it during the penitential seasons and on all occasions of mourning. According to St. Jerome, St. Basil the Great, Tertullian, and others, these rules were derived from the Apostles themselves; but because some would sit when they ought to stand, and some stand when they ought to kneel, the Sacrosanct Council of Nicæa, in order to establish uniformity, thus decreed in its twentieth canon: "In order that all things may be done alike in every parish, it has seemed good to this Holy Synod [to decree] that the people pour out their prayers standing" (*Summa Conciliorum*, p. 35; Selvaggio, 8). Of course this rule did not affect the Public Penitents, who were obliged to remain kneeling during the entire time that they were permitted to be present in the house of God. The fourth Council of Carthage strictly forbade them ever to change this posture.

Whenever any important prayer or lesson was to be read, and the people had been kneeling beforehand, the deacon invited them now to stand by the words, "Erecti stemus honeste"—that is, "Let us become erect and stand in a becoming manner." During the penitential season the congregation were invited to kneel by saying, "Flectamus genua," and to stand up afterwards by "Levate." The same custom may yet be observed in Lent and on some other occasions. The Catholic reader need not, of course, be told that during the actual celebration of Mass the priest is always standing. At Solemn High Mass he and his ministers are allowed to sit down while the choir are chanting the "Kyrie eleison," "Gloria in excelsis," and "Credo," but never at any other part of the service. Two singular instances of saying Holy Mass in a sitting posture are upon record. Pope Benedict XIV. did so in his declining years, when through great feebleness of health he could neither stand nor kneel, and the same is recorded of the saintly and ever-memorable pontiff, Pope Pius VII.

Praying towards the East.—The custom prevailed very generally with the Christians of early days of turning to the east in prayer, whether at Mass or out of Mass, and the majority of ancient churches were built with a view to favor this custom. The reasons given for this practice are the following: First, because the east is symbolic of our Lord, who is styled in Scripture the "Orient from on high," the "Light," and the "Sun of Justice." Secondly, the Garden of Eden was situated in that region, and thence did the Magi come to lay their gifts at the crib of our Lord on Christmas morning. Thirdly, according to St. John Damascene, when our Lord hung on the cross his back was turned to the east and his face to the west; we therefore pray to the east that we may, as it were, be looking in his face. Fourthly, the ancients prayed in this direction, in order not to resemble the pagans, who moved in every direction—now praying towards the sun at mid-day, now towards the moon, and again towards the stars; the Saracens prayed towards the south, the Jews towards Jerusalem, and the Mahometans towards Mecca. Fifthly, it has always been looked upon as an established thing that at the last day our Lord, with his effulgent cross sparkling in the heavens, will come to judge mankind from the eastern quarter (see Bona, *Divina Psalmodia*, p. 441; Riddle's *Christian Antiquities*, p. 795).

NUMBER OF COLLECTS SAID IN THE MASS.

On occasions of great solemnity the general rule prescribes but one Collect, but on ordinary occasions three is the number. It is forbidden to say more than seven at any time, and this number is rarely reached unless when some special commemorations are made. According to liturgical commentators, one prayer mystically represents the unity of our faith; three are said in honor of the Blessed Trinity, and in memory of our Lord's praying thrice in the Garden of Olives; five commemorate his five wounds; and by seven we are reminded of the seven gifts of the Holy Ghost (Bouvry, ii. 128; Durandus, *Rationale Divin.*, p. 181).

Whatever be the number of the Collects, none others may be said unless those given in the missal. As far back as the year 416 laws were made by the Council of Milevi, in Africa, forbidding under severe censures the introduction of any prayers into the Mass except those approved of by legitimate authority. This discipline is yet strictly observed.

Prayers of the Oriental Church.—The prayers used by the Orientals are much more numerous than ours, as may be readily seen from any one of their liturgies. In length, too, they far exceed those that we employ, for which reason alone the service of Mass in the East occupies nearly twice the time that ours does. The Copts generally add prayers for the favorable flow of the Nile, which is to them one of the chief sources of temporal blessings, for the entire vegetation and fecundity of Egypt depends upon its inundations.[5] The "Oratio fluminis," or Prayer of the River, is thus worded: "Remember, O Lord! the waters of the river, and bless and increase them according to their measure."

AMEN.

At the conclusion of the prayers the server answers "Amen," a Hebrew word meaning "may it be so." The custom of thus answering amen at the end of the prayers is evidently derived from the old law, for we find it in nearly every book of the Old Testament, and it is also very common in the New. According to Cardinal Bona (*Divina Psalmodia*, p. 532), it is one of those words which the translators of the Bible left untouched, lest by rendering it in any other

---

[5] There is an instrument for measuring the rise of the Nile in the isle of Rhoda, called the nilometer, but by the Arabs *Dir-el-Mekias*—place of measure. According to Kalkasendas, if the river rose but twelve pikes there would be a famine; fourteen pikes caused a year of plenty; sixteen gave abundance for two years; and when it reached seventeen it had attained its full limit. Great fears were always entertained of its going beyond this boundary, for a serious inundation would be the result; and hence the earnestness with which the Copts prayed for a due disposition of these waters (cfr. Pococke's *Travels in Egypt*).

language but its native Hebrew its power and beauty might be lost.

THE EPISTLE.

The reading of the Epistle immediately follows the last Collect. To this end, instead of keeping his hands spread out as heretofore, the priest now rests them on the missal-stand, while he reads the Epistle in an audible tone. Nor is this change in the position of the hands without a mystic meaning. By it the priest is made aware of the obligation he is under of not only *reading* the law, but also of *doing* what it prescribes, the hands being indicative of labor (Romsee, iv. 101).

The particular part of Scripture from which the Epistle is taken, as well as the Apostle's name to whom it is accredited, both of which form the title, are first read before the text itself; thus, for example, "the reading of the Epistle of blessed Paul the Apostle to the Corinthians," "to the Hebrews," "to the Romans," etc., as the case may be. If the lesson to be read be taken from any one of the three books, viz., Proverbs, the Canticle of Canticles, or Ecclesiasticus, its title is always, "the reading of the Book of Wisdom," without any further specification, for the reason that these three books were always denominated the "Sapiential Writings" by the ancient Fathers (De Herdt, *Sacr. Liturg.*, ii. No. 63).

The ancient Hebrews—and the practice is yet kept up by the modern Jews—always began the reading of the Law with the forty-fourth verse of the fourth chapter of Deuteronomy, viz., "this is the law that Moses set before the children of Israel" (Burder, *Relig. Cerm. and Customs*, p. 39). Before the Epistles were in circulation, the custom of reading portions of the Old Testament was always observed in the early Church, as can be proved by numberless testimonics. The Acts of the Apostles refer frequently to this practice. But as soon as the Epistles were written the custom of reading the Old Testament gradually died away, and gave place to the custom which is now in vogue. St. Paul strictly ordained that his Epistles should be read in all the churches under his charge. In his Epistle to the Colossians, chapter iv., he writes thus: "And when this Epistle shall have been read with you, cause that it be read also in the Church of the Laodiceans." And at the end of his first Epistle to the Thessalonians he thus expresses himself: "I charge you by the Lord that this Epistle be read to all the holy brethren." St. Justin Martyr (second century) informs us that this practice was general in his time (*Apol.*, 2); and Tertullian refers to it also (*Apol.*, c. 39).

In many of the churches of early days it was customary to read first a lesson from the Old Testament, and then an Epistle from the New, in order to show that both the one and the other are entitled to much respect; and that although the new law is much more perfect than the old, still the moral teaching of the latter remains yet in all its vigor. This custom is yet kept up in the Mozarabic and Ambrosian rites; and the Carthusians and Dominicans observe it on Christmas day and its vigil. A vestige of the practice may be seen in our own missal, also, in the Masses of the Quarter Tenses—with this difference, however: that instead of one lesson several are read, in order to show the aspirant for the holy ministry the necessity he is under of becoming thoroughly conversant with the law and the prophets, as well as with what the New Testament contains; for it was during these days that orders were conferred in ancient times, and even according to the present discipline of the Church they are yet set apart for this purpose in the majority of places in Europe (Gavantus, *Thesaur. Sacr. Rit.*, p. 338). The Council of Laodicea, held in the fourth century, and the third Council of Carthage forbade the reading of anything in the Mass which was not taken from Holy Scripture. An exception, however, seems to have been made in some cases, for we see that the letters of the Supreme Pontiffs and the Acts of the Martyrs, also the letters of the bishop of the diocese, used to be read very frequently (Martène, *De Antiquis Eccl. Ritibus*).

With the ancient Hebrews, the Pentateuch, or *Sepher Tora*,* as they called it, was held in such high estimation that they made it a practice to read as much of it on every Sabbath as would enable them to finish it in the course of a year. · For which reason they divided the entire five books into portions called *parshizoth*, fifty-three or fifty-four in number, corresponding with the entire number of service days, and read one at every service. The Jews of to-day keep up this custom (Bannister, *Temples of the Hebrews*, p. 351).

It is universally admitted, we believe, that the series and order of the Epistles read to-day in the Mass were drawn up by St. Jerome at the request of the Sovereign Pontiff Pope Damasus (Cardinal Bona, *Rer. Liturg.*, p. 324). They were first inserted in a book by themselves, called by St. Jerome the *Companion*, but when plenary missals came into use the *Companion* was superseded by them, and in this way it lost its individuality.

At High Mass the Epistle is chanted by the subdeacon in a loud tone of voice, with only one modulation at the con-

---

* We deem it well to inform the reader at this place that the Hebrews made three great divisions of the entire Bible, which they denominated respectively *Sepher Tora*, or the Book of the Law—*i.e.*, the Pentateuch; *Nebiim*, or the Book of the Prophets; and *Ketobiim*, or the Sacred Writings. This last division was what the ancient Fathers called *Hagiographa*. The reading of the Sepher Tora began at Nisan, the first month of the Jewish ecclesiastical year, and continued up to the end of Adar, the last month. Much display attended this reading.

clusion. It is chanted facing the altar and not the congregation, as is the case when the Gospel is chanted, because the latter, being the words of our Lord, is entitled to more respect, and, besides, it is principally designed for the instruction of the people. The custom of sitting down during the reading of the Epistle is very ancient, being evidently derived from the synagogue and early Christians (Romsee, iv. p. 103). According to Durandus, the Epistle is read before the Gospel on account of its symbolizing the mission of St. John the Baptist, who was the precursor of our Lord (*Rationale*, p. 183).

Deo Gratias.—At the conclusion of the Epistle the server answers, "Deo gratias"—"Thanks be to God"—as an evidence of the gratitude we owe to our Creator for the spiritual nourishment of his sacred words. According to the Mozarabic Rite, this response is made as soon as the title of the Epistle is announced.

In ancient times the expression "Deo gratias" was in very common use among the faithful. It was, in fact, one of their principal forms of salutation whenever they met, as we learn from St. Augustine, who also tells us that the impious Donatists endeavored to turn it into ridicule. When the proconsul Galerius Maximus read out the decree, "Thasius Cyprianus shall die by the sword," the saintly bishop received the sentence by exclaiming, "Deo gratias!"

Epistle in the Eastern Church.—The practice of reading the Epistle in the Mass is also observed by all the Oriental churches, as their liturgies show us. The Copts at this place read five different portions of the Sacred Writings, each of which, in accordance with Oriental usage, they denominate the *Apostle*. These five portions are taken respectively from the Epistles of St. Paul, the Catholic Epistles, the Acts of the Apostles, the Psalter, and the Evangels

(Renaudot, *Liturg. Orient.*, i. 186). Their canons are so strict in this matter that, were a priest to omit any of these designedly, he would subject himself to excommunication; and as the ancient Coptic, or that in which their service is carried on, is entirely unknown among the people, after the Epistle has been read in that tongue, it is again read in Arabic, the language of the day in those parts. All through the East the Apostle—as they call the Epistle—is listened to and read with a very great amount of respect.

The Ambo.—Whenever there was Solemn High Mass, which was the case nearly always in the early Church, the Epistle used to be chanted, not in the sanctuary as now, but from an elevated lectern or pulpit known as the Ambo, from the Greek $\dot{\alpha}\nu\alpha\beta\alpha\iota\nu\omega$—*anabaino*, I ascend—placed generally in the nave of the church. In some places there were as many as three appurtenances of this kind: one for the reading of the Epistle, another for the reading of the Gospel, and the third for the Prophecies. Specimens of these may yet be seen in that ancient church at Rome known as St. Clement's. Though many churches possessed two of these amboes, one set apart for the chanting of the Epistle, the other for the chanting of the Gospel, still the general rule was to make one ambo serve for both these purposes; and we find but one employed in the great church of Holy Wisdom at Constantinople, which all regarded as the most perfect temple of worship then in existence.

Material of which the Amboes were made.—The material as well as the workmanship of the amboes varied, of course, according to the means of the church. Some were plain and made wholly of wood, while others were formed of the costliest materials. That in the Church of Holy Wisdom was constructed of pure alabaster, and enriched with columns of silver and gold sparkling with gems (Neale, *Holy Eastern Church*, i. 203). The celebrated ambo of the ancient Cathedral of Durham, in England, was made of solid brass, and so beautifully finished was it that persons came from afar to see it. It is described in the *Ancient Monuments of Durham* as having a gilt pelican, feeding its young with blood from its breast. These annals describe it as the "goodlyest letteron of brass that was in all the countrye" (*Church of Our Fathers*, vol. iii. 191). (The reference in the figure of the pelican is to a vision had by St. Gertrude, where our Divine Lord appeared to her in the form of this bird with his Precious Blood flowing from his Sacred Heart for the nourishment of mankind. The pelican is said to open its breast with its bill when all other means of feeding its young fail, and keep them from utter starvation by administering its life-blood for their food.) Many of the ancient amboes had curious figures engraved and constructed upon them. In some the Archangel St. Michael with the last trumpet could be seen; in others a huge eagle with its eyes turned aloft, to signify the sublimity of the Word of God. This was generally the device used in the Gospel ambo.

But the ambo was not exclusively used for the Epistle and Gospel. Sermons were preached from it sometimes, and in the churches of Egypt it was thence that the announcement regarding the time of Easter and the other movable feasts was made. The ambo was also the place where the diptychs were read; and at Constantinople it was there that the emperors were generally crowned (Neale, *Holy Eastern Church*, i. 205).

Although these ancient appurtenances have long been discontinued, traces of them may yet be seen in some of the European churches, particularly in those of Rome. At Lyons, too, not only are amboes seen, but the old custom of chanting the Epistle and Gospel from them is still strictly observed.

THE GRADUAL.

After the Epistle comes the Gradual, so called not, as some suppose, from the steps of the altar—for it was never read from these—but rather from the steps of the ambo, which was the place always assigned it. The Roman Ordo is very explicit on this point. "After the lesson has been finished," it says, "let those who are going to sing the Gradual and Alleluia stand on the lower step by the pulpit" (*i.e.*, the ambo). The remarks of Cassander regarding this are to the same effect. "The responsory," says he, "which is said at Mass is called, in contradistinction to the others, the Gradual, because this is sung on the steps, the others wherever the clergy please" (Bona, p. 325). It is called a responsory from the fact that it is a kind of reply to the Epistle, after which it is sung to stir up the hearts of the people to the salutary truths the latter contains (Kozma, p. 178).

The principal literal reason for introducing singing at this place was to keep the attention of the people from flagging in the interval that elapsed while the procession for the chanting of the Gospel was forming (*ibid.*, and Romsee, iv. 105).

• The Gradual is made up of two verses taken from the Psalms or some other part of Holy Scripture, followed by an Alleluia repeated twice, to which is added another verse with one Alleluia at the end of it.

Alleluia.—Alleluia is a Hebrew word translated generally by "praise the Lord." Its precise derivation is "allelu," to praise with jubilation, and "Jah," one of the names of the Almighty. This sacred word was held in so much esteem by the early Christians that it was only pronounced on very solemn occasions. St. Jerome tells us in his twenty-seventh Epistle that in a convent founded at Jerusalem by the pious St. Paula it used to be the signal for assembling all the nuns to their exercises of devotion. To this end it used to be chanted along the corridors several times in a loud tone of voice.'

St. Anselm, Archbishop of Canterbury from 1093 to 1109, held a strange opinion regarding the origin of this word. According to him, it belonged to no language upon earth, and could not be properly rendered into any one, but was altogether angelic in its formation. Cardinal Bona, wondering at this strange deception, humorously writes (*Divina Psalmodia*, p. 511) : "Omnis homo aliquid humanum patitur, et quandoque bonus dormitat Homerus"— that is, "Every man has a little of the frailty of human nature in him ; even the good Homer sometimes nods."

During the penitential seasons and on occasions of mourning Alleluia is not said, according to the Roman Rite, but in the Mozarabic it is always said even in Masses for the dead ; and this is the rule, too, in the Greek Church.

The Tract.—When the Alleluia is not said, what is known as the Tract is added to the Gradual in its place. This Tract, which is made up of three or four verses taken from the Psalms—though sometimes the entire psalm is recited, as on Palm Sunday and Good Friday—derives its name from the Latin *trahere*, to draw, agreeably to which liturgical writers inform us that in ancient times it used to be drawn out in a slow, measured tone without any interruption whatever on the part of the choir (Romsee, iv. 105; Durandus, *Rationale*, book iv. chap. xxi.)

---

[7] According to St. Jerome, Almighty God was known to the ancient Hebrews under ten different names, viz. : " El " or " Al," the *Strong One ;* " Eloah," the *Adorable ;* " Adonai " (plural of Adon), the *Great Lord ;* " Tsabaoth," *God of Hosts ;* " Jah," the *Ever-Living ;* " Nghelion," the *Most High ;* " Elohim," *Gods* (plural form—suggestive, as some maintain, of the Blessed Trinity) ; " Havah," *He who is ;* " Shaddai," the *All Mighty ;* and " Jehovah," or *He who is, was, and will be.* This last name the Jews would never pronounce, out of the great respect they had for it, but would always use Adonai in its stead.

SEQUENCES.

On particular occasions of the year there are added immediately after the Gradual certain rhythmical pieces of composition called by the several names of *Proses, Jubilations,* and *Sequences.* They are denominated *Proses* because, though written like verse, yet they are destitute of the qualifications that are looked for in regular metrical compositions, for they are formed more with a view to accent than quantity—a very striking characteristic of the poetry of the early ages of the Christian Church. The name *Jubilations* was given them from their having been for the most part employed on occasions of great solemnity and rejoicing; and that of *Sequences,* or *Sequels,* from their following the Alleluia (Bona, p. 326). Formerly it was customary to prolong the singing after the last note of the Alleluia for quite a considerable time, without using any words whatever, but merely the notes themselves. This was what received the name of the *Pneuma,* or breathing; and, strictly speaking, it was the origin of what we now call *Jubilations* or *Sequences* (*ibid.*)

For a considerable time every Sunday in the year, except those of the penitential season, had a Sequence of its own, as may be seen from any ancient missal, and the rite observed at Lyons keeps up this custom yet. But as a great deal of abuse crept in on account of having to use such a multiplicity of Sequences, and as many were carelessly written, the Church thought it well to subject the entire number to a rigid examination, and retain only those which were remarkable for their rare excellence. The principal step in this matter was first taken by the Council of Cologne, held in A.D. 1536, and its measures were seconded by that of Rheims in 1564; so that of the entire number which obtained in the Church up to these dates five only were deemed worthy of a place in the Mass, viz.: 1, the "Victimæ Paschali," proper to Easter ; 2, the "Veni Sancte Spiritus," proper to Pentecost ; 3, the "Lauda Sion," proper to Corpus Christi ; 4, the "Stabat Mater," proper to the Feast of the Seven Dolors of B.V.M. ; 5, the "Dies Iræ," proper to Masses for the dead. In addition to these it may be well to add that which the Friars Minor were allowed to retain on the Feast of the Holy Name of Jesus, the first lines of which begin thus (Gavantus, p. 355) :

"Lauda, Sion, Salvatoris
Jesu Nomen et Amoris."

Authors of the Sequences.—Much variety of opinion exists regarding the authors of these Sequences, but, as we are unable to settle the question, we shall simply name those to whom they have been attributed from time to time.

The first, or the "*Victimæ Paschali*," is, we believe, by the vast majority of critics accredited to a monk, Notker by name, of the celebrated monastery of St. Gall, in Switzerland, who flourished in the ninth century, and attained to much renown by his talent for writing sacred poetry. According to some, he is said to have been the first who caused this species of composition to be introduced into the Mass; and, if we are to believe Durandus, he was encouraged in this by Pope Nicholas the Great (858–867). Others ascribe its introduction to Alcuin, the preceptor of Charlemagne. The "Victimæ Paschali" is also sometimes attributed to Robert, King of the Franks.

"*Veni, Sancte Spiritus.*"—This beautiful hymn is generally accredited to the Blessed Hermann, usually styled *Contractus*, or the *Cripple*, from the deformity of his limbs. As the early history of this remarkable man is very interesting, we presume that the reader will not think it amiss if we give a brief sketch of it, as it bears much upon our subject :
"Hermannus Contractus, the son of Count Weringen, in

Livonia, was, at the age of fourteen, sent to the monastery of St. Gall to be educated. He was lame and *contracted* in body, and made little progress in learning on account of his slowness of mind. Hilperic, his master, seeing how bitterly he bewailed his misfortunes, pitied him, and advised him to apply himself to prayer, and to implore the assistance of the Immaculate Virgin, Mother of God. Hermannus obeyed his master, and about two years after thought he saw the holy Virgin one night whilst he was asleep, and that she thus addressed him: 'O good child! I have heard your prayers, and at your request have come to assist you. Now, therefore, choose whichever of these two things you please, and you shall certainly obtain it: either to have your body cured, or to become master of all the science you desire.' Hermannus did not hesitate to prefer the gifts of the mind to those of the body, and such from this period was his progress in human and divine science that he was esteemed the most learned of his contemporaries. He excelled them all in philosophy, rhetoric, astronomy, poetry, music, and theology; composed books upon geometry, music, and astronomy, the eclipses of the sun and moon, the astrolabe, the quadrant, the horologue, and quadrature of the circle; wrote commentaries on Aristotle and Cicero; translated some Greek and Arabic works into Latin; composed a chronicle from the creation of the world to the year 1052, a treatise on physiognomy, and several hymns, amongst which the 'Salve Regina,' 'Alma Redemptoris,' and 'Veni, Sancte Spiritus' are enumerated. He died in 1054, aged forty-one years" (*Dublin Review*, vol. xxx., June, 1851; Gavantus, ii. p. 166). The "Veni, Sancte Spiritus" is also ascribed to Pope Innocent III., to St. Bonaventure, and to Robert, King of the Franks.

"*Lauda Sion.*"—All are unanimous in ascribing this to the "Angelic Doctor," St. Thomas Aquinas, who, at the request of Pope Urban IV., composed it for the solemnity of Corpus Christi, of which we have already spoken at length.

"*Stabat Mater.*"—A good deal of dispute has arisen regarding the author of this sublime production, some ascribing it to Pope Innocent III., some to Jacoponi (1306)— sometimes called Jacobus de Benedictis, a Franciscan monk —and others to St. Bonaventure. We follow the majority, however, in ascribing it to Pope Innocent III. To our mind Jacoponi's claims to this hymn are not very strong; and if there were no other reason to justify our opinion but that founded on his hymn for Christmas morning, beginning with

"Stabat Mater speciosa
Juxta fœnum gaudiosa
Dum jacebat parvulus,"

we think that would be sufficient.

"*Dies Iræ.*"—The authorship of the "Dies Iræ" seems the most difficult to settle. This much, however, is certain : that he who has the strongest claims to it is Latino Orsini, generally styled *Frangipani*, whom his maternal uncle, Pope Nicholas III. (Gaetano Orsini), raised to the cardinalate in 1278. He was more generally known by the name of Cardinal Malabranca, and was at first a member of the Order of St. Dominic (see *Dublin Review*, vol. xx., 1846; Gavantus, *Thesaur. Sacr. Rit.*, p. 490).

As this sacred hymn is conceded to be one of the grandest that has ever been written, it is but natural to expect that the number of authors claiming it would be very large. Some even have attributed it to Pope Gregory the Great, who lived as far back as the year 604. St. Bernard, too, is mentioned in connection with it, and so are several others ; but as it is hardly necessary to mention all, we shall only say that, after Cardinal Orsini, the claims to it on the part of Thomas de Celano, of the Order of Franciscans Minor, are the greatest. There is very little reason for attributing it to Father Humbert, the fifth general of the Dominicans, in 1273 ; and hardly any at all for accrediting it to Augustinus de Biella, of the Order of Augustinian Eremites. A very widely circulated opinion is that the "Dies Iræ" as it stands now is but an improved form of a Sequence which was long in use before the age of any of those authors whom we have cited. Gavantus gives us, at page 490 of his *Thesaurus of Sacred Rites*, a few stanzas of this ancient Sequence, which we deem well to place before the reader :

> " Cum recordor moriturus,
>   Quid post mortem sim futurus,
>   Terror terret me venturus,
>   Quem expecto non securus:
>   Terret dies me terroris.
>   Dies iræ, ac furoris,
>   Dies luctus, ac mœroris,
>   Dies ultrix peccatoris,
>   Dies iræ, dies illa," etc., etc.

As late as 1576 the "Dies Iræ" was forbidden to be said by the Dominicans of Salamanca, in Spain. Maldonatus, also, the great Jesuit commentator, objected to its use in Masses for the dead, for the reason that a composition of that kind was unsuited to mournful occasions. Others, too, made similar complaints against it. To repeat what learned critics of every denomination under heaven have said in praise of this marvellous hymn would indeed be a difficult task. One of its greatest encomiums is that there is hardly a language in Europe into which it has not been translated ; it has even found its way into Greek and Hebrew—into the former through an English missionary of Syria named Hildner, and into the latter by Splieth, a celebrated Orientalist. Mozart avowed his extreme admiration of it, and so did Dr. Johnson, Sir Walter Scott, and Jeremy Taylor, besides hosts of others. The encomium passed upon it by Schaff is thus given in his own words : "This marvellous hymn is the acknowledged masterpiece of Latin poetry and the most sublime of all uninspired hymns. The secret of its irresistible power lies in the awful grandeur of the theme, the intense earnestness and pathos of the poet, the simple majesty and solemn music of its language, the stately metre, the triple rhyme, and the vocal assonances, chosen in striking adaptation—all combining to produce an overwhelming effect, as if we heard the final crash of the universe, the commotion of the opening graves, the trumpet of the archangel summoning the quick and the dead, and saw the King of 'tremendous majesty' seated on the throne of justice and mercy, and ready to dispense everlasting life or everlasting woe" (see *Latin Hymns*, vol. i. p. 292, by Professor March, of Lafayette College, Pa.) The music of this hymn formed the chief part of the fame of Mozart; and it is said, and not without reason, that it contributed in no small degree to hasten his death, for so excited did he become over its awe-enkindling sentiments while writing his celebrated "Mass of Requiem" that a sort of minor paralysis seized his whole frame, so that he was heard to say : "I am certain that I am writing this Requiem for myself. It will be my funeral service." He never lived to finish it; the credit of having done that belongs to Sussmayer, a man of great musical attainments, and a most intimate friend of the Mozart family (*Dublin Review*, vol. i., May, 1836).

The allusion to the sibyl in the third line of the first stanza has given rise to a good deal of anxious enquiry; and so very strange did it sound to French ears at its introduction into the sacred hymnology of the Church that the Parisian rituals substituted in its place the line "Crucis expandens vexilla." The difficulty, however, is easily overcome if we bear in mind that many of the early Fathers held that Almighty God made use of these sibyls to promulgate his truths in just the same way as he did of Balaam of old, and many others like him. The great St. Augustine has written much on this subject in his *City of God;* and the reader may form some idea of the estimation in which these sibyls were held when he is told that the world-renowned Michael Angelo made them the subject of one of his greatest paintings. In the Sistine Chapel at Rome may yet be seen his celebrated delineation of both the sibyl of Erythrea and that of Delphi. In the opinion of the ablest critics it was the first-mentioned, or the Erythrean sibyl, that uttered the celebrated prediction about the advent of our Divine Lord, and his final coming at the last day to judge the living and the dead. This prediction, it is said, was given in verse, and written as an acrostic on one of the ancient designations of our Divine Lord in Greek—viz., ἰχθύς, *ichthus*, a fish, referring to our spiritual regeneration through the efficacy of the saving waters of holy Baptism established by our Saviour for our sakes. The letters of this word when taken separately form the initials of the sacred name and official character of our Divine Lord, thus: "*I*" stands for *Jesus;* "*X*" for *Christ;* "*Θ*" for *Theos*, or *God;* "*Υ*" for *Υἱός*, or *Son;* and "*Σ*" for σωτήρ, or *Saviour*—that is, "Jesus Christ, Son of God, the Saviour." The part of the sibyl's response which referred particularly to the Day of Judgment was written on the letters of *Soter*, or Saviour. It is given as follows in the translation of the *City of God* of St. Augustine (edited by Clarke, of Edinburgh, 1871):

"Sounding, the archangel's trumpet shall peal down from heaven
Over the wicked who groan in their guilt and their manifold sorrows;
Trembling, the earth shall be opened, revealing chaos and hell.
Every king before God shall stand on that day to be judged;
Rivers of fire and of brimstone shall fall from the heavens."

There are in all twenty-seven lines.

The "Stabat Mater," too, deserves more than a mere passing notice, for, in the estimation of able critics, it is one of the most pathetic hymns ever written. Hogarth called it "a divine emanation of an afflicted and purified spirit," and the encomiums lavished upon it by other men of genius are numberless. As far as concerns its musical merits, the chief credit is due to Pergolesi and Rossini, both of whom immortalized themselves in their rendition of it.

The precise merits of the "Lauda Sion" lie in this: that it is one of the most able theological exegeses that have ever been written on the doctrine of the Real Presence. Every possible objection that could be raised concerning the Blessed Sacrament is comprehended in it.

Sequences of the Oriental Church.—By way of compensating for the entire absence of all instrumental music from the service of the Oriental Church, sacred hymnology is made to act a far more conspicuous part there than it is with us. Not a Mass is celebrated without at least half a dozen of *Troparia*, as they are called, nearly all of which end with a doxology in honor of the Mother of God, to whom, as we have already said, the Orientals are very devout. To give the reader an idea of the intrinsic beauty of some of the Oriental Sequences, we copy the following, inscribed "for a Sunday of the First Tone." It, of course, is written and sung in Greek, and the work from which we copy it (*Hymns of the Eastern Church*, by Rev. Dr. Neale) ascribes it to St. Anatolius, A.D. 458. It refers to that scene on the Sea of Galilee where the disciples are out in a boat and our

Lord comes to them walking upon the waters (Matthew xiv.):

> "Fierce was the wild billow,
>   Dark was the night;
> Oars labored heavily,
>   Foam glimmered white
> Trembled the mariners,
>   Peril was nigh;
> Then said the God of God,
>   'Peace! it is I.'
>
> Ridge of the mountain-wave,
>   Lower thy crest!
> Wail of Euroclydon,
>   Be thou at rest!
> Sorrow can never be,
>   Darkness must fly,
> Where saith the Light of Light,
>   'Peace! it is I.'
>
> Jesu, Deliverer!
>   Come thou to me
> Soothe thou my voyaging
>   Over life's sea!
> Thou, when the storm of death
>   Roars sweeping by,
> Whisper, O Truth of Truth!
>   'Peace! it is I.'"

"MUNDA COR MEUM."

After the Epistle and the responses following it have been read, the priest goes to the middle of the altar, and, having bowed profoundly, recites the prayer "Munda cor meum," by which he begs of God to purify his heart and lips, as he did those of Isaias of old, in order that he may announce the good truths of the Gospel in a befitting manner. In the meantime the missal is removed by the server from the

Epistle to the Gospel side, and so placed that the priest may be a little turned towards the congregation while reading it, and this to preserve a vestige of the ancient custom of reading the Holy Evangel from the ambo in the hearing and sight of all.

The literal or natural meaning of removing the missal at this place is that the Epistle corner of the altar may be entirely free for receiving the gifts presented and placed there by the people at the Offertory, and to make room for the paten, which in former times was much larger than it is now (Romsee, iv. 107 ; Kozma, p. 182). Mystically, this ceremony is intended to remind us of the translation of the word of God from the Jews, represented by the Epistle side, to the Gentiles, represented by the Gospel side, in accordance with what is said by SS. Paul and Barnabas in the Acts of the Apostles (xiii. 46) : "To you it behoved us first to speak the word of God ; but because you reject it, and judge yourselves unworthy of eternal life, behold we turn to the Gentiles." The bringing back of the missal afterwards denotes the final return of the Jews to Christianity at the preaching of Enoch and Elias (Durandus, *Rationale*, p. 195).

We have said that the Missal is placed at the Gospel side, a little turned towards the congregation, and that this is with a view to preserve a vestige of the ancient practice of reading the Gospel from the ambo. As it may be objected that the Epistle, too, was formerly read there, and why not now be read as the Gospel is ? we reply by saying that whenever the Epistle was read from the ambo it was always from an inferior stand to that set apart for the Gospel, generally from the steps themselves, and always facing the altar ; for it was not, at its introduction into the Mass, designed so much for the instruction of the people as the Gospel was, nor did it ever occupy the same place of honor, although the honor shown it was very great (Martène, *De Antiquis Eccl. Ritibus*, f. 24).

THE GOSPEL.

When the priest has arrived at the missal after the prayer "Munda cor meum," he pronounces in an audible tone the salutation, "Dominus vobiscum," without, however, turning to the people—for he is partly turned already—and then announces the title of the Gospel he is going to read. Together with doing so he makes the sign of the cross with his thumb on the missal itself at the beginning of the Gospel, and then upon himself in three separate places—viz., on the forehead, mouth, and breast respectively. That made upon the book is intended to teach us that the Holy Gospel contains the words of Him who died upon the cross for our salvation; that made upon the forehead is intended to remind us that we must never be ashamed of the Word of God, for our Lord himself says : "He who is ashamed of me and of my words, of him shall the Son of Man be ashamed when he shall come in his majesty" (*Luke* ix. 26); and the cross upon the breast reminds us of the holy admonition in the Canticle of Canticles : "Put me as a seal upon thy heart" (chap. viii.) (For other mystical meanings see Durandus, p. 202.) When the priest has announced the title of the Gospel, the server answers : "Gloria tibi, Domine"—Glory be to thee, O Lord—and the congregation sign themselves after the manner of the priest. The response, "Glory be to thee, O Lord," is made to thank God for the spiritual blessings contained in the holy Gospel. The Acts of the Apostles, chap. xiii. 48, tell us how the Gentiles glorified the word of God, and expressed their heartfelt thanks to SS. Paul and Barnabas for having brought them the salutary truths which the Jews rejected.

Standing up at the Gospel.—At the reading of the Holy

Gospel all stand up out of respect for the sacred words of our Divine Lord, as well as to testify their readiness to follow out all that the Gospel teaches. This custom is very ancient, as we find the Jews observed it when Esdras the Scribe read them the Law after the return from the Babylonian captivity (2 *Esdras*, viii. 4). When the custom was in vogue of bringing staves to church for the purpose of leaning on them during certain parts of the service, their use was never permitted during the reading of the Holy Gospel. They were at that time to be put aside, and with them all insignia of royalty, such as sceptres, crowns, and things of that sort, in order that all might appear in the humble posture of servants before the Lord (Bona, p. 328; Romsee, p. 114). Certain military knights, and among others the Knights of St. John,[8] were accustomed to unsheath their swords at this place, as evidence of their readiness to defend the interests of the sacred words even unto the shedding of blood (Bona, *ibid.*)

When the priest has finished reading the Gospel he kisses the sacred text out of reverence for the words of our Lord—for the Gospel is pre-eminently " Christ's Book," as it used to be styled in ancient times—and as he performs this act he says : "In virtue of the evangelical words may our sins be blotted out." The Carthusians kiss the margin of the missal instead of the text itself. Should some great dignitary

---

[8] The Knights of St. John, established first at Jerusalem about the year 1098, were also known by the several names of *Hospitalers*, from the fact that their first house was a hospital specially built for the care of the sick ; *Knights of Rhodes*, from their temporary residence in that island ; and *Knights of Malta*, from their last stronghold at Malta, in the Mediterranean Sea. They exist no longer as a distinctive military body, but several yet bearing the name, and observing to a great extent their original vows of poverty, chastity, and obedience, may be met with throughout Italy, England, and other parts of Europe, and their honorary grand-master has a right to the high title of " Most Eminent." Their patron saint is St. John the Baptist ; and their badge a white cross, with eight points in it, in memory of the eight beatitudes (see *Lives of the Saints*, vol. i. 571, note ; Ferraris. *Bibliotheca ; Knights of Malta*, bp Taaffe).

be present in the sanctuary, it is the rule to present him the book first, in which case the priest celebrating would not kiss it at all. In ancient times not only did the priest kiss the book at this stage of the Mass, but every member of the congregation did so (Bona, p. 329). In the Sarum Rite a special codex was set apart for this purpose (*Church of Our Fathers*, iii. 192). The custom of kissing documents of importance is very ancient, and prevails yet in the majority of royal courts, especially in those of the East. Those that come direct from our Holy Father the Pope are always shown this mark of respect; and that the pious practice of kissing not only the book of the Gospels, but almost every utensil in the house of God, even the very door-posts and pillars, was generally observed by the primitive Christians we learn from numerous sources (Riddle, *Christian Antiquities*, p. 739; *Life of Cardinal Ximenes*, by Hefele, p. 37).

At the conclusion of the Gospel the server answers, "Laus tibi, Christe"—"Praise be to thee, O Christ!"—but in the Mozarabic Rite the old custom of answering "Amen" at this place is yet kept up (see *Liturgia Mozarabica*, ed. Migne). Another ancient custom—viz., that of making the sign of the cross here—is still retained by the Carmelites.

At Solemn High Mass.—At Solemn High Mass, where the Gospel is chanted in a loud tone of voice, the ceremonies are imposing and full of deep meaning: As soon as the celebrant has passed from the middle of the altar, after the "Munda cor meum," to the Gospel side, the deacon receives from the master of ceremonies the book of the Holy Evangels, which he carries to the altar with much reverence, and places in front of the tabernacle in a horizontal position. He does not return immediately, but remains there to assist the celebrant at the blessing of the incense for the forthcoming procession. The incense having been put in the censer and blessed, the deacon descends one step and recites the prayer "Munda cor meum," at the conclusion of which he rises from his knees, and, having taken the book from the altar, kneels down with it before the celebrant and asks the latter to bless him. Having received the blessing, he kisses the celebrant's hand, and then descends to the floor, where he awaits the signal for the procession to move to that part of the Gospel side of the sanctuary where the Holy Evangel is chanted. A full corps of acolytes with lighted candles, incense, etc., head the procession, and the deacon, walking immediately behind the subdeacon, moves in a slow and dignified manner, carrying the sacred codex elevated before his face. This is afterwards given to the subdeacon, who holds it resting against his forehead during the entire time of chanting. Having given the usual salutation of "Dominus vobiscum," and announced the title of the Gospel, the deacon receives the thurible, or censer, and incenses the book in three different places—viz., in the centre, at the right, and at the left. He then chants the text in a loud tone of voice, and, having finished, receives the censer again and incenses the celebrant at the altar, who stood facing the Gospel the whole time that the deacon was chanting it.

Explanation.—The taking of the book of the Gospels from the altar is intended to remind us, according to Pope Innocent III., that *the law has come forth from Sion, and the word of the Lord from Jerusalem;* not so much the law of Moses, but the law of the New Covenant, of which the prophet Jeremias wrote: "Behold the days shall come," saith the Lord, "and I will make a NEW COVENANT with the house of Israel, and with the house of Juda. . . . I will give my law in their bowels, and I will write it in their heart, and I will be their God, and they shall be my people" (chap. xxxi.) The deacon, kneeling at the feet of the priest in the manner of an humble suppliant to receive his blessing, teaches us the necessity of first asking permission to preach the Gospel, and then a blessing for the sacred work in order that it may produce the proper fruit. To take upon ourselves the heavy onus of preaching without having been divinely called to that sacred office would be to incur God's wrath, and, instead of a blessing, draw down his condemnation. The Apostle St. Paul lays particular stress upon the necessity of receiving a special call to discharge this duty (*Romans*, chap. x.) Then, again, this taking of the book from the altar and reading it aloud in the hearing of the people forcibly recalls to mind what Moses did of old on Sinai, whence he brought down the tables of the law and read them before the chosen people at the mountain's edge. The subdeacon goes before the deacon to the place where the Gospel is chanted to remind us that John the Baptist, whose ministry the Epistle, and consequently the subdeacon, typifies, went before our Lord, who is represented by the Gospel (Durandus, p. 199). Incense is used on this occasion to commemorate what St. Paul says (2 *Cor.* ii.), that we are the good odor of Christ unto God in every place. And lighted candles are employed to testify our joy at receiving the glad Gospel tidings, as well as to show our respect for Him who is the "Light of the World" (Innocent III., *Sacrif. Miss.*, p. 141). Finally, the Gospel is chanted at the corner of the sanctuary, with the sacred text facing the north, to show that the preaching of our Lord was specially directed against Lucifer, who said, "I will establish my seat in the north, and will be like the Most High" (*Isaias; ibid.*) When, according to the ancient discipline, the Gospel was chanted from those elevated pulpits called amboes, it was in remembrance of that sacred admonition of our Lord to his disciples when he charged them regarding the ministry of the word. "That which I tell you in the dark," said he, "speak ye in the light; and that which you hear in the ear, preach ye on the housetops" (*Matthew* x.; Durandus, *Rationale*, p. 200). The last-named author speaks of the custom that prevailed in his day (thirteenth century) of chanting the Gospel from the eagle, referring to the appurtenance in the shape of this bird that used to be employed in the embellishment of the ancient book-stands, and this with a view to the fulfilment of the words, "He flew upon the wings of the wind" (*Ps.* xvii.); for the wings of the eagle are aptly compared to the wings of the wind, as that bird can fly highest of all the feathered race, and the Gospel is the highest of all the inspired writings. For many other interesting facts about what we have been speaking the reader is referred to Durandus, chap. xxiv., *Rationale Divinorum*.

Respect shown to the Gospels in Ancient Times.—The respect shown to the Gospels in ancient times is evinced from the fact that the sacred codex used to be bound in massive covers of gold, silver, and precious stones, as we learn from many sources. The cases, too, in which the sacred volumes used to be enclosed when not in use, were made of the costliest materials, often of beaten gold, and the most exquisite workmanship was displayed in finishing them (Kozma, p. 105). Dr. Rock (*Church of Our Fathers*, iii. 31) tells us that sheets of gold, studded with large pearls and precious stones, were not thought too good to be the binding of these books, and that their printing used to be often in letters of gold upon a purple ground. At all great ecclesiastical meetings the holy Gospels were assigned a very conspicuous position. At the General Council of Ephesus, held in the Church of St. Mary in that city A.D. 431, the book of the Gospels was placed upon an elevated throne in view of all the assembled Fathers (Bona, p. 329). At a Solemn High Mass celebrated by the Pope the Epistle and Gospel are first chanted in Latin, then in Greek, to express the union of the two churches (Kozma, p. 183).

The Gospel in the Oriental Church.—The ceremonies attending the reading of the Gospel in the East resemble our own very closely. In the Liturgy of St. Chrysostom the deacon, kneeling down at the feet of the celebrant before the procession moves, asks the customary blessing in these words : "Sir, bless the preacher of the holy Apostle and Evangelist N." (here the name of the Gospel is mentioned); then the priest, making the sign of the cross upon him, says : " May God, through the preaching of the holy and glorious Apostle and Evangelist N., give the word with much power to thee, who evangelizest to the accomplishment of the Gospel of his beloved Son, our Lord Jesus Christ." After this the procession moves to the ambo, and everything goes on much in the same way as with ourselves at Solemn High Mass. With the Abyssinians, the deacon makes a circuit of the entire church at this place, saying with a loud voice as he goes along : " Arise ! hear the Gospel and the good tidings of our Lord and Saviour Jesus Christ." This circuit is intended to signify the promulgation of the Gospel by the Apostles throughout the entire globe, in accordance with the sacred text, " Their sound has gone forth into every land, and their words unto the end of the world " (*Ps.* xviii. 5).

The Copts, instead of making the circuit of the church in this way, go around the altar in a procession, headed by an immense number of acolytes and other ministers bearing torches and incense. The display is very imposing. After the Gospel has been chanted it is first kissed by the clergy, it is then covered with a silken veil and presented to be kissed by the people (Renaudot, *Liturg. Orient.*, i. 190). It is customary also with the Coptic prelates, should any be present, to put aside their mitres and crosiers at this time, and remain slightly bowed down during the entire chanting.

The Greek bishops, besides rising up to hear the holy Evangel, also put aside their *omophorion*,[9] testifying thereby, according to St. Simeon of Thessalonica, their total subjection to the Lord (Goar, *Euchol. Græc.*, p. 223).

[9] The omophorion of the Greeks serves the same end as our pallium, only that it is common to every bishop, instead of being restricted to archbishops, as with us. Like the pallium it is made of wool, but is much broader, and, instead of hanging down freely, is fastened round the neck in a knot. It is usually ornamented with silver and silken threads, and symbolizes the "Lost Sheep" (Neale, *Holy Eastern Church*, i. 312; Romanoff, *Greco-Russian Church*, p. 400).

CHAPTER XXII.

THE SERMON.

ACCORDING to the present discipline of the Church, regulated in a great measure by the General Council of Trent, it is required that at every parochial Mass on Sundays and holydays of obligation a sermon touching the great truths of our holy faith should be preached to the people. To do this the more effectually it is recommended to follow the line of thought expressed in the Gospel of the day, as it is the wish of the Church that this portion of the sacred writings should be carefully expounded and developed in all its bearing.

The custom of thus preaching at Mass is of the highest antiquity, the ablest critics maintaining that it is of apostolic origin; and the Holy Scriptures themselves would seem to warrant this assertion. St. Justin Martyr (A.D. 167) tells us in his *Apology*, i. 67, that it was the practice in his day to read portions of the Sacred Scriptures first in the assemblies of the people, and then explain their application and meaning afterwards. The ancient Hebrews always preached to the people after the reading of the *Sepher Tora*, or book of the Law (Bannister, *Temples of the Hebrews*, p. 351).

WHOSE DUTY IT WAS TO PREACH.

Whenever the bishop presided, as used to be the case in nearly all the cathedral churches, the duty of preaching devolved upon him. This duty was, indeed, regarded in early times as so peculiar to a bishop that whenever a priest addressed the people in any public church it was looked upon as a sort of great concession and favor. "Episcopi proprium munus," says St. Ambrose (*De Off. Sac.*, lib. i. c. i.), "docere populum"—"It is the peculiar office of the bishop to teach the people"; and St. Chrysostom, commenting on this faculty, says that the bishop who does not possess it should be deposed from his office (*Hom. x. in I. Ep. ad Tim.*)

During the prevalence of the early heresies, the greatest care was taken to see that no one should ascend the pulpit unless he possessed the rarest qualities as a preacher and theologian. This was especially the case when the heresy of Arius broke out. So dangerous was this considered to be that it was thought well all through the East to confine preaching solely to bishops, and forbid priests under severe penalties to take upon themselves this task. The Council of Chalcedon (A.D. 451), as is well known, interdicted preaching to monks, on account of the fall of Eutyches, one of the heads of this body (*Comment. in Pontif. Romanum*, Catalani; Mühlbauer, i. 133).

LAYMEN ALLOWED TO PREACH.

Although the ancient Fathers were very strict on the subject of preaching, and always insisted on having it entrusted to men of tried ability and worth among the higher grades of the hierarchy, still we find a little relaxation of this rigor in certain rare cases; for not only did members of the inferior orders of the clergy discharge this duty, but even those who were not ranked among the clergy at all. The celebrated Origen, as we learn from Eusebius, preached frequently in Jerusalem while yet a layman; and we are assured by the same author that this permission was also granted on certain occasions to Constantine the Great (*De Vita Const.*, lib. iv. c. xxix.–xxxiv.)

DEPORTMENT OF THE PEOPLE DURING THE SERMON.

The behavior of the people during the sermon was nearly always of the most edifying kind. Sometimes a little inattention or carelessness would be observed in some, while others in rare instances might be seen engaged in frivolous conversation. Whenever this was noticed it was the duty of the deacon to stand up in the sanctuary and call for attention and order by exclaiming: "Silentium habete!"— "Keep silence." St. Ambrose had frequent occasion to give this order at Milan, and many bitter complaints did he make of the people of that city for their want of propriety in this respect.

POSTURE OF THE PREACHER.

As a general rule, the preacher stood while delivering his sermon, and this generally in the sanctuary. The custom of preaching from the ambo, where the Gospel used to be read, is said to have been introduced by St. John Chrysostom (Socrates, *Hist. Eccles.*, lib. vi. c. v.; Sozomen, *Hist. Eccl.*, viii. v.) When, through feebleness of health or other causes, the preacher could not stand, he was allowed to sit upon a chair. This practice was often resorted to by St. Augustine in his declining years, and many of the early Fathers rather favored it, even when there was no special need of having recourse to it, in memory of our Lord's Sermon on the Mount. Bishops of the present day observe this practice yet in many places. But, whether the preacher stood or sat, the general rule was, as we learn from St. Gregory Nazianzen, Eusebius, and St. Chrysostom, that the people of the congregation should stand. Whenever the preacher said anything that deserved special approbation slight indications of appreciation used to be manifested, such as bowing the head, making gestures with the hands, sometimes even clapping the hands or waving the garments. The people were so carried away upon one occasion by the golden eloquence of St. Chrysostom that they cried out with one acclaim : " Thou art worthy of the priesthood ; thou art the thirteenth apostle ; Christ hath sent thee to save our souls " (Riddle, *Christian Antiquities*, p. 455).

The custom of offering up a short prayer before the sermon was observed by the early Fathers. Sometimes this was nothing more than an ejaculation or a salutation to the people, under such forms as "Peace be to you," "May God bless you," "The Lord be with you" (*ibid.*) The custom now in vogue in many countries, especially in France, of saying a "Hail Mary," or some other prayer to Our Blessed Lady, was introduced by St. Vincent Ferrer in the fifteenth century as a protest against the indignities offered the Mother of God by the heretics of that time (see Manahan's *Triumph of the Catholic Church*).

Regarding the delivery of the sermon the ancient Fathers were very exact. Earnestness on the part of the preacher and sympathy with his people were looked upon as the great redeeming features of every discourse. Too much gesticulation was always severely reprehended ; and if the preacher manifested any signs of levity in the pulpit, or indulged in any actions which were not considered entirely in keeping with the dignity of the place and occasion, he was at once commanded to desist, and silence was imposed upon him ever afterwards. It is said of the heretic Paul of Samosata that he carried gesticulation so far as to stamp the pulpit with his feet, beat his thighs with his hands, and act while preaching in a most unbecoming manner, for which reason the Council of Antioch, in A.D. 272, bitterly complained of him to Pope Dionysius, the reigning pontiff.

INFLUENCE OF THE DISCIPLINE OF THE SECRET ON THE PREACHING.

We wish here to call the particular attention of the reader to a fact which is too often lost sight of in treating of the customs of the early Church. We refer to the *Disciplina Arcani*, as it was called, or the Discipline of the Secret, in virtue of which the principal mysteries of our holy faith and the nature of many of the public prayers of the Church were carefully concealed from all who were not considered as belonging to the household of faith, and this with a view to follow out to the letter that sacred admonition of our Divine Lord himself, viz.: not to "cast pearls before swine or give what was holy to dogs." "The mysteries," says St. Athanasius, " ought not to be publicly exhibited to the uninitiated, lest the Gentiles, who understand them not, scoff at them, and the catechumens, becoming curious, be scandalized" (*Apol. contra Arian.*, p. 105).

The caution which was to be observed during the prevalence of this discipline—which, as we have said in another place, lasted during the first five centuries—influenced the preachers of those days very considerably, from the fact that their audiences were often made up of Jews, Gentiles, pagans, and others who were wholly ignorant of the nature of our belief, and who would, had they but understood it in all its bearings, have made it a pretext for inciting fresh persecution. This accounts for the thick veil of mystification that hung over many of the sermons of the early Fathers, and for the abruptness with which several of them ended. Many a time did St. Chrysostom break off his discourse with some such expression as this: "The initiated know what I mean." This he would do if he saw any persons in the audience who did not belong to the faithful. "I wish to speak openly," said he upon a certain occasion while addressing his flock, "but I dare not on account of those who are not initiated. These persons render explanation more difficult by obliging us to speak in obscure terms or to unveil the things that are secret; yet I shall endeavor, as far as possible, to explain myself in disguised terms" (*Hom. xl. in I. Corinth.*) Tertullian, who lived in the second century under the Emperors Severus and Caracalla, says upon this subject: "'The profane are excluded from the sight of the most holy mysteries, and those are carefully selected who are permitted to be spectators" (*Apol. adversus Gentes*).

The extreme reserve of St. Epiphanius (fourth century) when speaking upon the Blessed Eucharist is very remarkable. Lest he might make use of the slightest expression that would be calculated to excite the curiosity of the uninitiated, he has recourse to the following guarded language: "We see that our Lord took a *thing* into his hands, that he rose from the table, that he resumed the *thing*, and, having given thanks, said: '*This is that of mine.*'" "We should rather shed our blood," says St. Gregory Nazianzen, "than publish our mysteries to strangers" (*Orat.*, pp. 35 and 42).

Nor must we omit to mention that during those times swift-hand writers (ὀξυγράφοι) were sent around in bands by the pagans to take down whatever they heard preached in the Christian assemblies. Frequent mention of these is made by Sozomen and other historians; and, according to the testimony of St. Gregory Nazianzen (*Thirty-third Sermon*), he himself, while preaching, saw men of this kind stealing among the people and hiding, so as not to be detected in their work; and when they could hear nothing worthy of noting they would fabricate something, and often make the preacher say what was farthest from his intention. St. Gaudentius (427) bitterly inveighed against this clandestine practice (Riddle, *Christian Antiquities*, p. 457).

We have designedly dwelt upon this subject for the reason

that Protestants are fond of saying that the early Fathers say little or nothing about the Real Presence of our Lord in the Holy Eucharist. Let them but remember that until the sixth century it was strictly forbidden to teach this doctrine openly, in virtue of the Discipline of the Secret, and they will cease to be surprised at this prudent silence. The historian Sozomen had so scrupulous a regard for this sacred Discipline that he would not commit to writing the Creed framed by the Council of Nicæa in A.D. 325, for this also came under the Secret.

PREACHING IN THE ORIENTAL CHURCH.

If we are to credit the reports of travellers and tourists, preaching in the Oriental Church has gone almost into desuetude, at least among the schismatics; and at this we cannot wonder when we see the superficial training that candidates for the sacred ministry there receive. They are ordained in some places upon the sole qualification of being able to recite a few prayers in addition to the Creed; and so low is their status among the Copts that it has been found necessary to print all the rubrics of the missal in Arabic, in order that they might know what to do. (For a corroboration of this statement concerning the wide-spread ignorance among the Oriental clergy see Smith and Dwight, *Researches in Armenia,* vol. ii. p. 34 et passim.)

So careless are the Russians in regard to preaching that they entrust the duty not unfrequently to the most illiterate persons, even to laymen, and attach very little importance to the orthodoxy of the preacher's views.

DISMISSAL OF THE CATECHUMENS.

The moment the sermon was ended, or, in the absence of a sermon, at the end of the Gospel, the catechumens were dismissed from the church, and then the Mass of the Faithful began with closed doors. "Ecce post sermonem," says St. Augustine, "fit missa catechumenis; manebunt fideles"—that is, "After the sermon the catechumens are dismissed; the faithful will remain" (*Sermo* 237). Together with the catechumens were also dismissed the *energumens*, or those troubled with unclean spirits; the *lapsed*, or those who had denied the faith openly; public sinners whose term of penance had not yet expired; and, finally, Jews, Gentiles, and pagans. As the going out of these caused no small commotion in the church in the early days —for their number was very great—it was usual to place porters at the outer doors to see that the strictest decorum was observed, and that nothing was done out of keeping with the dignity of the place. The forms of dismissal varied with different churches. Sometimes it was, "Si quis est catechumenus exeat foras"—"If there be any catechumen present let him go out"—at other times, "Catechumens depart! Catechumens depart!" This was vociferated several times by the deacon. For a while the phrase used to be, "Si quis non communicat det locum"—"If any one does not intend to communicate let him depart." We shall see by-and-by that all who assisted at Mass in the early days were expected to approach Holy Communion, or be considered among the excommunicated. According to the Liturgy of St. James, the form of dismissal was, "Let none of the catechumens remain; let none of the uninitiated, let none of those who are not able to join with us in prayer, remain!" After which the deacon cried: " The doors! the doors! All upright!"

The Mozarabic is the only rite in the Latin Church which yet retains in divine service the appellations of "Mass of the Catechumens" and "Mass of the Faithful." Neither in the East nor in the West are these dismissals anything more now than mere commemorations of an ancient practice.

CHAPTER XXIII.

THE CELEBRATION OF MASS.

THE SYMBOL, OR CREED.

THERE are few words that have a greater variety of meanings than the word *symbol*, but there seems to be an almost unanimous opinion that its application to the Creed has been owing to the fact that it was at its formation the joint contribution of the Apostles before their separation to evangelize the different portions of the globe. In its original acceptation, coming as it does from the Greek σύν (*sun,* or *syn,* with or together) and βάλλω (*ballo,* I throw), it means the portion subscribed by any one individual towards some common fund. Thus, with the ancient Romans the part contributed by a person in getting up a public dinner or banquet went by this name. The application, then, of the term to the Creed is very appropriate, seeing that it has been formed, as the constant tradition of the Church and the unanimous consent of the early Fathers testify, by the Apostles themselves, from whom it derives its name (Bona, *Rer. Liturg.,* p. 330; *Divina Psalmodia,* p. 501).

THE PART COMPOSED BY EACH APOSTLE.

At the end of the Missal of St. Columbanus (an Irish saint of the sixth century) there is a very curious tract on the Creed, which, among other things, assigns the portion composed by each of the twelve Apostles. The order is as follows :

1st, St. Peter—*I believe in God the Father Almighty, Creator of heaven and earth.*
2d, St. John—*And in Jesus Christ, his only Son, our Lord.*
3d, St. James—*Who was conceived by the Holy Ghost, born of the Virgin Mary.*
4th, St. Andrew—*Suffered under Pontius Pilate, was crucified, dead, and buried.*
5th, St. Philip—*He descended into hell.*
6th, St. Thomas—*The third day he arose again from the dead.*
7th, St. Bartholomew—*He ascended into heaven, and sitteth at the right hand of God the Father Almighty.*
8th, St. Matthew—*From thence he shall come to judge the living and the dead.*
9th, St. James, son of Alphæus—*I believe in the Holy Ghost.*
10th, St. Simon Zelotes—*The Holy Catholic Church, the Communion of Saints.*
11th, St. Thaddeus—*The forgiveness of sins.*
12th, St. Matthias—*The resurrection of the body and life everlasting.*

According to Ferraris, this analysis of the symbol was worked out by Duns Scotus, familiarly known as the "Subtile Doctor" on account of his keen intellect; but as the Missal of St. Columbanus was composed long before the thirteenth century, when Scotus flourished, it is not easy to see how he could be accredited with this work.

As the Creed was one of the public prayers of the Church which the catechumens were not allowed to hear, it was not recited until they had left the house of God, and prior to the Council of Nicæa it was never committed to writing, but only confided by word of mouth. This we clearly learn from St. Cyril among others, who in his catechetical instructions (v. 1–12, pp. 77, 78) thus addresses his pupils : "This [*i.e.*, the Creed] I wish you to remember in the very phraseology, and to rehearse it with all diligence amongst yourselves, not writing it on paper, but graving it by memory on your hearts, being on your guard in your exercise lest a catechumen should overhear the things delivered to you." St. Ambrose speaks to the same effect : "This warning I give you," says he, "that the symbol ought not to be written" (*Explanatio Symb. ad Initiandos*).

According to several authors of note, the Apostles' Creed was used in the Mass up to the year 325, when that framed by the Fathers of the Council of Nicæa superseded it, as being more explicit and complete on the dogmas of our holy faith (Gavantus, *Thesaur. Sacr. Rit.*, p. 86).

CREED OF NICÆA.

This was framed in the year 325 at the General Council of Nicæa, a town of Bithynia, in Asia Minor, where three hundred and eighteen Fathers assembled at the call of Pope Sylvester for the purpose of condemning the heretic Arius, who denied the divinity of our Lord.

Among the Fathers present at this famous synod, known throughout the East as the "Council of the three hundred and eighteen," were several upon whose persons could yet be seen the wounds they had received for the faith in the previous persecutions. The great Paphnutius, Bishop of the Thebaid, was there with his right eye plucked out, and his right hand burned into the very socket of the arm, in the persecution of Maximilian. So deeply affected was the Emperor Constantine the Great at the appearance of this saintly hero of the faith that he never took leave of him without first having kissed his wounds. Another venerable spectacle was St. Paul of Nova Cæsarea, whose two hands were burned off by order of Licinius. There was present, too, the great St. Potamon, Bishop of Heraclea, whose right eye was plucked out during another persecution. All these venerable men, old and feeble as they were, braved the perils of sea and land in order to defend the integrity of the apostolic faith against the most daring heresy that was ever broached in the Church.

The Council; Constantine the Great, etc.—Pope Sylvester was the reigning pontiff at this time, but he did not preside in person. Vitus and Vincent, priests of Rome, and Hosius, Bishop of Cordova, in Spain, represented him. It is generally believed that the last-named prelate presided over the deliberations of the Fathers; and there is an almost unanimous agreement among ecclesiastical historians that it was he who drew up the famous Creed, which the reader need hardly be told was written in Greek.

Constantine the Great was present a few moments after the Fathers had assembled. When his arrival was announced all rose to their feet to welcome him, and he was forthwith conducted to the magnificent golden throne prepared for him in the assembly-room. The emperor forbade any of his court to follow him, except those who had been baptized. The entire scene is so beautifully described by Eusebius that we cannot refrain from giving it in full: "The emperor appeared as a messenger of God, covered with gold and precious stones—a magnificent figure, tall and slender, and full of grace and majesty. To this majesty he united great modesty and devout humility, so that he kept his eyes reverently bent upon the ground, and only sat down upon the golden seat which had been prepared for him when the bishops gave him the signal to do so. As soon as he had taken his place all the bishops took theirs" (*Vita Constan.*, iii. p. 10). After the congratulatory address had been delivered to the emperor, the latter in a gentle voice addressed the Fathers. He spoke in Latin, which a scribe at his side immediately turned into Greek. At the end of the speech the articles touching the heresy of Arius were read and examined, and then the heretic himself was called to stand at the tribunal.

Description of Arius.—Arius is described as tall and thin, of austere appearance, serious bearing, but yet of very fascinating manners. He is represented as a learned man, a clever and subtle logician—proud, ambitious, insincere, and cunning. St. Epiphanius called him a perfidious serpent.

What his Error really was.—Like Philo, Arius admitted an intermediate being, who, being less than God, was the divine organ of the creation of the world, like the gods of Plato. Furthermore, he transferred the idea of time which rules every human generation to the divine generation, and drew from that, as he himself supposed, by logical necessity, the proposition that the Son could not be co-eternal with the Father. It was precisely this that condemned him.

Regarding the celebrated word that the Fathers employed as the great weapon of defence against his heresy—viz., ὁμοούσιος (*Homoousios*)—a very considerable amount of discussion has been set on foot, owing to its different shades of meaning, for in its own language it may be interpreted in various ways; nor can it be proved so easily that the Fathers of Nicæa intended it to signify, in a theological point of view, all that it really does, for it is well known that the numerical unity of the three Persons of the Adorable Trinity was not defined until the Fourth Council of Lateran, in 1215, condemned the opposite error of the Abbot Joachim.

To translate "Homoousios" by *consubstantial* is not enough without considerable explanation, for it is equally true that the Son of God is consubstantial with his Blessed Mother and with us. His consubstantiality with God the

Father must be something higher. Neither will it do to translate it, as may be done, by *the same being*, for this would be the heresy of Sabellius, who maintained that the Father and the Son were one and the same person, but differing in name only. But although it is not certain what the exact ground was that the Fathers of Nicæa intended to cover by their use of Homoousios, this much we know and believe, that no better word could have been chosen under the circumstances as a crucial test for the heresy of Arius ; and this Arius himself perfectly understood, for he moved heaven and earth to escape its force. The least ambiguous term for rendering this celebrated word into English is *co-eternal*, or *co-equal*, as the word *consubstantial* is very liable to be misinterpreted (see *Dublin Review*, June, 1845, vol. xviii., art. "Difficulties of the Ante-Nicene Fathers"; Alzog's *Church History*, vol. i., "Arian Controversy," translated by Pabisch and Byrne ; *History of the Christian Councils*, by. Hefele, vol. i.; and *Tracts, Theological and Ecclesiastical*, by Rev. Dr. Newman).

We must remark here that the Nicene Creed had for its basis the Apostles' Creed, and that only those clauses were added which bore upon the heresy of Arius and his heretical predecessors. Another remark, too, that it will not be amiss to make is this: that although Arianism at one time shook the whole earth to its foundations, still it never formed a church of itself, as did Nestorianism and Eutychianism. There are thousands in the East to-day who belong to both of these sects, but not an Arian can be found anywhere.

We shall now give the principal clauses of the Creed that the Fathers of Nicæa inserted in their new symbol of faith, as well as the names of the principal heresies against which they were directed :

Creed of Nicæa.

"Θεὸν ἀληθινόν ἐκ Θεοῦ ἀληθινοῦ."
Deum Verum de Deo Vero.
True God of True God.

This was inserted against the Arians and Eunomians, both of whom denied that our Divine Lord was very God by natural property, but only in the same way in which certain classes of men are styled gods in the Scripture; as, for instance, in the Eighty-first Psalm.

"Γεννηθέντα οὐ ποιηθέντα."
Genitum, non factum.
Begotten, not made.

This is to show that our Lord was not a creature, as some heretics implied by their phraseology, and others, such as Arius, asserted.

"Ὁμοούσιον τῷ Πατρί."
Consubstantialem Patri.
Consubstantial with the Father.

The "ὁμοούσιος," as we have said already, was the weapon which prostrated Arius, for it took from him the last prop upon which his heresy rested. Besides his, there were also included in the anathema fulminated by this council the teachings of the Manichæans, Basilians, Ebionites, Simonians, and those of Paul of Samosata.

"δι' οὗ τὰ πάντα ἐγένετο."
Per quem omnia facta sunt.
Through whom all things were made.

Many of the early heretics maintained that God the Father was the maker of all things, to the total exclusion of the Son, contrary to what our Divine Lord himself says in St. John, chapter v.: "What things soever he [*i.e.*, the

Father] doth, these the Son also doth in like manner." In their works *ad extra*, say theologians, the three divine Persons are concerned and united.

"Καὶ σαρκωθέντα, καὶ ἐνανθρωπήσαντα."
Et incarnatus est, et homo factus est.
And became incarnate, and was made man.

This was inserted against the many who maintained that our Lord's body was not, strictly speaking, a real human body, and that his divinity supplied the place of a human soul.

According to Cardinal Bona (*Rer. Liturg.*, p. 331), as soon as this famous Creed was promulgated all the churches of the East adopted it; the faithful and the catechumens were taught it; and those who did not profess it openly were stigmatized at once as Arians.

CONSTANTINOPOLITAN CREED.

We have just seen how Arius was condemned at Nicæa for denying the divinity of our Lord. Another great heretic now started up, Macedonius by name, denying the divinity of the Holy Ghost, for which he was condemned at the second general council—viz., that of Constantinople, held in the year 381. This council was entirely Oriental in its nature, and only became general, or œcumenical,[1] by a subsequent decree of the Roman Pontiff, or, as theologians say, *ex post facto*. In the condemnation of Macedonius were included also Apollinaris, Bishop of Laodicea, and Eunomius, of whom we have spoken already.

As the Symbol of Faith received an additional accretion at this Council, and as it was considered a very important

---

[1] The word *œcumenical*, coming from the Greek οἰκέω (*oikeo*, to dwell), in its original acceptation means *habitable;* but as the habitable globe is, in a certain sense, the whole world, it has in a secondary way come to mean universal or general.

one at that period of the Church's existence, it was deemed advisable to construct a new Creed on the basis of the Nicene, in which the distinctive prerogatives of each of the three Persons of the Adorable Trinity would be fully set forth. The opinion is almost universal that the composition of this Creed was the work of St. Gregory Nazianzen. After this had been drawn up and submitted to the council for inspection it is said that all the Fathers cried out with one acclaim: "This is the faith of all; this is the orthodox faith; this we all believe" (St. Liguori, *History of Heresies*, i. 84).

This Creed is more specific, too, than the Nicene on the incarnation, death, and resurrection of our Saviour; for it inserts the clauses in italics of " born *of the Virgin Mary*," "suffered *under Pontius Pilate*," "rose on the third day *according to the Scriptures*."

In its Latin form the Creed of Nicæa contains in all ninety-five words, whilst that of Constantinople has as many as one hundred and sixty-seven. The two are frequently confounded; and even to-day it is believed by many that the Creed we use in the Mass is that which was framed at Nicæa. Strictly speaking, it is neither the Nicene nor Constantinopolitan, but the one which was prepared by the Fathers of the Council of Trent in the sixteenth century. Of course we must not be understood as saying that this council added anything new to the Creed in the way of a dogma. The changes that it made wholly respected its grammatical construction (see Ferraris, *Bibliotheca*, art. "Symb.")

WHEN THE NICENE CREED BECAME PART OF THE MASS.

According to Renaudot (*Liturg. Orient.*, i. p. 200), the Nicene Creed was introduced into the Mass of the Eastern Church immediately after its formation by the "Three hundred and eighteen," and its recital was never interrupted. But it did not find its way into the Mass of the Western Church at so early a period, for the reason, given by some, that this Church never fell into any of the errors spoken of, and that, therefore, since its faith was evident to all, there was no necessity of making open profession of it. Indeed, it may be asserted without fear of contradiction that the Nicene Creed, strictly so called, was never recited in the Mass of the Western Church; for when the practice of reciting one at all came into use, which, according to Pope Benedict XIV. (*De Sacr. Miss.*, p. 46), was soon after the year 471, the Creed was not the Nicene but that of Constantinople. The custom of *singing* the Creed at Mass was not, according to the same pontiff, introduced into the Roman Church until the time of Benedict VIII. (1012–1024), and it was only introduced then in order to gratify the most earnest wishes of Henry II., Emperor of Germany. Previous to this, the Creed was simply *recited*.

ADDITION OF THE "FILIOQUE."

We have now come to one of the most interesting questions that we possibly could be engaged in considering, and the most difficult, perhaps, that has ever been raised in the Church; but, inasmuch as we are not writing an ecclesiastical history or dealing with purely dogmatical questions, we think our duty will be discharged if we give the reader the leading facts of the great controversy that this celebrated clause gave rise to.

We preface our remarks by correcting an error which too many have fallen into for want of a thorough examination of the case—to wit, that of ascribing the separation of the Eastern Church from the Western to the doctrine involved in the "Filioque." Every student of ecclesiastical history knows that the original cause of this separation was the refusal on the part of Rome to acquiesce in the impious action of the Emperor Bardas, who thrust into the See of Constantinople the audacious Photius, a mere layman, in place of St. Ignatius, the legitimate bishop. This happened about the year 858, and from this dates the separation of the two churches.[1] Photius, finding that his sacrilegious act would not be countenanced at Rome, moved heaven and earth to stir up as bitter feelings as he could between the two churches, and so began to arouse the suspicions of the Greeks by representing to them that the Latins were favoring the Manichæan heresy, inasmuch as they admitted two principles in the Deity; furthermore, that the Latin Church, in holding that the Holy Ghost proceeded from the Father and the Son, acted contrary to the express wishes and declarations of the previous general councils, and that, in consequence, it had fallen from the faith and become heretical. The Latin Church foresaw from the beginning that the state of affairs in the Greek Church would eventually take this turn, for the Greeks were always hot-headed and difficult to manage; but she wisely abstained from aggravating the case by making any public parade of the "Filioque" until things would assume a more tranquil appearance.

It is now very well understood that there never existed anything more between these churches on the doctrine involved in the clause in question than a mere misunderstanding in regard to some theological technicalities. "The

---

[1] To show how fickle-minded the Greeks were, and how very ill they bore being separated from the Western Church, which they well knew contained the centre of unity and the divinely-appointed teacher and expositor of all that pertained to faith and morals, they sought to be reunited no less than fourteen different times prior to the General Council of Florence, where the last union between the two churches was effected. Unhappily for themselves, none of these unions lasted long. The Greeks returned again to their errors, and so they remain to-day, like the Jews, a spectacle to the rest of mankind.

Greeks," says the late Dr. Brownson in an article in the *Ave Maria* of June, 1868, "never denied that the Holy Ghost proceeds from the Son as medium; what they denied was—what they understood by the 'Filioque'—that he proceeds from the Son as a principle distinct from the Father. . . . There was a misunderstanding between the Latins and the Greeks. The Latins supposed that the Greeks excluded the Son, and made the Holy Ghost proceed from the Father alone without any participation of the Son, which is unquestionably a heresy; the Greeks, on the other hand, supposed that the Latins by their 'Filioque' represented the Holy Ghost as proceeding from the Father and the Son as two distinct original principles, which was equally a heresy." The depositions made at the Council of Florence in 1439 clearly show that both Greeks and Latins were alike orthodox on this celebrated question.

When the Filioque was inserted.—The reader need hardly be told, but we think it well to call his particular attention to the fact, that the early ages of the Church and those we now live in differ very widely. There were no swift ships then to cross the ocean and bear despatches from place to place; nor had such things been heard of as railroads and telegraphs. News travelled very slowly; and things went on in their own way, unknown and unobserved by any save those in whose locality they occurred. That Rome, the centre of unity and orthodoxy, always kept a vigilant watch over the whole of Christendom nobody attempts to deny; but as Rome was often very far away, it could not be expected that she would become cognizant of local events as soon as they occurred. For this reason customs were introduced into many remote churches and allowed to take deep root there before the Holy See even knew of their existence. The "Filioque" first took rise in this way, and forced itself into the Creed without either the knowledge or consent of

Rome. The precise date at which this happened remains yet among the disputed points—some say in the year 400; others, 589. All, however, are unanimous in saying that the addition was first made in Spain; that thence it made its way into France; from France it was introduced into Germany, and so continued its course until it was deemed necessary at last to authorize its final insertion.

When the Spanish Church was called upon to answer for its conduct in this matter, it alleged as a plea that it was necessitated to place the divinity of our Lord in as strong a light as possible, in order to check the rapid strides that Arianism was making in its territories at the hands of the Goths and Visigoths, who had then almost undisturbed possession of the country, and who were avowed professors of this dangerous heresy. As the French Church had some misgivings about the propriety of following the example of the Spanish in a matter so very delicate, a council was summoned at Aix-la-Chapelle, in December, 809, by order of Charlemagne, to see what steps should be taken. Pope Leo III. was the reigning pontiff at the time. The council unanimously agreed that the proper way to act was first to consult the Holy See and abide by its decision. Bernhar, Bishop of Worms, and Adelard, Abbot of Corby, were accordingly despatched to the Pope with instructions to ask whether it would be pleasing to his Holiness or not to have the Church of France, after the example of its Spanish sister, add the "Filioque" to the Creed. From the manner in which the Holy Father, Pope Leo, acted with the legates it is easy to see how displeased he was at learning that any Church should dare to tamper with the Creed without the supreme authority of the Holy See. He did not say to the legates that they might add it, nor did he say that they might not. If he said the first, he clearly foresaw the unpleasant results that would ensue when the thing came to the knowledge of the troublesome Greeks, who would not hear of any intermeddling whatever with the Creed of Nicæa or Constantinople; and if he said the second, he feared very much that the Spaniards and others might accuse him of favoring the Arians. He evaded a direct answer by saying to the legates: "Had I been asked before the insertion took place, I should have been against it; but now—which, however, I do not say decidedly, but merely as discussing the matter with you—as far as I see both things may thus be accomplished: Let the custom of singing that Creed cease in the palace, since it is not sung in our holy Church, and thus it will come to pass that what is given up by you will be given up by all; and so, perhaps, as far as may be, both advantages will be secured." The legates departed satisfied with this response, and Pope Leo, to evince his determination to preserve the Creed inviolate, caused two silver plates to be cast, upon which he had the symbol engraved in Latin and Greek and affixed to the gate of the Church of St. Paul. For a full and interesting account of the entire interview between the legates of Charlemagne on this occasion and the Sovereign Pontiff, the reader is requested to consult Baronius, tome ix., or Neale's *Holy Eastern Church*, ii. p. 1163.

According to some, the final insertion of the "Filioque" was made by Pope Nicholas the Great somewhere between the years 858 and 867; others maintain that this was not authoritatively done until the time of Pope Benedict VIII.—that is, about the beginning of the eleventh century (see Perrone, *Prælectiones Theol.*, iv. p. 346, note 8). It will interest the reader to know that the Uniat Greeks, or those in communion with Rome, are not required to recite the "Filioque" in the Creed at the present day, even though saying Mass in presence of the Supreme Pontiff. All that the Holy See requires of them in this matter is that they believe in the doctrine involved in it, and be ready to make open profession of it when called upon to do so (*ibid.* p. 350, note 16).

PART OF THE MASS AT WHICH THE CREED IS RECITED.

According to the Roman Rite, the Creed is recited immediately after the Gospel, or after the sermon, if there should have been one. In the Mozarabic Rite it is recited just before the "Pater Noster," in accordance with a decree of the third Council of Toledo, A.D. 589, and this in order that the people may receive the Body and Blood of our Lord in Holy Communion with hearts full of fresh faith and love (*Summa Conciliorum*, p. 124; *Liturg. Mozar.*, Migne, p. 118, note).

Eastern Practice regarding its Recital.—The Armenians recite the Creed at the same part of the Mass that we do— viz., after the Gospel. In the Liturgy of St. James it follows soon after the expulsion of the catechumens. It is a little further on in the Liturgy of St. Chrysostom. The Nestorians recite it close upon the Canon, and the Copts immediately before the prayer of the "Kiss of peace." So great a veneration has the Russian Church for the Creed that the great bell of the Kremlin tolls the entire time of its chanting, and with many of the nobles of the land it is customary to have it worked in pearls upon their robes of state (*Holy Eastern Church*, by Neale and Littledale, p. 32).

Ceremonies attending the Recital of the Creed.—With very little exception the Creed is recited precisely as the "Gloria in excelsis." When the priest has come to the "et incarnatus est" he begins to incline the knee so as to touch the ground at "homo factus est," and this to recall more intimately to mind the profound humility of our Divine Lord in coming upon earth for our sakes and taking our nature upon him (Romsee, iv. 118). The Carthusians make only a simple bow of the knee at this place, without touching the ground. According to the Roman Rite, the priest says the entire Creed at the middle of the altar before the crucifix. The Dominicans begin its initial words there, but finish the rest of it at the Gospel side, where the missal is. When they come to the place where the genuflection is to be made they move to the middle, and, having spread out the anterior part of the chasuble on the altar in front of them, kneel down and touch the ground as we do. They then return to the missal and finish the rest there. In the Masses that are said in the Church of the Holy Sepulchre at Jersusalem—which, it is well to state, are always *de Resurrectione*—instead of simply saying "et sepultus est," it is of obligation to add the adverb "hic," and say "was buried here" by way of specification of place (Vetromile, *Travels in Europe and the Holy Land*, p. 211).

TO WHAT MASSES THE CREED IS PROPER.

The Creed is said on all the Sundays of the year, in memory of our Lord's resurrection on that day, and also out of deference to the Adorable Trinity, to whom Sunday, as being the principal liturgical day, is dedicated. During the rest of the week the Creed, as a general rule, is not said. Formerly it was not said on the feasts of the Holy Angels, inasmuch as they had nothing to do with it, but it is said now because they come under the "invisibilium omnium" (Ferraris, p. 751). It will interest the reader to know that St. Mary Magdalene is the only female saint in heaven—the Mother of God alone excepted—who enjoys the privilege of having a Credo in her Mass, and this because, in the language of the Church, she is styled "Apostola Apostolorum" —*the Apostle of Apostles*—for it was to her, as the Scriptures testify, that our Lord first appeared after his resurrection.

The other occasions upon which the Credo is said are, with few exceptions, comprehended under the old dictum of rubricists, "Muc non credunt." Taking the letters of *Muc* apart, we have "m," which stands for *martyrs;* "u," or "v," for *virgins, widows,* and *non-virgins;* and "c," for *confessors,* all of whom have no Credo special to them. As exceptions to this rule may be mentioned the feasts of the apostles and doctors of the Church, also those of our Lord and his Blessed Mother. With us the Creed is never said in Masses for the dead, but it is with the Greeks, who also on such occasions celebrate in red vestments instead of black, as is our custom.

CHAPTER XXIV.
THE CELEBRATION OF MASS.

THE OFFERTORY.

THE word *Offertory*—from the Latin *offerre*, to offer—is now used in two special senses, the first, meaning the prayer called in the Missal the *Offertorium*, which the priest reads immediately after the Creed; the second, all that takes place at the altar from the end of this prayer to the end of the oblation of the bread and wine.

In the early ages of the Church it was customary for the people to present here bread and wine for the use of the altar, oil for the sanctuary-lamp, incense for Solemn High Mass, and ears of corn and clusters of grapes as the first-fruits of the land (Bona, p. 332). By the third of the Apostolic Canons, nothing but what was required for the Holy Sacrifice could be placed on the altar; all the other offerings were usually received on a side-table prepared for the purpose, and called in ancient books, and yet so styled by the Greeks, the *Gazophilacium*. The Council of Trullo,[1] in the year 692, forbade the offering of milk and honey. The Council of Carthage, in 397, allowed these commodities to be offered once a year—viz., at Easter—because it was customary at that time especially to give milk and honey to the newly baptized; a custom which is yet almost universally observed in the East. In presenting these gifts the

---

[1] So called because the room of the emperor's palace at Constantinople where this council was held was shaped after the manner of a *trulla*, or basin. It was this council that forbade the making of the cross on the pavements, lest people walking upon it may desecrate it.

people usually gave in their names also, in order that they might be recorded among those for whom the priest made a special memento; and it served, too, for determining who it was that intended going to Holy Communion on that occasion, for, as a general rule, all who presented offerings approached the Blessed Eucharist (*ibid.*, p. 333).

This ancient custom is yet kept up in many European churches, at Lyons especially; and vestiges of it may be seen in the Masses of ordination, where the elect to orders present wax candles at this place to the ordaining bishop; also in the Mass of the consecration of a bishop-elect, where the newly-appointed offers two lighted candles, two loaves of bread, and two ornamented small barrels of wine. According to Kozma (p. 186), this ancient custom continued, with little interruption, up to the thirteenth century, when it gave place to that in vogue to-day of receiving the people's offerings in the pews throughout the church.

THE ORDER IN WHICH THE OFFERINGS WERE PRESENTED.

The Roman Ordo, describing the Offertory as it was observed in the ninth century, tells us that the people presented their gifts in a clean linen cloth, the male portion of the congregation leading the way, and the females after them with their cakes of fine flour and cruses of wine. The priests and deacons presented gifts after the people, but these were of bread simply. When the bishop was present the onus of receiving the gifts devolved always upon him. For this reason, as soon as the time for presenting them had arrived, his lordship walked over to the end of the altar-rail, followed by an archdeacon, a subdeacon, and two acolytes. The subdeacon, with an empty chalice, followed immediately after the archdeacon, who, upon receiving the offerings of wine from the hands of the bishop (who himself had received them first from the people), poured them into the large chalice held by the subdeacon. The offerings of bread were handed direct by the bishop to the subdeacon, who placed them in a large linen cloth carried by two acolytes. When all was ended the bishop washed his hands (a custom yet observed in a Bishop's Mass), and, having returned to the altar, there received the offerings of the priests and deacons. All that remained over and above what was necessary for the immediate wants of the altar on these occasions, went into a common fund for the sustenance of the clergy and the poor of the parish (Kozma, *ibid.*)

A question that is not easily settled is this: Did any of the congregation approach the altar at the Offertory and place their gifts upon it, instead of presenting them at the rails, as we have described? The discipline of allowing no one inside the sanctuary but the ministers of the altar was always very strictly observed in the Greek Church, except in case of the emperors of Constantinople, in whose favor an exception was made; and that it was strictly observed, too, in the Latin Church, at least for quite a long time, may be clearly seen from the conciliar statutes that were made concerning it. But that there were places and times when a relaxation of this discipline was allowed to be made, there is every reason to believe, and it is generally understood that at least the male portion of the congregation went up with their gifts to the altar itself, but that the female portion presented them at the rails. This, certainly, was the custom throughout the diocese of Orleans, in France, as we learn from the capitulary of Theodulf, bishop of that see. Cardinal Bona says that in course of time this whole discipline was so relaxed that both males and females approached the altar indiscriminately when the Offertory was at hand (*Rer. Liturg.*, p. 336).

ANCIENT LOCAL CUSTOMS REGARDING THE OFFERING OF GIFTS.

As late as the sixteenth century a very singular custom prevailed in England—viz., that of presenting at the altar during a Mass *of Requiem* all the armor and military equipments of deceased knights and noblemen, as well as their chargers. Dr. Rock (*Church of Our Fathers*, ii. 507) tells us that as many as eight horses, fully caparisoned, used to be brought into the church for this purpose at the burial of some of the higher nobility. At the funeral of Henry VII., in Westminster Abbey, after the royal arms had first been presented at the foot of the altar, we are told that Sir Edward Howard rode into church upon "a goodlie courser," with the arms of England embroidered upon his trappings, and delivered him to the abbots of the monastery (*ibid.*) Something similar happened at the Mass *of Requiem* for the repose of the soul of Lord Bray, in A.D. 1557, and at that celebrated for Prince Arthur, son of Henry VII. (*ibid.*)

MUSIC DURING THE OFFERTORY.

Up to the fourth century the presentation of gifts took place in silence, but after this period the custom of singing psalms at this place, in order to relieve the tedium of the people, was introduced (Kozma, pp. 186, 187). St. Augustine alludes particularly to this custom in his works (see *Retract.*, l. ii. c. xi.), and a precedent for it may be seen in the old law, where the sons of Aaron, while the high-priest was offering the blood of the grape, sounded their silver trumpets, and the singers lifted up their voices and caused the great house to resound with sweet melody (*Ecclesiasticus*, chap. l.)

The custom very generally prevails here to-day of singing,

instead of the *Offertorium* itself, a certain musical composition called a *motet*,[2] in which several voices join, accompanied by instruments. These motets must be always sung in Latin, never in English, or any other language, without the permission of the Holy See. They must be characterized, too, by gravity and dignity both as to wording and rendition, so as to be qualified to raise the feelings to a contemplation of heavenly things rather than excite in them earthly desires (Benedict XIV., l. c., § 89).

The *Offertorium*, according to the present disposition of the Roman Missal, is, for the most part, very short, seldom exceeding half a dozen lines. It is generally taken from the Psalter of David, and was formerly called an *antiphon*, for the reason that in the *Antiphonary* of Pope Gregory the Great certain verses used to be attached to it after the manner of a versicle and response. Whenever the offering of the gifts on the part of the people took up more time than usual, it was customary to sing the entire psalm here, or at least as much of it as would occupy the whole time that elapsed from the reading of the *Offertorium* by the priest to the end of the offering of gifts (Romsee, iv. 125; Kozma, pp. 186, 187).

The *Offertorium* common to all Masses for the dead is yet formed after the ancient manner of an antiphon, a versicle, and a response, though it is not, like the great majority, taken from the psalms. In fact, it is from no part of

---

[2] The word *motet* comes originally from the Latin *movere*, to move; but whether this name has been given it from its *moving* effect upon the feelings, or from its somewhat lively and more sprightly nature in opposition to the slow, measured motion of plain chant, authors are not prepared to say. Morley, in his *Introduction to Harmony*, p. 179, thus writes of it: "A motet is properly a song made for the Church, either upon some hymn or anthem, or such like; and that name I take to have been given to that kind of musicke, in opposition to the other, which they call 'canto firmo,' and we do commonlie call *plain chant*; for as nothing is more opposite to standing and firmness than motion, so did they give the motet that name of moving, because it is, in a manner, quite contrarie to the other."

Holy Scripture. As this same *Offertorium*, on account of its strange wording, has given rise to much curious questioning, some going so far as to say that the Church intends by it the liberation of the souls of the damned from hell, we deem it well to give it entire to the reader, and make the necessary comments afterwards: "Lord Jesus Christ, King of glory, deliver the souls of all the faithful departed from the pains of hell and the deep lake; deliver them from the mouth of the lion, lest Tartarus swallow them up, lest they fall into the dark place; but let the standard-bearer, St. Michael, bring them into the holy light which thou didst of old promise to Abraham and his posterity."

In a secondary way all this may be applied to Purgatory; but to our mind the intrinsic beauty and effect of the whole prayer would be lost if this were its exclusive application. Its true explanation is this: In the very early days of the Church Masses for the faithful departed were accustomed to be celebrated the moment it became known that any given soul was in its last agony, and, consequently, past all chance of recovery. It made no difference what time of the day this happened, or whether the priest who said the Mass was fasting or not. The virtue of the Holy Sacrifice was then supposed to ascend before the throne of God simultaneously with the departure of the soul of the deceased to the tribunal of judgment, and the merciful God was besought, in consideration of this, not to condemn it to hell's flames. (The authors who say that this view may be taken of it are Pope Benedict XIV., *De Sacros. Missæ Sacrif.;* Romsee, iv. 126; Cavalieri, tom. iii. dec. 19; Grancolas, *De Missis Mortuorum*, p. 536; Gavantus, *Thesaur. Sacr. Rit.*, p. 92.) A moment's consideration would enable any one to see that Purgatory never could have been directly meant by the wording of this *Offertorium*. For what fear, it might be asked, could there be entertained of having a soul swallowed up by Tartarus, or drowned in the "deep lake," who was already secure in that middle state, and whose eternal happiness was certain? The souls in Purgatory are in a state of grace, and, as there is no danger of their ever falling from it, it would be idle, nay, heretical, to pray for them as if such danger existed.

To this interpretation it is sometimes objected that the entire tenor of these Masses would lead a person to suppose that the soul for whom they are designed to be offered had been some time dead; how, then, it is asked, can this view be reconciled? Although the ancient custom of saying these Masses when the soul was in its last agony no longer exists, still the Church has not deemed it necessary to change their wording, inasmuch as it may yet be easily verified by supposing the time at which these Masses are now offered withdrawn to that very moment in the past when the soul was leaving the body. Instances of thus withdrawing from the present time, and representing an event as yet to take place which has really already taken place, is by no means uncommon in the offices of the Church. The whole of Advent time, for example, is framed upon this principle. We pray then for the coming of the great Messias with as much earnestness as if he were yet to appear. We ask the heavens to open and rain down the Just One. We beg of God to send us a Redeemer, and we ask the aid of His divine grace to enable us to prepare in our hearts a suitable dwelling into which to receive Him. Many more examples may be cited to show that this mode of praying is by no means unusual. St. Michael is here styled God's standard-bearer because chief of the heavenly host; and it was to him, as ancient tradition states, that the duty of hurling Satan and the rest of the fallen angels from heaven was entrusted. He is called the "Winged Angel," and is generally represented in art with a shield and lance. When depicted as the conqueror of Satan he stands in armor with his foot upon the demon, who is represented prostrate in the shape of a fierce dragon. As lord of souls St. Michael holds a balance in his hand. According to an ancient legend, it was he who appeared to our Blessed Lady to announce the time of her death, and conduct her afterwards to the throne of her Divine Son in heaven. It may interest the reader to be told that the old English coin called an *angel* received its name from the fact that St. Michael was depicted upon it (see *Legends and Stories Illustrated in Art*, by Clara E. Hemans, p. 228).

After the priest has recited the *Offertorium* he proceeds without delay to the Offertory proper. The chalice, which had stood up to this time on the corporal in the centre of the altar, is now uncovered, and the oblation of the Host, resting on the paten, is made with the following words: "Accept, Holy Father, Omnipotent, Eternal God, this immaculate Host which I, thy unworthy servant, offer thee, my living and true God, for my innumerable sins, offences, and negligences, and for all who are present; moreover, for all faithful Christians, living and dead, that it may avail both me and them unto salvation and life everlasting." Having finished this prayer, the priest lowers the paten, and, having made the sign of the cross with it over the corporal, places the Host upon the latter, near its anterior edge, where it remains until the time of Communion.[3] He places the paten itself at his right, partially covering it with the corporal, and lays the purificator over the rest of it. At Solemn High Mass the paten is not placed here, but is wrapped up by the subdeacon in a corner of the humeral veil, and held

---

[3] The reader must not suppose that it remains so undisturbed until the time of Communion. This would not be true, for at the consecration the priest takes it in his hands, and does so frequently afterwards.

partially elevated by him below near the altar-rails until the end of the "Pater noster." This ceremony is intended to preserve a vestige of a very ancient rite, the explanation of which is generally given as follows: For the first six centuries of the Christian Church it was on the paten that the Hosts used to be consecrated and broken, and from it distributed to the people at Holy Communion. This we clearly see from the words of the *Sacramentary* of Pope Gregory the Great, to wit : "We consecrate and sanctify this paten for confecting in it the Body of our Lord Jesus Christ." But when this custom ceased, in order that the paten might not lie uselessly on the altar and impede the operations of the priest (for in ancient times, as we have already stated elsewhere, it was of very large proportions), it used to be given in charge to the subdeacon until it was needed again. Why the subdeacon held it rather than any of the other ministers was to remind him of his office, because it was his duty to see always to the bread of oblation, as may clearly be understood from the words addressed him at his ordination; and then, again, he was more free from this part of the Mass to the time of Communion than any of the rest in the sanctuary (see Romsee, ii. 32, note ; Catalanus, *Comment. in Pontif. Romanum;* Mühlbauer, *De Ordin. Subd.*, i. 41).

Regarding the expression "immaculate host," applied here to what is as yet but mere bread, enquiries are often made ; the answer to all of which is that the appellation is given solely by way of anticipation of what is going to take place at consecration. "We do not call the bread and wine an immaculate host," says Hofmeister, "but the Body and Blood of the Lord which they are changed into. Therefore, not from what they now are, but from what they are going to be, are they dignified with such a title" (Bona, *Rer. Liturg.,* p. 337).

Having completed the oblation of the bread, the priest takes the chalice in hand and goes to the Epistle corner to receive the wine and water from the server. The amount of wine placed in the chalice on the occasion is, as a general rule, about as much as would fill a small wine-glass, and the water added seldom exceeds two or three drops. To approach as nearly as possible to the proper quantity, and have an exact measure to go by, it is customary to use a small spoon in many places of Europe for this purpose. The wine is poured into the chalice without either a blessing or a prayer; but as the water is added the priest makes the sign of the cross over it and recites the following prayer in the meantime: "O God! who didst wonderfully form the substance of human nature, and more wonderfully still regenerate it, grant us, by the mystery of this water and wine, to be united with the divinity of Him who deigned to become partaker of our humanity, thy Son, Jesus Christ, our Lord, who liveth and reigneth with thee in the unity of the Holy Ghost, God, world without end. Amen."

Liturgical writers seem to be unanimous in holding that the literal reason for mixing a few drops of water here with the wine is to commemorate what our Lord himself most probably did at the Last Supper; for it was always customary in his time, and the custom remains yet unchanged throughout the entire East, to temper the wine, before drinking it, with a little water. A neglect of this was looked upon by the Jews as a great breach of etiquette.⁴ But besides this literal reason there are several mystical reasons for this very ancient ceremony. In the first place, as the prayer recited while adding the water implies, it is intended to remind us

---

⁴ Bannister, in his *Temples of the Hebrews*, p. 233, tells us that water was always mingled with the wine at the Feast of the Passover, and that the master of the assembly offered a form of thanksgiving on the occasion by using these words: "Blessed be thou, O Lord! who hast created the fruit of the vine."

of the very close union that exists between ourselves and our Lord—so close, indeed, that we are said to partake in a measure of his divinity, as he partook of our humanity and became *like unto us in all things*, as the apostle says, *sin alone excepted*. Secondly, this mixture recalls to mind the blood and water which issued from our Lord's side on the cross when pierced by the spear. Thirdly, it has a reference, according to some, to Holy Baptism, in virtue of which we are all regenerated. The small quantity of water added on this occasion is said to be intended as a reminder of the fewness of the elect at the last day (Gavantus, p. 199).

WHY THE WATER IS BLESSED BEFORE PUTTING IT INTO THE CHALICE.

It will always remain a wonder to us why the blessing of the water here has occasioned so much anxious enquiry, and given rise to an almost interminable amount of discussion, when the reason is so close at hand. It is blessed here simply because it cannot be found by itself afterwards. The wine is not blessed until immediately before the consecration—that is, when the priest makes the sign of the cross over it at the word "benedixit." It is at this part of the Mass that the bread also receives its special blessing, and not at the Offertory. Formerly the water was not blessed at this place—and is not even now in Masses for the dead—but was let fall into the chalice in the form of a cross, a custom which we see yet in vogue with the Carthusians. The Carmelites and Dominicans place the wine and the water in the chalice at the beginning of Mass ; the Carthusians put the wine in at that time, too, but not the water until the Offertory. The reason usually alleged for putting the wine and water into the chalice at this early stage is that sufficient time may be given for the water to be converted into the substance of the wine before consecration takes place. A rubric to this effect thus reads in the Dominican Missal: "Tantam quantitatem aquæ distillet in calicem, quæ facillime tota possit in vinum converti"— "He drops as much water into the chalice as may very easily be converted, in its entirety, into the substance of the wine." Few questions gave rise to more spirited argumentation in the middle ages, especially towards the latter part, than that which respected the mingling of the water with the wine, as here alluded to; some holding that the water was immediately taken up by the wine and made part of its own substance, while others maintained that the water always remained as it was, even after consecration, and was not transubstantiated at all, as the wine was. Pope Innocent III. discusses the question at full length in his treatise on the Mass, but abstains from giving any definite decision in the matter. According to St. Thomas Aquinas (par. 3., quest. 74, art. 8) and St. Bonaventure (dis. ii. par. 2, art. 1, q. 3), the water is not converted *immediately* into the Body and Blood of our Lord in this case, but *mediately* only—that is, it is first converted into wine, and then both, as one entire body, are transubstantiated. All the Thomists and Scotists alike held this.

Local Customs.—The priests of the Ambrosian Rite, in pouring the water into the chalice, say: "Out of the side of Christ there flowed blood and water at the same time. In the name of the Father, and of the Son, and of the Holy Ghost. Amen." The priests of Lyons Cathedral say: "From the side of our Lord Jesus Christ there issued blood and water at the time of his Passion; this is a mystery of the Blessed Trinity. John the Evangelist saw it and bore witness of the fact, and we know that his testimony is true." In the Mozarabic Rite the formula is: "From the side of our Lord Jesus Christ blood and water are said to have flowed; and, therefore, we mix them, in order that the merciful God may vouchsafe to sanctify both for the salvation of our souls."

OBLATION OF THE CHALICE.

The priest, in making this oblation, holds the chalice with both hands raised before his face while he recites the following prayer : " We offer thee, O Lord! the chalice of salvation, beseeching thy clemency that it may ascend in the sight of thy divine Majesty with the odor of sweetness for our salvation and for that of the whole world. Amen." He then lowers the chalice, and, placing it on the corporal immediately behind the Host, covers it with the pall. Up to the fifteenth century the practice was very much in vogue of placing the chalice not behind the Host, as now, but at the right of it—that is, opposite the left of the priest—and this with a view to catch the Precious Blood, as it were, as it flowed from the body of our Lord when opened by the soldier's spear. The tradition in the Eastern Church as well as the Western, has always been that it was our Lord's right side that was pierced on the cross, and not the left (Rock, *Church of Our Fathers*, i. 261 ; *Translation of the Primitive Liturgies*, p. 182, note 12, by Neale and Littledale). The plural form "we offer" used in this prayer, instead of the singular "I offer," is retained here, some say, from Solemn High Mass, where the deacon touches the chalice with his hand while the celebrant is making its oblation, and thus offers it conjointly with him (Romsee, iv. 141). Others see in the retention of the plural a special reference to the duty of the deacon—viz., of dispensing the chalice to the people when the custom of communicating under both species was in vogue (Bona, *Rer. Liturg.*, p. 338). And as to the retention of the plural form when no deacon assists, as is the case in Low Mass, authors tell us that Pope Gregory the Great was very fond of employing the plural instead of the singular, and that very likely he allowed this to stand untouched, as he did the form "benedicite, Pater reverende," instead of "benedic, Pater" (Le Brun, *Explication des Prières et des Cérémonies de la Messe*, ii. p. 60, note *a*).

After the oblation of the chalice the priest inclines slightly, and, placing his hands united, palm to palm, on the altar, recites the following prayer: "In a spirit of humility and with contrite heart may we be received by thee, O Lord! and grant that the sacrifice we offer this day in thy sight may be pleasing to thee, O Lord God!" The priest then becomes erect, and presently, raising, then lowering his hands, invokes the Holy Ghost, saying: "Come, O Sanctifier, Omnipotent, Eternal God! and bless this sacrifice prepared to thy holy name." Upon saying "bless" he makes the sign of the cross over the Host and chalice conjointly. This prayer affords the only instance in the whole Mass where the Holy Ghost is invoked expressly by name, for which reason some have supposed that it is God the Father who is meant; but, as Romsee very well says, we do not apply the term *come* to the Father, but only to God the Son, or God the Holy Ghost, both of whom are always *sent*, or implored that they might come; but God the Father, who sends them, is never addressed in this way (Romsee, iv. p. 146). In many ancient missals the Holy Ghost used to be mentioned in this prayer expressly, and is so mentioned yet in the Mozarabic Rite, where the prayer of invocation thus begins: "Come, O Holy Ghost, Sanctifier!" etc. In commenting on this prayer Pope Benedict XIV. says, in his treatise on the Mass, that it is addressed to the Third Person of the Blessed Trinity, in order that, as the Body of our Blessed Lord was formed by the power and operation of this Holy Spirit in the chaste womb of the Blessed Virgin, it may be formed anew by the same Spirit upon the altar of God (*Enchiridion de Sacrif. Missæ*, p. 53).

At Solemn High Mass incense is brought on the altar after this prayer, and the oblation, as well as the altar itself and its ministers, are incensed. Then follows the incensing of all in the sanctuary, and, finally, of the people of the congregation. We have not deemed it necessary to enter more minutely into this ceremony, as our book is not a treatise on rubrics.

Having recited the prayer "Come, O Sanctifier!" the priest goes to the Epistle corner, and there washes the tips of his fingers—not of all his fingers, but only of the thumb and index-finger of each hand, as it is these, and these only, that are allowed to touch the Blessed Sacrament, for which reason they are sometimes called the canonical fingers; and it is they which were anointed with holy oil by the bishop when the priest was ordained. While performing this ablution the priest recites that portion of the twenty-fifth Psalm which begins with "I will wash my hands among the innocents." Besides the literal reason of this ablution, there is a beautiful mystical reason also —to wit, that in order to offer so tremendous a sacrifice as that in which the victim is none else than the Son of God himself, the priest's conscience must be free from the slightest stain of sin. "This signifies," says St. Cyril of Jerusalem, in his fifth book of *Catechesis*, "that our souls must be purified from all sins and wickedness. For, as the hands are the instruments of action, the washing of them shows the purity of our desires." St. Germanus says to the same effect: "The washing of a priest's hands should remind him that we must approach the holy table with a clean conscience, mind, and thoughts (the hands of the soul), with fear, meekness, and heartfelt sincerity." It is worth noting here that the priest does not remain at the middle of the altar while washing his hands, but goes to the Epistle corner, and this out of respect for the Blessed Sacrament enclosed in the tabernacle and for the crucifix. In case the Blessed Sacrament should be exposed, to show a still greater degree of respect, he descends one step at the Epistle side, and, standing so as to have his back turned to the wall and not to the altar, performs the ablution there. The Church is very particular in all that concerns the reverence due to the Holy Eucharist.

Having performed this ablution, the priest returns to the middle of the altar, where, bowing down slightly, he recites the following prayer: "Receive, O Holy Trinity! this oblation, which we offer thee in memory of the passion, resurrection, and ascension of our Lord Jesus Christ; in honor of Blessed Mary ever Virgin; of blessed John the Baptist; and of the holy Apostles Peter and Paul, of these and of all the Saints, that it may tend to their honor and to our salvation, and that they whose memory we celebrate upon earth may deign to intercede for us in heaven. Through the same Christ our Lord. Amen." During the first four centuries the Church was very careful in alluding to the Blessed Trinity, for the reason that she feared it might lead the pagans and infidels to suppose that she worshipped a plurality of Gods. She wisely abstained, therefore, from addressing her public prayers to any of the three Divine Persons but the Father only. This prayer, although not of as high antiquity as some of the others, is yet very old, for we find it in the so-called Illyric Missal, supposed to date as far back as the seventh century (Romsee, p. 156).

"ORATE FRATRES."

Having finished this prayer, the priest turns round to the congregation and salutes them with "Orate fratres," or "Pray, brethren," which he continues reciting as follows: "That my sacrifice and yours may be acceptable to God the Father Almighty." The reason generally assigned for only saying the first two words of this prayer in an audible tone is that the singers may not be disturbed while going through their offertorial pieces (*ibid.*) To this prayer the server answers, "May the Lord receive this Sacrifice from thy hands, to the praise and glory of his name, for our benefit also, and that of his entire holy Church." At the end the priest says "Amen" secretly.

Although there should be none but females assisting at a priest's Mass, as is frequently the case in convents, still the form of salutation must not be changed from the masculine gender; nor must any addition whatever be made to it by reason of the attendance of the opposite sex. In ancient times, however, such a change used to be made in some places, for we find that the Sarum Rite used to say, "Orate fratres et sorores"—"Pray, brethren and sisters"; and the form may also be seen in a Missal of Cologne [5] edited in the year 1133.

THE "SECRETÆ," OR SECRET PRAYERS.

Having said "Amen" after the server's response to the "Orate fratres," the priest, standing at the centre of the altar, reads from the missal, placed at his left (Gospel side), the prayers called "Secretæ," which always correspond in number with the collects read at the beginning of Mass. As to how the term *secret* came to be applied to these prayers much diversity of opinion exists. According to some, this

---

[5] The Cathedral of Cologne is the finest specimen of Gothic architecture in the world. It was begun in 1248, and is yet in process of building. Its two massive towers will, when completed, be each 500 feet high—that is, about 50 feet higher than St. Peter's at Rome, and 25 feet higher than the tower of the great Cathedral of Strassburg, which ranks now as the highest structure in the world. The Cathedral of Cologne has the rare privilege of possessing the skulls of the Magi who came to adore our Lord on Christmas morning. They are preserved in silver cases studded with gems, and their names—viz., Gaspar, Melchior, and Baltassar—are wrought upon them in rubies.

name was given them because they were the first prayers recited after the catechumens had been dismissed or set apart (*secreti*) from the rest of the congregation, the Latin origin of the word—viz., *secernere*—favoring this interpretation. Others say they are so called from the fact that they are recited over that part of the offerings presented by the people, according to the ancient rite, which was *separated* and set aside from the rest for altar purposes. The great weight of authority, however, inclines towards attributing their name to the fact that they were recited *secretly*—that is, in a sort of whisper—in order not to disturb the singers, who in ancient times were stationed in the choir quite close to the altar. In order to have as little difference as possible between one kind of Mass and another, the Church has allowed many things to remain in Low Mass which really had their origin in High Mass, and, as we have taken care to state already, the majority of Masses in the early days were of the latter kind (Romsee, p. 162; *Enchiridion Sac. Missæ, ex Opere Bened. XIV.*, p. 55). At the end of the last secret prayer the Offertory is said, strictly speaking, to conclude.

OFFERTORY IN THE ORIENTAL CHURCH.

From what we have said in another place regarding the singular care which is taken by the Orientals in the matter of the sacrificial oblations, it will be easy to understand why the custom so long prevalent in the Western Church—viz., of receiving bread and wine from the people for altar purposes—never gained any ground with them. The Orientals take nothing for the holy Mass except what has been first prepared and presented by their own clergy. There is, then, strictly speaking, no offering on the part of the people in the Oriental Church, but donations in the shape of money are handed in for the sustenance of the clergy. " Before they go to the Prothesis" (the cruet-table), says Dr. Covel, "to begin the liturgy, all good people who are disposed to have their absent friends, living or dead, commemorated go to them that celebrate and get their names set down—there being two catalogues, one for the living, one for the dead— for which they deposit some aspers, or richer presents in silver or gold, as they are able or disposed, this being a great part of the common maintenance of a priest, especially in country villages" (Neale and Littledale, *Primitive Liturgies*, p. 186, note). This offering, then, takes place in the East at the beginning of Mass, at what is called the *Little Entrance*, or Introit, and there is no offering whatever made at the Offertory proper.

Before we pass on to the next portion of the Mass we beg to delay the reader here a while, in order to say a few words about certain liturgical appurtenances that were in quite general use in days gone by. We refer to the *Holy Fan* (*Sacrum Flabellum*), the *Colum* or Strainer, and the *Comb*.

THE HOLY FAN.

For quite a long time the custom prevailed in the Western Church, and we see it continues yet in the Eastern, of employing a fan at the Offertory, and up to the end of Communion, for the purpose of driving away flies and other troublesome insects from the priest and the sacred oblation. The charge of this fan was entrusted to the deacon, and its delivery to him at his ordination formed, in early days, one of the necessary things, and is still so considered in the Greek Rite.

In the ancient Rite of Sarum these fans were remarkable for the beauty and costliness of their workmanship, being sometimes made of the purest silver and gold curiously wrought. In an inventory found in the Cathedral of Salisbury, in 1222, a fan of pure silver is mentioned. In the great Cathedral of York there was a precious fan which exhibited on one side an enamelled picture of the bishop of that see (*Church of Our Fathers*, iii. p. 200). Sometimes these fans were made of parchment finely wrought, and sometimes again of peacock's feathers. They had a long handle attached, which was, for the most part, made of ivory. Hano, Bishop of Rochester, gave a fan to his cathedral in 1346 which was made of precious silk, with an ivory handle (*ibid.*)

The earliest definite account that we have of these fans is that which is furnished by the so-called *Apostolic Constitutions*. These give the following directions concerning their use: "Let two deacons stand on both sides of the altar, holding a small fan made of parchment, peacock's feathers, or fine linen, and with a gentle motion let them keep away the flies, in order that none of them may fall into the chalice" (Riddle, *Christian Antiquities*, p. 603).

We have said that the use of the fan is yet kept up by the Orientals during divine service. That employed by the Maronites is circular in shape, and has a number of little bells round its rim. It is generally made of silver or brass (*Church of Our Fathers*, p. 179). The Greek fan—of which Goar gives a full account, with a print on the opposite page, in his *Euchol. Græc.*, p. 136—is made in the shape of the winged face of a cherub. In the Western Church fans were symbolic of the Holy Spirit, and the flies and other troublesome insects which the fan was made to banish were supposed to be vain and distracting thoughts (Durandus, *Rationale Divinorum*, iv. p. 35). As the fan of the Greek Church resembled a cherub in shape, its motion during Mass symbolized the flitting about of these blessed spirits before the throne of God (*Prim. Liturgies*, by Neale and Littledale, Introduction, p. xxix.)

THE STRAINER.

In order to have the wine for the service of the altar wholly free from all manner of impurity, it was customary in the early days to pass it into the chalice through a liturgical appurtenance called a *colum*, or strainer. This strainer, like all the other sacred utensils used about the altar, was frequently made of the most costly material, and was looked upon as filling a very important part in the service of the Mass. As a general rule it was made of silver, shaped like a spoon, and perforated with a number of very minute holes through which the pure wine was passed into the chalice in a filtered state. Cardinal Bona speaks at some length of these in his *Rer. Liturg.*, p. 293.

THE COMB.

Another ancient liturgical utensil, which perhaps we should have spoken of sooner, was the comb, employed for the purpose of keeping the celebrant's hair in order during divine service. These were for the most part made of ivory. but we find them of silver and gold very frequently, and studded in many cases with pearls. The Cathedral of Sens has yet among its ancient curiosities a liturgical comb of ivory, with the inscription, "Pecten sancti Lupi"—"The comb of St. Lupus"—engraved upon it. St. Lupus was bishop of this place in the year 609, from which we see that the comb is of a very high antiquity (*Church of Our Fathers*, ii. p. 124).

The Cathedral of Sarum, in England, had a vast number of ivory combs of this nature beautifully finished; and as a curious bit of information we mention that among the spoils carried away from Glastonbury Abbey by the English Nabuchodonosor, Henry VIII., there is mentioned "a combe of golde, garnishede with small turquases and other course stones" (Dugdale, *Mon. Ang.*, tom. i. p. 63, from Dr. Rock).

When the bishop officiated the deacon and subdeacon combed his hair as soon as his sandals had been put on; when the celebrant was a priest the office of combing was first performed for him in the vestry, and then at stated times during Mass. The rule in this respect was that whenever the officiating minister stood up after having been seated for some time, and took off his cap, his hair was combed before he ascended the altar. While the process of combing was going on a cloth was spread over the shoulders to prevent the sacred vestments from being soiled.

Durandus, who is always ready with a mystic meaning for everything, says that the stray hairs which lie upon the head now and then are the superfluous thoughts which trouble us from time to time and hinder us from paying the attention that we ought to our sacred duties (*Rationale*, pp. 149, 150).

The use of the comb in the Western Church is now entirely unknown, but it may yet be seen in some churches of the East, for nearly all the Eastern clergy allow the beard to grow freely down the face after the manner of the ancient patriarchs (see Romanoff, *Rites and Customs of the Greco-Russian Church*, p. 401), for which reason combing becomes frequently necessary in order to present a neat and becoming appearance.

CHAPTER XXV.

THE CELEBRATION OF MASS.

THE PREFACE.

AT the end of the last secret prayer the priest raises his voice and says, "Per omnia sæcula sæculorum," to which the server answers, "Amen." He then says, "Dominus vobiscum," without, however, turning to the people, and now enters upon the Preface, so called because it is, as it were, a preparation for the most solemn part of the whole Mass— viz., the Canon. The reason why the priest does not turn round to the people at this place when he says "Dominus vobiscum" is founded on that ancient custom which once prevailed in the West, and still continues in the East, of drawing aside the sanctuary curtains so as to hide the altar from the congregation the moment the Preface began. As there were no persons in sight then to salute, it was not deemed necessary to turn round, and a vestige of this ancient practice is here kept up (Kozma, p. 193).

After the "Dominus vobiscum" the priest raises his hands aloft and says, "Sursum corda"—"Your hearts upwards"; that is, "Lift your thoughts to heaven"—to which the server responds, "We have lifted them up to the Lord." The "Sursum corda" is, no doubt, taken from the Lamentations of Jeremias (iii. 41), and is found in all the liturgies of the East and West. The solemn motion of the priest's hands, as he raises them on high while pronouncing this sacred admonition, is aptly compared by several liturgical writers to the outspreading wings of a dove when going to fly, and forcibly recalls to mind that beautiful saying of King David, " Who will give me the wings of a dove, and I will fly and be at rest?" (*Ps.* liv.) After the "Sursum corda" the priest says, "Gratias agamus Domino Deo nostro"—" Let us return thanks to the Lord our God"— to which the server answers, "Dignum et justum est"— " It is meet and just." The priest then enters on the Preface proper, and continues reciting it to the end without further interruption.

The question is sometimes asked, Where does the Preface really begin? Strictly speaking, not till the "Sursum corda," for the " Per omnia sæcula sæculorum" belongs to the conclusion of the last secret prayer, and the "Dominus vobiscum" is a salutation to the people ; but as all our missals begin the Preface at the " Per omnia sæcula sæculorum," it is well that this should be considered its true beginning.

In the Mozarabic Liturgy the Preface is called the *Inlatio*, or *Inference*, from the fact, as Cardinal Bona conjectures, that the priest infers from the responses of the people that it is *meet and just to give thanks to the Lord*. In some ancient manuscripts it is called the *Immolation*, for the reason that it is, as it were, an introduction to that most sacred part of the Mass where Christ our Lord, the Immaculate Lamb, is newly immolated as on Calvary of old.

ANTIQUITY OF THE PREFACE, AND THE NUMBER OF PREFACES NOW USED.

The use of the Preface in the Mass is, according to the best authorities, of apostolic origin. For quite a long time it was customary to have a special one for every feast that occurred, so that the number was once very great. According to Neale, as many as two hundred and forty are yet preserved.

In the Mozarabic Rite there is still a proper Preface for every Sunday and festival; and the Ambrosians, or Milanese, have a different one every day in the week (Neale, *Holy Eastern Church*, i. p. 467). Towards the eleventh century the Roman Church reduced the entire number to nine, to which two others were subsequently added, making in all eleven, which is the number of distinct Prefaces that we use to-day. Their names are as follows: 1st, the Preface of the Nativity, or Christmas day; 2d, the Preface of the Epiphany, or 6th of January; 3d, the Preface of Quadragesima, or Lent; 4th, the Preface of the Cross and Passion; 5th, the Preface of Easter Sunday; 6th, the Preface of the Ascension; 7th, the Preface of Pentecost; 8th, the Preface of the Blessed Trinity; 9th, the Preface of the Blessed Virgin; 10th, the Preface of the Apostles; 11th, the Preface of the Common.

Preface of the Blessed Trinity.—It is admitted by all that this Preface is a masterpiece of composition. It reads very like a work of inspiration, and is, as far as its theology goes, the most profound of the eleven. We subjoin a translation of it in full, but we beg to remind the reader that to be fully appreciated it must be read in its original tongue, the Latin. When rendered into English much of its sublimity is lost: "It is truly meet and just, right and salutary, that we should always, and in all places, give thanks to thee, O Holy Lord, Father omnipotent, Eternal God, who, together with thy Only-Begotten Son and the Holy Ghost, art one God and one Lord; not in the singularity of one Person, but in a Trinity of one substance. For what we believe of thy glory as thou hast revealed, the same we believe of thy Son and of the Holy Ghost, without any difference or distinction. So that in the confession of the True and Eternal Deity we adore a distinction in the Persons, a unity in the Essence, an equality in the Majesty.

Whom the Angels and Archangels praise, the Cherubim also and the Seraphim, who without ceasing cry out daily with one accord, Holy, holy, holy, Lord God of Hosts. Heaven and earth are full of thy glory. Hosanna in the highest! Blessed be he who cometh in the name of the Lord! Hosanna in the highest!" Looking at this Preface from a theological point of view, it would appear that some of its phraseology must have been changed subsequent to the General Council of Nicæa, held in the year 325, for it is a well-known fact that, prior to that period, the Church, as we have already intimated in another place, wisely abstained from giving too much publicity to her doctrine concerning the exact relations existing between the three Persons of the Adorable Trinity. She declared, it is true, by her solemn definition against Arius at the above-mentioned council, that the Son of God was *homoousios*—that is, consubstantial with the Father; but it was not until nine hundred years and more had passed away that she openly defined as *de fide Catholica* that the unity of the Godhead was a *numerical* unity, and not a *generic* or *specific* unity, as the writings of many of the ancient Fathers would be apt to lead one to suppose. "Not till the thirteenth century," says Dr. Newman, "was there any direct and distinct avowal on the part of the Church of the numerical unity of the Divine Nature, which the language of some of the principal Greek Fathers, *prima facie*, though not really, denies" (*University Sermons*, p. 324). The cause that led to the definition of this numerical unity in the thirteenth century —that is, at the fourth Council of Lateran, A.D. 1215—was the opposite teaching of the Abbot Joachim (*Dublin Review*, 1845, "Difficulties of the Ante-Nicene Fathers").

The Preface of the Blessed Virgin.—This is called the *Miraculous Preface;* for, as the story goes, the greater part was miraculously put in the mouth of Pope Urban II. as he was one day singing High Mass in the Church of our Blessed Lady at Placentia. He began by chanting the Common Preface, but when he had come to that part where the Prefaces generally turn off to suit the occasion he heard angels above him singing as follows : " Who, by the overshadowing of the Holy Ghost, conceived thine Only-Begotten Son, and, the glory of her virginity still remaining intact, brought into the world the Eternal Light, Christ Jesus, our Lord." The holy pontiff caused these words to be afterwards inserted in the Common Preface at the council held in the above place in 1095, and for this reason the Preface of the Blessed Virgin is ascribed to him (Ferraris, *Bibliotheca;* Bona, p. 341; Merati, *Thesaur. Sacr. Rit.*, p. 94). A custom once prevailed in many places of bowing solemnly to the ground at the words, " Adorant dominationes." There was a rubric to this effect in a Roman ordo of the eighth century, composed for the use of monasteries (Martène, *De Antiq. Eccl. Rit.*, f. 31).

TERMINATION OF THE PREFACE.

All the Prefaces terminate with the " Holy, holy, holy, Lord God of Hosts," etc. This is called the *triumphal* hymn, sometimes the *seraphic,* and is taken from Isaias, vi. 3 ; St. John also mentions it in the fourth chapter of his Apocalypse. The Mozarabics recite the termination of the Preface—that is, the " Holy, holy, holy," etc.—in Greek as well as in Latin.

At Solemn High Mass, as the reader knows, the Preface is chanted throughout by the celebrant. The music is of the simplest kind of plain chant, but very soul-stirring. We have shown in our chapter on " Church Music " how deeply affected some of the ancient Fathers used to be when singing this part of the Mass, and what abundance of tears its celestial melody often drew from their hearts. The chant used at Lyons and Milan differs a little from ours, as does also the Mozarabic, but the same divine fascination is inherent in all of them.

PREFACES OF THE ORIENTAL CHURCH.

The Orientals have no variety of Preface at all. Every liturgy has one peculiar to itself, and this is employed the whole year round without any change whatever. It is called by the Easterns the *Anaphora* (although this word also includes the Canon of the Mass), and begins and ends almost precisely like our own. According to a ritual of Gabriel, Patriarch of Alexandria, directions are given to the priest to make the sign of the cross three different times at the "Sursum corda": first, upon himself; secondly, upon the attending deacons; and, thirdly, upon the congregation (Renaudot, i. p. 206). In the East, as well as in the West with ourselves, it is customary to stand up always the moment this portion of the Mass begins, and this as a testimony of the great respect that is due it. At Low Mass, however, the rule is to remain kneeling.

The Greeks call the "Holy, holy, holy," etc., the *Triumphal Hymn*, as we do. The "Gloria in excelsis" they call the *Angelic Hymn*. Their *Trisagion*, or Thrice Holy, which we recite on Good Friday, and of which we have given a full history already, is that which begins with "Holy God, Holy Strong One, Holy Immortal One." They have another hymn, called the *Cherubic*, which they recite in the Mass soon after the expulsion of the catechumens. It is worded as follows: "Let us, who mystically represent the Cherubim, and sing the Holy Hymn to the Life-giving Trinity, lay by at this time all worldly cares, that we may receive the King of glory invisibly attended by the angelic orders. Alleluia, alleluia, alleluia."

In the Ethiopic Liturgy four archangels are particularized

in the Preface—viz., Michael, Gabriel, Raphael, and Suriel, or, as he is more commonly styled, *Uriel*. The Syriac Liturgy of Philoxenus mentions the celestial spirits after a somewhat singular manner, thus: "The jubilees of Angels; the songs of Archangels; the lyres of Powers; the pure and grateful voices of Dominations; the clamors of Thrones; the thunders of Cherubim; and the swift motion of Seraphim." Immediately before the conclusion of the Preface in the Liturgy of St. Chrysostom mention is made of the celestial spirits as *singing* ($ᾄδοντα$), *bellowing* ($βοῶντα$), *crying* ($κεκραγότα$), and *speaking* ($λέγοντα$). According to some Oriental commentators, the four Evangelists are here mystically represented. The *singing* with a loud voice alludes to St. John, who, on account of the lofty flight of his genius, is aptly compared to the eagle, and is generally represented in art with this bird by his side. The *bellowing* refers to St. Luke, who, on account of his setting forth the priesthood of our Lord so conspicuously, has been always represented by an ox, the symbol of sacrifice. By the *crying* or *roaring* like a lion St. Mark is meant, as he is said to be pre-eminently the historian of our Lord's resurrection; and an Eastern tradition has it that young lions are born dead and are brought to life after three days (the time our Saviour was in the grave) by the roaring of their sire. And by the *speaking*—that is, like a man—St. Matthew is meant, on account of his dwelling so much on the human nature of our Lord. In art he is generally represented by the figure of a cherub, which is supposed to resemble a human being so much (Neale, *Holy Eastern Church*, i. p. 470; *Symbolism in Art*, by Clara E. Clement, p. 18; also St. Jerome on the Four Evangelists).

At the conclusion of the Preface the little sanctuary bell is rung to remind the people of the approach of the most solemn part of the Mass, in order that their attention may be fixed upon it more earnestly.

CHAPTER XXVI.

THE CELEBRATION OF MASS.

THE CANON.

WE have now come to the most sacred portion of the entire Mass—sacred by reason of its great antiquity, for it carries us away back to the days of the apostles; and doubly sacred because it contains those blessed words uttered by our Divine Redeemer at the Last Supper, in virtue of which the bread and wine are changed into his own Body and Blood. For the latter reason alone the Canon should be treated of on bended knees.

WHY CALLED BY THE NAME OF CANON.

The word *Canon*, from the Greek $\kappa\alpha\nu\grave{\omega}\nu$, was used in a variety of senses by ancient authors. Originally it meant a rule or contrivance by which other things were kept straight; but in a secondary sense it was variously applied according to the nature of the case, always, however, preserving the idea inherent in its original meaning. In architecture it was the plumb-line or level; in weights and measures it was the tongue of the balance; in chronology it was the chief epoch or era; in music it was the monochord, or basis of all the intervals; and when applied in a literary sense it served to designate those writings which were to be distinguished from all others by the elegance and excellence of their diction. The *Doruphoros* of Polycletus was called by this name, and for this reason also the select extracts of many of the ancient Greek authors (Müller, *Archäol. d. Kunst*, § 120, 4; Ruhnken, *Hist. Crit. Orat. Græc.;* Quintilian, *Inst. Rhet.*, 10). To this last acceptation of the word the Canon of the Mass has a thousand claims, for all admit that it is a work of rare worth—in fact, a model of perfection; for which reason, to pass over many others, it used to be formerly written in letters of gold (Martène, *De Antiquis Eccl. Rit.*, f. 34). Many writers, however, say that it is called the *Canon* because of its unchangeable nature; but to our mind this has never seemed a good reason, nor is it strictly true. The Canon *does* change on some occasions.

THE EXTRAORDINARY CARE TAKEN BY THE CHURCH OF THIS PART OF THE MASS.

So careful is the Church to prevent innovations from entering into this part of the Mass that she forbids any one to meddle with it under pain of incurring her most severe censures. She will not even permit a correction to be made in it for fear of destroying its antiquity. We shall mention a few cases in point. It is a well-known fact that the Canon terminates at the "Pater noster"; yet we find the word *Canon* printed in every missal from the first prayer, or "Te igitur," to the end of the Gospel of St. John. This is evidently a printer's blunder; but because it is of a very ancient date the Church has allowed it to stand, and printers to the Holy See are strictly forbidden to change it in printing new missals. A still more striking instance is the following: As far back as the year 1815, when devotion to St. Joseph, the spouse of the Blessed Virgin and foster-father of our Divine Lord, was making rapid headway, the Sacred Congregation of Rites was earnestly besought to grant permission to add the name of this venerable patriarch to this part of the Mass, one of the reasons assigned for making the request being that many persons had a particular devotion to him. The request was not granted, the reply to the petition being *negative;* and this was denominated a response *urbis et orbis*—that is, one binding in Rome and everywhere else.

ITS GREAT ANTIQUITY.

That the Canon is of very great antiquity all writers and critics admit. The precise date at which it was composed, and who its real author was, still remain among the disputed questions. Certain it is, however, that a hand has not touched it since the time of Pope Gregory the Great—that is, since the early part of the seventh century—and what that pontiff added to it was so very little that we would be almost justified in saying that it takes us back, in its present form, to those days in the past when we could converse with men who spoke face to face with our Divine Lord himself and his blessed apostles. The Church possesses nothing more venerable than this sacred memorial.

NAMES BY WHICH THE CANON WAS FORMERLY KNOWN.

The Canon was known in early times by a variety of names. Pope Gregory the Great always called it the *Prayer;* by St. Cyprian it was styled the *Oration;* by St. Ambrose, the *Ecclesiastical Rule;* and by St. Basil, the *Secret.* To indicate its great excellence, many of the ancient Fathers called it the *Action,* and we see this word yet retained as the heading of the prayer "Communicantes."

WHERE THE CANON ANCIENTLY BEGAN.

That the Canon formerly included the Preface, just as it does to-day in the Oriental Church, we have the most indubitable proofs. In the *Sacramentary* of Pope Gelasius, for instance. it is thus introduced · "Incipit canon actionis;

Sursum corda; habemus ad Dominum," etc. (Le Brun, *Explicat. de la Messe*, ii. p. 111, note).

MANNER OF READING THE CANON.

Out of the great respect that is due to this most solemn portion of the Mass, as well as to secure the utmost recollection on the part of the priest and people, it has been customary from time immémorial to recite it throughout in secret. Another reason, too, that is often given for this laudable practice is that the sacred words may be kept from becoming too common—a thing which could hardly be avoided if they were read in a tone audible to all; for, inasmuch as the Canon seldom changes, the same words would be heard upon every occasion, and in process of time thoughtless persons would have committed them to memory, and perhaps might use them in common parlance, to the great disedification of our holy religion. (For a very low misapplication of the sacred words of institution, which originally took rise in the way we are speaking of, the reader is referred to Disraeli's *Amenities of Literature*.)

A very singular story touching the silence observed in reciting the Canon is related in the *Spiritual Meadow*, a book written about the year 630 by a holy recluse named John Moschus. The book received the encomiums of the Fathers of the seventh General Council, held at Nicæa in 787, and it therefore carries some authority with it. It is therein stated that a party of boys guarding flocks in Apamea, in Syria, took it into their heads one day to while away a portion of their time by going through the ceremonies of Mass. One acted as celebrant, another as deacon, and a third as subdeacon. All went along pleasantly, as the story relates, until he who personated the celebrant pronounced the sacred words of consecration, when suddenly a ball of fire, rapid and fierce as a meteor, fell down from heaven, and so stunned the boys that they fell prostrate on the ground. When this singular occurrence was afterwards related to the bishop of the place, he went to examine the spot, and, having learned all the particulars of the case, caused a church to be built thereon to commemorate so remarkable an event. From this circumstance, it is said, the Church derives her custom of reciting the Canon in secret. Be this as it may, the ablest liturgical writers maintain that the Canon has been recited in secret from its very institution (Romsee, iv. p. 175).

As a precedent for this solemn silence many examples may be adduced from Holy Writ. On the great day of Atonement, for instance, while the high-priest was offering incense to Jehovah on the golden altar, a deep silence prevailed throughout the entire temple, and all the people recited their prayers in secret. To this solemn silence St. John evidently alludes when he says that at the opening of the seventh seal "there was silence in heaven, as it were for half an hour" (*Apoc.* viii. 1). Mention is also made of it in the Mishna in describing the "drink offering": "Then came the time of the drink offering, when, having given him the wine of which it consisted, the Sagan,[1] who stood beside the horn of the altar, observed the time for pouring it out, and with a napkin gave the signal for the music to begin. The reason of their being so long was that the perfect sacrifice might be before God, and that silence best suited so solemn a duty" (Bannister, *Temples of the Hebrews*, pp. 211, 329; see also *Habacuc*, ii. 20).

---

[1] The *Sagan*, though not mentioned by name in the Holy Scriptures, was nevertheless looked upon as a very important minister by the Jews, for it was he who discharged the duties of the high-priest whenever the latter, through any indisposition or legal defilement, was unable to act (Bannister, p. 190).

THE PICTURE AT THE BEGINNING OF THE CANON.

In all the missals of the present day a picture representing our Lord crucified, and gazed at in sorrowful contemplation by the three Marys—viz., Mary of Cleophas, Mary Magdalene, and Mary the Mother of God—is inserted, in order to recall vividly to the mind of the priest that, at this most solemn part of the Mass, he should be wholly intent on his crucified Redeemer. That the practice of inserting a picture here is very ancient may be seen from several early manuscripts, and almost every liturgist of note refers to it. Honorius of Autun, who flourished towards the beginning of the twelfth century, thus writes of it: "Hic in libris crucifixum ideo depingitur quia per illud passio Christi oculis cordis ingeritur" (*Gemma Animæ*, cap. 103, "De Canone")—that is, Here a crucifix is painted in the missals, in order that by it the Passion of Christ may be fixed in the eyes of the heart. Pope Innocent III. also alludes to the practice, and dwells particularly on the striking coincidence that the very first prayer of the Canon begins with one of the ancient representations of the cross—viz., the letter T. In many early missals this letter was beautifully illuminated and made very large, in order that the eye of the priest might rest upon it, and, in doing so, that he might remember the mysterious *Thau* of the prophet Ezechiel, which was ordered to be made on the foreheads of the men "that sigh and mourn for all the abominations that are committed in the midst." In Leofric's Missal, of Anglo-Saxon times, this letter is splendidly illuminated in gold, and so very long that it nearly stretches the whole length of the page. In a folio vellum copy of the Salisbury Missal, which was written towards the middle of the fourteenth century, the letter is so drawn out as to hold within it an illuminated picture of Abraham about to sacrifice his only son, Isaac (*Church of Our Fathers*, i. p. 103).

In many churches the custom prevailed of kissing the picture at the beginning of the Canon, when the priest came to that part, and at Milan, where the Ambrosian Rite is kept up, the custom is in vogue of washing the hands here.

"TE IGITUR."

While reciting the opening words of this prayer the priest is profoundly inclined, with hands resting upon the altar; but when he comes to the words, "these gifts, these presents, these holy and unspotted sacrifices," he becomes erect and makes three crosses over the oblation. The crosses made at this place now more strongly than ever remind us that we are fast approaching that solemn moment at which He who wrought our salvation on the cross of Calvary will be present on our altar. The reader who wishes to see their various mystic interpretations will do well to consult Durandus (*Rationale Divin.*, p. 241). The literal meaning of these three crosses is, according to De Vert (*Explic. Rub. Miss.*, tome iii. p. 1, rub. 122), founded on a very ancient custom yet in vogue with the members of the Carthusian Order—viz., of making two equal divisions of the Hosts used for Communion, and placing one on each side of the large Host. When the breads were so arranged the priest would make a separate cross over each portion and over the large Host placed in the centre, thus forming three crosses in all. Although this custom went into desuetude soon after its introduction, De Vert still maintains that the three crosses have been retained as a vestige of it.

There was great diversity of usage in former times about the number of crosses made here, as may be seen from some of the ancient sacramentaries. In the Gallican there was but one cross prescribed. In the Gelasian there were as many as five, and these, it is supposed, in memory of the

Five Wounds. So great was the diversity of practice in this matter that St. Boniface, the Apostle of Germany, wrote for advice upon the subject to Pope Zachary (741 to 752), and received a response to the effect that wherever a cross was required to be made it would be marked for him in the Canon. According to Romsee, whenever there is but one cross it signifies the unity of the Divine Essence; when two are made, the duality of natures in our Divine Lord is signified; three crosses are typical of the Blessed Trinity, and five of the Five Wounds (iv. p. 180).

In the first prayer of the Canon the priest prays for the Universal Church at large, and for its visible head upon earth, the Supreme Pontiff, by name; then for the bishop of the diocese in which he is celebrating; and, finally, for all the orthodox upholders of the Catholic Faith. In mentioning the reigning Pope he gives him the first part of his official title, without adding anything else to particularize him—thus, "Pius," "Gregory," "Leo," or whatever else the name be—and makes a slight bow to the missal as he pronounces it, out of reverence for the name of the Vicar of Christ. The bishop of the diocese is mentioned in the same way, but without any bow of the head. In case the diocese should be ruled by a bishop administrator or coadjutor while the real bishop, through some indisposition, is unable to attend to it, the name of the indisposed bishop must, nevertheless, be inserted, and not that of the administrator or coadjutor. When a bishop himself says Mass, instead of saying, "and our bishop, N.," he says, "and I, thy unworthy servant," without expressing his name. When the Holy Father celebrates he says, "I, thy unworthy servant, whom thou hast wished should preside over thy flock." If the Mass be celebrated at Rome no bishop's name is mentioned after the Pope's, for there is no other bishop of Rome but the Holy Father himself.

What has been said here of bishops, of course, applies also to archbishops, patriarchs, and cardinals, no matter of what grade. The members of religious orders are not permitted to insert here the name of their superior, but must, like secular priests, add that of the bishop of the diocese.

" Pro omnibus orthodoxis "—
" For all the orthodox."

Since there are two expressions in the latter part of this first prayer which mean one and the same thing, many writers have supposed that by the word *orthodox* are here meant all those who are outside the visible unity of the Church by schism only; according to which the present Greek Church with its offshoot, that of the Russian Empire, would be included. The reader need hardly be told that any given Church may be *schismatic* without being heretical at the same time. The one neither means nor necessarily implies the other. The one may, theologically speaking, be sound in the faith; the other never can be. A heretic, from the very derivation of the word ($\alpha i \rho \acute{\epsilon} \omega$), is one who constitutes himself a judge and *chooses* his faith upon the strength of his own private authority. A schismatic, strictly speaking, is one who separates or cuts himself off ($\sigma \chi i \zeta \omega$) from the outward unity of the Church by refusing assent to some point of discipline, or authority to the chief pastor. Now, although the so-called Greek Church has been schismatic since the ninth century, with little exception, still it has never by any formal act been declared heretical by the Holy See; and until the Holy See passes judgment upon it and pronounces it heretical no private authority has a right to do so. Some think, therefore, that it is no distortion of the meaning of this prayer to suppose that it refers to, or at least includes, schismatics when it speaks of the *orthodox*, for, as they say, a person may be orthodox—that is, sound in the faith—and still be outside the visible unity of the Church. The principal objection to this interpretation is, that the Church is not accustomed to share the Holy Sacrifice of the Mass with those who are wilfully out of her Communion. (See the *Catholic World* for the months of March and April, 1877; articles, "The Russian Chancellor" and "Natalie Narischkin.")

PRAYING FOR TEMPORAL RULERS.

In countries where Catholicity is the established religion it is customary in this prayer to add the name of the sovereign on the throne immediately after that of the diocesan bishop. The Venetians used to insert the name of the grand doge here. For some time the Hungarians prayed at this place for the king, but by a recent decree of the Holy See the title of *emperor* has been substituted instead (Kozma, p. 198). A priest celebrating in any part of the Austrian dominions, therefore, is bound to observe this rule. It is hardly necessary to add that without the express permission of the Holy See it is unlawful to insert any name whatever in this place.

CANON OF THE ORIENTAL CHURCH.

We have already stated that the Canon of the Oriental Church begins at the Preface. That of the Liturgy of St. Basil the Great is ushered in with this solemn admonition: "Come forward, O men! Stand with trembling awe and look towards the east." According to nearly all the Oriental liturgies, some such warning precedes the Canon, and the moment the people hear it they become at once erect and attentive. The Maronite laity, who use staves in church to lean upon, as the modern custom of sitting down at Mass is not in vogue with them, are required to stand up here without any support whatever, as a mark of great respect for this most solemn part of divine service. The form of prayer for the spiritual and temporal ruler with the Armenians is thus worded: "For our lord the most holy Patriarch N., for his health and the salvation of his soul." Then the minor clergy are mentioned: "for all vartabeds,[2] priests, deacons, and subdeacons." After this comes the name of the sovereign on the throne: "the emperor, the imperial family, the court, and the camp." This prayer assumes formidable proportions in the Russian Church, for every member of the imperial family must be mentioned in it by name, and woe to the poor priest or bishop who would dare to omit one of them; for the czar is supreme in spirituals as well as in temporals throughout that empire, and arrogates the right to himself of having his name and title, wherever they appear, always written in capital letters (Tondini, *The Pope of Rome and the Eastern Popes*, p. 95).

The prayer for the temporal ruler in the Liturgy of St. Mark is very beautiful. It runs thus: "The orthodox and Christ-loving king: . . . lay hands upon the shield and buckler, and stand up to help him; . . . cover his head in the day of battle; speak good things to his heart for thy Holy Catholic and Apostolic Church, and all the people that loveth Christ."

The prayer in St. Clement's Liturgy is thus expressed: "For every episcopate under heaven of those who rightly divide the word of thy truth let us make our supplication; and for our Bishop James and his parishes let us make our supplication; for the Bishop Clement and his parishes let us make our supplication; for our Bishop Evodius and his parishes let us make our supplication, that the merciful God may vouchsafe them to their holy churches, safe, hon-

---

[2] By *Vartabed* the Armenians understand a monastic or celibate priest. They are generally the preachers of the Word in the East.

orable, full of length of days, and may afford them an honorable old age in piety and righteousness."

THE SECOND PRAYER OF THE CANON, OR THE MEMENTO FOR THE LIVING.

As the priest begins this prayer he moves his hands slowly before his face, and, having united them, rests in meditation awhile, pausing over those for whom he intends to pray particularly. He is at liberty to remember here —privately, of course—whomsoever he pleases, no matter whether he be in the Church or out of it; for the prayer is *private*, and the Church exercises no jurisdiction over private prayers. This memento is worded as follows: "Remember, O Lord, thy servants, male and female, N.N. [pause], and all here present, whose faith is known to thee and devotion manifest; for whom we offer, or who offer to thee, this sacrifice of praise, for themselves and all that belong to them, for the redemption of their souls, for the hope of their salvation and safety, and who render their vows to thee, the Eternal, Living, and True God."

Regarding the expression, "who offer to thee," as applied to the people, the reader must not suppose that the right or power of offering sacrifice in the true sense is meant, for the people cannot do this, but only the priest. The expression is a familiar form for signifying co-operation in the sacred mystery, and directly refers to the ancient practice of receiving offerings from the people in the shape of bread and wine for altar purposes. According to Romsee (p. 187), the particle "or" in this prayer must be considered a *copulative* conjunction, and not a *disjunctive* one; and that hence the wording in its true sense would be, "for whom we offer, and who offer unto thee," etc. Regarding the word "vota," translated by us as *vows*, it is well to remark that what are technically called by that name, whether they be simple vows or solemn ones, are here meant only in a very remote sense; the direct application of the word is to be taken in the sense of *pious desires, thanksgivings,* and *private intentions* (Romsee, p. 189).

Formerly it was customary to read aloud at the letters "N.N." of this memento the names of all those who were entitled to special mention. In Solemn High Mass the duty of doing this devolved upon the deacon, who would stand for this purpose on the altar-steps, or ascend the ambo, which was the more general way; but in Low Mass the duty devolved upon the priest, who turned round to the congregation at this place, and read the names from folded tablets called diptychs. According to the general opinion of liturgists, this custom lasted, with little interruption, up to the eleventh century, when, on account of the excessive vainglory that many indulged in at hearing their names and offerings read out in public, the Church thought well to discontinue it (Romsee, p. 185).

DISSERTATION ON THE DIPTYCHS.

The diptychs, from the Greek $δις$, twice, and $πτύσσω$, I fold, were, agreeably to their derivation, tablets folding in two somewhat after the manner of a writing portfolio, and having three separate columns of equal extent. In the first of these columns were inscribed the names of the holy martyrs who openly died for the faith, and who, from the fact of their being mentioned here, were said to be *canonized*—that is, worthy of being named in the Canon of the Mass. This was the primitive way of bringing about canonization; and a vestige of it is yet kept up, for, according to the present discipline, when any servant of God has been declared a saint it is customary for our Holy Father the Pope to invoke him in the Mass said on that occasion, after the other saints mentioned

(*Hierurgia*, p. 480, note). The second column contained the names of those who were illustrious among the living, or held places of eminence either in the temporal or spiritual order, such as the Supreme Pontiff, the patriarch, archbishop, or bishop of the diocese, and after these the ruling prince or sovereign. In this same column were also inserted the names of those for whose special intention the Mass was offered, or who contributed bountifully towards the wants of the altar and the support of its sacred ministers. As it was strictly forbidden to receive gifts from those whose lives were in any way scandalous, or who were not considered, strictly speaking, practical Catholics, so it was also forbidden to insert their names in the sacred tablets, no matter how exalted a position in life they otherwise held. In the third column of the diptychs were enrolled those of the dead who departed life in full communion with the Church, but who were not otherwise in any degree remarkable. The substance of these three columns is now distributed among the following prayers, viz.: the first memento, the "Communicantes," the "Nobis quoque peccatoribus," and the second memento.

Here we call the reader's attention again to yet another proof of the reluctance of the Church to make any alteration in the Canon. Although the custom of reading the names of the living and the dead has long since ceased, still the letters "N. N.," where this reading occurred, have never been removed, although they serve no particular purpose now, nor is the priest required to pause at them in celebrating, as he was of old.

Ceremonies attending the Reading of the Diptychs.—In many of the ancient cathedral churches a very great display used to be made—almost as great as that made at the Gospel—when the time for reading the diptychs had arrived. We have said that, as a general rule, they were read from the ambo. For this reason it was customary for the entire congregation to turn their eyes in this direction; and such of them as could conveniently do it would flock around the ambo and remain there until all the names had been read. Whenever any name was read out which was entitled to special veneration it was usual to exclaim: "Gloria tibi, Domine"—"Glory be to thee, O Lord"—as if to thank God for the favors bestowed on such individuals. This was done at a Mass celebrated during the session of the fifth General Council, held in 553 at Constantinople, when the names of Pope Leo the Great and those of the saintly bishops Macedonius and Euphemius were read out (Selvaggio, i. p. 21; Bona, p. 345). Sometimes, too, the names of these general councils in which some remarkable dogma of faith was defined or heresy condemned were also read for the gratification of the people (*ibid.*) When the names of the persons to be prayed for reached a very high figure, in order not to increase the tedium of the people, a catalogue of them was drawn up and placed on the altar before the eyes of the priest, who would remember them in this manner: "Remember, O Lord! thy servants, male and female, and those also who have a special claim to be mentioned in the sight of thy Divine Majesty; of those, too, whose names we are looking at or express in words." Martène tells us that in some churches the practice prevailed through the ninth century of having the subdeacon recite, in a low whisper, to the celebrant the names of those who deserved special commemoration (*De Antiquis Eccl. Ritibus*, f. 37). The only rite which yet retains the reading of the diptychs in the Latin Church is the Mozarabic.

Diptychs of the Oriental Church.—That the reading of the diptychs is yet kept up in all the churches of the East may be seen from a glance at any of their liturgies, where we find special directions given on this head to the deacon of the Mass. The order of the memento in the Coptic diptychs is, first, for the Church at large, then for bishops in general, after this for their patriarch and all the orders of the clergy, and, finally, for the favorable flow of the Nile. In the Greek Liturgy of St. Basil mention of the Pope is made; but this is not, as some have supposed, the Pope of Rome, but rather the Patriarch of Alexandria, to whom this title is always given in the East. In some of the churches of Syria it is customary to say "Kyrie eleison" after every name read from the diptychs (Renaudot, *Liturg. Orient.*, ii. p. 96). As there is nothing else of any great importance in this second prayer of the Canon, we now pass on to the third prayer, or the "Communicantes."

THIRD PRAYER, OR THE "COMMUNICANTES."

The priest, remaining in the same place and preserving the same attitude, with outstretched hands recites the third prayer of the Canon, which, in English, may be rendered as follows : " Communicating and venerating the memory, in the first place, of the ever glorious Virgin Mary, Mother of God, our Lord Jesus Christ, as also of thy blessed Apostles and Martyrs, Peter and Paul, Andrew, James, John, Thomas, James, Philip, Bartholomew, Matthew, Simon and Thaddæus, Linus, Cletus, Clement, Xystus, Cornelius, Lawrence, Chrysogonus, John and Paul, Cosmas and Damian, and of all thy saints; by whose merits and prayers grant that we may be aided in everything, and fortified by thy help ; through the same Christ, our Lord."

The Saints mentioned in this Prayer.—As is just and proper, because she has the proud title of Queen of Saints and Martyrs, our Blessed Lady's name heads the list in this sacred catalogue, where she is commemorated as the "ever glorious Virgin Mary, Mother of God, our Lord Jesus

Christ." There is not a liturgy in the East or West in which our Heavenly Queen, with her singular prerogatives, is not mentioned. In the Liturgy of St. James she is styled "the most holy, immaculate, exceedingly glorious, blessed Lady, Mother of God, and ever Virgin Mary." In that of St. Chrysostom she is denominated " the most holy, undefiled, exceedingly laudable, glorious Lady, Mother of God, and ever Virgin Mary." The Liturgy of St. Basil the Great styles her " the all-holy, immaculate, super-eminently blessed, glorious Lady, Mother of God, and ever Virgin Mary"; and in the Coptic version of the same she is commemorated in the following manner : "Above all, the most holy, most glorious, immaculate, blessed Lady of ours, Mother of God, and ever Virgin Mary." Nor are the Nestorians, who deny her the title of *Mother of God*, behindhand, for all that, in showing her every other mark of reverence and respect. They invoke her as follows : "The prayers of the Virgin Mary, Mother of Jesus our Saviour, be to us at all times a wall of defence by day and by night." And in another place they say of her : "Rejoice and exult, O thou who art full of grace, holy and chaste Virgin Mary, Mother of Christ, because the archangel became a heavenly messenger unto thee, O thou, Mother, who in virginity didst bring forth the Wonderful, the Counsellor, and Saviour of the world." The Rev. Mr. Badger, from whose work (*The Nestorians and their Rituals*, ii. p. 249) we copy these words, declares his utter astonishment at the intense devotion manifested by these heretics to our Blessed Lady ; he is forced even to confess—with much reluctance, we may be sure, for he is a Protestant of the first water—that they do not scruple to apply to our Lady, now and then, the epithet *Theotokos*—that is, *Mother of God*—of which so much was said at the General Council of Ephesus in the year 431, where Nestorius himself was condemned. The reader will see in this work of Badger many good points on the devotion of the Eastern heretics to our Blessed Lady.

Before we enter on a history of the other saints mentioned in the "Communicantes" we deem it well to inform the reader that it is only those who are ranked as martyrs who have a place in the Canon; and this is another proof of its great antiquity, for it was not until the fourth century that the Church instituted feasts in honor of the other classes of saints.

St. Peter.—The Prince of the Apostles was a native of Bethsaida, and, as tradition goes, was our Divine Lord's senior in age by about ten years. He received at his circumcision the name of Simon, or Simeon, meaning in Hebrew "Jehovah hath heard," but this was afterwards changed by our Lord to "Kipho," generally written *Cephas* in English, from the Syriac ܟܐܦܐ — a *rock*. St. Peter was a married man, but a very ancient tradition, upon which St. Jerome lays particular stress, assures us that after his call to the apostleship he and his wife (a very holy lady) agreed to live continent the rest of their lives. He had a daughter named Petronilla, whom the Church honors as a saint on May 31. Our glorious apostle, as is well known, suffered death under Nero on the Vatican Hill, where, at his own request, he was crucified head downwards. He is represented in most of the early paintings as bald on the crown of the head, but having a thick circle of hair growing round the under part, after the manner of some of the clerical tonsures worn by members of religious orders. In Anglo-Saxon art he is always beardless, to favor a long-standing tradition that the pagans, in order to make him as despicable-looking as possible in the eyes of the people, shaved his head closely. Ever since the eighth century it has been customary to represent him with a pair of keys in hand, symbolic of his power in heaven and on earth. Many will have it appear that the ecclesiastical tonsure, so-called, owes its origin to the indignity practised on our apostle by the pagans—viz., shaving his head.

St. Paul.—St. Paul was a native of Tarsus, a city of Cilicia, in Asia Minor. After his miraculous conversion to the faith he went to Jerusalem, where, through the mediation of his companion, St. Barnabas, he made the acquaintance of SS. Peter and James. With the former he became associated in the see of Rome, and together with him suffered martyrdom about the year 67 of our era and the twelfth of the reign of Nero. The two holy apostles are generally named together, for, as the Church sings of them, "in life they loved each other; in death they are not separated." According to some, our apostle changed his first name, *Saul*, to *Paul* through respect for the Proconsul Sergius Paulus, whom he converted to the faith. Others say that he took the name from the Latin *paulus*, "little," because, as he says in his own profound humility, *he was the least of the apostles*.

St. Andrew, November 30.—St. Andrew was St. Peter's brother, but whether his senior in years or not the New Testament does not say. Upon the portioning out of the globe among the twelve Scythia was assigned as the field of his labors. He finally penetrated Cappadocia, Galatia, Bithynia, and the parts around the Euxine Sea, and ended his days, like his Divine Master, by dying on the cross. This, according to the best authorities, happened at Patras, a city of Achaia. In the fourth century some of his relics were taken to Scotland by St. Regulus, from which fact he has been venerated as the patron of the country and of its first order of knighthood, or that known as the "Order of the Thistle."[3] He is also the patron of the

---

[3] The collar of the Order of the Thistle is made of thistles and rue. The one cannot be touched without hurt; the other is an antidote against poison.

"Order of the Golden Fleece" of Burgundy, founded by Philip the Good in 1429, and of the entire empire of Russia, together with its great order, known as the "Order of the Cross of St. Andrew." In heraldry our saint is generally represented with a cross *decussate*, or *saltier*. When blended with the cross of St. George and the saltier gules of St. Patrick this cross forms the English flag familiarly known as the "Union Jack."[4]

St. James, July 25.—This blessed apostle, generally known as St. James the Greater, because of his seniority in years to St. James, commonly styled the "brother of the Lord," was son of Zebedee and Salome, and brother of St. John the Evangelist. It was this apostle who, in company with St. Peter and St. John, formed the three that were present on Thabor at our Lord's Transfiguration and in the Garden of Olives when his agony began. By command of Herod Agrippa, who, as the Acts of the Apostles relate (chap. xii.), "stretched forth his hands to afflict some of the Church," he was "killed with the sword." This happened about the year 43. The body of the apostle was first interred at Jerusalem, but was finally removed to Spain, where it is alleged he once preached the Gospel, and deposited at Iria Flavia, now El Padron, on the confines of Galicia. By order of Alphonsus the Chaste, King of Leon, it was subsequently transferred to Compostella (a corruption of Giacomo Postolo), in whose cathedral it lies at present. From this circumstance our blessed apostle has been chosen as the Patron of Spain under the name of Sant Iago di Compostella. A military order, known as that of "St. James the Noble," was established in his honor by Ferdinand II. in 1175.

---

[4] The name "Jack," as used here, is nothing else but a corruption of the French "Jacques," James, and had its origin in the fact that, at the accession of King James I., the cross of St. George and that of St. Andrew were united in one, thus forming the original "Union Jack."

St. John, December 27.—This holy apostle and Evangelist, called in the New Testament "the disciple whom Jesus loved," was a Galilean by birth. According to a tradition of long standing, he is said to have dwelt at Jerusalem until the death of our Blessed Lady, which took place, it is said, about the year 48, and that then he journeyed into Asia, where he is said to have founded the seven churches mentioned in his Apocalypse. Authentic accounts say that he died and was buried at Ephesus when about one hundred years of age. According to Polycrates, St. John always wore the golden plate of the Jewish high-priest upon his forehead, upon which was engraved "Kodesh le Jehovah"— "Holiness to Jehovah." The Greeks generally style him "St. John the Divine." From his great purity, having always led a single life, and from his singular intimacy with our Divine Lord, many of the Oriental Fathers held that he was taken up, body and soul, to heaven like Enoch and Elias. Though he died a natural death, he is by all esteemed a martyr from the fact that he submitted to martyrdom when cast by order of Domitian into a caldron of boiling oil, from which he escaped unhurt.

St. Thomas, December 21.—According to the most general opinion, this apostle was by birth a Galilean. Parthia was given as his field of labors when the portioning out of the globe was made among the twelve. He is said to have met death by being run through with a spear by the Brahmins of India. As he is universally styled the "Doubting Disciple" (from the fact of his saying that he would not believe the other apostles, who told him they had seen our Lord after he had risen from the dead on Easter Sunday, unless he saw him with his own eyes and examined his wounds), it is commonly said that the shortest day in the year was assigned as his feast day, to remind us of the *shortness of his faith*.

St. James, May 1.—The second apostle mentioned by the

name of James is he who is generally styled the "brother of our Lord," from a Hebrew usage of thus naming cousins-german. He is called "James the Less" from being younger than the other of the same name, and "James the Just" on account of his great sanctity. He is said to be the son of Alphæus and Mary (sister of the Blessed Virgin). It is the general opinion that he was the first bishop of Jerusalem, having been appointed to that see soon after our Lord's Ascension. Like the "Beloved Disciple," he is said to have always worn the plate of gold peculiar to the Jewish high-priest, as an ensign of his consecration to the Lord. According to Hegesippus, quoted by St. Jerome, and others, he met death by being cast by the Jews from the battlements of the Temple and afterwards despatched with a blow from a fuller's club. It is said that the resemblance of this apostle to our Lord was so great that it was difficult to tell the two apart, for which reason Judas found it necessary to tell his band to seize upon him whom he would address. "Whomsoever I shall kiss," said he, "that is he; lay hold of him and lead him away carefully" (*Mark* xiv. 44). According to the legend, St. James said he would eat nothing from the time he partook of the Last Supper until our Lord had risen from the dead. Soon after the Resurrection it is said that our Lord appeared to him and asked for a table and some bread, whereupon he said to the saint: "My brother, eat thy bread, for the Son of Man is risen from among them that sleep." According to St. Gregory of Tours, our saint's remains were interred on Mount Olivet in a tomb which he had built for himself. He is the author of the Catholic Epistle called after his name, and which the disdainful heretic Luther denominated "Epistola straminea"—an "Epistle of straw"—because it says very pointedly that *faith without good works is dead*, for which reason Protestants rejected it formerly.

St. Philip, May 1.—St. Philip was born at Bethsaida, and received as the place of his apostolic labors, upper Asia. He finally came to Hierapolis, in Phrygia, where he suffered martyrdom at a very advanced age. One of his arms was brought from Constantinople to Florence in the year 1204; the rest of his body is kept in the Church of SS. Philip and James at Rome.

St. Bartholomew, August 24.—According to the most exact commentators, our saint and Nathanael are one and the same person. He is said to have been born at Cana of Galilee. His name, Bartholomew, comes from the Syriac *bar*, a son, and *Tolmai*, a proper name.[5] As to the precise manner of this apostle's death authorities are not agreed, but all hold that he died a martyr, and this, according to St. Gregory of Tours, in Greater Armenia. One of his arms, it is said, was sent by the Bishop of Benevento to St. Edward of England (Edward the Confessor), who deposited it in the Cathedral of Canterbury. In art he is generally represented with a butcher's flaying-knife, the supposed instrument of his torture, in commemoration of which the strange custom of bestowing such knives as gifts on the recurrence of the feast once prevailed at Croyland Abbey.

St. Matthew, September 21.—St. Matthew was, according to the most general opinion, a native of Nazareth, and a publican by profession. His original name was Levi, but this he abandoned when he became an apostle. Ethiopia is generally assigned as the field of his apostolic labors—not the African Ethiopia, but that which corresponds with the ancient Chaldea. At Nadabar, a city of this region, he is said to have ended his days by martyrdom.

---

[5] Before the Captivity, when the Jews spoke the true Hebrew, the name for son was "Ben," thus: Benjamin—son of my right hand; Benoni—son of my anguish; but after the Captivity, when the pure Hebrew was no longer spoken, but only the Aramaic or Syriac, a son was designated by the term "Bar," thus: Bar-Jona—son of Jonah; Bartimeus—son of Timeus; Barabbas (strangely enough)—son of his father.

St. Simon, October 28.—To distinguish this saint from the Prince of the Apostles, who was called Simon Peter, and from St. Simon, brother of St. James the Less, he is generally known as Simon the Cananean, and sometimes Simon Zelotes. According to St. Jerome, the epithet last mentioned is the Greek equivalent of the Hebrew *Chanaanite*, a zealous imitator, so that it must not be supposed that our apostle was a native of Cana from having this epithet attached to his name. According to the Greek menology, our apostle passed over into Britain towards the end of his career, and was there crowned with martyrdom.

St. Thaddeus, October 28.—This apostle is known in the New Testament by three different names—viz., *Jude, Thaddeus,* and *Lebbæus.* By the last-mentioned name he is called in the Greek text of St. Matthew. It is generally understood that our apostle changed his first name, *Jude,* to his second, *Thaddæus,* in order not to have the same name as the traitor Judas Iscariot. Others say that he did so out of respect for the ineffable name of Jehovah, which the Jews would never pronounce. His field of labor was first Samaria, then Syria and the eastern parts. His martyrdom is said to have occurred in Persia. He wrote an Epistle, which, like that of St. James, is denominated *Catholic,* from the fact that it was addressed to no Church in particular, but to Christendom at large.

St. Linus, September 23.—St. Linus was the immediate successor of St. Peter in the Roman see, over which he reigned twelve years, and suffered martyrdom about the year of our Lord 87.

St. Cletus, April 26.—St. Cletus succeeded St. Linus as pope, and ruled the Church for about thirteen years. His martyrdom is said to have taken place about the year 91. There has always been much dispute as to whether this saint and Anacletus are two distinct persons or one and the same. Most probably they were different. In the *Gerarchia Cattolica* Anacletus is reported to have governed the Church from A.D. 100 to 112, and that then he died a martyr. The two are also distinguished in the Liberian Calendar.

St. Clement, November 23.—St. Clement, the companion and fellow-laborer of St. Paul, was, according to the most reliable accounts, a Jew by birth. He is specially mentioned by the Apostle of the Gentiles as having his name in the "Book of Life." An epistle written by him to the Christians of Rome in their severe hours of trial has been looked upon by many as a work of inspiration; and, from its great resemblance to St. Paul's Epistle to the Hebrews, the authorship of the latter has been often called into question. St. Clement met death, it is said, by decapitation, under the persecution of Trajan.

St. Xystus, August 6.—He suffered martyrdom under Valerian in 258.

St. Cornelius, September 16.—St. Cornelius was pope from A.D. 254 to 255. He is styled by St. Cyprian "a blessed martyr."

St. Cyprian, September 16.—This saint was born at Carthage, in Africa, and suffered martyrdom about the year 258. When the decree concerning his torture was read to him he is reported to have exclaimed in a transport of holy joy, "Deo gratias!"—"Thanks be to God!" Our saint's name will be ever held in remembrance from the celebrated controversy he had with the bishops of Numidia about the validity of baptism given by heretics. Pope St. Stephen pronounced such baptism valid, and forbade any steps whatever to be taken to reiterate it, saying: "Nihil innovetur nisi quod traditum est"—that is, "There must be no innovation upon what has been handed down by traditional authority."

St. Laurence, August 10.—It is generally supposed that St. Laurence was by birth a Spaniard. All are unanimous in saying that he suffered martyrdom in A.D. 258, and this on an instrument made after the manner of a gridiron, which was heated to redness and then the saint placed upon it. One of the most celebrated monuments built in honor of him now in existence is the famous palace of the Escurial, fifteen miles from Madrid, in Spain, which was founded by Philip II. in 1557, out of gratitude for a victory over the French at St. Quentin, in Picardy, on the feast of St. Laurence. The palace is built in the shape of a gridiron, the royal apartments forming the handle, and the church the body of the instrument. It is built of solid granite, 700 feet long, 564 wide, and 330 feet high. Over one of its main grand entrances are six beautifully-finished statues, each seventeen feet high, of Kings David, Solomon, Josaphat, Ezechias, Manasses, and Josias. This structure is one of the greatest curiosities, perhaps, in the world.

St. Chrysogonus, November 24.—Very little is recorded of this saint, further than that he was slain by the sword and then cast into the sea. His body was afterwards found and is now said to be kept at Venice. A church was built to his memory in the Trastevere in A.D. 599.

SS. John and Paul, June 26.—These two saints were brothers and officers in the Roman army together under Julian the Apostate. They received the crown of martyrdom about the year 362.

SS. Cosmas and Damian, September 27.—There were three pairs of saints who bore the names of Cosmas and Damian, but it is almost universally admitted that the two mentioned here were those who suffered at Rome during the persecution of Diocletian.

The reader will remark that in the enumeration of the apostles in the "Communicantes" SS. Mark and Luke do not occur, and this because it is not certain whether they were martyrs or not, and none but such are named in the Canon.

"**Communicantes**" **in the Eastern Church.**—Protestants would fain have it believed that "saint-worship," as they term the holy practice, is entirely confined to the Church of Rome and has no place at all in the churches of the East; but evidence too strong to be rejected, or even called in question, proves that such is not the case; that the Eastern Church as well as the Western believes, confesses, and practises the doctrine that the saints of God, as such, ought to be revered, venerated, and invoked.

"I believe and confess," says the Ritual of Russia in its article on adult unction, "according to the understanding of the Holy Eastern Church, that the saints who reign with Christ in heaven are worthy to be honored and invoked, and that their prayers and intercession move the all-merciful God to the salvation of our souls" (*Rites and Customs of the Greco-Russian Church*, by Romanoff, p. 308). Part of the Armenian "Communicantes" reads as follows: "O Lord, through the intercession of the immaculate parent of thine only-begotten Son, the holy Mother of God, and the entreaties of all thy saints, and of those who are commemorated this day, accept our prayers" (Smith and Dwight, *Researches in Armenia*, i. p. 185). The following extract will show that the Nestorians are sound on this doctrine also: "O ye saints, prophets, apostles, doctors, confessors, martyrs, priests, and hermits, pray to Christ your strength for us all; that through your prayers we may receive out of his treasure an answer to all our prayers as may be profitable to us" (from the collection of Collects at the end of the *Khudrah*; Badger, ii. p. 138). We could thus go on reciting at pleasure testimonies from all the churches of the East, to show how sacred a duty the veneration of the saints is considered to be in all those regions, and how very efficacious before the throne of God; but as what we have said is sufficient to convince any unbiassed mind of this fact, we do not think it necessary to continue the subject further.

FOURTH PRAYER, "HANC IGITUR."

The priest, while reciting this prayer, keeps his hands spread out over the oblation, after the manner of the priests of the ancient law, who observed a similar usage in regard to the victims offered in sacrifice (*Exod.* xxix.; *Levit.* i. 4). As this prayer comes close upon consecration, it is customary for the server to ring the little bell at the beginning of it, in order to remind the people of the near approach of that moment when our Divine Lord will be present on the altar. According to Durandus (*Rationale*, p. 249), Pope Leo the Great composed and inserted the first part of this prayer down to the words "placatus accipias." The remainder was added by Pope Gregory the Great, in order to beg of God to avert the horrors of war and pestilence that threatened Rome in his time (Romsee, p. 199).

An ancient Roman ordo prescribed this prayer to be recited with hands raised aloft—a ceremony which the Dominicans yet keep up, and which was formerly observed in all those places of England where the Sarum Rite was followed. The Carmelites recite it lowly bowed down with hands resting upon the altar. According to Romsee, our present custom dates no further back than the fifteenth century, and we see that the Orientals do not observe it.

FIFTH PRAYER, "QUAM OBLATIONEM."

This prayer is worded thus: "Which oblation we beseech thee, O Lord! that thou wouldst vouchsafe in all respects to bless, approve, ratify, make rational and acceptable, that it may become the Body and Blood of our

Lord Jesus Christ." The Latin word "rationabilem" is here sometimes rendered in English by *reasonable*, sometimes by *rational*. The latter is the better word, because less liable to be misunderstood, for the epithet is evidently given with a view to distinguish the effect which is about to be produced on the bread and wine from the sacrifices of the old law, all of which were *irrational*, inasmuch as they were constituted of nothing but of bulls, goats, etc. (Durandus, p. 253).

In reciting the latter part of this prayer the priest makes five crosses over the oblation, three over the Host and chalice conjointly, and one over the Host and chalice singly. As to the peculiar import of these five crosses there is want of agreement among liturgical writers. No one, so far as we have seen, has attempted any other explanation of them than a purely mystical one. Some say they are commemorative of the Five Wounds; others that they are intended to recall to mind the threefold delivery of our Lord—viz., to the Jewish priests, to the scribes, and then to the Pharisees—and the duality of his nature. A very nice interpretation of them is that they are intended to remind us, now that consecration is about to take place, that the Blessed Victim who is going to be present on our altars suffered in his five senses during his bitter Passion—in his *seeing*, when the Jews veiled his face; in his *hearing*, when they laughed him to scorn; in his *taste*, when they gave him vinegar and gall to drink; in his *smelling*, when they conveyed him to Calvary, a hill used as a receptacle for dead bodies, whence its name when interpreted from the Hebrew, "a place of skulls"; and, finally, he suffered in his *touch*, when his hands and feet were nailed to the cross and his side pierced with a lance (*Enchiridion de Sacr. Sacrif. Miss. Ben. XIV.*, p. 71).

CHAPTER XXVII.

THE CELEBRATION OF MASS.

THE CONSECRATION.

HAVING concluded the last-mentioned prayer, the priest rubs the thumb and index finger of each hand over the corporal, in order to free them from any dust or defilement that may have adhered to them up to this time, and all this out of respect for the Sacred Host which he is going to handle at the moment of Consecration.

Taking up the Host, he says: "Who the day before he suffered took bread into his holy and venerable hands, and with eyes uplifted to heaven to thee, O God! his Father Almighty, giving thanks to thee, he blessed, broke, and gave to his disciples, saying: 'Take and eat ye all of this: FOR THIS IS MY BODY.'" The consecration of the bread is now effected, and, to adore our Lord present on the altar, the priest makes a profound genuflection the moment he has pronounced the sacred words. After this he raises the Host on high for the adoration of the people, and, having then placed it on the corporal before him, goes on to the consecration of the chalice. He first takes off the pall which had been covering the mouth of the chalice since the Offertory, and rests it against the altar-card in front of him. Then, taking the chalice, he continues thus: "In like manner after he had supped, taking this goodly chalice into his holy and venerable hands, also giving thanks to thee,

LARGE BREAD OF THE LATIN CHURCH.

PARTICLE

he blessed and gave to his disciples, saying : ' TAKE AND DRINK YE ALL OF THIS, FOR THIS IS THE CHALICE OF MY BLOOD OF THE NEW AND ETERNAL TESTAMENT ; THE MYSTERY OF FAITH, WHICH SHALL BE SHED FOR YOU AND FOR MANY UNTO THE REMISSION OF SINS.' " This is the form by which the consecration of the chalice is effected, after which the priest kneels down in adoration as before, and recites while he is doing so the words, "As often as you do these things you shall do them in remembrance of me." He then elevates the chalice as he did the Host, and after the last genuflection covers it again with the pall.

With the exception of a few words, both forms of consecration are taken from Holy Scripture. What is added over and above we shall now point out and explain according to the most approved authorities. We preface our remarks by reminding the reader that the essential form of the consecration of the bread is, THIS IS MY BODY, and of the wine, THIS IS THE CHALICE OF MY BLOOD, or, simply, *This is my Blood*. The rest, however, must be said under pain of mortal sin.

" *Who the day before he suffered.*"

These words are not Scripture, but were added very early by some of the popes. Walfridus and Micrologus ascribe them to Pope Alexander, who ruled the Church from A.D. 121 to 132 ; but Cardinal Bona and others are in favor of attributing them to some one of the apostles. They are to be found in the Liturgies of SS. James and Clement.

" *The day before he suffered.*"

This was what we now call Maundy Thursday, which, according to the best authorities, fell at the period of our Lord's Passion on the 22d of March [1] (Romsee, iv. p. 207).

[1] The Jews always celebrated the Passover on the fourteenth day of Nisan, the first month of their ecclesiastical year. To avoid agreeing with them in our celebration of

"Took bread into his holy and venerable hands."

The words "took bread" are given by the Evangelists, but the remaining ones are not. They are, however, of very high antiquity, and are found also in the liturgies of the East.

"With eyes uplifted to heaven to thee, O God! his Father Almighty."

These words are not found in Scripture, but it has been a constant tradition that whenever our Lord was about to perform any solemn act he always looked up to heaven. St. Matthew (xiv. 19) records that he did so when he performed the miracle of the multiplication of the loaves; and St. John records the same of him at the resuscitation of Lazarus (xi. 41). The particle *enim*, "for," in both forms of consecration, is also a subsequent insertion. St. Thomas Aquinas says (*Quæst.* 78, 3) that it was added by St. Peter.

In the language which our Lord spoke at the Last Supper and during his life upon earth—viz., the Syriac—the consecration of both species was effected by uttering two

---

Easter, it was decided at the Council of Nicæa, in A.D. 325, that the latter should be celebrated the first Sunday after the first full moon that set in after the 21st of March; according to which, Easter cannot be earlier than the 22d of this month nor later than the 25th of April. By the Gregorian style (so-called from Pope Gregory XIII.), the mode of reckoning Easter is not the *astronomical*, but rather the *absolute mode*, in order that the celebration may take place on the same day throughout the entire Church, which, owing to the difference of time between countries far apart, could not happen if the astronomical mode were followed. Still, for all, the Gregorian mode is not wholly free from faults. A somewhat defective cycle in regard to the months was selected on account of its great simplicity, which clashes very considerably with the astronomical computation, for by the latter mode the Easter full moon may rise two hours after the time calculated by the calendar. Thus, it may be at one o'clock on Sunday morning, whilst announced to take place at eleven o'clock on Saturday night by the calendar: in which case Easter would be celebrated on that same Sunday, when it ought not to be until the Sunday following. The Gregorian Calendar, too, in some very rare cases, makes our Easter and the Jewish Passover agree; as, for example, happened in the year 1825. It is impossible, in fact, to avoid an occurrence of this kind now without upsetting the whole new style of reckoning.

words each time; the form of the consecration of the bread being ܗܵܢܲܘ ܦܲܓܪܝ — *honau pagri*, and of the wine, ܗܵܢܲܘ ܕܹܡܝ — *honau demi*. Whereupon it is worth remembering that the verb "is" does not stand separate by itself, but is incorporated, in each case, with the demonstrative pronoun "this," thus leaving no room for doubt as to what our Divine Lord meant when he pronounced the sacred formula.

"*Benedixit*"—*he blessed*.

Touching the word "benedixit" employed upon this occasion, and in virtue of which both bread and wine are blessed by the priest, some curious opinions have been advanced. Ambrosius Catharinus,[2] the great Dominican theologian who proposed so many intricate questions at the Council of Trent, held that the moment our Lord pronounced the blessing over each element at the Last Supper consecration took place, and that the words, "This is my Body," etc., were merely added to point out the change which had been effected. Catharinus, it seems, preferred to take this view of the matter, in order not to make it appear that consecration did not take place until the disciples had the bread and wine in their own hands, which would certainly involve an incongruity. St. Augustine, who evidently foresaw the same difficulty, advanced the opinion that the order of the words may have been different from that given by the Evangelists, and that probably they were as follows: "He blessed, saying, 'This is my Body'; then he broke and gave to his disciples." According to this, consecration took place the moment "This is my Body" was pronounced. St. Thomas Aquinas, the great Doctor of the Blessed Eucharist,

---

[2] Catharinus was Archbishop of Compsa, in Italy, in the year 1552. He made himself famous at the Council of Trent for the very intricate theological questions he proposed to the Fathers. His opinions regarding the intention of the minister who conferred baptism are well known.

follows the same line of thought as St. Augustine, and gives the order of words as follows : "Taking bread into his hands, he blessed it, saying, 'This is my Body'"; so that, according to the Angelic Doctor, the blessing uttered on this occasion was also the formula of consecration. There is yet another view. According to Fromondus and others, it cannot be presumed that in a matter of such grave moment the Evangelists would omit the slightest particular, and that inasmuch as all of them agree in narrating the order of the words on this occasion, it is not lawful to change this order from the way in which the Gospels give it; and that, therefore, we must read as follows : "He blessed" by invoking the name of his Father upon the bread in order that it should become his Body ; "he broke" into as many parts as there were persons to communicate; and, thirdly, "he gave to his disciples"—that is, into their hands—saying, "Take ye and eat; this is my Body." Whether the order of words was different or not, at the Last Supper, from that given by the Evangelists makes but little matter to us, since it is the teaching of the Church that the essential form of consecration is, "This is my Body," and of the chalice, "This is my Blood" or "This is the chalice of my Blood," which amounts to the same thing (see Romsee, iv. p. 209). As far as relates to the other question sometimes asked—viz., whether our Lord made the sign of the cross or not when he blessed, as we do—it is hardly necessary to delay, for whether he did or not matters little. Most probably he did not make this sign upon that occasion, for as yet the cross had not obtained its efficacy.

"Fregit"—He broke.

It is generally held that our Lord on this occasion made thirteen divisions of the Holy Eucharist, and that he himself communicated, and permitted the traitor Judas to communicate with the rest. The Fathers of the Eastern Church, as well as those of the Western, have always held this. It is also surmised that our Lord must have broken the Sacred Host at this time with peculiar and impressive ceremonies; for it is narrated of the disciples who supped with him at Emmaus that *their eyes were opened, and that they knew him in the breaking of bread.*

The Ambrosians, or Milanese, immediately before the "qui pridie"—that is, a moment or two before they pronounce the sacred words of institution—go to the Epistle side of the altar and wash their hands, out of respect for the Host which they are soon going to handle. This is the only rite in the Church where such a custom prevails.

A very important question that calls for consideration here is, whether the words of consecration are pronounced by the priest at this moment *narratively, historically,* or *significatively.* According to Pope Benedict XIV., they are pronounced in the last-mentioned way, that is, *significatively—significativè;* and that hence the priest who pronounces them does so as effectively in what relates to consecration as if they were pronounced by our Lord himself (*Enchiridion de Sacrif. Miss.,* p. 71). St. Thomas agrees with this, but adds that they are also pronounced *recitatively—recitativè (ibid.)*

We should have said before, perhaps, that immediately after the priest has placed the Sacred Host on the corporal after the elevation, he joins the thumb and index finger of both hands, and never separates them from that time until Communion is over, unless when touching the Sacred Host. This is done out of respect for the Blessed Sacrament, as well as to avoid the danger of losing any minute particles that may have adhered to these fingers.

CONSECRATION OF THE CHALICE.

As much of what we have said of the consecration of the bread applies to that of the chalice also, it will be only necessary to dwell upon what refers to the chalice directly in the following remarks:

"*This is the Chalice of my Blood.*"

By a figure of speech called metonymy the container is here put for the thing contained, so that, according to St. Thomas (*Quæst.* 78, iii. art. 3), the real form would be: "This is my Blood contained in the chalice."

"*Æterni Testamenti*"—*Eternal testament.*

These words are not in the Holy Scripture, but it is the universally received opinion that they were added by some of the apostles, and this to point out directly that the sacred priesthood of our Divine Lord would continue for ever, in accordance with the prophecy expressed in the One hundred and ninth Psalm, "Thou art a priest for ever according to the order of Melchisedech." There is also allusion here, by way of opposition, to the "Old Testament" which was ratified by the blood of bulls and goats only, not by the Blood of Christ.

"*The mystery of faith.*"

The Holy Eucharist is called the "mystery of faith" from the fact that its real greatness is hidden from the senses, and nothing is left to enable us to form a judgment of the extraordinary change which has been wrought any more than if no such change had ever taken place. All is left to pure faith; and, therefore, well may it be called a mystery. How beautifully this is expressed in the *Lauda Sion* of St. Thomas Aquinas:

" Quod non capis,
   Quod non vides,
   Animosa firmat fides,
   Præter rerum ordinem."

" *Which for you and for many shall be shed.*"

According to the best authorities, and Pope Benedict XIV. among others (*Enchirid.*, p. 72), the word " many" is here to be taken as meaning *all*, a mode of expression by no means uncommon in the Holy Scripture. St. Thomas Aquinas also interprets it in this way. If taken in any other sense it would hardly be possible to keep free of the Calvinistic error that our Lord died only for a certain class of persons.

At each elevation the little bell is rung to remind the people that our Lord is now present on the altar; and the end of the priest's chasuble is lifted up by the server, who kneels for this purpose (just as consecration is about to take place) on the highest step. This ceremony of lifting the end of the chasuble is not observed now through any necessity whatever—for, if so, there would be as strong a reason for doing it at every other part of the Mass at which the priest genuflected—but is kept up merely as a vestige of that ancient custom of having the deacon and subdeacon hold up the priest's robes at this place when the ample and long-flowing form of chasuble was in use. This was required to be done then in order that the priest might not be impeded in any way at the solemn moment of consecration, when the slightest accident might cause an incalculable amount of distress. In some places the practice of lifting the chasuble here is going, or has already gone, into desuetude; but this should not be tolerated for a moment, for it is a flagrant act of supreme disobedience which no authority in the Church, short of the Pope himself, could sanction. We do not know an instance in which the Rubrics are departed from without a sacrifice of real beauty, for which reason alone, to pass over many others, the slightest innovation in this respect should be looked upon as a species of sacrilege, and should in no case be allowed.

THE ELEVATION.

We have stated that immediately after the consecration the blessed Body of our Lord is elevated on high for the adoration of the people. Before the eleventh century the elevation did not take place at this part of the Mass, but only at the "Omnis honor et gloria," a little before the "Pater noster," which we now call the minor elevation. The present discipline was introduced as a solemn protest against Berengarius, who had the audacity to deny Transubstantiation. It first began in France, for Berengarius was a native of that country, and archdeacon of Angers; from France it was introduced into Germany, and from Germany it found its way into the other countries of Europe, until at last it came to be an established law of the Church, binding everywhere. It must not, however, be supposed that when the new discipline of elevating the Sacred Species here was first introduced both the Host and chalice were elevated. Not so; for quite a long time there was no elevation at all here of the chalice, but only of the Host—a custom which we yet see in vogue with the Carthusians.[3] The elevation of one species was considered enough, inasmuch as our Lord was as complete under one kind as under both by what is termed *concomitance;* but that the elevation of the chalice soon followed that of the

---

[3] It must not be supposed that the Carthusians have no elevation of the chalice at all. They have, and that, too, at the regular place, but it is no higher than what we observe at the minor elevation.

Host there is every reason to believe, for Durandus, Bishop of Mende, whose death is placed at 1296, makes mention of it in his *Rationale Divinorum* (p. 265, No. 52). Then, again, as to the manner of elevating, local customs varied. Some covered the chalice with the pall, as we see the Mozarabics still do.

The question is sometimes asked, Has it been customary from the beginning to have an elevation of some kind ? All are agreed that it has, but Cardinal Bona says that it is impossible to tell, from the data given, whether the Sacred Species were raised any higher than they are now at what we call the minor elevation. As a precedent for our custom of elevating the Sacred Species may be mentioned the practice which obtained in the old law of lifting the victims on high at the regular sacrifices (*Exod.* xxix. ; *Levit.* vii. and xxiii.)

CONSECRATION IN THE EASTERN CHURCH.

We have mentioned in our Preface that where validity of orders prevails the power of consecration exists independently of either schism or heresy ; and that, consequently, in all the churches of the East a true sacrifice of the Mass may be looked for, and as veritable a Real Presence as that which we have the happiness to enjoy.

Strangely enough, nearly all the Oriental liturgies mention the mingling of water with the wine in the form of consecration. "Thou didst take," says the Liturgy of St. Gregory of the Alexandrine family, "the chalice and mingle it of the fruit of the vine and water"; "In like manner, also," says the Syro-Jacobite Liturgy of St. Marutas, "he took wine, and when he had mingled it in just proportion with water," etc., and so on with several others.

It is customary all through the East for the priest to pronounce the words of consecration aloud, and for the people to answer "Amen" after each assertion of the narrative portion. Thus, according to the Liturgy of St. Basil, the arrangement is as follows: "Priest: He blessed it; People: Amen. Priest: And sanctified it; People: Amen. Priest: And tasted it, and gave to his disciples." Whereupon it is also worthy of remark that nearly all the Eastern liturgies mention our Lord's communicating upon this occasion as well as his disciples.

In an Ethiopic Liturgy, called the *Athanasian*, the sacred words of consecration are thus given: "This bread is my Body, from which there is no separating"; and of the chalice: "This cup is my Blood, from which there is no dividing. As often as ye eat this Bread and drink this Chalice, set forth my death and my resurrection, and confess my ascension to heaven and my coming again with glory whilst ye await." The Armenian form thus reads: "Taking bread into his holy, divine, spotless, and venerable hands, he blessed, and gave to his holy, elect, and fellow-disciples, saying, 'This is my Body, which for you and for many is given for remission and pardon of sins.'" The consecration of the chalice is worded in nearly the same way. According to the Liturgy of St. Basil, the narration thus goes on: "In the night when he gave himself up for the life of the world, taking bread into his holy and spotless hands, having shown it to thee, his God and Father, having given thanks, blessed, hallowed, and broken it, he gave it to his disciples and apostles, saying, 'Take, eat; this is my Body, which is broken for you unto the remission of sins.'" And of the chalice: "Likewise taking the chalice of the fruit of the vine, having mingled, given thanks, blessed, and hallowed it, he gave it to his holy disciples and apostles, saying, 'Drink ye all of it, for this is my Blood of the New Testament, which is shed for you and for many for the remission of sins.'" In the Coptic Liturgy of St. Cyril the form is worded as follows : "He took bread into his holy, immaculate, pure, blessed, and quickening hands, and looked up to heaven, to thee his God and Father, and Lord of all, and gave thanks, and blessed, and sanctified it, and broke it, and gave to his holy disciples and pure apostles, saying, 'Take, eat ye all of this; for this is my Body, which shall be broken for you, and for many shall be given for the remission of sins.'" The form according to the Liturgy of St. James is almost word for word like this; and as that of the Liturgy of St. Chrysostom differs hardly in anything from our own, we do not deem it necessary to give it.

The Elevation in the Eastern Church.—Nowhere in the East does the elevation take place immediately after consecration, as with ourselves, but only before the Communion. As the solemn moment draws near, the deacon turns round to the people and cries with full compass of voice, "Attendamus!"—"Let us be attentive." In some places this admonition is worded: "Let us attend with the fear of God." The Ethiopians say, "Inspiciamus!" After the admonition follows the elevation, which all the churches of the East observe just as we do, with this difference: that while perfect silence pervades our congregations at this solemn moment, in theirs the noise is deafening, for both priest and people are shouting at the highest pitch of their voices.

When the Sacred Host is first raised on high, the priest cries aloud, "*Ἅγια ἁγίοις*," *Hagia hagiois*—that is, "Holy things for holy people"—to which the people, or rather the choir, respond, "One Holy, one Lord, Jesus Christ to the glory of God the Father." According to the Syriac Liturgy of St. James, which all the Jacobites follow, the priest exclaims, "Holy things are given for holy persons in perfection, purity, and holiness"; to which the people respond, "One Holy Father, one Holy Son, one Holy Ghost; blessed be the name of the Lord, for he is one in heaven and on earth; glory be to him for evermore." At the elevation which takes place with the Maronites the priest, raising the sacred Host aloft, cries out, "Holy things are given for holy people in perfection, purity, and sanctity"; to which the people respond, "One Holy Father, one Holy Son, one Holy Ghost; glory be to the Father, to the Son, and to the Holy Ghost." When elevating the chalice the priest says, according to the same rite, "Thus, O Lord! in truth we verily believe in thee just as believes in thee the Holy Catholic Church, that thou art one Holy Father, to whom belongeth glory, Amen; one Holy Son, to whom belongeth glory, Amen; one Holy Spirit, to whom belongeth glory and thanksgiving for ever, Amen." The elevation with the Maronites takes place at the same time as it does all over the East—viz., before Communion. In some of the Oriental churches it is customary for the priest to turn round to the people and bless them three times before the elevation takes place, and after the elevation to move around, with the sacred Host in his hands, at the centre of the altar, just as we do when giving benediction of the Blessed Sacrament. This especially obtains throughout Syria (Renaudot, *Liturg. Orient.*, ii. p. 114).

The words, "One Holy Father, one Holy Son, one Holy Ghost," common to all the Oriental liturgies with hardly an exception, is employed as a profession of faith in the Adorable Trinity. The Copts at this place make a profession of faith in the Real Presence, which, on account of its singular beauty, we give word for word. It is as follows: "I believe, I believe, I believe, and confess to the last breath of my life, that this is the real, life-giving flesh of thy Only-Begotten Son, our Lord, God, and Saviour Jesus Christ; he received it from the blessed Lady of us all, the Mother of

God, and ever Virgin Mary." It is customary, too, in the East, as with many of our own congregations, to strike the breast with the hand as the Host is elevated. In one of the Coptic versions of the Liturgy of St. Basil a rubric on this head thus reads: "Then [that is, at the elevation] the priest will take the Isbodicon [*i.e.*, the Holy Body] in his hands, and will raise it aloft as far as he can stretch his arms, with head inclined, and will shout with full compass of voice, 'Holy things for holy people!' All the people will incline their heads, adoring their Lord in fear and trembling, and asking with tears, with earnestness, and with the striking of their breasts the remission of their sins, and their confirmation in the orthodox faith unto the last breath of life" (Renaudot, i. p. 245). On Sundays the rubric calls for only a simple genuflection, but on week-days the Copts are required to bow their heads down to the ground at this place. The crying out at the elevation, which varies slightly with the different churches, is intended by the Orientals to commemorate the cry of the penitent thief when our Lord was raised on the cross beside him. In many places they exclaim: "O God, be merciful to me a sinner!" Sometimes the very words of the holy thief are used, viz.: "Lord, remember me when thou reachest thy kingdom" (*ibid.* i. p. 246). That the ringing of bells, also, is observed in the East when consecration takes place we learn from various writers. Neale makes special mention of this practice as prevailing among the Ethiopians and Syrians (*Hist. of the Holy Eastern Church*, i. p. 517).

The Orientals say but little about the elevation of the chalice, for the reason that they look upon itself and the Host as one and the same thing; but that the elevation of it is observed by them their liturgies clearly show. In that of St. Xystus, for example, the chalice is elevated with these words: "O Lord! we believe, and believe in truth, just as thy Holy Catholic Church believes in thee, that there is one Holy Father; one Holy Son; one Holy Ghost; glory to the Father, and to the Son, and to the Holy Ghost, who are one for ever and ever." This agrees almost wholly with what is said at the elevation of the chalice in the Maronite Church.

We have said that the words of consecration are pronounced aloud in the East. It must not, however, be supposed that the rest of the Mass is pronounced in this manner. Not so; for the Orientals say a great number of prayers in secret, as we ourselves do, and only break silence at those places where the people are accustomed to join in and respond. Nothing is more common in the liturgies of the East than the admonition, "Let all in fear and silence stand and pray."

"UNDE ET MEMORES."

This is the first prayer the priest recites after the elevation has taken place, and he does so with hands extended as when reciting the collects, only that, as we have already stated, the thumb and index finger of each hand are joined together. The Carthusians, Carmelites, and Dominicans recite it with outstretched arms in the form of a cross—a custom which was also in vogue under the Sarum Rite. At the words "a pure Host, a holy Host, an immaculate Host; the holy Bread of life eternal, and the Chalice of perpetual salvation," the sign of the cross is made five different times —three times over the Host and chalice conjointly, and once over each of them singly. Many curious questions are asked about the meaning of these crosses at this place. That they are not intended as blessings all are agreed, because neither Host nor chalice needs a blessing now; but as to their precise import opinions vary very much. According to the majority of liturgists, they must be accounted for wholly in a mystic manner, as commemorative of the Passion of our

Lord, the five recalling to mind, as St. Thomas Aquinas says, and others repeat after him, the Five Wounds. Father Le Brun, in that truly excellent work of his entitled *Explication des Prières et des Cérémonies de la Messe*, tom. ii. p. 232, gives as beautiful an explanation of these crosses as any that we have seen. His words are: "When we make five signs of the cross at this prayer, the *first*, in saying 'Hostiam puram,' points out that there lies the pure Victim which was nailed to the cross; the *second*, in saying 'Hostiam sanctam,' indicates that there lies the Victim which was offered up on the cross; the *third*, in saying 'Hostiam immaculatam,' indicates that this is the Victim without blemish which was immolated on the cross; the *fourth*, at 'Panem sanctum,' shows that we have before us the holy Bread of Life—that is to say, Him who said, 'I am the true Bread of Life, who descended from Heaven and died upon the cross to give you life'; and the *fifth*, at 'Calicem salutis,' is intended to show that the Blood which is contained in the chalice is the very same that was shed upon the cross for the redemption of the world." In one word, then, crosses made before consecration are always symbolic of blessing or are such in reality; after consecration they signify that the blessed Victim who suffered on the cross is now lying before us on the altar.

Crosses made after Consecration in the Oriental Church.—From the fact that many, even within the Church, have looked upon these crosses as an idle and useless observance it is a great relief to us to find that they are also employed by the Orientals. A rubric on this head in the Liturgy of St. Basil reads as follows: "Then the deacon, bowing his head, points to the holy bread with his stole and says secretly, 'Sir, bless the holy bread,' and the priest, standing up, signs the holy gifts, saying secretly, 'This bread is the Precious Body itself of our Lord and God and Saviour Jesus Christ.'" Deacon : "Sir, bless the chalice." Priest : "This chalice is the Precious Blood itself of our Lord and God and Saviour Jesus Christ." After this both Host and chalice are blessed conjointly, as with ourselves; so that, in fact, our interpretation of these crosses entirely agrees with that of the Orientals. We do not deem it necessary to lengthen our pages by giving any more examples of this practice; let it suffice to say that it may be seen in all the Eastern liturgies.

"SUPRA QUÆ PROPITIO."

The only thing that deserves special notice in this prayer is the allusion made to the sacrifices of Abel, Abraham, and Melchisedech ; and these are mentioned because they refer more directly than any of the other sacrifices of the old law to the sacrifice we offer in the Mass. For, in the first place, the blood of Abel, the just man, wantonly shed by his brother Cain, very forcibly recalls to mind the iniquity of the Jews in shedding the blood of our innocent Saviour, who, according to the flesh, was a kinsman of their own. Then, again, as Abel offered to God the firstlings of his flock (*Genesis* iv. 4), he aptly prefigures our Lord, who, as St. Paul says, "*was the first-born among many brethren*" (*Rom.* viii. 29). The holy Patriarch Abraham leading up his only son, Isaac, to immolate him on the mount, specially prefigures the Eternal Father immolating his Only-Begotten Son, our Lord and God, for our sake ; and Isaac carrying the wood upon which he was to be sacrificed represents our Saviour carrying his cross to Calvary.

The allusion to the sacrifice of Melchisedech is full of import. He is mentioned in Scripture as a priest of the Most High, without father or mother, without genealogy of any kind, and without beginning or end of days. Herein he is a most striking figure of our Lord, of whom the Scripture says : "Who shall declare his generation?" But there is yet a still closer resemblance between Melchisedech and our Lord. The former was king and priest at the same time. Our Lord is king and priest also. The king of Salem offered bread and wine in virtue of his being a priest of the Most High; our Lord offers himself in the Holy Mass under the same species, and is styled by the royal Psalmist "*a priest for ever according to the order of Melchisedech*" (Ps. cix.) The last words of the prayer—viz., "Sanctum sacrificium, immaculatam Hostiam"—were added by Pope Leo the Great (fifth century). They refer, as is evident, not to the sacrifices of the old law here mentioned, but to the Holy Sacrifice of the Mass, where our Lord, the Immaculate Lamb, is the victim.

"SUPPLICES TE ROGAMUS."

Whilst reciting the first part of this prayer the priest is bowed profoundly, with his hands resting upon the altar, and when he comes to the words, "ex hac altaris participatione," he kisses the altar, and, having become erect, makes the sign of the cross upon himself at the same time that he pronounces the words, "omni benedictione cœlesti et gratia repleamur." In English this entire prayer is rendered as follows : "We humbly beseech thee, O Almighty God! that thou wouldst command these gifts to be carried by the hands of thy holy angel to thy altar on high, before the sight of thy Divine Majesty, that all of us who by this participation shall receive the most holy Body and Blood of thy Son may be enriched with every heavenly blessing and grace, through the same Christ our Lord. Amen." As to who the holy angel mentioned here is, a diversity of opinion exists. Some say that it is the angel deputed by God to watch over the Sacrifice after the manner in which blessed spirits of this name were appointed to watch over the sacrifices of the old law, as we read in various parts of Scripture (see *Genesis* xxii. 11; *Judges* vi. and xiii.; and *St. Luke* i.); but, according to the vast majority of commentators, the holy angel referred to is none other than our Lord himself, who is styled "the Angel of the Great Council" in Holy Writ (Romsee, iv. p. 231). The Carmelites and Dominicans, while reciting the first part of this prayer, bow down and cross their arms one over the other (*brachiis cancellatis*) before their breast.

When an explanation was demanded of the Greeks at the Council of Florence, in 1439, of their prayer which asks God to make the bread the Precious Body and the chalice the Precious Blood of Christ, and all this after they had become such already by consecration, they objected the wording of the prayer now under consideration—viz., the "Supplices te rogamus"—contending that theirs could be as easily defended as this. As they fully acquiesced, however, in the teaching that the sacred words of institution—viz., "$τοῦτο\ γάρ\ ἐστι\ τὸ\ σῶμα\ μοῦ$," *touto gar esti to soma mou*—are alone the efficient cause of transubstantiation, the Fathers of the Latin Church did not deem it necessary to push the motion before the council any further, and so they allowed the prayer alluded to to stand where it was in all the Greek liturgies, instead of changing it to some earlier part of the Canon.

MIXING WARM WATER WITH THE PRECIOUS BLOOD AFTER CONSECRATION.

Another strange custom which prevails with the Greeks is the mixing of warm water with the chalice after consecration. They mingle a few drops of ordinary water with the wine at the beginning of Mass, as we do, and for the same literal and mystical reasons; but the adding of warm water besides, and that, too, after consecration has taken place, is, to say the least of it, very strange—we were about to say very offensive. There was a spirited discussion about this ceremony at the Council of Florence, for the Latin Fathers severely reprehended it, and were at first fully determined to compel the Greeks to abolish it before the decree for the reunion of the churches would be made out and ratified. Dorotheus, Bishop of Mitylene, however, made so eloquent and satisfactory a defence of the practice that he gained all the Fathers to his side; and as the Pope himself expressed his admiration of the defence, the custom was approved of, and so it is still kept up by the Greeks.

The words employed in adding this warm water suggest its mystic meaning. They are: "The fervor of faith, full of the Holy Ghost. Amen." This is repeated thrice, and the water is poured in in the form of a cross. Speaking of this ceremony, St. Germanus writes as follows: "As blood and *warm* water flowed together from the side of Christ, thus hot water poured into the chalice at the time of consecration gives a full type of the mystery to those who draw that holy liquid from the chalice as from the life-giving side of our Lord" (*Translation of the Primitive Liturgies*, p. 120, by Neale and Littledale; Goar, *Euchol. Græc.*, p. 148). As the latter-named author gives a full history of this rite, he may be consulted with advantage.

MEMENTO FOR THE DEAD.

As he begins to recite this prayer the priest moves his hands slowly before his face, so as to have them united at the words, "in somno pacis." This gentle motion of the hands is aptly suggestive here of the slow, lingering motion of a soul preparing to leave the body, and the final union of the hands forcibly recalls to mind the laying down of the body in its quiet slumber in the earth. As this prayer is very beautiful, we transcribe it in full. It is thus worded:

"Remember also, O Lord! thy servants, male and female, who have gone before us with the sign of faith and sleep in the sleep of peace, N. N.; to them, O Lord! and to all who rest in Christ, we beseech thee to grant a place of refreshment, light, and peace; through the same Christ our Lord. Amen." At the letters "N. N." the names of the particular persons to be prayed for among the departed were read out from the diptychs in ancient times. When the priest comes to them now he does not stop, but pauses awhile at "in somno pacis" to make his private memento of those whom he wishes to pray for in particular, in which he is to be guided by the same rules that directed him in making his memento for the living, only that here he cannot pray for the conversion of any one, as he could there, for this solely relates to the dead who are detained in Purgatory. Should the Holy Sacrifice be offered for any soul among the departed which could not be benefited by it, either because of the loss of its eternal salvation or its attainment of the everlasting joys of heaven, theologians commonly teach that in that case the fruit of the Mass would enter the treasury of the Church, and be applied afterwards in such indulgences and the like as Almighty God might suggest to the dispensers of his gifts (Suarez, *Disp.* xxxviii. sec. 8).

We beg to direct particular attention here to the expression "sleep of peace." That harsh word *death* which we now use was seldom or never heard among the early Christians when talking of their departed brethren. Death to them was nothing else but a sleep until the great day of resurrection, when all would rise up again at the sound of the angel's trumpet; and this bright idea animated their minds and enlivened all their hopes when conversing with their absent friends in prayer. So, too, with the place of interment; it was not called by that hard name that distinguishes it too often now—viz., the *grave yard*—but was called by the milder term of *cemetery*, which, from its Greek derivation, means a dormitory, or sleeping-place. Nor was the word *bury* employed to signify the consigning of the body to the earth. No, this sounded too profane in the ears of the primitive Christians; they rather chose the word *depose*, as suggestive of the *treasure* that was put away until it pleased God to turn it to better use on the final reckoning day. The old Teutonic expression for cemetery was, to say the least of it, very beautiful. The blessed place was called in this tongue *Gottes-acker*—that is, God's field—for the reason that the dead were, so to speak, the seed sown in the ground from which would spring the harvest reaped on the day of general resurrection in the shape of glorified bodies. According to this beautiful notion, the stone which told who the departed person was that lay at rest beneath, was likened to the label that was hung up on a post by the farmer or gardener to tell the passer-by the name of the flower that was deposited beneath. This happy application of the word *sleep* to death runs also through Holy Scripture, where we frequently find such expressions as "He slept with his fathers"; "I have slept and I am refreshed," applied from the third Psalm to our Divine Lord's time in the sepulchre; the "sleep of peace"; "he was gathered to his fathers," etc. (For a very interesting article on this subject see *The Catholic World*, November, 1872.)

Memento of the Dead in the Oriental Church.—The prayers of the Orientals for the faithful departed are singularly touching. In the Coptic Liturgy of St. Basil the memento is worded thus: "In like manner, O Lord! remember also all those who have already fallen asleep in the priesthood and amidst the laity; vouchsafe to give rest to their souls in the bosoms of our holy fathers Abraham, Isaac, and Jacob; bring them into a place of greenness by the waters of comfort, in the paradise of pleasure where grief and misery and sighing are banished, in the brightness of the saints." The Orientals are very much attached to ancient phraseology, and hence their frequent application of "the bosom of Abraham" to that middle state of purification in the next life which we universally designate by the name of Purgatory. In the Syro-Jacobite Liturgy of John Bar-Maadan part of the memento is worded thus: "Reckon them among the number of thine elect; cover them with the bright cloud of thy saints; set them with the lambs on thy right hand, and bring them into thy habitation." The following extract is taken from the Liturgy of St. Chrysostom, which, as we have said already, all the Catholic and schismatic Greeks of the East follow: "Remember all those that are departed in the hope of the resurrection to eternal life, and give them rest where the light of thy countenance shines upon them." But of all the Orientals the place of honor in this respect must be yielded to the Nestorians; for, heretics as they are, too much praise cannot be given them for the singular reverence they show toward their departed brethren. From a work of theirs called the *Sinhados*, which Badger quotes in his *Nestorians and their Rituals*, we take the following extract: "The service of the third day of the dead is kept up, because Christ rose on the third day. On the ninth day, also, there should be a commemoration, and again on the thirtieth day, after the example of the Old Testament, since the people mourned for Moses that length of time. A year after, also, there should be a particular commemoration of the dead, and some of the property of the deceased should be given to the poor in remembrance of him. We say this of believers; for as to unbelievers, should all the wealth of the world be given to the poor in their behalf it would profit them nothing." The Armenians call Purgatory by the name *Gayan*—that is, a mansion. The Chaldeans style it *Matthar*, the exact equivalent of our term. By some of the other Oriental churches it is called *Kavaran*, or place of penance; and *Makraran*, a place of purification (Smith and Dwight, i. p. 169).

We could multiply examples at pleasure to prove that there is no church in the East to which the name of Christian can be given that does not look upon praying for the faithful departed, and offering the Holy Mass for the repose of their souls, as a sacred and solemn obligation. Protestants who would fain believe otherwise, and who not unfrequently record differently in their writings about the Oriental Christians, can verify our statements by referring to any Eastern liturgy and examining for themselves. We conclude our remarks on this head by a strong argument in point from a very unbiassed Anglican minister—Rev. Dr. John Mason Neale. Speaking of prayers for the dead in his work entitled *A History of the Holy Eastern Church* (geneeral introduction, vol. i. p. 509), this candid-speaking man uses the following language: "I am not now going to prove, what nothing but the blindest prejudice can deny, that the Church, east, west, and south, has with one consentient and universal voice, even from apostolic times, prayed in the Holy Eucharist for the departed faithful." Would that we had more of such candid-speaking men instead of those modern sciolists who travel east and west and afterwards record their observations as if they had eyes and saw not!

"NOBIS QUOQUE PECCATORIBUS."

At the initial words of this prayer the priest breaks silence for the first time since he began the Canon, but only while he is saying the words "to us also sinners," at which he strikes his breast as the poor publican in the Gospel did when he went up to the temple to pray. In many parts of

Ireland it is customary for the person serving Mass to answer, "Parce nobis, Domine"—"Spare us, O Lord!"—at this place; but the origin of the custom we have never been able to trace, nor is it spoken of by any liturgist whom we have consulted. The precise reason for breaking silence here has never been satisfactorily explained. All that liturgical writers say of it is that it is intended to commemorate the humble cry for mercy of the penitent thief on the cross; but from all we have seen about it in the ancient Roman ordinals, and in other works of a like nature, we are inclined to think that it was originally intended as a sort of signal for the minor ministers of the Mass to attend to some particular duty at that time. Romsee intimates that it might have been used as an admonition for the people to enter into themselves and bewail their offences together with the priest. An ancient Roman ordo has the following words upon this matter, from which our opinion derives some strength: "When he shall say, 'Nobis quoque peccatoribus,' the subdeacons rise." The Carthusians do not raise their voice here at all, but simply strike the breast; and this is also the custom at the cathedral church of Lyons.

The force of the word *quoque*, "also," employed here, depends on the connection of this prayer with the preceding one, as if it were said, "We have prayed for a place of rest and peace for our departed brethren; we also pray for a similar favor in behalf of ourselves, in order that we may become associated with thy holy apostles and martyrs," etc. As it is necessary for a priest to know exactly who the saints are that are mentioned in this prayer, and also in the "Communicantes," in order to be able to bow the head when Mass is celebrated on the recurrence of their festivals, or a commemoration is made of them in another Mass, we have deemed it proper to give a brief sketch of their lives.

First, as to who the St. John is that occurs here. For

quite a long time it remained undecided whether this was St. John the Evangelist or St. John the Baptist, and many weighty opinions lay on both sides. Pope Innocent III., speaking as an ordinary liturgical scholar, maintained that it was St. John the Evangelist. He was named first, according to this Pontiff, as an apostle in the prayer "Communicantes," and here, again, as a virgin disciple. Others held, too, that it was the Evangelist who was mentioned, not on account of his virginity, but simply because he was looked upon as having, in a manner, died twice: first, when plunged into the caldron of boiling oil by order of Domitian, from which, however, he was miraculously preserved; and, secondly, when he died a natural death at Ephesus. This latter opinion never had many supporters, and, we think, deservedly. The principal objection to naming St. John the Baptist here was that he was not, strictly speaking, a saint of the new law, having been put to death before the Passion of our Lord. The question remained thus unsettled for a long time, with opinions on both sides (by far the weightier, however, on the side of the Evangelist), until at last the decision of the Sacred Congregation of Rites was asked in the matter. When the question was first proposed—viz., in April, 1823—it responded, "Dilata," that is, that the answer was held over for further consideration. In March, 1824, it replied that the saint mentioned, and at whose name a reverence should be made, was St. John the Baptist. After this decision had appeared all further discussion ceased. The question was settled. The Church has instituted two special feasts in honor of the Baptist: the one, that of his nativity, on June 24; the other, of his decollation, or beheading, on August 29. Part of the precursor's head is said to be kept in the Church of St. Sylvester at Rome, and another part at Amiens, in France.

St. Stephen, December 26.—This saint is generally distinguished by the title of protomartyr, from the fact that he was, strictly speaking, the first martyr of the new law who suffered publicly for the faith. His relics were conveyed from Jerusalem to Rome some four hundred years after his death; and when deposited beside those of the holy martyr St. Lawrence, a pious legend says that the latter moved to the left in order to yield the place of honor to the protomartyr, for which reason the Romans styled St. Lawrence *Il cortese Spagniolo*—that is, *the polite Spaniard*—for he was of that nation. The Feast of St. Stephen used anciently to be called "straw day" in the South of France, from a custom that prevailed there of blessing straw on that day. Throughout England and Ireland it was known as "wrenning day," from the very singular custom of hunting and stoning a wren to death in commemoration of St. Stephen's martyrdom. Wren-boy day in the South of Ireland was a regular gala-day for the young folks; it is still celebrated to some extent in many places.

St. Matthias, February 24.—A vacancy having occurred among the twelve by the apostasy of Judas, Matthias was chosen by lot to fill it. The manner of his death is not exactly known, but it is generally believed that he ended his days by crucifixion. The reason for not naming this apostle with the others in the "Communicantes" is that he was not associated to the apostolic band until after the Passion of our Lord; nor is he named in any of the Gospels. And if it be objected to this that St. Paul was neither an apostle nor even a Christian until after the Passion, and still he is mentioned in the "Communicantes" with the other apostles, we reply that this was done in order not to separate him from St. Peter; for the Church sings of both of them: "In life they loved each other; in death they are not separated." This is the reason given by all.

St. Barnabas, June 11.—St. Barnabas was a native of Cyprus. His first name was Joses, which he himself changed to Barnabas, an Aramean name meaning " son of consolation." He was the friend and companion of St. Paul in the holy ministry. The Feast of St. Barnabas was, according to the old style,[4] the longest day in the year, and hence the familiar rhyme:

> " Barnaby bright, Barnaby gay,
> The shortest night and the longest day."

St. Ignatius, February 1.—According to a pious tradition, it was this saint whom our Lord took into his arms when he said to his apostles : " Whosoever shall receive one of such children in my name receiveth me." He became Bishop of Antioch in the early part of the second century, and suffered a glorious martyrdom under Trajan in the year 107. He is said to have been the originator of responsive singing in the Church—a practice which he learned, it is said, from the angels, whom he frequently heard chanting after this manner.

St. Alexander, May 3.—This saint succeeded Evaristus as Pope in the year 109, and is named as a martyr in the *Sacramentary* of St. Gregory the Great.

St. Marcellinus, June 2.—St. Marcellinus was a priest of Rome, who, with St. Peter the Exorcist, suffered martyrdom in the persecution of Diocletian, A.D. 304.

St. Peter, June 2.—This saint, generally styled " Peter the Exorcist "—for he was not in full orders—suffered mar-

---

[4] Russia is the only Christian country which yet retains the old style, or Julian Calendar. The principal error of this style consists in making the year 365¼ days, or about eleven minutes too much. The new style, or Gregorian Calendar (so called from Pope Gregory XIII.), began in 1582. In order to obtain the true date according to this style, we must deduct *ten* days for the sixteenth and seventeenth centuries, *eleven* days for the eighteenth century, and *twelve* for the nineteenth. It is well to bear this in mind, as a neglect of it has often occasioned much perplexity.

tyrdom under the Emperor Diocletian, together with St. Marcellinus, in A.D. 304.

St. Perpetua, March 7.—St. Perpetua suffered martyrdom at Carthage, in Africa, in the year 202, at the age of twenty-two. The instrument of her torture was a wild cow let loose upon her, by which she was tossed about and frightfully mangled in the amphitheatre. Her name and that of her companion, St. Felicitas, were added to the Canon of the Mass by Pope Gregory the Great.

St. Felicitas, March 7.—There is little to be said of this saint further than that she suffered martyrdom with St. Perpetua. She must not be confounded with the St. Felicitas who suffered under the Emperor Antoninus Pius.

St. Agatha, February 5.—She is said to have been a Sicilian by birth, and to have suffered martyrdom in the persecution of Decius, about the year 251.

St. Lucy, December 13.—St. Lucy was a native of Syracuse, in Sicily, and suffered martyrdom about the year 304. Her body is said to be preserved at Metz, where it is exposed for the veneration of the faithful on certain occasions of the year. In art she is generally represented with a palm-branch in one hand, and in the other a burning lamp expressive of her name, which comes, it is said, from the Latin *lux*, light.

St. Agnes, January 21.—There are two saints of this name in the calendar, but the one named here is the saint generally meant when St. Agnes is spoken of. She is said to have suffered martyrdom about the year 305. Her church on the Via Nomentana, at Rome, gives title to a cardinal, and furnishes the lambs annually from whose wool the palliums of archbishops are made. In ancient art she is represented in her miraculous snow-white garment, with an executioner by her side armed with a halberd. Her feast was once a holyday of obligation in England.

St. Cecilia, November 22.—According to the best accounts, this saint suffered martyrdom in the year 230. From the great love she manifested for singing the divine praises she is generally looked up to as the patroness of music, and is always represented in art with a lyre in her hand. So eminent a saint was she held to be in the early Church that a special preface was composed for her feast and inserted in the *Sacramentary* of Pope Gregory the Great. She is said to have always carried a copy of the Gospels with her—a pious custom very prevalent among the primitive Christians, and not entirely extinct yet.

St. Anastasia, December 25.—This saint is said to have met her death by being burnt at the stake by order of the prefect of Illyria in the year 304, during the persecution of Diocletian.

"PER QUEM HÆC OMNIA."

At each of the words "sanctify," "vivify," and "bless," of this prayer, a cross is made over the Host and chalice together. The chalice is then uncovered, and the priest, taking the sacred Host between the thumb and index finger of the right hand, makes three crosses with it over the chalice as he says "through him," "with him," and "in him," and two between the chalice and himself in a direct line at the expression "to thee, God the Father Almighty, in the unity of the Holy Ghost, be all honor and glory." As he says "all honor and glory" he raises the chalice and Host a few inches from the altar. This is called the *minor elevation*, and here the Canon ends.

According to Pouget (*Inst. Cathol.*, tom. ii. p. 869), when the ancient discipline of elevating the Host and chalice together at this place prevailed, they were raised high enough to be seen by the people. He is about the only author who ventures to assert this, but there is very good reason to think him right.

It was long customary in the early days to bless new fruits and products of various kinds at this part of the Mass, such as grapes, milk and honey, oil, wine, etc. This was done just before the "per quem hæc omnia," and the commodities to be blessed were placed on the altar by the deacon.

CHAPTER XXVIII.

THE CELEBRATION OF MASS.

THE PATER NOSTER.

In concluding the Canon the priest raises his voice and says aloud, "Per omnia sæcula sæculorum"; then, "Oremus"; and after this follows the "Pater noster," or Lord's Prayer, to which the following short preface is prefixed: "Being admonished by salutary precepts, and taught by divine institution, we presume to say, 'Our Father,'" etc. According to several authorities of note, the expression, "being admonished by salutary precepts," refers to the existence of the Discipline of the Secret, in virtue of which it was strictly forbidden to recite, among other things, the "Lord's Prayer" in the hearing of the catechumens; but inasmuch as none of this class could be present at this part of the Mass, there was no danger to be apprehended from reciting it aloud. At the Divine Office, however, it was never said but in *secret*, for catechumens as well as Christians could be present then. This discipline stands yet. The rest of this short preface refers to what our Lord said to his disciples on the quantity and quality of prayer, for the "Pater noster" was formulated by himself as a model for their guidance (*Enchiridion Sacrif. Missæ Bened. XIV.*, p. 95 ; J. Pleyer, S.J., *De Sacr. Miss. Sacrif.*, p. 7).

In the Liturgy of St. James this little preface is thus worded : "Grant us, O Lord, and lover of men ! with boldness, without condemnation, with a pure heart, with a broken spirit, with a face that needs not to be ashamed, with hallowed lips, to dare to call upon thee, our Holy God and Father in heaven, and say, 'Our Father,'" etc. All the Oriental liturgies have some preface of this kind here.

Throughout the Western Church it is the priest himself who says the "Pater noster," but in the Eastern Church it is said by people and priest together. The Mozarabics add "Amen" after each of its different petitions.

In the time of Pope Clement III. (1187–1191), while the Crusaders were engaged in fighting for the recovery of the sacred places of Palestine, it was customary to recite immediately after this prayer the psalm "Deus venerunt gentes" —"O God! the heathens are come into thy inheritance." Pope Innocent III. ordered the same psalm to be sung, together with a verse and a prayer, after the "Pax"; and by a decree of Pope John XXII. (1316–1334) the psalm "Lætatus sum" was to be recited in every Mass after the "Pater noster" for the extinction of heresies and schisms (Romsee, p. 255).

We had almost forgotten to mention that when the Pope celebrates on Easter Sunday, "Amen" is never responded to the "Per omnia sæcula sæculorum," immediately before the "Pater noster," and this to commemorate a miracle once wrought in favor of Pope Gregory the Great, to whom the angels responded at this place upon a certain Easter morning (*ibid.*)

SEQUENCE OF THE LORD'S PRAYER.

The moment the priest has finished the Lord's Prayer he wipes the paten with the purificator, in order to prepare it for receiving the sacred Host; and then, holding it in his right hand, resting erect on the altar, recites the sequence, or, as it is called, the *embolismus* (that is, something *added on*) of the "Pater noster." It is worded as follows: "Deliver us, O Lord! we beseech thee, from all evils, present, past, and future, and through the intercession of the blessed and ever-glorious Virgin Mary, Mother of God, with thy blessed Apostles Peter and Paul and Andrew, and all thy saints, grant of thy goodness peace in our days, that, being assisted by the help of thy mercy, we may be always free from sin and secure from all disturbance."

Many writers are of opinion that the name of St. Andrew was here added by Pope Gregory the Great, because he cherished a singular devotion to him and built several churches in his honor. In early times it was left entirely to the celebrant of the Mass what saints' names to add to this prayer after that of St. Andrew. He could name any one that his own devotion prompted; and this was the rule, with little interruption, until the eleventh century, when that now in vogue superseded it.

The *embolismus* is recited in secret, because, on account of all the saints' names that used to be added to it formerly, it could not be easily chanted in High Mass; and from that the custom found its way into Low Mass also. De Vert, however, says that this way of saying it was adopted in order not to interfere with the singing of the choir at this place (Romsee, p. 264).

When the priest comes to the words, "grant of thy goodness peace in our days," he makes the sign of the cross upon his person with the paten, and then kisses the latter at its rim. The paten is here kissed because it is about to receive our Divine Lord, who is pre-eminently the author of peace, and who makes the paten his throne at this solemn part of the Mass. Having come to the words, "being assisted by the help of thy mercy," etc., he places the paten under the Host, and then, removing the pall from the chalice, genuflects to adore our Lord. He then becomes erect, and, bringing the Host over the chalice, breaks it first into two equal parts, saying, "Through the same Jesus Christ our Lord, thy Son." The part held in the right hand is now placed on the paten, and from the part he holds in his left, still over the chalice, he breaks a minute particle, and places the remainder with the other large portion on the paten also, reciting during this action the concluding words of the prayer, "Who liveth and reigneth with thee in the unity of the Holy Ghost, God." Still holding the minute particle over the mouth of the chalice, he says aloud, "Per omnia sæcula sæculorum," and then, "Pax Domini sit semper vobiscum"—"The peace of the Lord be always with you." When reciting these last words he makes three crosses over the mouth of the chalice with the particle held in his right hand, and then lets it fall into the Precious Blood, saying at the same time, "May this commixture and consecration of the Body and Blood of our Lord Jesus Christ be to us who receive it unto life everlasting."

EXPLANATION OF THESE CEREMONIES.

The Host is broken in memory of what our Lord himself did at the Last Supper and on those occasions afterwards which are recorded in Holy Scriptures; but as regards the triple division, all we can say is that in ancient times there was much diversity of practice in this respect. Some broke it into three portions; some into four; and some, like those who follow the Mozarabic Rite, into nine. According to the ancient Roman Rite, it was first broken into three portions, one of which was cast into the chalice; another was reserved for communicating the celebrant, deacon, and subdeacon; and the third was kept for the sick. This custom was in vogue in the majority of churches, and a vestige of it is yet retained in Papal High Mass, where the Holy Father drops one part of the Host into the Precious Blood, communicates himself from another part, and the deacon and subdeacon from the third. The like, too, may be seen in the consecration of a bishop (Romsee, p. 273).

According to Durandus, the three crosses made over the chalice here with the small particle are intended to commemorate the three days that the blessed Body of our Lord remained in the sepulchre; and the casting in of this particle afterwards to unite with the Precious Blood forcibly recalls to mind the union of our Lord's Soul and Body after his resurrection.

We have said that the Mozarabics break the Host into nine parts. The first division made is into two equal portions; then a subdivision is made by which one portion is broken into four parts and the other into five, thus making nine in all, which are then arranged on the paten in the form of a cross, and a name given to each commemorative of the principal events in our Lord's life: thus, 1st, the Incarnation; 2d, the Nativity; 3d, the Circumcision; 4th, the Epiphany; 5th, the Passion; 6th, Christ's Death; 7th, his Resurrection; 8th, the Glory of Christ in heaven; 9th, the Kingdom of Christ. From Easter to Pentecost, and also on the Feast of Corpus Christi, while the priest of this rite holds the part called the "Kingdom of Christ" in his hand over the chalice, he says three times aloud, "The Lion of the tribe of Juda, the root of David, has conquered"; to which the choir responds, "Thou who sittest upon the cherubim, root of David, alleluia."

Division of the Host in the Oriental Church.—The Greeks divide the Host into four parts, one of which the priest casts into the chalice; another he receives himself; a third he puts aside and distributes among the communicants; and the fourth part he reserves for the sick. According to the Liturgy of St. Chrysostom, the rubrics touching this ceremony are worded as follows:

RUBRIC: *The deacon then girds his Orarion [stole]*

crosswise and goes into the holy Bema, and standing on the right hand (the priest grasping the holy Bread), saith:

Deacon : " Sir, break the Holy Bread."

RUBRIC : *And the priest, dividing it into four parts with care and reverence, saith:*

Priest : " The Lamb of God is broken and distributed; he that is broken and not divided in sunder; ever eaten and never consumed, but sanctifying those who receive him."

Before the particle is cast into the chalice by the Greeks the sign of the cross is first made with it, and it is then allowed to fall in with the words, " the fulness of the chalice of faith of the Holy Ghost," to which the deacon responds, " Amen."

In the Liturgy of St. James the particle is cast into the chalice with the words, "The union of the most Holy Body and Precious Blood of our Lord and God and Saviour Jesus Christ." The Copts first divide the Host when pronouncing the word *fregit*—" he broke "—just before they pronounce the exact words of institution, and make subdivisions of it afterwards a little before communion. The Nestorians divide it into three parts, using both hands, and saying during the ceremony, " We now approach in the true faith of thy name, O Lord! and through thy compassion we break, and through thy mercy we sign, the Body and Blood of our Lifegiver, the Lord Jesus Christ; in the name of the Father, and of the Son, and of the Holy Ghost"; and when putting the particle in the chalice, " May the Precious Blood be signed with the life-giving Body of our Lord Jesus Christ, in the name of the Father, and of the Son, and of the Holy Ghost. Amen." From all this we see how much the practice of the Eastern Church resembles our own in all that concerns the Holy Eucharist.

AN ANCIENT CUSTOM.

After the recital of the *embolismus,* or sequence of the " Pater noster," the archdeacon who assisted at Episcopal Mass was accustomed, in early days, to turn round to the congregation and intone " Humiliate vos ad benedictionem "—" Bow down for the benediction"; to which the rest of the clergy would respond, " Deo gratias." Then the bishop, before he said " Pax Domini," would turn to the people and impart his solemn blessing.

According to the Mozarabic Rite, this custom was also observed in Low Mass, and that by priests as well as by bishops. The fourth Council of Toledo, however, decreed that the custom should be abolished. The reason assigned by Mabillon (*De Liturgiis Gallicanis,* lib. i. cap. iv. Nos. 13 et 14) for this ceremony was that those who did not intend to communicate might leave the church. Hence the meaning of that invitation to depart mentioned by Pope Gregory the Great : " Si quis non communicat det locum "—" If any one does not intend to communicate let him make way."

AGNUS DEI.

During the recital of the "Agnus Dei " the priest strikes his breast three times in humble sorrow for his sins, saying the two first times, " Lamb of God who takest away the sins of the world, have mercy on us "; and the third time, " Lamb of God who takest away the sins of the world, grant us peace." In Masses for the dead the form is, " Lamb of God who takest away the sins of the world, grant them rest"; this is repeated twice, and the third time is said, "Lamb of God who takest away the sins of the world, grant them eternal rest"; but the breast is not struck at all at these Masses, inasmuch as they concern the dead and not the living. The expression "Lamb of God," as applied to our Lord, is taken from Holy Scripture, where we find it frequently occurring. From the relations between our Saviour and the Paschal lamb of the ancient law, a preference was given to the use of it in early days.

Before the time of Pope Sergius I. (A.D. 687 to 701), the chanting of the "Agnus Dei" was solely confined to the choir, but by a decree of this pontiff it was also extended to the clergy. This is the explanation that Mabillon gives; and it seems in accordance with what the *Pontifical Book* states about the pontiff named, for in its fourteenth chapter the following occurs: "He ordained that at the time of the fraction of the Body of the Lord 'Agnus Dei qui tollis peccata mundi, miserere nobis,' should be sung by the clergy and people" (Romsee, p. 281). It is for this reason that Pope Sergius is generally accredited with the introduction of the "Agnus Dei" into the Mass. But that it existed long before his time may be seen from the *Sacramentary* of Pope Gregory the Great.

The number of times, however, that it was to be said varied very considerably. Sometimes it was said but once, and this was all that Pope Sergius ordered in his decree concerning it. At other times it used to be kept up until the entire ceremony of the fraction of the sacred Bread had been gone through with; whence it was sung *once, twice, three times*—as often, in fact, as was necessary. Its double repetition was very frequent in the eleventh century; and Belethus (chap. xlviii.) alludes to its triple repetition in the century following. The same may be seen in the Missals printed at that period, from which it may be fairly inferred that the present discipline dates. Nor must we omit to mention that the celebrant did not say the "Agnus Dei" at all when first introduced, but only the choir. When the duty became incumbent on the priest also it is not easy to determine. According to Romsee, the pope used to say it in his Mass about the fourteenth century. Very likely it became obligatory on priests in general about this period also. Another variation that respected its recital was that in some places it used to be said once before the Preface and twice at the place where it is now recited (Romsee, p. 282).

The words "grant us peace," added to the last repetition, instead of "have mercy on us," have not been always in use, nor is it customary now to say them in the church of St. John Lateran at Rome. According to very creditable authorities (see Bona, p. 358), they were first introduced by directions received from the Mother of God, who appeared one day to a certain carpenter as he was felling trees in the forest, and gave him a medal with the image of our Lord upon one side, and the inscription, "Lamb of God, who takest away the sins of the world, grant us peace," on the other. The Blessed Virgin commanded the carpenter to show this medal to the bishop of the place, with the request that others might be made in imitation of it and be reverently worn, in order that God might restore peace to the Church of those days. The addition soon found its way into the Mass, where it has been retained ever since.

THE PAX.

Having recited the Agnus Dei, the priest bows a little, and, resting his hands upon the altar, recites three prayers without changing his posture. The first is a petition to Almighty God for that peace *which the world cannot give;* the second asks for deliverance from all iniquity in virtue of the Body and Blood of our Divine Redeemer; and the third, that the reception of the same Body and Blood may prove to be a remedy for all the infirmities of soul and body.

When the Mass is a Solemn High Mass a very ancient and interesting ceremony is witnessed here after the recital of the first of these prayers—viz., the imparting of the "Pax," or kiss of peace, which is kept up in the Mass to commemorate that tender-hearted and loving practice which our Divine Lord always observed in his intercourse with his disciples. And here it may be well to remark that although our Blessed Saviour said, "Do this in remembrance of me," only of what was done in regard to confecting the Holy Eucharist at the Last Supper, still the Church has thought fit to do not only what her Divine Founder did and commanded to be observed afterwards, but also many other things which, though not prescribed expressly, are yet recorded by the Evangelists as worthy of imitation. These she has introduced into the Mass as being the most fitting place to commemorate them; for what is the Mass itself but a mystic biography of our Lord's life upon earth? The moment, then, that the celebrant has recited the first of these prayers he turns to the deacon, and, having placed his hands upon his shoulders, inclines his head slightly as if about to kiss him, and says, "Pax tecum"—"Peace be with you"—to which the deacon responds, "Et cum spiritu tuo"—"And with thy spirit." The pious salutation is then taken up by all the other ministers of the altar and the clergy who are present, but it is no longer observed among the people of the congregation. It is not witnessed in Masses for the dead, on account of their lugubrious nature, and also for the reason that in former times it was not customary to communicate at such Masses, and the "Pax" was intended principally as a ceremony of reconciliation between man and man previous to the reception of the Holy Eucharist (Bona, p. 359).

In ancient times, when the male portion of the congregation was separated from the female portion, the kiss of peace went through the entire church; and this discipline continued, with little interruption, up to the time of Pope Innocent III.—that is, until the thirteenth century—when, on account of the increasing depravity of morals, and from other causes, it was deemed prudent to discontinue the practice in its primitive spirit, and substitute another form of holy salutation in its stead. A small instrument made of silver or gold, and having a representation of our crucified Redeemer upon it, was accordingly introduced, and denominated the *osculatorium*, which all kissed, even the celebrant, at this part of the Mass. Though once very common, this instrument of peace is now seldom seen, at least in American churches, the general practice being to approach each other as above described, and salute with "Pax tecum." In the ordination of priests the "kiss of peace" is commanded to be given as of old by the ordaining bishop to the newly-ordained. Many religious orders observe it, too, in private life.

In ancient times it was customary for the priest, before he gave the "Pax" to any one else, to stoop down first and kiss the sacred Host lying on the paten before him, to signify that it is from our Divine Lord that he received that peace which he wished to communicate to others. This practice was, however, soon abrogated, as it was considered somewhat unbecoming, and there was always danger attending it on account of the liability of some particles of the sacred Host adhering to the lips.

The custom prevailed in some places, too, of first kissing the chalice, and then sending the salutation around in the ordinary way among the clergy of the sanctuary. This was long in vogue with the Dominicans, and is, to a certain extent, observed by them yet; for their ceremonial directs that the priest first kiss the rim of the chalice, and afterwards the paten, or the regular instrument of peace presented him by the deacon, and say: "Peace to thee and to the Holy Church of God." The practice of first kissing the missal on this occasion, as containing the sacred words of our Lord, was in vogue at Cologne, and in many churches of France, in the beginning of the sixteenth century.

Pax in the Oriental Church.—In the Liturgy of St. James the "Pax" follows closely upon the recital of the Creed, at some distance from the Preface. The time of its observance is thus announced by the deacon: "Let us kiss one another with a holy kiss; let us bow our heads to the Lord." When the Maronites are giving the "Pax," which, like all the Orientals, they do before the Preface, the celebrant first kisses the altar and the sacred oblation placed upon it, saying: "Peace to thee, altar of God, and peace to the mysteries placed upon thee"; then gives it to the attending minister with the words: "Peace to thee, minister of the Holy Ghost." The whole congregation then go through the ceremony, beginning with a general shaking of hands. The only Western rite which gives the kiss of peace before the Preface is the Mozarabic. The salutation in many of the ancient churches when imparting it used to be: "May the peace of Christ and his Church abound in you" (Bona, p. 358). Cardinal Bona is of opinion that it was the Franciscans who induced the Holy See to discontinue giving the "Pax" according to the primitive mode, on account of certain abuses that were gradually creeping into the ceremony. This opinion is also sustained by Pope Benedict XIV. (*Enchiridion Sacr. Missæ*, p. 106).

COMMUNION OF THE PRIEST.

At the end of the last of the three prayers mentioned the priest genuflects, and, upon becoming erect, says: "I will receive the Bread of heaven, and call upon the name of the Lord"—words taken from the one hundredth and fifteenth

Psalm, with the exception of "Bread of heaven." Formerly the words used here varied very much, nor was it until the thirteenth century that anything like uniformity was established concerning them. The Carmelite priests say here at the present day: "Hail, Salvation of the world, Word of the Father, Sacred Host, Living Flesh, Perfect God, Perfect Man!"

Having recited the words above given, the priest takes the sacred Host from the paten, and, supporting the latter under it with his left hand, raises it a little from the altar and says: "Lord, I am not worthy that thou shouldst enter under my roof; say but the word and my soul shall be healed."[1] This solemn protest, taken from the reply of the centurion mentioned in the Gospels, he repeats three times, striking his breast at each repetition; and then raising the Host to about the height of his eyes, and tracing with it the sign of the cross in front of him, says: "May the Body of our Lord Jesus Christ preserve my soul to life everlasting. Amen." He then stoops down, and, resting his elbows reverently on the altar, receives the sacred Host. After this he becomes erect and pauses awhile in solemn meditation with his hands joined before his face.

It is well to remark here that the teeth must never be applied to the sacred Host when it enters the mouth. It must be swallowed by the sole aid of the tongue; and if a difficulty should be experienced in this respect, on no account must the finger be introduced to overcome it.

Next follows the communion of the chalice. To this end the priest removes the pall from the mouth of the chalice, and, having made a genuflection as before, recites the words,

---

[1] In the Latin form as used here the expression for "say the word" is *dic verbo*, where we would naturally expect *dic verbum*. In using the ablative instead of the accusative form the Church has followed the Greek of St. Luke—viz., εἰπὲ λόγῳ—in preference to the εἰπὲ λόγον of St. Matthew. In the Syriac (the language in which St. Matthew is supposed to have written his Gospel) both forms are the same.

"What shall I render to the Lord for all the good things that he has rendered me?" (Psalm cxv.) He then takes the paten in hand, and gathers up with it, from the corporal, any loose particles that may have remained upon the latter from contact with the sacred Host, all of which he allows to drop into the chalice by the aid of the thumb and index finger of his right hand. After this he places his hand on the Chalice, saying, "I will receive the Chalice of Salvation, and call upon the name of the Lord ; praising I will invoke the Lord, and will be safe from my enemies" (Psalm cxv.) Then placing the paten under his chin with his left hand, and taking the chalice in his right, he makes the sign of the cross and communicates with the words, "May the Blood of our Lord Jesus Christ preserve my soul to life everlasting. Amen."

CHAPTER XXIX.

THE CELEBRATION OF MASS.

COMMUNION OF THE PEOPLE.

IN order to give such members of the congregation as may be desirous of communicating timely notice of this sacred work, it is customary for the server of the Mass to ring the little hand-bell each time that the priest says, "Domine non sum dignus," just before he communicates. The people then advance to the sanctuary rails, where they take a kneeling posture, and, having placed the communion cloth immediately under their chins, await the approach of the priest. The server, in the meantime, recites in their behalf the same form of Confession that was said at the beginning of Mass, while the priest is getting ready the Sacred Particles for distribution. To this end he opens the tabernacle, and, having made a genuflection, takes therefrom the ciborium in which these Particles are kept, and places it on the corporal in front of him. He uncovers it immediately, and, having made another genuflection, turns a little towards the communicants and pronounces over them the two following prayers: 1st, "May the almighty God have mercy on you, forgive you your sins, and bring you to life everlasting." 2d, "May the almighty and merciful God grant you pardon, absolution, and remission of your sins." When pronouncing this form of absolution he makes the sign of the cross over all at the rails, and, having made a third genuflection, takes the ciborium in his left hand,

and, holding a Particle over it with his right, says in an audible tone, "Behold the Lamb of God; behold who taketh away the sins of the world. Lord, I am not worthy that thou shouldst enter under my roof; say but the word and my soul shall be healed." This latter protestation he pronounces three times, and then descends to the rails, where he distributes the Sacred Particles to the communicants, always beginning at the Epistle side. At this part of divine service all are on a level—rich and poor, learned and illiterate, king and peasant. All kneel together at the same rail, and, side by side, receive their Lord at the same time without any distinction of ceremony by reason of rank or title; and so careful is the Church of the reputation of her children that she forbids the priest to pass any one by at the rails, no matter how unworthy that person be, provided his criminality is secret; thus imitating that singular charity of her Divine Founder, who allowed Judas to communicate at the Last Supper, although he knew that he would soon betray him. In administering the Blessed Particle to each person the priest says, "May the Body of our Lord Jesus Christ preserve your soul unto life everlasting. Amen." Unless in danger of death, Holy Communion must be always received fasting.

Having communicated all, the priest returns to the altar and encloses the ciborium in the tabernacle with the customary genuflections. He then holds out the chalice to the server, and receives about as much wine in it for the ablution as was first put into it for consecration. While doing this he says: "What we have taken with our mouth, O Lord! may we receive with pure mind; and from being a temporal gift may it become for us an eternal remedy." The Holy Eucharist is here called "a temporal gift," inasmuch as received here below by wayfaring men. It is denominated "an eternal remedy" in accordance with what our Lord himself says of it: "If any man eat this Bread he shall live for ever." The wine is taken into the chalice in order to purify it from all traces of the Precious Blood, and is drunk by the priest instead of being thrown into the *sacrarium*, as was the custom in early times (Bona, p. 371). Having drunk this first ablution, the priest takes the chalice with both hands, and proceeds to the Epistle corner of the altar to receive the second ablution from the server, consisting of wine and water, which he allows to fall into the chalice through the tips of the thumb and index finger of each hand held over the chalice's mouth, and this to purify them from any particles of the sacred Host that may have adhered to them. He drinks this second ablution also; and having then purified the chalice with the purificator—instead of which the Greeks use a sponge—arranges it in the centre of the altar, putting all that belongs to it in the proper places.

HOLY COMMUNION IN ANCIENT TIMES.

In the early days of the Christian Church's existence the people were accustomed to communicate every time they assisted at Mass; and many would do this frequently on the same day, if they assisted at more Masses than one and were still fasting. St. Jerome says in his Epist. l. to Pammachius that this praiseworthy custom prevailed throughout Spain and at Rome in the fourth century. By degrees, however, the practice went so much into desuetude that St. John Chrysostom, who died in the early part of the fifth century, bitterly complained of it to his people. "In vain," said he when Bishop of Constantinople, "is there a daily oblation when there is no one present to communicate." Notwithstanding all attempts to check it, coldness in this respect went on increasing from day to day and from year to year, until the Church found it necessary to enact laws requiring all to approach Holy Communion at least on Sundays and festivals. We see a statute in the *Capitulary* of Charlemagne (l. v., No. 182) strictly enjoining this practice. In course of time still greater latitude was given, for it was only required that a person should communicate at three special periods of the year —viz., on Christmas day, Easter Sunday, and Pentecost. The decree specifying these three occasions was promulgated by the Council of Tours in the ninth century, during the pontificate of Pope Leo III. The Council of Agatho, held some time before, ordained that those who did not approach the Blessed Eucharist on these occasions should not be looked on as Catholics at all (Romsee, p. 309). This practice continued until about the thirteenth century, when the fourth Council of Lateran, A.D. 1215, held under the auspices of Pope Innocent III., solemnly declared and decreed, under pain of excommunication, that all the faithful who had reached the years of discretion should confess their sins at least once a year and approach Holy Communion within the Paschal time.[1] This solemn injunction was confirmed and renewed by the Council of Trent,[2] which said in its twenty-second session that it desired that the faithful should communicate not only once a year, but every time they assisted at Mass, if their consciences were pure and guiltless before God. Practical Catholics now, as a general rule, approach Holy Communion the first Sunday of every month and on every intermediate festival of note. Many have the pious practice of going once a week; and it is

---

[1] The Paschal time commences, strictly speaking, on Palm Sunday and ends on Low Sunday. The time in Ireland, by an apostolic indult, is from Ash Wednesday until the Feast of SS. Peter and Paul (June 29); in England, by a similar indult, from Ash Wednesday till Low Sunday; and in America from the first Sunday in Lent to Trinity Sunday.

[2] The Council of Trent opened on December 13, 1545, and lasted, but with considerable interruption, until the year 1563.

not unfrequent, thank God! to meet tri-weekly communicants.

COMMUNION UNDER BOTH KINDS.

Up to the twelfth century Holy Communion was administered to the faithful under both kinds, as we see from numerous testimonies (Kozma, p. 236; Romsee, p. 311). After this time it began to be restricted to the celebrant, but the restriction did not become a universal law of the Church until the Council of Constance, in A.D. 1414, declared it such. We shall see what prompted this declaration.

It is worth observing that whenever any of the Church's adversaries taught as a matter of dogma what she herself only considered a matter of discipline, to confound their impiety she either dropped the practice altogether or strenuously exerted herself in an entirely opposite direction. The Ebionites, for example, held that the Holy Eucharist could be confected with no other kind of bread but unleavened, or azymes; to confound these the Church allowed for some time the use of leavened bread also. The Armenians maintained that it was wholly unlawful to mix even the smallest drop of water with the wine used for consecration; the Church said that it was not so, and that, rather than grant dispensation in this respect to this people, she would suffer the entire body of them to separate from her communion; still, she looked upon the observance as entirely disciplinary. The arch-heretic Luther said that those Masses at which only the priest himself communicated were idolatrous and should be abolished at once. The Church, on the other hand, approved of them, and granted full faculties to the priests of those days to celebrate them at pleasure. This brings us to the question under consideration. John Huss held such fanatical views about the necessity of Communion under both kinds that the whole land was disturbed by his teaching. According to him, the Church could not dispense with the obligation of receiving both species, for Communion under one kind was no Communion at all, and that all who received in that way were damned. Huss was supported in these views by his disciples, Jerome of Prague, Jacobellus of Misnia, and Peter of Dresden. To confound these heretics, and for other very wise reasons, the Council of Constance, assembled in A.D. 1414, declared that Communion under one species was as true a participation of the Body and Blood of the Lord, in virtue of what theologians called *concomitance*, as if both species were received; and that all who held differently were to be anathematized as heretics. A decree was then issued by said council abrogating Communion under the species of wine; and from this dates our present discipline in this respect (Kozma, p. 236). But the practice of receiving under both kinds, even after this decree, was enjoyed, as a particular favor of the Holy See, by certain persons and in a few particular places. It was granted, for instance, 1st, to the kings of France on the day of their coronation, and also at the point of death; 2d, it was allowed to the deacon and subdeacon of Papal High Mass; 3d, the deacon and subdeacon of the Monastery of St. Dionysius, near Paris, communicated under both kinds on Sundays and festivals, as did also the monks of Cluny (Romsee, p. 306).

Four principal reasons, not including the heresy of John Huss and his followers, induced the Church to abandon Communion under the species of wine: 1st, the great danger the Precious Blood was exposed to in communicating so many; 2d, the scarcity of wine in certain regions, and the difficulty in procuring genuine wine in northern climates; 3d, the nausea that this species creates in some people; 4th, the great difficulty of reserving the Holy Eucharist under this kind in warm climates, where the tendency to acidify is very great.

COMMUNION UNDER THE SPECIES OF BREAD.

Some of the ablest commentators see in the "breaking of bread from house to house," and in other similar expressions of the New Testament, Communion under one species only; and it is admitted by all that in this way did the two disciples communicate whom our Lord met on the way to Emmaus on Easter Sunday after his Resurrection, for, as the narrative has it, "they knew him in the breaking of bread." Communion under one kind has been common ever since the days of the apostles, especially in case of sick persons and of those who lived a great distance from the church; and we shall see a little further on that the Orientals have practised such Communion from time immemorial.

Order of Receiving in Ancient Times.—After the celebrant had communicated, the sacred ministers attending him communicated next in order—first the deacon, then the subdeacon, and after him the rest of the clergy. The Communion of the people, which took place at the rails, was arranged in the following order: deaconesses, virgins consecrated to God, children, then the grown people of the congregation—the men first, and then the women (Kozma, p. 240). This order is fully set forth in the Apostolic Constitutions.

Manner of Receiving.—With very little exception, it was customary during the first five or six centuries to place the sacred Host in the hands of the communicant and let him communicate himself. The male portion received the

Blessed Particle in their naked hands, one placed over the other in the form of a cross, and the palm of the right bent a little so as to have it hollow-shaped, in order that there might be no danger of letting the Particle fall off. The females never received the Host in the naked hands, but were always required to bring with them, when they intended to communicate, a clean linen cloth called a *dominical*, with which they covered their hands when about to receive the consecrated Particle. The rule in this respect was so rigid that, should a female present herself for Communion and be without this hand-cloth, she would be obliged to leave the rails and defer receiving until another occasion. The custom of thus receiving the sacred Host in the hands was instituted to commemorate what was done at the Last Supper, when the apostles received in this way. But as the custom was open to many dangers and abuses in places where large numbers approached the Holy Table, it was abrogated about the beginning of the ninth century (Kozma, p. 241).

Form used in giving the Holy Eucharist.—In early times the words used by the priest in giving Holy Communion were, for the species of bread, "Corpus Christi"—"the Body of Christ"—to which the receiver answered, "Amen"; and for the species of wine, "Sanguis Christi poculum Salutis"—"the Blood of Christ, the cup of Salvation"—to which "Amen" was also answered. About the time of Pope Gregory the Great (sixth century) the form had changed into "Corpus Domini nostri Jesu Christi conservet animam tuam"—"May the Body of our Lord Jesus Christ preserve your soul"—to which the receiver would respond, as before, "Amen." With Alcuin, preceptor of Charlemagne, we find the form, "May the Body of our Lord Jesus Christ preserve you unto life everlasting."

PERMISSION GRANTED TO BRING THE BLESSED SACRAMENT HOME.

During the days of persecution permission was granted the faithful to bring the Blessed Sacrament to their houses and communicate themselves in case of imminent death. St. Basil speaks of this custom as prevailing throughout all Egypt. Tertullian and St. Cyprian frequently allude to it also. The Holy Eucharist on these occasions used to be carefully put away in little boxes specially made for the purpose, on the lids of which some such pious devices as IHS (Jesus) or XP (Christ) used to be engraved. These boxes were generally made of gold or silver when owned by the wealthy classes, and had a ring attached to their lids, through which was passed a string, in order to fasten them to the neck (see *Hierurgia*, p. 194, note).

THE HOLY EUCHARIST CARRIED ON JOURNEYS.

According to the present discipline of the Church, permission is enjoyed by no person, no matter how exalted his dignity, unless it be the Holy Father himself, to carry the Blessed Sacrament on his person when travelling, except for the purpose of communicating the sick. In ancient times, however, this permission was often granted, but generally in case of very long and dangerous journeys; and we see that many of the Orientals make it a practice yet to bring it with them whenever they intend to set out on any hazardous voyage. This is especially the case with the Maronites (Denzinger, *Ritus Orient.*, p. 99). When the Pope conveys the Blessed Sacrament publicly on any long journey from Rome, a sort of procession is generally organized of the Noble and Swiss Guards, and of the other functionaries and officials who usually attend him; but there is no demonstration whatever made when the Holy Father is travelling privately. He then carries the Blessed Sacrament around his neck, as Pope Pius IX., of blessed memory, did in his flight from Rome to Gaeta in 1848.

The Armenians (that is, the schismatic Armenians) are much to blame for allowing the Blessed Sacrament to be carried on caravan expeditions through the country, and that, too—to their shame be it said—by lay persons, by the merchants who organize these caravans for the purpose of selling their wares.

HOLY COMMUNION GIVEN TO CHILDREN.

For a long time it was customary to communicate children, under the species of wine, immediately after their baptism. This used to be done by the priest dipping his finger in the Precious Blood and then putting it into the child's mouth to suck. The custom is still kept up in the East, where Baptism, Holy Eucharist, and Confirmation are administered on the same occasion. Romsee says (iv. p. 309) that this custom prevailed, at least in some churches of the West, up to the eleventh century. According to the practice of the modern Greek Church, infants are now generally given the Precious Blood in a spoon.

THE BLESSED EUCHARIST BURIED WITH THE DEAD.

So great was the faith of the primitive Christians in the virtue of the Holy Eucharist that, not content with giving it to the living, they also placed it in the grave with the dead, in order that it might be a safeguard against the wiles of the devil, and as a companion for that body which had been through life, in virtue of the participation of the sacraments of the Church, the temple of the Holy Ghost, as blessed Paul the Apostle says. But there were other reasons for this strange practice. Many believed, in simplicity of mind, that the Blessed Sacrament in this case would answer as a substitute for the last rites of the Church, should it happen that the person had died suddenly or otherwise unprepared.

It is generally said that a stop was put to this practice by a miracle which was witnessed at the grave of a person recently buried. The Blessed Sacrament, as the story goes, was interred with the corpse, but the moment the grave was covered the earth burst open, and after some time the coffin was exposed to view. As no miracle was apprehended at first, the earth was gathered up and the grave made over anew; but the same thing happened again—the earth was scattered, as before, in all directions. This led to an examination as to the probable cause, and as it was found that the Blessed Sacrament sprang forth from the body of the deceased person, it was concluded that it was a portent of the displeasure of God. The custom, it is said, ceased from that time. (The reader must take our own statement of this story instead of better authority, as we find it impossible to recall the name of the work in which we read it.) Be this story true or false, the practice, as bordering on irreverence, was very early condemned, first by the third Council of Carthage, in A.D. 393, and afterwards by those of Auxerre, in France, and Trullo, at Constantinople.

In examining ancient customs we must be careful not to form hasty conclusions, and condemn our fathers in the faith for what may seem irreverent to us, but was never so intended by them.

HOLY COMMUNION WHEN GIVEN BY THE BISHOP.

Whenever the bishop administered Holy Communion he gave the kiss of peace first to the ministers assisting him, and then to those whom he communicated, who also in turn saluted him. There is a vestige of this ancient practice yet in vogue; for, according to our modern discipline, whoever receives Holy Communion from a bishop is required to kiss his ring first. The true origin of this ceremony is founded on the fact that in ancient times all the faithful were regarded as forming one common family with the bishop as their head, and as a pledge of this spiritual union the kiss of peace used to be imparted upon receiving the great Head and Father of all (Mabillon, *Comment. in Ord. Rom.*; Valesius, *Not. ad Eusebii Hist.*, l. vi. c. xliii. ; Kozma, *Liturg. Sacr. Cathol.*, p. 243, note ; Bona, p. 359). The modern practice of kneeling down to kiss the bishop's ring is derived from this ancient custom.

RESPECT SHOWN TO THE BLESSED EUCHARIST.

Nothing can exceed the singular care that the Church always manifests in everything that concerns the Blessed Eucharist. We have spoken already of the minute directions she has given about the vessels in which it is kept— the chalice, the ciborium, the pyx, and the tabernacle ; how clean and precious they must be, how they are to be touched, and who has the right to touch them ; and then, again, the sacred linens, and the extraordinary care that must be taken of them in Mass and out of it. Every imaginable accident, too, that could happen to the Blessed Sacrament is provided for ; and directions on this head of the most minute kind are printed in all the missals, in order that every priest may know what to do in each case. Should a Particle fall to the ground, for instance, it is ordered that the spot where it fell should be carefully marked by a strip of linen, and afterwards scraped and washed and the ablution thrown into the sacrarium. It was the consideration of all this care bestowed on the Blessed Sacrament by the Church, coupled with the magnificent and solemn grandeur of the ceremonies of Holy Mass, that drew from Frederick the Great that noble and magnanimous saying :

"The Calvinists treat Almighty God as a servant; the Lutherans as an equal; the Catholics as a God" (Kozma, *Liturg. Sacr. Cathol.*, Præfatio).

In Spain, whenever the Blessed Sacrament is borne through the streets on a sick-call, red curtains hang in all the principal windows, and the people fall on their knees at their doors until "His Majesty" (the common appellation in that country of the Blessed Sacrament) has passed by (*Impressions of Spain*, by Lady Herbert). At Seville the choir dance before the Host on the Feast of Corpus Christi, in imitation of David's dancing before the Ark of the Covenant; and so exceedingly devout is this dance in all respects that persons who have witnessed it describe it as singularly touching. Lady Herbert tells us, on page 137, that no one could speak of the holy dance of Corpus Christi at Seville without emotion. Spain is pre-eminently the land of the Blessed Sacrament. It is by no means unusual to see in the streets of some of its principal cities little children cluster together in groups, and cry out one to another, as the Most Holy is borne to the sick, " Sale su Magestad " —" His Majesty is going out ! "

HOLY COMMUNION IN THE EASTERN CHURCH.

According to the Liturgy of St. Chrysostom, the celebrant of the Mass communicates first, under the following form of words: "The blessed and most holy Body of our Lord and God and Saviour Jesus Christ is communicated to me, N., priest, for the remission of my sins and life everlasting." When receiving the chalice he says: "I, N., priest, partake of the pure and holy Blood of our Lord and God and Saviour Jesus Christ, for the remission of my sins and life everlasting." When communicating the deacon the priest says: "N., the holy deacon, is made partaker of the precious, holy, and spotless Body of our Lord and God and Saviour Jesus Christ, for the remission of his sins and life everlasting." In giving the Precious Blood to the deacon the form is the same as when the priest receives. According to the Coptic Rite, the priest first kisses the sacred Host before he receives it, and then communicates the rest (Renaudot, p. 261). The form, according to the Nestorian Rite, for communicating a priest is, "The Body of our Lord to the chaste priest for the forgiveness of sins." The form of giving the chalice is the same.

Communion of the People in the Eastern Church.—As we have said already, it is customary all through the East, with Catholics and schismatics alike, to administer Holy Communion under both species. There are three particular ways of performing this ceremony: According to the first, the sacred Host is given by itself, then the communicant drinks from the chalice; according to the second, the sacred Host is given by the priest to each communicant, and the chalice is administered by the deacon through the aid of a small spoon, which he dips into it and afterwards puts into the mouth of the receiver; and according to the third way, which is the most common, the Holy Bread is broken into many minute particles, and, having been steeped in the wine, is afterwards given to the communicant in a spoon. In this last case there is no separate receiving of the Precious Blood. The first way here spoken of is peculiar to the ministers of the altar; also to the patriarch, if he should be present. The minor clergy receive in the second way, and the laity in the third. In some of the Syro-Jacobite churches the priest goes down to the laity with the paten and the deacon with the chalice, upon which occasion the priest dips the Particles in the Precious Blood and distributes them to the people. In many places in the East a lighted taper is borne by some of the assistant ministers at this time.

With the Nestorians the method of communicating the laity is rather peculiar. The priest first comes out with the Holy Bread in a napkin fastened around his neck, and the deacon carries the Precious Blood in a large bowl with a cloth under it, intended as a purificator. Each communicant in succession stands up before the priest and holds his hand under his chin to receive any loose particles that may fall from the sacred Host. After he has partaken of the latter he goes to the deacon and sips a little from the bowl, then wipes his mouth on the napkin carried for this purpose. He then returns to his place, keeping his hand up to his mouth for some time (Smith and Dwight, *Researches in Armenia*, ii. p. 262). The formula of distribution among the laity, according to the Liturgy of St. Chrysostom, is : "N., the servant of God, is made partaker of the pure and holy Body and Blood of our Lord and God and Saviour Jesus Christ, for the remission of his sins and life everlasting." The rubric on this head directs the receiver to draw near with reverence and hold his arms crossed upon his breast. It is not customary in any part of the East to kneel while receiving; all stand up, but bow the head a little as the Blessed Sacrament approaches.

The directions given in the Coptic rituals about the administration of Holy Communion to the laity are exceedingly praiseworthy. Nothing can exceed the singular reverence that the Copts show our Lord upon these occasions. According to their rubrics, the priest and deacon descend from the altar, the one with the Holy Bread, the other with the chalice, and advance to where the communicants are, all of whom the priest blesses with the paten when he arrives there. An assistant deacon bears a lighted candle before the sacred Host. The moment each person is communicated he retires to his place, moving so as not to turn his back on the Blessed Sacrament, as Judas is said to have done, according to the tradition of the Copts. When the Communion of the male portion of the congregation has been administered in this way, that of the females begins. Exceeding great care is required to be taken in the latter case, for, as all the females of the East are veiled in church and out of it, it is often impossible to discern who the person is that you have to deal with, and, according to the Coptic canons, the Blessed Eucharist must not be given to any unknown person (Renaudot, i. p. 205). When all the females are communicated the sacred ministers return to the altar.

Form used in Communicating.—The form of Communion in use with the Copts is : "The Body and Blood of Emanuel our God is really here"; and he who receives says, "Amen." It is worthy of remark that the Copts always communicate the laity by dipping the Host in the chalice, and not by administering both separately. He who receives Holy Communion must shut his mouth and be very careful not to rub the Precious Particle with his teeth ; he must have his head uncovered, his hands disposed in the form of a cross ; must be humble in his bearing, with eyes cast down, and profound recollection depicted on his countenance.

The Abyssinians, too, are very strict in their discipline regarding Holy Communion. With them it is customary for all who are going to receive to wash their hands first, and afterwards approach with great humility and recollection. Just before distributing the sacred Particles the priest stands in front of the communicants, and, holding the Host in his hand, says aloud : "Behold the Bread of the Saints ! Let him who is free from sin approach ; but let him who is stained with sin retire, lest God strike him with his lightning ; as for me, I wash my hands of his sin." Out of respect for the Holy Eucharist, the communicants are cautioned against expectorating during the entire day.

Communion under one Kind in the East.—Outside of Mass the Orientals rarely administer Holy Communion under any other form than that of bread. There is hardly any exception to this rule throughout the entire East when the Communion is intended for the sick. The discipline of the Greeks in this respect is very singular. They do not celebrate regular Mass on any of the days of Lent, except Saturdays, Sundays, and the Feast of the Annunciation. In order, then, that a sufficiency of consecrated Particles may be always on hand for the sake of the sick, they consecrate on these occasions a large quantity of bread, which they steep in the chalice before the Precious Blood is consumed. They then take this sacred bread out, and, having placed it on a large paten, apply heat to the latter until it becomes warm enough to cause all the moisture of the Host to evaporate. By this means the Holy Bread becomes almost as hard as flint, and is rendered proof against all danger of corruption, so that it may be put away with safety for an entire year, if necessary. When communicating the sick afterwards with this, ordinary wine is sprinkled over it in order to soften it (Goar, *Euchol. Græc.*, p. 208).

Throughout the entire East the general term for a consecrated Particle is *Margarita*—that is, a pearl. The Syrians call it *Margonita*, but both words are the same. The term *Carbo*, a coal, is frequently applied to the large Host on account of its vivifying nature.

We shall now return to the end of the Communion according to the Latin Rite.

After the priest has adjusted the chalice he goes to the Epistle side, and there reads from the missal the prayer called the " Communio," which is a short antiphon bearing upon the feast of the day, and generally taken from the Psalter. In former times this prayer was denominated "Antiphona ad Communionem," and it was customary to sing it, together with some portions of a psalm, or, if necessary, the entire psalm, while the priest was communicating the people. Having read the "Communio," the priest goes to the centre of the altar, kisses it, and, having turned round to the people, says: "Dominus vobiscum." He goes to the missal again, and reads from it, in an audible tone, as many prayers called "Post-Communions" as he read collects at the beginning of Mass. In many ancient missals the "Post-Communion" is inscribed "Oratio ad complendum," or the concluding prayer, because the moment it was said the people were dismissed from church. During the Lenten season it was customary to add a prayer for the sake of those who could not, for legitimate reasons, approach Holy Communion with the rest. This used to be called the "Oratio super Populum," and in the Sacramentaries of Pope Gelasius and Pope Gregory the Great we find it prescribed for every occasion on which any of the people did not communicate. Now the "Oratio super Populum" is confined solely to Lent, and is always the same as the prayer said at Vespers, for the reason that, according to the ancient discipline, Vespers and Mass formed one joint act during this season—a vestige of which we have to-day in the service of Holy Saturday—and the last prayer of the one was made to serve for the other also. It must be borne in mind that up to the twelfth century it was the rule during Lent to defer the celebration of Mass until the ninth hour of the day—that is, until three o'clock in the afternoon, the time at which regular Vespers began. Up to this hour all were obliged to remain fasting. When the discipline of the Church was changed in this respect the afternoon meal was appointed for midday, and Mass was changed to the forenoon. The "Oratio super Populum," however, was left as it stood, and this is why itself and the prayer at Vespers are the same to-day. This prayer is never said on Sunday, because that day was never kept as a fasting day.

After the last prayer the priest closes the book, and, having turned round at the middle of the altar to the people, salutes them for the last time with "Dominus vobiscum," and, if the Mass of the day admit of it, subjoins, without changing his position, "Ite missa est"—"Go, the dismissal is at hand." If the occasion should not admit of the dismissal of the people, he says instead of this, but facing the altar, "Benedicamus Domino"—"Let us bless the Lord." According to the arrangement of Pope Pius V., the rule to be guided by in this respect is that whenever the "Te Deum" is said in the Divine Office "Ite missa est" is said in the Mass; but when the "Te Deum" is not said, then "Benedicamus Domino."

The "Ite missa est" was originally an invitation to leave the church; but it is not so now, for Mass is not finished until the end of the last Gospel. It is, therefore, like many other things, merely kept up to preserve a vestige of an ancient rite. The precise force of the "Benedicamus Domino" said at this place will be readily seen when we bear in mind that during the penitential seasons it was customary to say some part of the Divine Office after Mass; and as the people generally were present at this, they were not dismissed at the regular place, but were invited to remain and continue their devotions to the Lord. Durandus tells us that in many places it was customary to say "Benedicamus Domino" instead of "Ite missa est" after the first Mass on Christmas morning, for the reason that the office of Lauds immediately followed, at which the people always assisted. This custom is yet kept up at Lodi (Romsee, p. 330).

"ITE MISSA EST."

Touching the exact rendition of these words into English a diversity of opinion exists. According to some, the full form is, "Ite missa est Hostia"—"Go, the Host has been sent on high"; according to others, it is, "Ite missa est ecclesia"—"Go, the church, or assembly, is dismissed." The great majority, however, interpret the words in an entirely different way, and in doing so they are supported by the strongest authority. The word "missa" here has precisely the same meaning—and is, in fact, the same word, only in a different form—as "missio," or "dimissio," the Latin noun for *dismissal;* and therefore, according to this, "Ite missa est" is nothing else but "Ite missio est"—that is, "Go, the dismissal is at hand." The practice of using the participial form in such cases as this, instead of the real substantive, was very common with the early Fathers, and we find instances also of it in Cicero, Horace, Ovid, Virgil, and Suetonius. Tertullian and St. Cyprian both use "remissa" instead of "remissio." The first says, for example, "Diximus de remissa peccatorum" (lib. iv. *ad Marcionem*); the second, "Dominus baptizatur a servo, et remissam peccatorum daturus," etc. (*Hierurgia*, by Dr. Rock, p. 210, note).

Having said the "Ite missa est," the priest turns to the altar, and, with hands placed upon it, recites the prayer, "Placeat tibi, Sancta Trinitas," to the Holy Trinity, asking that his service may be pleasing on high. After this prayer he turns and blesses the people in the name of the Father, and of the Son, and of the Holy Ghost. In Masses for the dead there is no blessing, for reasons that we shall presently see; nor is there any dismissal, because the people are supposed to remain for the absolution of the body and its interment. The priest, on such occasions, turns to the altar and simply says, "Requiescant in pace."

Dismissal in the Eastern Church.—The forms used in the Eastern Church vary with the different liturgies. In some places the dismissal is, "Go in peace"; in others, "Let us depart in peace"; and in a number of places, "Let us go in the peace of Christ." In the Liturgy of St. James the expression is, "In the peace of Christ let us depart." In most of the Oriental churches a long prayer is sometimes read, called the prayer of dismissal, after which all the people leave the church. According to the Liturgy of St. Chrysostom, this prayer is worded as follows : "The grace of thy lips, shining forth like a torch, illuminated the world, enriched the universe with the treasures of liberality, and manifested to us the height of humility; but do thou, our instructor, by thy words, Father John Chrysostom, intercede to the Word, Christ our God, that our souls may be saved."

END OF MASS IN ANCIENT TIMES.

That Mass formerly terminated at the "Ite missa est" is too well known to need proof, for the Gospel of St. John is a late introduction. The old custom is yet kept up by the Carthusians, who neither say the "Placeat tibi," as we do, nor bless the people at this place.

The custom of blessing the people at this part of the Mass only goes as far back as the tenth century. Before this time the only blessing given was that spoken of as taking place before the "kiss of peace" (Bona, p. 372 ; Romsee, p. 334). Some writers, from not having borne this carefully in mind, have fallen into the strange blunder of saying that in ancient times the blessing used to be given before the "Ite missa est." If by *before* they mean, in this case, what used to take place at the "Pax," they are right; but as they cannot mean this, their mistake is a great one. This error arose from the fact that the prayer now called the "Post-

Communion" used to be anciently called the "Benedictio," inasmuch as it was said to invoke a blessing on all who had communicated that day. No particular ceremonies attended its recital, and no blessing was imparted before or after it. Strabo makes this very clear when he says : "It was decreed by the Council of Orleans that the people should not go away from Mass before the blessing of the priest, by which blessing is understood the last prayer that the priest recites" (Bona, p. 372).

When the custom of blessing the people at the end of Mass was introduced every priest blessed with a triple cross, as bishops do now ; and this continued to be the rule until the sixteenth century, when it was abrogated by Pope Pius V., yet so as not to abolish it altogether, for he allowed it at Solemn High Mass. Pope Clement VIII., however, entirely restricted the triple form to bishops, and ordained that priests should bless only with a single cross (Romsee, p. 336). The old custom of not blessing the people at all is yet kept up in Masses for the dead. In the old law it was customary, too, to pronounce a blessing over the people before they were dismissed. This was generally worded as follows : "May the Lord bless thee and keep thee ; may the Lord show thee his face and have pity on thee ; may the Lord turn his countenance to thee and grant thee peace" (Bona, p. 373 ; *Reasons of the Law of Moses*, by Maimonides, notes, p. 402). The Jews even at the present day are dismissed from their synagogues with this blessing, which they all look upon with the greatest reverence. According to many liturgical scholars of note, the triple blessing now peculiar to bishops is founded on the three divisions made of this ancient mode of blessing in use with the Jews, which, as we see, is taken from the Book of Numbers, vi. 24–26 (Bona, *ibid.*) When the priests of the Carmelite Rite have given the last blessing they kneel down on the upper step of the altar and recite aloud the "Salve Regina," or "Regina Cœli" if it be Paschal time.

THE GOSPEL OF ST. JOHN.

After the priest has imparted his blessing he turns to the Gospel corner of the altar, and there, standing with his face a little turned towards the people, as at the first Gospel, reads the "In principio," or Gospel of St. John. He kneels so as to touch the ground at the words "et Verbum caro factum est"—"And the Word was made flesh"—to remind us of the profound humility of our Lord in becoming man for our sake.

At the end of the Gospel the server answers, "Deo gratias," and the Mass is ended. The priest then takes the chalice with him into the sacristy, and, having unrobed himself, remains some moments in acts of thanksgiving and prayer.

History of the Gospel of St. John.—From the surpassing sublimity of this Gospel many ancient philosophers used to say that it ought to be written in letters of gold and conspicuously hung up in every church, in order that all might be able to see it (Bona, p. 373). From the remotest days of Christianity it has been held in the deepest veneration by all classes of people, and many pious Catholics now, as well as of old, carry their reverence for it so far as to wear it on their persons. But it has not been always a part of the Mass. Up to the time of Pope Pius V. a priest could say it or omit it, just as he pleased, for it was then only a private prayer, just like the "Benedicite." This holy Pontiff, however, finding how very much attached the people were to it, inserted it in the missal which was drawn up by his orders, and so made its recital obligatory on all, with certain special exceptions. The bishop does not recite it at the altar in Solemn High Mass, but only on the way back to his throne, and it is never recited by the Carthusians, Cistercians, the monks of Monte Casino, or those of Cluny. At Lyons it is recited by the priest on his way back from the altar, and at Clermont it is said at the sacristy door (Romsee, p. 341). It has no place in the Mass of the Orientals, nor is it customary to say it in the Pope's Chapel at Rome.

THE ANTIDORON.

For the reason that many Protestants who travel in the East are fond of saying when they come home that the Orientals allowed them to partake of the "consecrated wafer," meaning Holy Communion, we do not think that our work would be complete if we failed to expose this deception. From time immemorial it has been customary all through the East to bless, before regular Mass begins, a large quantity of bread at one of the side altars, and keep it for distribution, after service is over, among all who, for some legitimate reason, could not approach regular Communion on that day. From the fact that it was given as a sort of substitute for ordinary Communion it used to be called the *Antidoron*—that is, something in lieu of the *Doron*, or gift, as the Holy Eucharist was generally styled; and all could receive it at pleasure. Its use is still kept up in the East, and at one time it was also employed in the Western Church. The French call it *pain benit*. This is the true account of what Protestant tourists are pleased to call the "consecrated wafer" of the Oriental Church, and which they often boast of having received. To them it certainly ought to be something sacred, for it is, to say the least of it, *blessed*, and therefore far superior to any bread that they have in their service; for the power of blessing resides not in their ministers, but is enjoyed by those of the East, notwithstanding that they may be heretical and schismatical at the same time.

A LIST

OF THE PRINCIPAL AUTHORS CONSULTED IN WRITING THE PRESENT WORK.

Augustine, Saint, *City of God.*
Bona, Cardinal, *Rer. Liturg.* Antwerp, 1739.
" " *Divina Psalmodia.*
Benedict XIV., Pope, *De Sacrosanct. Missæ Sacrif. et Enchiridion.*
Bouvry, *Expositio Rubricarum Missalis et Ritualis.*
" " " *Breviarii.*
Bannister, *Temples of the Hebrews.* London, 1861.
Burder, *Religious Ceremonies and Customs.* London, 1841.
Badger, *The Nestorians and their Rituals.* London, 1852.
Brerewood, *Enquiries on the Diversity of Languages and Religions.* 1674.
Bingham, *Antiquities of the Christian Church.*
Barry, *The Sacramentals.*
Breviary, Syriac Maronite. Rome, 1863.
Catalanus, *Comment. in Pontifical. Romanum.*
Cæremoniale Episcoporum.
" *Prædicatorum seu Dominicanorum.*
" *Carthusianorum.*
" *Carmelitarum.*
Ceremonial of the Papal Chapel.

Denzinger, *Ritus Orientalium.*
Durandus, *Rationale Divinorum Offic.* Naples, 1859.
De Herdt, *Praxis Pontificalis.* 3 vols.
" *Sacr. Liturg. Praxis.* 3 vols.
De Conny, *Les Cérémonies de l'Église.*
" *Recherches sur l'Abolition de la Liturg. Ant. dans l'Église de Lyon.*
De Montor, *Lives of the Popes.*
De Carpo, *Cæremoniale juxta Ritum Romanum.*
Ferraris, *Bibliotheca.*
Goar, *Euchologium Græcorum.* Paris, 1647.
Gavantus and Merati, *Thesaur. Sacr. Rit. Missalis.* Venice, 1749.
" " *Thesaur. Sacr. Rit. Breviarii.* 1749.
Gagarin, *The Russian Clergy.*
Hefele, *History of the Christian Councils.*
Hemans, *Catholic Italy.* 2 vols. Florence, 1862.
Holy Days of the English Church.
Innocent III., Pope, *De Sacro Altaris Mysterio.*
Kozma, *Liturgia Sacra Catholica.*
Lobera, *El Porque de todas las Ceremonias de la Iglesia.* 1781.
Liturgia Mozarabica.
Lingard, *History and Antiquities of the Anglo-Saxon Church.*
Lamy, *De Fide Syrorum et Disciplina in re Eucharistica.*
Le Brun, *Explication de la Messe.* 2 vols.
Merati and Gavantus, *Thesaur. Sacr. Rituum.*
Martinucci, *Manuale Sacr. Cæremoniarum.* 4 vols.
Maimonides, *Reasons of the Laws of Moses.*
Maringola, *Institutiones Liturgicæ.* 2 vols.
Manuale Decretorum (up to 1866).
Moran, *Origin, Doctrine, and Discipline of the Early Irish Church.*

Morinus, *De Sacris Ecclesiæ Ordinationibus.*
Mühlbauer, *Comment. in Pontif. Romanum.*
Martène, *De Antiquis Ecclesiæ Ritibus.* Venice, 1783.
Neale, *Holy Eastern Church, General Introduction.* 2 vols.
" *Hymns of the Eastern Church.*
Neale and Littledale, *Primitive Liturgies.*
Northcote, *The Roman Catacombs.*
Newman, *Tracts, Ecclesiastical and Theological.* London, 1874.
Poetæ Christianæ.
Pococke, *Travels in Egypt,* etc.
Pleyer, *De Sacrosancto Missæ Sacrificio.*
Pope, *Holy Week in the Vatican.*
Palma, *Historia Ecclesiastica.*
Riddle, *Christian Antiquities.*
Romanoff, *Rites and Customs of the Greco-Russian Church.*
Renaudot, *Liturgiarum Orientalium Collectio.* 2 vols.
Romsee, *Sensus Lit. Moralis ac Histor. Rit. ac Cær. Missæ.*
Rock, *Church of our Fathers.* 4 vols.
" *Hierurgia.*
Schild, *Manuale Liturgicum.*
Semita Sanctorum.
Selvaggio, *Institutiones Christianorum Antiquorum.* 2 vols.
Smith and Dwight, *Researches in Armenia.* 2 vols.
Tondini, *The Pope of Rome and the Eastern Popes.*
Vetromile, *Travels in Europe and the Holy Land.*

GENERAL INDEX.

(The numbers refer to the pages.)

Abaneth—name given by Moses to the cincture, 41.
Ablution—ablution of the hands, 178; of the chalice, 370; how often a bishop washes his hands when celebrating, 179; ancient practice in this respect, 179.
Abouna—origin of the word—an Abyssinian prelate, 28.
Abyssinians—how governed in spirituals—present orthodox population—number of the schismatics—their spiritual head—their ordinations doubtful as to validity—celebrate Mass in the ancient Ethiopic—its two dialects—why sometimes called the Chaldaic—their singular devotion to the Mother of God, 28, 29; their strange tradition regarding the Ark of the Covenant—keep the Holy Eucharist in it—prayers and ceremonies used in blessing it, 89.
Adar—last month of the Jewish ecclesiastical year, 217.
Adrian II., Pope, gives permission to have Mass said in the Sclavonic language, 24, 25.
Agnus Dei, 361; who introduced it into the Mass—its triple repetition, 362; apparition of the Mother of God regarding the "dona nobis pacem," 363.
Alb—why so called, 36; antiquity of its use—formerly made of silk—its ornamentation—the alb presented to St. Peter's at Rome by the father of Alfred the Great—silken albs for Holy Thursday and Holy Saturday—those of cloth-of-gold worn by the monks of Cluny—albs of green, blue, and red in the Monastery of Peterborough—one of a black color used on Good Friday—figurative meaning, 37; Alb of the Greeks—its material, 38; prayer said by the Russian priests in donning it, 39.
Alleluia—its derivation and meaning—how esteemed by the early Christians, 221; what St. Anselm said about its celestial origin—when omitted in the Mass, and why, 222.
"Alma Redemptoris"—its author—see *Hermannus Contractus.*

Altar—its derivation—dimensions—material—the one used at the Last Supper, 113; wooden altars of St. Peter yet preserved at Rome—inscription upon one of them—the first Pope who made stone altars obligatory—altars of gold, silver, and precious stones, 114; silver altars presented to St. John Lateran by Constantine the Great—altar of gold and gems bestowed by the Empress Pulcheria—the marvellous altar of the Church of Holy Wisdom (Sancta Sophia) at Constantinople—inscription upon its front, 115; tombs of the martyrs used as altars—why called "Memoria," "Confessio," etc., 121; symbolism of altars, 116; altars of the Oriental Church, 117; altar coverings, 117.

Altar cards—how many required by the rubrics, 119, 120.

Ambo—its use in ancient times—origin of the name—more than one used in some churches—materials of which made, 219; devices used upon them—where they are yet employed, 220.

Ambrosian Liturgy—its full history and peculiarities, 110, 111.

Amen—its meaning—antiquity of its use—same in every language, 214; not answered at the end of the "Canon" on Easter Sunday when the Pope is the celebrant, why, 356.

Amharic—see *Ethiopic* or *Abyssinian*.

Amice—origin of the name—its various appellations—not in use with the Greeks—custom in regard to it with the Ambrosians and Maronites—what the Armenians call it—description of theirs—its early history, and the office it formerly served—how long this continued—practice of the Capuchins and Dominicans regarding the manner of wearing it—its mystical meaning, 35, 36.

Angel, a coin—why so called, 273.

Antidoron—its derivation—what it means—how Protestants travelling in the East mistake it frequently for the Blessed Eucharist—what the French call it, 392, 393.

Antimens—what they are—their use by the Orientals—how consecrated, 117, 118.

Antipendium—when used, and why so called—its color, etc., 113.

Apse—see frontispiece.

Aquarians—why so called—their heresy—what they offered in the chalice, 165.

Arabic—the ·pure Arabic of the Koran a dead language—liturgical language of all the Mahometans, 32; the vernacular of the Maronites, Copts, etc.—the Gospel of the Mass read in it after it has first been read in the liturgical language, 23, 30.

Arabs—divided into three special classes—names and meaning of each class, 109.

Archimandrite—origin and application of the word, 71.

General Index. 399

Arius—his personal appearance—his real error—condemned at the General Council of Nicæa in A.D. 325, 253.

Ark of the Covenant, 80; strange tradition of the Abyssinians concerning it, 88.

Armenians—use unleavened bread in the Holy Eucharist—liturgical language—patriarch—residence—their great monastery of San Lazaro—do not mix water with the wine in the chalice, and why, 25, 26.

Artophorion—name of the receptacle in which the Blessed Sacrament is reserved by the Greeks—where situated, 88.

"Aufer a nobis"—when said—meaning and reference of the expression *Holy of Holies*, 190; antiquity of the prayer, 191.

Bali language—its relation to the Sanscrit—though now a dead language, yet is used by the natives of Ceylon, Bali, Madura, and Java in their religious service—language of Lamaism, 32.

Baradai, James—one of the reformers of Eutychianism—the Jacobites, or *Monophysites*, of Syria, so called from him, 26.

Beca—one of the ancient insignia of the doctorate—what it is—its color, etc., 55.

Bells—their use in divine service—mentioned in the old law—large ones described in the Mishna, 146; the first who introduced them into the Christian Church—why called *campanæ*, why *nolæ*—ancient substitute for bells, 147; different kinds of semantrons—why the Mahometans prohibit bells to be rung in their dominions, 147; concessions in this respect to the Christians of the East—bells of the church of the Holy Sepulchre at Jerusalem—the Syrians ascribe their invention to Noe—their explanation of this, 148; bells of the Nestorians, Armenians, and Abyssinians—when first introduced into the Eastern Church, and by whom, 149, 150; Cretan ballad regarding their ringing—those used in the Russian Church—the great monster bell of Moscow, 150; serves now as a chapel, 151; bells silent the last days of Holy Week, and why, 152; names and dimensions of the largest bells in the world, 151.

Benedict XIV., Pope—how he used to say Mass sitting down during his last sickness, 212.

Berretta—clerical cap—origin of the word—shape of berretta, 52; its primitive form—date of its introduction as an article of clerical attire—what its corners symbolize—its color—who may wear a red one—description of a Cardinal's—that worn by doctors of divinity—when it may be employed—ceremonies employed in conferring it, 53; the oath taken—names of the institutions in the United States which have the privilege of conferring it—when cardinals first received permission to wear a red one, 54, 55; what the red color is intended to call to mind—substitute worn by the Pope for a berretta—its material—description—when doffed—number of corners worn to the berretta by the clergy of France, Spain, and Germany—ornamental one of the French universities for a doctor of divinity, for a canon—singular privilege granted by the Holy See to the Catholic missionaries of China regarding the use of the berretta at Mass, 56; berretta of the Orientals, 56, 57; the kind worn by the schismatical Patriarch of Alexandria, who never doffs it during Mass—this right also arrogated by the Patriarch of the Nestorians—the one used by the Copts, 57.

Bible—how the ancient Hebrews divided it, 217.

Bishop—why he vests at the altar, 180; the Greek bishops wear no mitre like ours, 57; his blessing, 361.

"Black Clergy"—why so called by the Russians, 56.

Blessed Eucharist—brought home during the days of persecution—brought on journeys sometimes, 877; given to children—buried with the dead, 878; why this practice was discontinued—miracle recorded, 879; ceremonies observed when given by the bishop, 879, 880; respect shown to it by the Church, 880; the great reverence shown it all through Spain, 881; inserted formerly in the altar instead of relics. See *Relics*, also *Holy Communion*, for further particulars.

Blessed Virgin—how represented in mediæval art, 6; a letter supposed to be written by her inserted as a relic in the Cathedral of Messina, 124.

Blessing of nuptials, according to the Rite of York, 6; see also *Bridal Mass*.

Book—see *Missal*.

Borromeo, St. Charles—chosen by the Council of Trent as one of the committee to examine church music, 99.

Bread used at Mass—leavened and unleavened—how baked, 153, 155; devices used on the irons—the various interpretations of "I H S" —its true meaning, 155, 156; breads, by whom made—story of St. Wenceslaus, Duke of Bohemia, 157; size of the bread—form—breads of the Oriental Church, 158; ceremonies attending their making, 159; how strict the Oriental canons are on this head, 160; bread used by the Greeks—ceremonies attending its preparation at the Prothesis—meaning of its quadrangular shape—inscription stamped upon it, 161, 162, 164; inscription of the Coptic bread—history of the *Trisagion*, 162, 163.

Breaking of the Host—explanation and history of this rite—into how many parts it is broken by the Mozarabics—their different names,

General Index. 401

358, 359; the breaking of the Host in the Eastern Church, 359, 360.
Burse—its material and use, 85.
Cabala—what the word means with the rabbins, 188.
Caliph—origin and application of the word, 41.
Calotte—see *Zucchetto*.
Canon—origin of the word—its various applications, 295; care taken by the Church of this part of the Mass—instances of her unwillingness to change any part of it, 296; its great antiquity—names given it by the early Fathers—where it anciently began, 297; why read in secret—singular story upon this head related in the *Spiritual Meadow* of John Moschus—a precedent for this silence —what the Mishna says about it, 298, 299; picture at the beginning of the Canon—ancient customs, 300.
Canonical fingers—why the thumb and index-finger are so called, 280; how the priest joins these fingers after the consecration of the Host—the reason of this practice, 329.
Cap, clerical—see *Berretta*.
Cardinal's berretta—full history of it, 53, 54.
Cardinal's red hat—date of its introduction—to whom first granted, 55.
Cardinal Vitelozzi—chosen by the Council of Trent as one of the committee to examine church music, 99.
"Care-cloth"—what it was used for, and when, 6.
Carmelites—by whom founded, 61; their history and the manner in which they say Mass, 106, 107.
Carthusians—why so called—who founded them, 61; the peculiarities of their manner of celebrating Mass—other privileges enjoyed by them, 104, 105.
Cassock—ancient name—material, 60; color—the kind given by the University of Paris to doctors of theology and canon law—who empowered them to do this, 61; Oxford said to enjoy the same privilege—cassocks with pendants to them—meaning of this custom—color and material of the cassock worn by our Holy Father the Pope—antiquity of this practice, 62.
Catacomb—what the Catacombs are—origin of the word, 70.
Catechumen—origin of the word—its application—how many classes of catechumens in the early Church—where their Mass began and ended—their expulsion from the church, 2, 247, 248.
Cenacle of Sion—account of it—indulgences granted to all who visit it with the proper dispositions, 18.
Ceremony—origin of the word, 3.
Chaldaic language—has eighteen alphabets—by whom used in the Mass —how the word is used in the East, 24.

Chalice—its present form—why made formerly in shape of an apple—chalice used by our Lord at the Last Supper, 69, 70; material of the chalice—chalices of pewter—why those of brass, glass, and wood forbidden—glass chalices used in the very early days, 70, 71; also those made of wood—what St. Boniface said when questioned upon this head—wooden chalices interdicted by the canons of King Edgar of England—chalices of marble, 71; of precious stones—of horn and ivory—those of horn prohibited by the Synod of Calcuith—decree of the Council of Rheims regarding their material—ornamentation of chalices formerly—the various devices employed in them, 72; ministerial chalices, 72; to whose charge entrusted—offertorial chalice—baptismal chalices—chalices with tubes or reeds attached—how adjusted, 73, 74; vestige of this custom yet in Papal High Mass, 74; chalices of the Orientals—those used by the Copts—why their consecration is not generally observed in the East, 75; miracles recorded on this head—form and ceremonies of the consecration of a chalice according to the Coptic Ritual—always consecrated in the Latin Church—opinion of Diana upon the necessity of this, 76.

"Charter-House Monks"—see *Carthusians.*

Chasuble—why so called—ancient form—material—when the present kind came into use—how introduced—upon what authority, 49, 50; chasuble of the Orientals—the one used by the Maronites—Coptic chasuble—chasuble worn by the Greeks—that in use among the bishops of Russia—Nestorian chasubles, 51; that used by the Hungarian Greeks—its name among the Syrians—what called in ancient Latin—how named by the Greeks, 52; St. Peter's, 21.

Chorepiscopus, 175.

Christians, ancient—how they assisted at Mass, 211.

Christmas day—mystical meaning of its three Masses—who instituted them, 169.

Ciborium—why so called—when used—its ancient meaning, 77.

Cincture—antiquity of its use—its various names -ancient form, material, color, etc., 39; the one found at the ruins of Durham—mentioned in Holy Scripture, 40; description of the Aaronic cincture as given by Josephus, 41; that worn by our Lord yet preserved at Aix-la-Chapelle—when exposed for veneration—our Blessed Lady's kept at Prato, in Tuscany, 42; cincture of the Orientals—what the Mahometan rulers of Egypt used to enact regarding its daily use by the Christians of that country—name given it by Moses, 41; cincture of the Russian priests—moral signification, 41, 42.

Clergy—origin of the word, 32.

Cœur de Lion—Richard I., King of England—his zeal in leading the choir at Mass, 101.

Collar, Roman—when introduced—custom regarding its use among the religious orders generally—its ancient form—laws relating to it passed in France, Belgium, and Italy, 59; how it varies in color with the rank of the wearer—the kind worn by cardinals—by bishops—by monsignores—by canons, 60.

Collects—number generally said—why so called, 213; collects of the Orientals, 214.

Cologne—history of its great cathedral—possesses the skulls of the Magi —how preserved, 282.

Comb—when used in the Mass—full history of it, 286, 287.

"Communicantes"—how our Blessed Lady is here styled—how styled in the Oriental liturgies, 310, 311; brief history of the saints herein mentioned, 312 to 321; why none but martyrs are mentioned, 312; why SS. Mark and Luke are not named, 321.

"Communio"—how this prayer was designated in ancient times, 386.

Communion—see *Holy Communion*.

Concelebration—what it means—how long practised in the Latin Church —what Pope Innocent III. says concerning it—vestiges of it remain unto this day, 173; questions started concerning it, 174; the Orientals practise it yet, 175.

Confession—see *Confiteor*.

Confiteor—its antiquity—when reduced to its present form—the Confiteor of the Sarum Rite, how worded—form used by the Dominicans, 187; why the priest strikes his breast three times when saying it—ancient precedents for this practice—confession in the old law, 188; form of wording—nothing can be added to the Confiteor without the permission of the Holy See—what orders have the privilege of adding the name of their founder—confession in the Oriental Church—its form with the Maronites, 189.

Consecration—explanation of both forms, with comments on the words of the narration and those of institution, 324 to 330; strange opinion of Ambrosius Catharinus about "benedixit"—what happened, according to his views, when our Lord pronounced the blessing in each case—views upon this head of St. Thomas Aquinas and St. Augustine, 327, 328; what Fromondus says—into how many parts our Lord broke the bread on this occasion, 328; custom of the Eastern and Western Church in this respect, 329; consecration of the chalice—full explanation of all the ceremonies and actions—comments on the form and on its different clauses, 330,

331; consecration in the Oriental Church—words pronounced aloud—people answer, 333, 334.

Constantinopolitan Creed—see *Symbol*.

Coptic language—its connection with the ancient Egyptian—who say Mass in it—origin of the word *Copt*—liturgies used by this people, 26, 27.

Corporal—why so called—its material and size—decree of Pope Silvester concerning its material, 83; of the Council of Rheims also, 83, 84; who first prescribed linen corporals, and why—corporals of the Orientals, 84.

"Corpus Christi"—full account of the institution of this feast—the author of its Mass and office, 78.

Council of Trent—what it enacted concerning Private Masses, 8.

Creed—see *Symbol*.

Cross—ancient customs regarding the manner of making it, 181; how the Spanish peasantry make it—the various ways of holding the fingers while making it in former times, 182; custom of the Orientals in this respect, 182, 183; singular way in which the fingers are disposed by the Greeks—meaning of this practice, 183; formula used by the Maronites in making it, 184; different kinds of crosses, 126, 127; triple cross a misconception—history of the double cross, or that generally called the *Archiepiscopal*, 127; the two prelates who have a special right to carry a double cross to-day—Jansenistic crosses—why so called—how formed, 128; crosses after consecration, what they mean, 338, 339; made also by the Orientals at this part, 339.

Cunegunda, St.—her trial for suspected adultery by the so-called *Mass of Judgment*—her innocence, 16.

Cuthbert, St.—how he wept when chanting the Preface, 97.

Dagon—false god—falls to the ground before the Ark of the Covenant, 80.

"Deo gratias"—when said—custom of the ancient Christians regarding it, 218.

De Vert—his great work on the ceremonies of the Church—his singular views regarding the literal meaning of the ceremonies of the Mass, 50.

Diana—his opinion regarding the necessity of consecrating the chalice before using it at Mass, 76.

"Dic verbo"—why used instead of "Dic verbum" in the form of Communion, 367.

"Dies Irae"—its history, author, and merits—see *Sequences*.

Dikerion, 183.

Diptychs—why so called—dissertation on them, 307 to 309; their use in the Oriental Church, 309.

Discipline of the Secret—what it was and how long it prevailed in the Eastern and Western Church—what came under it, 1. See also *Sermon*.

Doctorate—its insignia, 53; doctor's cap—ceremonies gone through in conferring it—the oath taken—what institutions in the United States have the right to confer the degree and its insignia, 53, 54; custom of Salamanca, 55.

Dominicans—their history and manner of saying Mass, 107, 108.

" Dominus vobiscum "—whence taken—different forms of salutation among the ancient Hebrews—how careful they were to have God's name or some of his peculiar prerogatives mixed up in each, 208; how the Oriental priests salute the people at Mass, 209; how bishops salute after the " Gloria in excelsis "—see *Pax vobis*.

Duns Scotus—his analysis of the Creed, 250.

Easter Sunday—how regulated so as not to be celebrated with the Jewish Passover, 326.

Eckius—his erroneous notions about the language in which Mass was first celebrated, 20.

Elevation—when it took place formerly—origin and cause of the present discipline in this respect, 332, 333; elevation in the Oriental Church—impressive demonstrations of the Orientals at this part of the Mass, 335; beautiful profession of faith in the Real Presence made on this occasion by the Copts, 336; additional particulars, 337, 338.

Ely—description of its ancient cathedral, 167.

Embolismus—addition to the " Pater noster "—see *Pater noster*.

Ephesus—general council held here in 431—Nestorius condemned, 24.

Ephod, 35.

Epimanikia—maniples of the Orientals—their description and history —their material—how those worn by the bishops of the Eastern Church have images or icons upon them—what they are called by the Syrians—by the Armenians—by the Russians, 45.

Epistle—manner of reading it—mystic meaning of, 215.

Epitrachelion—Oriental stole, 48.

Esdras—one of the Introits taken from the apocryphal Fourth Book, 198.

Estrangelo—origin of the word, and comments upon it, 24.

Ethiopic canon—meaning of, 29.

Eucharist—how reserved in ancient times—how reserved now—manner of reserving it in the Oriental Church—Coptic custom, 87, 88, 89.

Evangelists—how symbolized in art, and why, 294.

" Exultet "—author of this anthem—its music, etc., 96.

Faithful—how summoned to church during the days of persecution, 151.

Fasting days in the Eastern Church—how rigidly they keep Lent, 171.

"Filioque"—who first inserted it in the Creed—why—when this was supposed to have been done—what Charlemagne did about it—what Pope Leo III. said to the emperor's legates—what the Holy Father did to preserve the Creed inviolate—to whom the authoritative insertion of the clause is ascribed—the Greek Catholics are not required to insert it now, even in the hearing of the Pope, 258 to 263. See also *Symbol*.
First Sunday of Advent—how regulated, 130.
Gallic Rite, 112.
"Gaudete Sunday"—why so called—what color cardinals wear on this day at Mass and out of Mass, 65.
Gemara—commentary on the Jewish Mishna, 146.
"Gloria in excelsis"—its author, 205; discipline of the early Church regarding it, 205, 206.
"Gloria Patri," etc.—how said in ancient times—what additions the Council of Nicæa made in it, 185, 186.
God Almighty—known to the Hebrews under ten different names—meaning of each name, 222.
Golden Rose—upon what occasion it is exhibited by the Pope—its full history, meaning, blessing, and to whom generally given, 65.
Gospel—ceremonies employed in reading it—why read sideways—the meaning of the crosses made, 233; why all stand up—what military knights are accustomed to do here—kissing the Gospel, ceremony of, 234; Gospel at Solemn High Mass, 235; ceremonies attending its chanting, and their meaning—full explanation, 236, 237; respect shown to the Gospel in ancient times—how the sacred volume used to be bound, 238; Gospel in the Oriental Church—ceremonies attending its reading, 239.
Gospel of St. John, 301; how reverenced in ancient times—what the primitive Christians used to do with it—encomiums passed upon it by pagan philosophers—when it became obligatory in the Mass, 302.
Gottes-Acker—meaning of this expression, and full history of how tenderly the primitive Christians spoke of the faithful departed, 344, 345.
Gradual—why so called, 221.
Grand Lama—how surrounded by lights, 135.
Gregorian Chant—see *Music*.
Gregorian Style—how Easter Sunday is determined by this mode, 326.
Gregory the Great, Pope—his reliquary, 47; what he did for church music—see *Music*.
Gudule's, St.—Golden Mass said there, 7.
Hagiographa—the books that were included under this name, 217.

"Hanc igitur"—how this prayer is recited, and why—its author—how recited formerly, and how the Carmelites now recite it—how old the present custom of reciting it is, 322.
Hebrew words retained in the Mass, 203.
Hegumenos—his position in the Oriental Church, 71.
Heliodorus—attempts to rob the Temple of Jerusalem—he is frightfully punished, 80, 81.
Heretic—origin and theological application of the word, 303.
Hermannus Contractus—apparition of the Mother of God enjoyed by him—his writings and history, 224, 225.
Hindoos—allow none but the Brahmins to read the Veda—read in a dead language, 32.
"Holiness to Jehovah"—inscription used on the golden plate of the high-priest, 42.
Holy Blood—relic of it sent from Jerusalem to Henry III. of England, and preserved for some time in St. Paul's, London, 64.
Holy Communion—Communion of the priest, 366 to 368; of the people, 369, 370; in ancient times, 371, 372; under both kinds, 373; when this practice was discontinued, and why—exceptions made in certain cases, 374; order of receiving in ancient times—manner of receiving, 375; Holy Communion in the Eastern Church, 381, 382; how distributed—extraordinary care of the Orientals regarding its distribution—how administered to the laity, 383, 384—Communion under one kind in the East, 385. See also *Blessed Eucharist*.
Holy Fan—its use in the Mass in the early days—to whom assigned—workmanship of these fans, 284 ; their full history in the Western Church—fans of the Oriental Church—the kind in use with the Maronites—the Greek fans, 285.
"Holy God, Holy Strong One," etc.—the *Trisagion*, 162, 163, 293.
"Holy Lamb"—what the Greeks mean by it, 161.
Holy of Holies, 190.
Holy Viaticum—Coptic custom regarding it, 11, 12; how carried to the sick, 90; Oriental usage regarding it—given in the East only under one kind—demonstrations made on the way before it—custom of the Syro-Jacobites, 90, 91; how the Spaniards act when they see it passing by, 381. See also *Blessed Eucharist* and *Holy Communion*.
Holy Wisdom—church of this name built at Constantinople by Justinian—history of it, 115; its marvellous altar—see *Altar*.
Homoousios—history of this celebrated word—what the Fathers of Nicæa meant by it—how Arius refused to accept it—its insertion in the Creed, 253, 254.

Host, sacred—dancing before it at Seville, 881.
"House of the Dove"—church so called—why, 87.
"I H S"—the various interpretations given it from time to time—its true meaning, 155, 156.
Incense—antiquity of its use in divine service—when employed now—the Maronites use it at Low Mass—its several spiritual significations—why used at the obsequies of the dead—its use with the Orientals, 92 to 94.
Introit—why so called—how recited—its name with the Ambrosians, Mozarabics, Carthusians, and Carmelites—who introduced it into the Mass, 195; who it was that arranged the present order of Introits, and according to what plan—the version of the New Testament employed on this occasion—difference in wording between the psalms of the Mass and those of the Divine Office—how accounted for—whence they are taken, 196; history of that which is taken from the apocryphal book of Esdras, 197; scope of the Introits—their mystical meaning, 198; Introits of the Eastern Church, and ceremonies attending them, 200.
Islam—origin and application of the word, 82.
"Ite Missa est"—various interpretations of the phrase—how it ought to be translated, 388, 389—end of Mass in ancient times, 390.
Jami—a Mahometan temple of worship—difference between it and a mosque, 183.
Jansenistic crosses—see *Crosses.*
Jews—why obliged in some countries to wear a yellow badge—how Judas was represented in mediæval art, 64.
John of Mount Cornelio—his Office of Corpus Christi suppressed, 78.
John VIII., Pope—his confirmation of the privilege of saying Mass in Sclavonic—upon what conditions, 25.
Jubilation—see *Sequence.*
Judas—why painted by all the ancient and mediæval artists with yellow hair, 64.
Julian the Apostate—sends his men to plunder the "Golden" Church at Antioch—frightful example made of them, 81, 82.
Juliana, Blessed—her vision of the Blessed Sacrament—what it led to—full history of everything concerning the feast, 78.
Kalkasendas—his account of the rising of the Nile, 214.
Kiss of peace—see *Pax.*
Knights of St. John—their several names and history, 234.
Koran—why so called—its language—how the Mahometans try to prove its miraculous nature—its construction—by whom the false prophet was aided in composing it, 31.
Kremlin—origin of the word—what the Kremlin is, 150.

Kyrie eleison—its ancient name—why said nine times—who introduced it into the Mass, 201; ancient customs regarding its recital—at how many different parts of the Mass the Ambrosians recite it—why said in Greek, 202; Oriental usage regarding its recital, 204.

" Lady Mary "—title given by the Abyssinians to the Blessed Virgin, 28.

Lætare Sunday—why so called—color of cardinal's dress on this day at Mass and out of Mass—full account of the blessing of the Golden Rose, 65.

Lamaism—language of, 32.

Languages in which Mass is celebrated to-day—brief account of each, and of the people who employ them, 21.

" Lauda Sion "—its author and history—see *Sequence.*

Leabhar Breac—its date, 65.

Legends regarding the Blessed Sacrament and the Feast of Corpus Christi, 78, 79.

Lent in the Eastern Church—see *Fasting days.*

Lights—antiquity of their use at Mass, 21; full history of them, 132, 133, 134.

Liturgy of St. Basil—when used in the East—see *Dissertation.*

Liturgy of St. Chrysostom—when used—see *Dissertation.*

Liturgy of St. James, 204; see also *Dissertation.*

Lyonese Rite, 112.

Maniple—its material—form—ancient names—primitive use, 43; how long it served this purpose—little bells often attached to it formerly, 44; maniple of the Orientals, 45.

Maronites—origin of the name—say Mass in Syriac—how governed—number of their clergy, secular and regular, 23, 24, 184.

Marriage of the Oriental clergy, 22.

Mass—why so called—not from *Massah, Myesis, Mes,* or *Messe*—not connected with the affix in *Christmas, Childermas, Michaelmas,* etc., 1; Mass of the Catechumens and Mass of the Faithful—meaning of these appellations—different names by which the Mass was anciently known, 2; explanation of each, 3; Solemn High Mass—Simple High Mass—Low Mass—Conventual Mass—Bridal Mass, 4; Golden Mass—Private Mass, 7; Dry Mass, 10; Evening and Midnight Mass, 11, 12; Mass of the Presanctified, 12; Solitary Mass, 8; Votive Mass, 9; Dry Mass, 10; Mass of Requiem—Mass of Judgment, 14; Bridal Mass according to the Sarum Rite, 5; number of Masses that a priest may say on the same day—ancient discipline in this respect—how many Pope Leo III. is said to have celebrated in one day, 168—Masses of Christmas day—of other privileged days—concession to the Spaniards in case of the Masses said on the commemoration of the faithful departed, commonly called *All Souls' day*, 168 when Mass cannot be celebrated, and why—reason given by St. Thomas Aquinas—the custom of the priests of the Ambrosian Rite in this respect, 17; Mass of Holy Saturday—its peculiar wording—how explained, 18; meaning of the expression "dies obitus seu depositionis" in the Mass of Requiem—why the departed souls are commemorated on the *third, seventh, thirtieth* day and anniversary of their death, 14; first Mass, by whom celebrated—when, where, and in what language, 18, 19; the nine different languages in which it is celebrated to-day—brief account of each, 21 to 28; must be said fasting—antiquity of this discipline —exceptions which it admitted formerly, 177; practice of the Oriental Church in this respect, 178; the priest who celebrates must wear shoes—those of the Nestorian Rite celebrate in naked feet after the manner of the Jewish high-priest—ancient rules regarding the color of the shoes worn while celebrating, 176; Mass in the Eastern Church—rules regarding its celebration— daily Mass very rare in the East—Dry Mass of the Nestorians, 170; Armenian discipline, 171; why Mass is said in Latin, 33; the missionaries of China say it with caps on—who granted this privilege, and why, 56; ancient custom of saying Mass for the dead at any time of the day, fasting or not fasting—Evening Mass in the Oriental Church, 11; Midnight Mass in Russia and in the Eastern Church, 12; where Mass ended in ancient times, 532.

Mayence, council of—what it decreed regarding Solitary Masses, 9.

Memento for the dead, 343; ancient customs, 344; dissertation on the word "sleep" as used here instead of "death," 344, 345; how the faithful departed are prayed for in the Eastern Church—specimens of the beautiful prayers used, 345 to 347.

Memento for the living—who may be prayed for here—ancient rites, 306.

Micrologus, 191.

Minor doxology—see *Gloria Patri*.

Minor elevation—when it takes place, 353.

Mishna, 146, 188.

"Missa Papæ Marcelli"—history of this Mass, 99.

Missal—how printed—where it begins, 139; how supported—spiritual signification of the cushion, 140—ancient missals—author of the first one, 140, 141; full history of the missal now in use, 142, 143; missals of the Oriental Church, 143, 144.

Monophysites—origin and application of the word—how they make the sign of the cross, and why, 26, 184.

Monstrance—its various names—what used for—when first introduced

77, 78; its early form—the kind now used by the Cistercians of France—what its present shape recalls to mind—its material, 79.
Moors, or Mauri, 109.
Moslem—same as Mussulman.
Motet—origin and application, 270.
Mount Athos—its monasteries—the Holy Mountain of the Eastern Church, 150.
Mozarabic Liturgy—its full history, 108 to 110.
Mozart's Mass of Requiem—228.
"Munda cor meum," 231.
Music, sacred—to whom we are principally indebted for its introduction into the Christian Church—to whom for its preservation, 95; the eight modes of Greek music, 96; full history of the Gregorian Chant, 96 to 99; musical instruments not in use with the Carthusians, Cistercians, Lyonese, or in any of the churches of the East, nor are they used in the Papal choir, 100.
Mussulman—see *Islam*.
Nails—the number by which our Lord was fastened to the cross—history of these nails, 129.
Nestorians—why so called—their other names, 24; their missals, 144.
Nicæa—council held there—history of its transactions—Constantine the Great attends it—description of him, 251, 252.
Nilometer, 214.
"Nobis quoque peccatoribus," 347; why silence is broken here, 348.
Œcumenical—derivation and application of this word, 256.
Offertory—why so called—early practice regarding it—rules regarding the offerings presented at this place, 266; where the ancient custom is yet kept up—how long it continued before abrogated—order in which the offerings were presented, 267; what was done with the *surplus*, 268; horses and the armorial bearings of knights and nobles sometimes offered in Masses for the dead, 269; why in the oblation of the chalice the plural form is used instead of the singular, 278; *Offertorium* in Masses for the dead—defence and explanation of its true meaning, 270 to 272; Offertory in the Oriental Church, 283, 284.
Omophorion, or Homophorion—why so called—its material and resemblance to our pallium—all Greek bishops wear it—its mystic meaning, 240.
Orarium—ancient name of the stole—origin of the word, 48.
"Orate fratres"—ancient mode of saying it and the variations it admitted—how said in the Sarum Rite, 282.
Order of the Thistle, 313.
Organ—when first introduced into the Christian Church, and by whom

—the monster organ of the ancient Cathedral of Winchester, in England, 100, 101.

Orsini, Cardinal—supposed author of the "Dies Iræ," 226.

Palestrina—his real name—what he did for church music—brief history of his labors, 99.

Pall—its material, dimensions, use—when introduced—Carthusian custom, 85.

"Pange lingua"—its author, 78.

Panhagia—the pectoral cross of the Eastern bishops, 47.

Papal choir—see *Sacred Music*.

Papal cross—see *Cross*.

Paschal time—its limits in England, Ireland, and the United States, 372.

Paten—its material—size in ancient times—the kind used by the Orientals—appalling punishment of a nobleman who washed his feet in one, 77—why the subdeacon takes the paten from the altar at the Offertory and holds it up before his face until after the "Pater noster," 273.

"Pater noster," 355; meaning of its short preface—how the Orientals recite it—how the Mozarabics—sequence of this prayer, 356.

Patriarch of Alexandria says Mass with cap on, 57; Patriarch of the Nestorians does the same thing, 57; the old title of patriarch yet retained in the Latin Church—names of the twelve sees that are ruled by patriarchs at the present day, 128.

Pax, or kiss of peace, 363; ceremonies attending it—ancient customs regarding it, 364, 365—Pax in the Oriental Church, 366.

"Pax vobis"—why said by the bishop—its history, 208, 209.

Pectoral cross—what it was originally—that of Pope Gregory the Great—substitute for it used by the Oriental bishops, 47.

Pergolesi—his famous "Stabat Mater," 99.

Pictures—used instead of statues all through the East, and why, 94.

Post-Communio, 386.

Preface—why so called—why the priest does not turn to the people here when he says "Dominus vobiscum," 288; what the Mozarabics call it—number formerly in use, 289; number in use to-day—remarks on the sublime Preface of the Blessed Trinity, 290, 291; miraculous Preface of the Blessed Virgin—when inserted among the others, and by whom, 291, 292—Preface of the Oriental Church, 293.

Profaners of sacred vessels and vestments—how punished by the hand of God, 80, 81, 82.

Purgatory—how styled by the Orientals, 346, 347.

Purificator—called also mundatory—its material and dimensions—when introduced—what the Greeks use as purificator, and why, 84, 85.

Pyx—what it is used for, 89; its shape—how carried on the person, 90.
Relics—by whom placed in the altar—when—how many—why, 122; Holy Eucharist used to be inserted very often in former times, 123; a letter supposed to have been written by the Blessed Virgin inserted in the cathedral altar at Messina—copy of this curious document and its history, 124, 125—relics inserted by the Orientals, 125.
Rheims, council of—its decree concerning the chalice and paten, 72.
Rites, varying, within the Church, 103 to 112.
Rubric—origin and meaning of the word, 139.
Saints, worship of, in the Oriental Church, 321.
Sarum Rite, 187.
Sancta Sophia, or Church of Holy Wisdom, at Constantinople—its history, 115.
Schismatic—origin and application of the word, 303.
Secretæ, or secret prayers—why so called—different opinions regarding the origin of their name, 282, 283.
Sequence—full history of the sequences—of those also in use with the Orientals, 223 to 231.
Sermon—full history of it in ancient times—why the early Fathers had to be so reserved in preaching on the Blessed Eucharist—short-hand writers in ancient times—preaching in the Oriental Church 241 to 247.
Shechinah—what the rabbins meant by it—its origin, 190.
Sibyls—their history, and the value placed upon their responses by some of the early Fathers, 229, 230.
Sponge—used by the Greeks instead of a purificator like ours—why, 85.
Stole, 46, 47, 48; stole worn by the Pope, 48.
Strainer—used in pouring the wine into the chalice in early times, 286.
Sura—the chapters of the Koran, so called—their number, 81.
"Suscipe, Sancta Trinitas"—remarks upon this prayer, 281.
Symbol—its full history, 249 to 257; how the Carthusians and others recite it—how said in the Church of the Holy Sepulchre at Jerusalem—to what Masses the Symbol is proper, 264.
Tabernacle—its form—full particulars concerning it, 137, 138.
Talmud, 146; the Jerusalem Talmud and the Babylonian, *ibid.*
Targum—origin of the name—different targums at present in existence, 31, 144.
Thurible—full history of it—ancient customs regarding it, 93, 94.
Tones—the eight tones of Greek music—character of each, 96.
Tonsure—different forms in ancient times, 57; present discipline—how the ceremony is performed—what the privileges of tonsure are, 58.

Tract—why so called, 222.
Trikerion—triple candle used by Greek bishops for blessing the people, 183.
Usher—his erroneous notions about saying Mass in the vernacular, 29.
Vestments—their various colors, 62 to 68.
Vartabed—an Armenian monastic priest, 305.
Waters of jealousy—history of this ordeal, 14, 15.
Wine—what sort required at Mass, 165; care bestowed upon it by the Orientals, 166.
Zucchetto—its form—color—when worn at Mass—privilege granted to bishops regarding its color by Pope Pius IX., 57, 58, 59.

H. J. HEWITT, PRINTER, 27 ROSE STREET, NEW YORK.